Understanding Clarence Thomas

Understanding Clarence Thomas

The Jurisprudence of Constitutional Restoration

Ralph A. Rossum

UNIVERSITY PRESS OF KANSAS

Published by the University Press of Kansas (Lawrence, Kansas 66045), which was organized by the
Kansas Board of Regents and is operated and funded by Emporia State University, Fort Hays State
University, Kansas State University, Pittsburg State University, the University of Kansas, and Wichita
State University

Library of Congress Cataloging-in-Publication Data
Understanding Clarence Thomas : the jurisprudence of constitutional restoration /
Ralph A. Rossum.
    pages   cm
Includes bibliographical references and index.
ISBN 978-0-7006-1948-1 (alk. paper)
1. Thomas, Clarence, 1948– 2. Constitutional law—United States. 3. Judges–United States.
4. United States. Supreme Court—Officials and employees. I. Title.
KF8745.T48R67   2014
342.730092—dc23

2013035682

British Library Cataloguing-in-Publication Data is available.

Printed in the United States of America
10 9 8 7 6 5 4 3 2 1

The paper used in this publication is recycled and contains 30 percent postconsumer waste.
It is acid free and meets the minimum requirements of the American National Standard for
Permanence of Paper for Printed Library Materials Z39.48-1992.

CONTENTS

PREFACE

Having written *Antonin Scalia's Jurisprudence: Text and Tradition*,[1] I thought it would be instructive to focus my research on the Supreme Court's other unabashed originalist, Clarence Thomas, and to compare and contrast the two jurists' approaches to constitutional and statutory interpretation. This book is the result of that research.

It is a detailed analysis of the close to 500 majority opinions, concurring opinions, and dissents Thomas has written during his twenty-two years of service on the Supreme Court. Thomas's opinions are invariably well crafted, extensively researched, and passionately argued. In them, as well as in his various speeches and law review articles, he has articulated a clear and consistent jurisprudence of constitutional restoration that seeks to restore the original general meaning of the Constitution. His original general meaning approach is considerably broader than Scalia's original public meaning approach. Thomas fully incorporates Scalia's narrower approach, and so he joins Scalia in asking what a particular constitutional text meant to the society that adopted it. But he then widens his originalist focus to consider evidence of the original intent of the framers of that text and the original understanding of those who ratified it so that he can answer the question of why the text was adopted. And if past precedents have departed from that original general meaning, Thomas understands that it is his "constitutionally assigned role" and responsibility to argue against them, to refuse to apply them in the case before him, and when appropriate to invite future cases that can overturn them so that the Constitution again means "what the delegates of the Philadelphia and of the state ratifying conventions understood it to mean."[2]

In this book, I attempt to understand Thomas as he understands himself. The focus is on Thomas—on what he himself has written, not on what others have written about him. I try to state affirmatively his understanding of federalism through an examination of his opinions on the Interstate, "negative," and Indian Commerce Clauses; federal preemption; the Necessary and Proper Clause; the Tenth Amendment; and state sovereign immunity. I explore his understanding of substantive rights through a consideration of his opinions on the Religion and Speech and Press Clauses of the First Amendment, the Second Amendment, the Takings Clause of the Fifth Amendment, and the Court's abortion jurisprudence. I study his understanding of criminal procedural rights through an analysis of his opinions on the Ex Post Facto Clauses, the Fourth Amendment, the three "witness" clauses of the Fifth and Sixth Amendments, the various questions posed by the right to trial by jury, and the proper reach of the Eighth Amendment's prohibition of cruel and unusual punishments. And finally, I describe his understanding of race, equality, and civil rights though an explication of his opinions on desegregration, racial preference, and voting rights.

I wish to acknowledge my gratitude to Paul Jeffrey, a student at Yale Law School, for serving as my research assistant on the book when he was an undergraduate at Claremont McKenna College; Professor Michael Uhlmann of Claremont Graduate School for his careful reading of various chapters and for his insightful comments; Stanford Law School, Rutgers School of Law–Newark, and the University of La Verne Law School for invitations to speak on my research on Thomas and for the opportunity they provided for me to receive valuable feedback; the law review staff at the University of Detroit–Mercy School of Law for inviting me to prepare an article for its symposium issue commemorating Thomas's twenty years of service on the Court and for allowing me to include here a modified version of that article as chapter 2; and to Claremont McKenna College for granting me a full-year sabbatical to work on this project. I also want to give special thanks to Joan W. Sherman, copy editor; Kelly Chrisman Jacques, production editor; and Fred M. Woodward, director, who make publishing with the University Press of Kansas such an honor and pleasure.

Ralph A. Rossum
Claremont, California
July 23, 2013

Introduction

When, on July 1, 1991, President George H. W. Bush nominated Clarence Thomas to serve as associate justice of the U.S. Supreme Court—predicting that he would be "a great justice," calling him "the best person for this position," and denying that Thomas's race had influenced his nomination—many Americans were skeptical. They doubted Bush's claims, just as they doubted his nominee. Among these doubting Thomas were individuals from the civil rights community, convinced that Thomas would abandon the lifelong campaign for racial justice undertaken by Thurgood Marshall, the first black justice, whose seat Thomas was to fill. Other skeptics included feminists, who thought that Thomas would vote in favor of overturning *Roe v. Wade*, and members of the political Left, who saw him as a partisan conservative of mediocre abilities whose original-ist approach to constitutional interpretation was simply a cloak for his policy preferences. Those doubting Thomas even came from the political Right, especially individuals worried that his unequivocal commitment to the principles of the Declaration of Independence would make him a judicial activist.

During his confirmation hearing, those who doubted Thomas were quick to believe Anita Hill's unsubstantiated claims that he had sexually harassed her. As a result of their doubts, Thomas was confirmed by a razor-thin margin of fifty-two to forty-eight votes.

Even after his confirmation, his critics continued to doubt him. They doubted his intelligence and independence, dismissing him as Justice Antonin Scalia's "sock puppet," who mindlessly agreed with and repeated Scalia's arguments, and labeling him, in racially charged language, Scalia's "lawn jockey" and "shoe-shine boy." They went so far as to doubt his very humanity, with the *New York Times* branding him "the Court's Cruelest Justice" during his first year on the bench. Left-wing law professors doubted his legitimacy, attempting to rescind invitations to speak that their law schools had extended to him and, if failing at that, boycotting his visits. One even argued that any five-to-four Supreme Court decision in which Thomas was in the majority should be regarded as nonbinding.

Thomas is now approaching a quarter century of service on the High Bench, during which he has written more than 475 majority, concurring, and dissenting opinions. This book undertakes a detailed analysis of these opinions, as well as of

1

his speeches and law review articles, and, on that basis, provides overwhelming evidence that there is no longer—and, in fact, there never was—any reason to doubt Clarence Thomas or what President Bush said about him. In these works, Thomas has articulated a clear and consistent jurisprudence of constitutional restoration that seeks to restore the original general meaning of the Constitution. It is an impartial, restrained jurisprudence that as often as not runs counter to the doubters' perceived sense of his policy preferences: his pro–criminal defendant opinions, his antibusiness preemption and negative Commerce Clause opinions, and his opinions interpreting various rights explicitly listed in the Bill of Rights, discussed in later chapters, will make this clear.

Clarence Thomas was born on June 23, 1948, in Pinpoint, Georgia, to M. C. Thomas and Leola Anderson. His people were Gullahs; they descended from West African slaves who lived on the barrier islands and coastal regions of South Carolina, Georgia, and Florida. As he reports in his memoir, *Gullah* was a derogatory term for those "who had profoundly Negroid features and spoke with a foreign-sounding accent similar to the dialects heard on certain Caribbean islands."[1] His father abandoned the family when Leola was pregnant with Thomas's younger brother, and Leola divorced him in 1950. Until his confirmation as a Supreme Court justice, Thomas had met his father only twice—once as a young boy, when M. C. broke his promise to send him a wristwatch, and then during a brief visit shortly after his graduation from high school.

Pinpoint was a town of no more than a hundred people on a tidal salt creek 10 miles southeast of Savannah. Until he was six, Thomas lived in "a shanty with no bathroom and no electricity except for a single light in the living room," but when his brother and cousin played with matches and burned the home down, he and his younger brother and mother were forced to move to Savannah, where Leola kept house for a man who drove a potato chip delivery truck. In Thomas's words, "Overnight, I moved from the comparative safety and cleanliness of rural poverty to the foulest kind of urban squalor."[2] He recalls, "I'll never forget the sickening stench of the raw sewage that seeped and sometimes poured from the broken sewer line." Unlike the shanty in Pinpoint, where rivers and the land provided his family "with a lavish and steady supply of fresh food: fish, shrimp, crab, conch, oysters, turtles, chitterlings, pig' feet, ham hocks, and plenty of fresh vegetables," their apartment in Savannah was often without food and adequate heat: "Never before had I known the nagging chronic hunger that plagued me in Savannah. Hunger without the prospect of eating and cold without the prospect of warmth—that's how I remember the winter of 1955." The apartment was also so cramped that his mother and brother shared the only bed, leaving him to sleep in a chair "too small, even for a six-year old." Thomas was enrolled in the first grade at Florance Street School, the first public school in Savannah built specifically for black students, but he was bored by the slow-moving and repetitive lessons and started skipping school and wandering the neighborhoods.[3]

On the ten dollars a week his mother earned, she was unable to support Thomas and his brother, and so she sent them to live with their grandparents, Christine and Myers Anderson. In his memoir, Thomas attributes his ability to overcome the many hurdles that stood along the way to achieving tremendous success in life to the grandfather who raised him from the age of seven. Thomas calls him "the greatest man I have ever known."[4]

Christine — Thomas and his brother always called her Aunt Tina — was small and thin, with a sixth-grade education. Myers — they called him Daddy, for he was the only father they knew — was tall, wiry, and "strongly muscled" and had a third-grade education, which really amounted to nine months of actual learning because he went to school for only three months a year. Myers ran a family business delivering fuel oil in the black community of Savannah; he made the deliveries, and Christine took orders over the phone and kept the books. This business allowed them to live in a two-bedroom, one-bathroom, cinder-block house with a kitchen filled with modern appliances. Myers raised Thomas and his brother with an "iron will" and by strict rules. Thomas concedes that it "would be too generous to call him semiliterate," but Myers did insist that the boys' first task was to get a good education so that they could get a "coat and tie job." And as Thomas recalls, "He wouldn't listen to any excuses for failure. 'Old Man Can't is dead — I helped bury him,' he said time and time again."[5]

And so, Myers, who had converted to Catholicism, sent Thomas to St. Benedict the Moor Grammar School, an all-black parochial school, and later to St. Pius X, Savannah's only Catholic high school for blacks. When Thomas was ten, Myers built a house on 60 acres of family land in Liberty County, Georgia, that had been passed down through the generations. And for the next decade, in an effort to keep Thomas and his brother off the alluring and dangerous streets of Savannah during the long, hot summer vacations, Myers saw to it that they spent their time, from the last day of one school year to the first day of the next, on the farm. There, he worked them hard, having them clear brush, build fences, hoe rows of corn, pick beans, and harvest sugarcane. "Our small soft hands blistered quickly at the start of each summer," Thomas writes, "[for] Daddy never let us wear work gloves, which he considered a sign of weakness. After a few weeks of constant work, the bloody blisters gave way to hard-earned calluses that protected us from pain." He would later reflect, "Long after the fact, it occurred to me that this was a metaphor for life — blisters come before calluses, vulnerability before maturity."[6]

After years of service as an altar boy, Thomas contemplated a religious vocation, and shortly before his sixteenth birthday, he decided to enter Saint John Vianney, a diocesan minor seminary located in Isle of Hope in affluent Chatham County, to prepare for the priesthood. The tuition at Saint John Vianney was four times as much as at St. Pius X, meaning Myers and Christine would have to make definite sacrifices for him to go there, but they agreed to the plan, with Myers laying down one condition: "If you go, you have to stay. You can't quit."[7]

Saint John Vianney was effectively an all-white boarding school (the only other black student when Thomas was there would drop out). It was a challenging experience for Thomas, in part because he still did not speak standard English, and he was required to repeat the tenth grade because he had not studied Latin at St. Pius X. But he mastered Latin, excelled in the classroom, and graduated with grades so good that the caption, courtesy of his classmates, under his yearbook photo for his senior year read: "Blew that test, only a 98."[8]

After Saint John Vianney, Thomas enrolled in Immaculate Conception Seminary in northwest Missouri, a Benedictine monastery. But he started to have second thoughts about the priesthood because of the failure of the Catholic Church to denounce racism with the same conviction that it denounced abortion. And when word spread in his dormitory that Martin Luther King had been shot, prompting a seminarian to shout, "That's good. I hope the son of a bitch dies," Thomas abandoned his vocation, lost his faith, and left the seminary at the end of the spring semester a month later. When he returned to Savannah and told his grandfather of his decision to leave the seminary, Myers reminded him of his pledge not to quit and ordered him to leave the house that very day.[9]

At the suggestion of Sister Mary Carmine, his chemistry teacher at Saint John Vianney, Thomas transferred to Holy Cross College in Worcester, Massachusetts, where he "excelled in his classes"[10] and majored in English "to fully master the fine points of standard English."[11] While there, he also embraced Black Nationalism, helped found the Black Student Union, lived on a black floor of a dormitory, became involved in the Black Panthers' free breakfast program for black children, and led a walkout over the issue of the college's divestment of funds from South Africa.[12] Accepted for admission by Harvard Law School, the University of Pennsylvania Law School, and Yale Law School, he chose Yale because it was smaller, more liberal, and "a better place for me to grow intellectually."[13] While at Holy Cross, he also met Kathy Ambush, a student at Anna Maria College; she accepted his proposal of marriage in Thomas's junior year, and they married the day after his graduation from Holy Cross on June 5, 1971.[14]

At Yale, their son, Jamal Adeen Thomas, was born.[15] Meanwhile, his militancy dwindled, and his opposition to affirmative action grew, for he felt stigmatized, perceiving that his accomplishments, especially in his corporate law and tax law courses, were dismissed as not based on his merits but on his race—a feeling reinforced by his failure to receive a job offer from any major law firm as he neared graduation.[16] He ultimately was obliged to accept a job working for John Danforth, a Yale Law School graduate and the attorney general of Missouri. He served initially in the criminal division and later in the civil division, where he argued many cases before the Missouri Supreme Court, representing the Department of Revenue and the State Tax Commission.[17] Three years later, he left Danforth's office in Jefferson City and joined the law department of Monsanto, a global chemical company headquartered in St. Louis.[18] Bored with corporate law, he accepted an offer in 1979 from Danforth, then serving as senator from Missouri, to join his staff in Washington, D.C., with responsibility for energy and environmental policies and public works projects.[19]

In 1981, President Ronald Reagan nominated Thomas to the position of assistant secretary of education for civil rights. One year later, he nominated Thomas to serve as chairman of the Equal Employment Opportunity Commission (EEOC), an agency in total shambles, giving him only one order: "[Keep] EEOC off the front pages of the newspapers."[20] Thomas's service over two four-year terms came at the expense of his first marriage, but his efforts succeeded; late in his second term, the *Washington Post* praised him for his "quiet but persistent leadership" whereby he had shifted the agency's focus from emphasizing group rights and imposing racial quotas and timetables on employers to ensuring that justice was done for the individual victims of employment discrimination.[21] In his second term, he hired as special assistants Kenneth Masugi and John Marini—both former students of Harry V. Jaffa, the finest scholar on the natural law of his generation. Their assignment was to assist Thomas in thinking through and expressing in speeches and articles the meaning of equality as it was articulated by Thomas Jefferson in the Declaration of Independence, as it was reaffirmed by Abraham Lincoln, and as Thomas wanted to enforce it at EEOC.[22] It was also during his second term that he met Virginia Bess Lamp, a devout Catholic and a labor-relations lobbyist for the U.S. Chamber of Commerce; they married on May 30, 1987. She was instrumental in leading Thomas back to the Catholic Church and rekindling his faith.

With George H. W. Bush's election as president in 1988, Thomas was approached by Michael Uhlmann, a senior member of the president-elect's transition team, who asked if he would be interested in becoming a federal judge. After consulting with friends and associates, Thomas eventually agreed to have his name considered, and in June 1989, President Bush nominated him to the Court of Appeals for the District of Columbia Circuit, widely considered the second most important court in the land.[23] He was confirmed by a voice vote of the

Senate in February 1990 and took his oath of office on March 12 of that year. As it turned out, his tenure on the court of appeals was brief; it was also unremarkable. Thomas wrote a total of nineteen opinions as a court of appeals judge — sixteen majority opinions, two concurring opinions, and one dissent — in cases that, for the most part, addressed questions about the decisions and rulemaking authority of the regulatory agencies of the federal government.

Fifteen months after Thomas took his seat on the D.C. Circuit, Justice Thurgood Marshall, the attorney who successfully challenged racial segregation in public schools in *Brown v. Board of Education*[24] and later was the first black to serve on the Supreme Court, unexpectedly announced his retirement. President Bush turned to Thomas once again, nominating him as Marshall's successor. In his memoir, Thomas reports that Boyden Gray, White House counsel to President Bush, told him several years after his confirmation that Bush had nominated him to the D.C. Circuit to position him for an appointment on the Supreme Court. But the plan at that time, Gray said, was to have Thomas replace Justice William Brennan in order to avoid appointing him to what was considered the Court's "black seat," which would have made his confirmation more contentious. Brennan, however, upended this plan when he retired earlier than expected and before Thomas had acquired sufficient experience on the nation's second highest court to be a credible nominee. As a result, Bush went with David Souter, who, though he also had very limited experience on a court of appeals (in his case, on the First Circuit), had served for seven years on the New Hampshire Supreme Court. Some time later when Marshall became the next justice to retire from the Court, Bush overlooked the fact that Thomas's race actually worked against him and nominated Thomas to the High Bench, declaring him "the best qualified" person for the position.[25]

Thomas's race worked against him because his publicly stated views on race and equality were diametrically opposed to those of Marshall. On the Court, Marshall routinely supported aggressive efforts to integrate public schools, defended the use of racial quotas in university admissions and government contracting, and interpreted the Voting Rights Act and the Fifteenth Amendment as authorizing proportional representation based on race. By contrast, Thomas was on record criticizing affirmative action; insisting that, based on the principles of the Declaration of Independence, the Constitution is color blind; and criticizing the Warren Court for basing its decision in *Brown* on the findings of social science rather than on the claim that the Constitution is color blind. Not unexpectedly, his nomination unleashed a torrent of harsh personal attacks. Because of his belief in a color-blind Constitution and his opposition to affirmative action, the National Association for the Advancement of Colored People (NAACP) and other leading civil rights organizations came out in opposition to his confirmation.

And making matters worse, Thomas also alarmed the defenders of *Roe v. Wade*, the 1973 decision holding that women have a fundamental right to abortion. Because of the views on natural law and the Declaration of Independence that he had expressed in speeches and articles during his tenure as chairman of EEOC, they feared he would provide the critical fifth Supreme Court vote to overturn this landmark decision.

A full-scale assault was mounted against his confirmation. Senator Joseph Biden, chairman of the Senate Judiciary Committee, delayed hearings for two and a half months, allowing ample time for Thomas's opponents to find any dirt on him and to lobby senators to oppose his confirmation. Thomas testified for three days before the Senate panel, and at the end, the committee split, with seven recommending his confirmation and seven opposing it. However, before the full Senate could vote on his confirmation, Anita Hill, a staff member Thomas was asked to hire when he was in the Department of Education—who had followed Thomas when he moved to the EEOC and whom Thomas had recommended for a faculty position at Oral Roberts Law School when she left government service—came forth with testimony that Thomas had sexually harassed her when she was in his employ. Thomas was obliged to spend two more days testifying that her allegations were utterly false and that he was the victim of "a high-tech lynching for uppity blacks who in any way deign to think for themselves, to do for themselves, to have different ideas."[26]

His final and powerful testimony ultimately won the day. Public opinion broke in his favor, and he was confirmed on Tuesday, October 15, 1991, by a vote of fifty-two to forty-eight, the narrowest margin for approval for a Supreme Court justice in more than a century. The final floor vote was mostly along party lines: forty-one Republicans and eleven Democrats voted to confirm Thomas, whereas forty-six Democrats and two Republicans voted to reject his nomination.[27] He was sworn in by Justice Byron White on Friday, October 18, and was administered the judicial oath by Chief Justice William Rehnquist on Wednesday, October 23.[28]

Using Thomas's speeches, law review articles, and majority, concurring, and dissenting opinions, the chapters that follow explore at length how Thomas employs an original general meaning approach to his interpretation of the Constitution and its various provisions. His nearly quarter century of service on the Supreme Court shows him to be an intelligent, hardworking, and conscientious justice who has a well-reasoned jurisprudential approach to constitutional and statutory interpretation, an approach that he consistently and often courageously pursues.

But for many, all of this has been overshadowed by his silence during oral argument, for he will go several years at a time without asking a single question from the bench. This has led Michael Sacks, an attorney from Georgetown University Law Center and therefore someone who should know better, to suggest that Thomas is silent because he "either does not care about the cases or cannot intellectually compete with his colleagues."[29] Scott D. Gerber is someone who does know better:

> The *Los Angeles Times* commissioned me to write an op-ed on the subject [of Thomas asking several questions during the 2002 oral argument about the Virginia cross-burning case], apparently believing that I too would find it odd that he does not ask many questions. I did not. Instead, I pointed out that Oliver Wendell Holmes, Jr.—the most influential theorist in the history of American law—did not ask many questions, and that Thomas likes to let the lawyers get a word in edgewise.[30]

Thomas explained his silence during oral argument in an interview with Susan Swain on C-SPAN on July 29, 2009. Swain noted that, earlier in the interview, Thomas had referenced the fact that he listened during oral argument, and she pointed out that "much has been made of that by court observers. We've read and heard from other justices that sometimes the arguments are used for the justices to communicate with one another, telegraphing their opinions through the kinds of questions and areas they explore. . . . Do you pick up cues from other justices about where they're going with a particular case from the questions they ask?" Thomas's answer was revealing:

> Not really. I think, I guess I view oral argument a little bit differently. I think it's an opportunity for the advocates, the lawyers, to fill in the blanks, to make their case, to point out things perhaps that were not covered in the briefs or to emphasize things or to respond to some concerns, that sort of thing. In other words, to flesh out the case a little better, to get into the weeds a little more. I think we're here, the nine of us, and we can talk to each other any time we want to. I just wouldn't use that thirty minutes of the advocate's time to do that, to talk to each other. But again as I said earlier, we all learn differently . . . I don't learn that way. When I first came to the Court, the Court was much quieter than it is now. Then perhaps, it was too quiet. I don't know. I liked it that way because it left big gaps so you could actually have a conversation. I think it's hard to have a conversation when nobody is listening, when you can't complete sentences or answers— perhaps that's southern thing. I don't know. But I think you should allow people to complete their answers and their thought, and to continue their conversation. I find that coherence that you get from a conversation far

more helpful than the rapid-fire questions. I don't see how you can learn a whole lot when there are fifty questions in an hour.[31]

The fact that Thomas wants to give opposing counsel time to make their case does not mean that he takes oral argument lightly or that he fails to spend a great deal of time preparing for it. John Eastman, the former dean of the Chapman University Law School and a former Thomas law clerk, has offered this valuable insight:

> This may no longer be true because there are a number of Justices on the Court now who were not there when I was a clerk, but I can tell you that Justice Thomas had a process that better equipped him for oral argument in every case than any of the other Justices on the Court. Here is the way it worked. Most of the Justices would assign a case individually to one of their clerks, and then at some point that clerk and that Justice would have a short meeting to discuss the case based on the bench memo that the law clerk provided. . . . Justice Thomas also assigned each case to a single clerk, but . . . the clerk did not just give the bench memo to the Justice, he instead gave it to all four clerks as well as the Justice. On every single case, we would have a clerk conference discussing the case that would last several hours. . . . In every single case, we explored parallel bodies of law—the implications of the case, . . . thinking very broadly and strategically about the importance of the case—recognizing, in a way that many lawyers and lower court judges do not—that the role of the Supreme Court is not so much resolution of a particular case, but to address the tectonic shifts that are going on in our overall jurisprudence. . . . Justice Thomas engaged in a process of thinking through that with his clerks, and it was an honor to be part of it. . . . He has an unbelievable grasp of both the broad constitutional theories, but also the technical details of every case. You do not get that from somebody on the bench who is lacking in confidence or lacking in intellect.[32]

Understanding Clarence Thomas is organized as follows. Chapter 1 provides a detailed explication of Thomas's original general meaning approach to interpretation. It gives scores of examples of how Thomas employs this approach to interpret both the Constitution and statutory law; by contrast, the remainder of the book focuses almost exclusively on how he applies the approach to questions of constitutional interpretation. The few exceptions to this focus involve analysis of his opinions on federal preemption, ex post facto laws, and the Voting Rights Act.

Chapters 2 and 3 explore how he brings this approach to bear on questions of constitutional structure as they relate to federalism. Thomas has written extensively on the Commerce Clause, and chapter 2 is devoted exclusively to his opinions and writings on that subject. Chapter 3 addresses how his original general meaning approach informs his opinions on such other federalism-related topics as federal preemption of state laws, the Necessary and Proper Clause, the Tenth Amendment and the reserved powers of the states, and state sovereign immunity. The other critical aspect of constitutional structure is, of course, separation of powers. As James Madison noted in *Federalist* No. 51, federalism and separation of powers together provide a "double security" for "the rights of the people."[33] Interestingly, few significant separation of powers cases have come before the Court during Thomas's tenure except those regarding the George W. Bush administration's treatment of Guantanamo Bay detainees. As a consequence, Thomas's only opinions directly addressing separation of powers are his dissents in *Hamdi v. Rumsfeld*[34] and *Hamdan v. Rumsfeld*,[35] both of which are briefly addressed in chapter 2.

Chapters 4 through 6 move from constitutional structure to the substantive, procedural, and civil rights secured by the Constitution. Chapter 4 assesses how Thomas employs his original general meaning approach to interpret the substantive rights found in the First Amendment's Religion and Free Speech and Press Clauses, exploring in detail his influential opinions expanding commercial speech and challenging campaign finance regulations. This chapter also considers his interpretive approach in relation to the Second Amendment's individual right to keep and bear arms for self-defense, the Fifth Amendment's requirement that private property can be taken only for public use, and the Fourteenth Amendment in regard to abortion rights.

Chapter 5 considers how Thomas applies his approach to the criminal procedural provisions found in the Ex Post Facto Clauses of Article I, § 9 and Article I, § 10 and the Bill of Rights. Analyzing his opinions in this area—especially concerning the three "witness" clauses found in the Fifth and Sixth Amendments, the various questions posed by the right to trial by jury, and the proper reach of the Eighth Amendment's prohibition of cruel and unusual punishments—makes clear how his original general meaning approach constrains his discretion and fosters his impartiality.

Chapter 6 explores Thomas's approach to questions of race, equality, and civil rights. Thomas grounds his original general meaning approach in the Declaration of Independence and its "self-evident" truth that "all men are created equal": that truth, he insists, "preced[es] and underl[ies] the Constitution."[36] The chapter traces out the many consequences that, for Thomas, flow from the centrality of that "self-evident" truth and how they shape his opinions in cases concerning desegregation, racial preference, and voting rights.

Chapter 7 reviews Thomas's voting patterns through the years and compares them with those of his colleagues. It highlights the areas of constitutional law on which Thomas has had a profound impact and provides evidence that his original general meaning approach not only has influenced his colleagues on the bench but also has won the respect and begrudging admiration of many of his onetime critics. The chapter closes confident that Justice Thomas will continue to guide in his direction "the tectonic shifts" occurring in the Court's overall jurisprudence.[37]

Chapter One

Thomas's Original General Meaning
Approach to Interpretation

During his nearly quarter century on the Supreme Court, Justice Clarence Thomas has pursued an original general meaning approach to constitutional interpretation. He has been unswayed by the claims of precedent—by the gradual buildup of interpretations that, over time, can distort the original meaning of the constitutional provision in question and lead to muddled decisions and contradictory conclusions.[1] As with too many layers of paint on a delicately crafted piece of furniture, precedent based on precedent—focusing on what the Court said the Constitution means in past cases as opposed to what the Constitution actually means—hides the constitutional nuance and detail he wants to restore. Of all the justices on the Court, Thomas is unquestionably the most willing to reject this buildup, this excrescence, and to call on his colleagues to join him in scraping away precedent and getting back to bare wood—to the original general meaning of the Constitution.[2]

The two Supreme Court justices who unabashedly identify themselves as originalists are Antonin Scalia and Clarence Thomas. Though their approaches have much in common, Scalia has a narrower view of originalism. Thomas fundamentally accepts Scalia's original public meaning approach to constitutional and statutory texts but then adds to it his original general meaning approach.[3]

Professor Gregory E. Maggs has identified three approaches to originalism. The first centers on original intent. This approach seeks to identify what the delegates to the Constitutional Convention in Philadelphia collectively intended to accomplish when they drafted the Constitution in the summer of 1787. Those who adopt an original intent approach believe that "interpreting a document means to attempt to discern the intent of the author."[4] Therefore, they focus on the records of the Constitutional Convention and on what the delegates said about the Constitution as it was being drafted. Madison's Notes figure most prominently for these individuals, but other delegates also took notes, and many wrote letters and essays during and after the convention. For those pursing an original intent approach, such materials provide insight into the framers' intentions.[5]

The second approach to originalism centers on original understanding. Here, the focus is on identifying the collective understanding of what the various provisions of the Constitution meant to the delegates of the state ratifying conventions of 1787 and 1788 that brought the Constitution into existence. Those who pursue an original understanding approach point out that delegates to the Constitutional Convention met in secret under a rule that "nothing spoken in the House be printed, or otherwise published, or communicated without leave,"[6] and as a consequence, the public did not become aware of the convention's records and what was said there until decades after ratification of the Constitution. Therefore, the best way to discern the original understanding of the Constitution, according to proponents of this second approach, is to look at what the delegates said at the ratifying conventions and at the arguments made by the various Federalist and Anti-Federalist writers attempting to influence the election of those delegates.[7] Advocates for an original understanding approach receive strong support from James Madison himself, who declared on the floor of the House on April 16, 1796:

> Whatever veneration might be entertained for the body of men who formed our Constitution, the sense of that body could never be regarded as the oracular guide in expounding the Constitution. As the instrument came from them it was nothing more than the draft of a plan, nothing but a dead letter, until life and validity were breathed into it by the voice of the people, speaking through the several State Conventions. If we were to look, therefore, for the meaning of the instrument beyond the face of the instrument, we must look for it, not in the General Convention, which proposed, but in the State Conventions, which accepted and ratified the Constitution.[8]

The third approach to originalism centers on original public meaning and is most closely associated with Justice Scalia. Proponents of this approach seek to ascertain the meaning of the particular constitutional text in question at the time of its adoption. They do so by consulting dictionaries of the era and other founding-era documents "to discern the then-customary meaning of the words and phrases in the Constitution."[9]

Thomas has incorporated all three of these approaches into his own distinctive original general meaning approach.[10] In a lecture entitled "Judging," delivered at the University of Kansas School of Law on April 8, 1996, as part of the Stephenson Lectures in Law and Government, Thomas declared, "I have said in my opinions that when interpreting the Constitution, judges should seek the original understanding of the provision's text, if that text's meaning is not readily apparent."[11] He went on to elaborate that for him, *original understanding* means what both "the delegates of the Philadelphia and of the state ratifying conventions understood it to mean."[12] He argued in *McIntyre v. Ohio Elections Commis-*

sion that this is the long-standing practice of the Supreme Court, quoting from an 1838 opinion: "We have long recognized that the meaning of the Constitution 'must necessarily depend on the words of the Constitution [and] the meaning and intention of the convention which framed and proposed it for adoption and ratification to the conventions . . . in the several states.' *Rhode Island v. Massachusetts*, 12 Pet. 657, 721 (1838)."[13]

So, in deciding cases, Thomas turns to founding-era documents not only to identify the original intention of the framers, the original understanding of the ratifiers, or the original public meaning of the Constitution's words and phrases but also to find agreement among these "multiple sources of evidence" and thereby ascertain the "general meaning shown in common by all relevant sources."[14] He does this because, although original intent, original understanding, and original public meaning typically lead to the same result, they do not always do so.[15]

Take, for example, Article III, § 2 of the Constitution. It declares, in part, that the judicial power shall extend to cases between a state and citizens of another state. The clear text would hold that the federal courts have jurisdiction whether the state is a plaintiff or a defendant; that is, the language does not announce the principle of state sovereign immunity. However, contrary to the original public meaning, the original understanding reaches a different conclusion. Alexander Hamilton, writing in *Federalist* No. 81, found the idea that Article III, § 2 implied the destruction of the principle of state sovereign immunity was altogether forced and unwarrantable, [16] and John Marshall declared in the Virginia Ratifying Convention, "I hope that no gentleman will think that a state will be called at the bar of the federal court. . . . The intent is, to enable states to recover claims of individuals residing in other states."[17] The issue was ultimately resolved by Congress and the states employing Article V of the Constitution. After the Supreme Court held in 1793 in *Chisholm v. Georgia*[18] that states could be sued in federal court without their consent, Congress began the process of repudiating that holding two years later by adopting the Eleventh Amendment to the U.S. Constitution — "The judicial power of the United States shall not be construed to extend to any suit in law or equity commenced or prosecuted against one of the United States by citizens of another State, or by the Citizens or Subjects of any Foreign State." The states completed the process of repudiation three years after that, in 1798, by ratifying the amendment by the requisite three-fourths of the state legislatures.

Another example is also telling, for it shows the tension between original intent and original understanding regarding the legal effect of treaties. James Wilson, one of the most prominent delegates to the Constitutional Convention (and the man who more than any other delegate shaped the executive branch), chaired the important Committee on Detail that turned the various resolutions approved by the delegates into a draft of the eventual Constitution. Wilson considered treaties to be self-executing, having "the operation of law" without requiring implementing legislation.[19] His original intent position differed completely from Hamilton's original understanding view as expressed in *Federalist* No. 75, where he wrote that treaties "are not rules prescribed by the sovereign to the subject [that is, they do not apply directly to the people and therefore do not have the operation of law], but agreements between sovereign and sovereign."[20]

Turning simultaneously to original public meaning, original intent, and original understanding allows Thomas to find the maximum agreement among these various sources and to identify what is, in fact, the original *general* meaning.

The differences between Scalia's original public meaning approach and Thomas's original general meaning approach need to be elaborated.

Since his elevation to the Supreme Court, Scalia has assiduously and consistently employed an original public meaning approach to interpretation.[21] He argues that primacy must be accorded to the text of the document being interpreted and that the job of the judge is to apply the clear textual language[22] of the Constitution or statute, or the critical structural principle necessarily implicit in the text.[23] If the text is ambiguous, yielding several conflicting interpretations, Scalia turns to the specific legal tradition flowing from that text[24]—to what it meant to the society that adopted it.[25] In fact, the phrase *text and tradition* fills Justice Scalia's opinions: judges are to be governed only by the "text and tradition of the Constitution," in other words, by its original public meaning, not by their "intellectual, moral, and personal perceptions."[26]

Given his original public meaning approach, Justice Scalia totally rejects reliance on legislative history or legislative intent and invariably refuses to join any opinion (or part of an opinion) that employs it.[27] He routinely criticizes his colleagues for turning to "committee reports, floor speeches, and even colloquies between Congressmen" to ascertain what a law means because, as he declared in *Thompson v. Thompson*, these "are frail substitutes for a bicameral vote upon the text of the law and its presentment to the President."[28] As he declared in *Crosby v. National Foreign Trade Council*,[29] these sources are not "reliable indication[s] of what a majority of both Houses of Congress intended when they voted for the statute before us. The *only* reliable indication of *that* intent—the only thing we know for sure that can be attributed to *all* of them—is the words of the bill that they voted to make law."[30]

Scalia argues, therefore, that the Court is to interpret the text alone and nothing else. Though he will occasionally turn to founding documents, especially *The Federalist*, he is quick to point out that he does so for a very narrow purpose. As he put it in *A Matter of Interpretation*:

I will consult the writings of some men who happened to be delegates to the Constitutional Convention—Hamilton's and Madison's writings in *The Federalist*, for example. I do so, however, not because they were Framers and therefore their intent is authoritative and must be the law; but rather because their writings, like those of other intelligent and informed people of the time, display how the text of the Constitution was originally understood. Thus, I give equal weight to Jay's pieces in *The Federalist*, and to Jefferson's writings, even though neither of them was a Framer. What I look for in the Constitution is precisely what I look for in a statute: the original meaning of the text, not what the original draftsmen intended.[31]

Scalia's refusal to consult even the debates over the drafting of the Constitution and the Bill of Rights occasionally keeps him from making as strong an argument as he otherwise could make.[32] One recent and high-profile example is his majority opinion in *District of Columbia v. Heller*.[33] In that case, Scalia gave a lengthy and detailed original public meaning argument that the Second Amendment "conferred an individual right to keep and bear arms" for purposes of self-defense.[34] In dissent, Justice John Paul Stevens argued that the Second Amendment protected only a "collective right" to possess and carry a firearm in connection with militia service; therefore, he said, the District of Columbia's total ban on handguns was constitutional, as was its requirement that lawfully owned long guns in the home be kept nonfunctional even when necessary for self-defense. Stevens insisted that the Second Amendment "was a response to concerns raised during the ratification of the Constitution that the power of Congress to disarm the state militias and create a national standing army posed an intolerable threat to the sovereignty of the several States"[35] and that Madison, who had offered in the First Congress a series of amendments that ultimately became what we refer to as the Bill of Rights, had intended it merely to amend the Militia Clauses of Article I, § 8, cls. 15 and 16.

Stevens knew better. He knew that Madison intended for his set of amendments to be incorporated into the text of the original Constitution—not appended at the end. Madison explained why in a speech on the floor of the House of Representatives on August 13, 1789: "There is a neatness and propriety in incorporating the amendments into the Constitution itself; in that case the system will remain uniform and entire; it will certainly be more simple, when the amendments are interwoven into those parts to which they naturally belong, than it will if they consist of separate and distinct parts. We shall then be able to determine its meaning without references or comparison."[36] Madison failed, however, to persuade his colleagues to do so. Roger Sherman successfully argued that the amendments should be added at the end of the Constitution, as any attempt to "interweave" these amendments into the Constitution itself would "be destructive of the whole fabric. We might as well endeavor to mix brass, iron, and clay."[37] Had Madison prevailed in his efforts to incorporate the amendments into the text of the Constitution, "the right of the people to keep and bear arms" would have been included in Article I, § 9 alongside other provisions securing individual rights, including the habeas corpus privilege and the proscriptions against bills of attainder and ex post facto laws, and it would have been there together with his proposed protections for speech, press, and assembly. Stevens knew all this because the respondent's brief expressly made this argument.[38] So, too, did Solicitor General Paul D. Clement during oral argument in response to a question from Stevens: "If the Second Amendment had the meaning that the District of Columbia ascribes to it, one would certainly think that James Madison, when he proposed the Second Amendment would have proposed it as an amendment to Article I, § 8, cl. 16. He didn't. He proposed it as an amendment to Article I, § 9, which encapsulates the individual rights to be free from bills of attainder and ex post facto clauses."[39]

This "placement" argument is powerful, but Scalia never used it in his majority opinion to refute Stevens's claim. Scalia's original public meaning approach keeps him from consulting any form of legislative history (including the debates in the Constitutional Convention or the state ratifying conventions or the work of the First Congress),[40] even when doing so would allow him to strengthen his overall argument.

Thomas, pursuing an original general meaning approach,[41] incorporates Scalia's narrower original public meaning approach, and thus he also asks what the text meant to the society that adopted it. But he then widens his originalist focus to consider evidence of the original intent of the framers and the original understanding of the ratifiers and to ask why the text (either constitutional or statutory)[42] was adopted. Concerning the Constitution and the Bill of Rights, Thomas reinforces Scalia's textualism by asking, when necessary to make his case most persuasively,[43] what ends the framers (and members of the First Congress) sought to achieve, what evils they sought to avert, and what means they employed to achieve those ends and avert those evils when they proposed and ratified those texts. To answer these questions, he readily turns to Farrand's *Records*, *The Federalist*, Elliot's *Debates*, *The Founders' Constitution*,[44] *The Complete Anti-Federalist*,[45] *The Documentary History of the Ratification of the Constitution*,[46] and the *Annals of Congress*. He then incorporates what he finds in these and other founding-era sources into his opinions.

For example, in his opinion for the Court in *United States v. International Business Machines*,[47] Thomas turned to Farrand's *Records* to refute the federal government's claim that the Export Clause of Article I, § 9, cl. 5 ("No Tax or

Duty shall be laid on Articles exported from any State") should not be understood to prohibit the assessment of nondiscriminatory federal taxes on goods in export transit. The government argued that the Export Clause should be sustained by the justices because it was originally proposed by delegates to the Federal Convention from the southern states, who feared that the northern states would control Congress and use taxes and duties on exports to raise a disproportionate share of federal revenues from the South, and because the nondiscriminatory tax in question before the Court did not conflict with the policies embodied in the Clause. But Thomas insisted,

> While the original impetus may have had a narrow focus, the remedial provision that ultimately became the Export Clause does not, and there is substantial evidence from the Debates that proponents of the Clause fully intended the breadth of scope that is evident in the language. See, Mr. King: "In two great points the hands of the Legislature were absolutely tied. The importation of slaves could not be prohibited—exports could not be taxed;" "Mr. Mason urged the necessity of connecting with the power of levying taxes . . . that no tax should be laid on exports;" Mr. Elseworth [sic]: "There are solid reasons agst. Congs taxing exports;" "Mr. Butler was strenuously opposed to a power over exports;" Mr. Sherman: "It is best to prohibit the National legislature in all cases;" "Mr. Gerry was strenuously opposed to the power over exports."[48]

In his concurring opinion in *Cutter v. Wilkinson*,[49] Thomas turned to the *Annals* of the First Congress to contradict Ohio's contention that § 3 of the Religious Land Use and Institutionalized Persons Act of 2000 (RLUIPA) impermissibly advanced religion by giving greater protection to religious rights than to other constitutionally protected rights, thereby violating the Establishment Clause. Thomas noted that the Establishment Clause "prohibits Congress from enacting legislation 'respecting an *establishment* of religion'; it does not prohibit Congress from enacting legislation 'respecting religion' or 'taking cognizance of religion.'"[50] He pointed out that "an unenacted version of the [Establishment] Clause, proposed in the House of Representatives," demonstrated the opposite of what Ohio was arguing: "It provided that 'Congress shall make no laws touching religion, or infringing the rights of conscience.' 1 *Annals of Cong.* 731 (1789)." The "original understanding"[51] of the Establishment Clause, based on the words that were ultimately adopted, was much "narrower" and simply declared that "'Congress shall make no law respecting an establishment of religion.'"[52] As Thomas saw it, that meant:

Even when enacting laws that bind the States pursuant to valid exercises of its enumerated powers, Congress need not observe strict separation between church and state, or steer clear of the subject of religion. It need only refrain from making laws "respecting an establishment of religion"; it must not interfere with a state establishment of religion. For example, Congress presumably could not require a State to establish a religion any more than it could preclude a State from establishing a religion.[53]

Scalia would view all of this as legislative history and outside his original public meaning approach. But there is perhaps an even bigger difference between Scalia's and Thomas's originalism—the Declaration of Independence.[54] In *A Matter of Interpretation*, Scalia derisively dismisses what he calls Professor Laurence Tribe's "aspirational" theory of constitutional interpretation by declaring: "If you want aspirations, you can read the Declaration of Independence, with its pronouncements that 'all men are created equal' with 'unalienable Rights' that include 'Life, Liberty, and the Pursuit of Happiness.' Or you can read the French Declaration of the Rights of Man." But, he continued, "there is no such philosophizing in our Constitution, which, unlike the Declaration of Independence and the Declaration of the Rights of Man, is a practical and pragmatic charter of government."[55]

By contrast, Justice Clarence Thomas takes seriously the Declaration of Independence and its claim that all men are created equal. In his Senate confirmation hearings, he explained why: "My interest started with the notion, with the simple question: How do we end slavery? By what theory do you end slavery? After you end slavery, by what theory do you protect the right of someone who was a former slave or someone like my grandfather, for example, to enjoy the fruits of his or her labor?"[56] Thomas believes that the Declaration's principles are foundational to the Constitution—they "preced[e] and underl[ie] the Constitution"[57]—and he grounds his opinions explicitly in them. In a 1987 article in the *Howard Law Journal*, he declared that "the 'original intention' of the Constitution [was] to be the fulfillment of the ideals of the Declaration of Independence, as Lincoln, Frederick Douglass, and the Founders understood it."[58] He noted that "the Constitution makes explicit reference to the Declaration of Independence in Article VII, stating that the Constitution is presented to the states for ratification by the Convention on 'the Seventeenth Day of September in the Year of our Lord one-thousand seven-hundred and eighty-seven and of the Independence of the United States of America the Twelfth.' . . . The Declaration marks a *novus ordo seclorum*, a new order of the ages."[59] And in a 1989 article in the *Harvard Journal of Law and Public Policy*, Thomas argued that the Declaration is the "higher law background" of the Constitution and that "if the Constitution is not the logical extension of the Declaration of Independence, important parts of the Constitution are inexplicable."[60]

For Thomas, the higher law principles of the Declaration not only offer insight into how to interpret the Constitution but also provide the "best defense of limited government, of the separation of powers, and of the judicial restraint that flows from the commitment to limited government."[61] They also offer "our best defense of judicial review—a judiciary active in defending the Constitution, but judicious in its restraint and moderation. Rather than being a justification of the worst type of judicial activism, higher law is the only alternative to the willfulness of both run-amok majorities and run-amok judges."[62]

Thomas asserts that "the fundamental principle of equality, one of the higher law principles [manifest in the Declaration and] informing the Constitution,"[63] requires a "color-blind" Constitution. In *Adarand Constructors v. Pena*, in which the Court held that the strict scrutiny standard applies to *all* government classifications based on race, Thomas declared in his opinion concurring in part and concurring in the judgment in part: "As far as the Constitution is concerned, it is irrelevant whether a government's racial classifications are drawn by those who wish to oppress a race or by those who have a sincere desire to help those thought to be disadvantaged." He pronounced "the paternalism that appears to lie at the heart of this [racial preference] program" to be "at war with the principle of inherent equality that underlies and infuses our Constitution. See Declaration of Independence ('We hold these truths to be self-evident, that all men are created equal, that they are endowed by their Creator with certain unalienable Rights, that among these are Life, Liberty, and the pursuit of Happiness.')."[64] He elaborated in his dissent in *Grutter v. Bollinger*,[65] noting that "the principle of equality embodied in the Declaration of Independence and the Equal Protection Clause"[66] was correctly identified by Justice John Marshall Harlan in his famous dissenting words in *Plessy v. Ferguson*: "Our Constitution is color-blind, and neither knows nor tolerates classes among citizens."[67] His fullest statement to date in a Court opinion is his opinion concurring in part and concurring in the judgment in part in *McDonald v. City of Chicago*:

> As was evident to many throughout our Nation's early history, slavery, and the measures designed to protect it, were irreconcilable with the principles of equality, government by consent, and inalienable rights *proclaimed by the Declaration of Independence and embedded in our constitutional structure.* See, e.g., 3 Records of the Federal Convention of 1787, p. 212 (M. Farrand ed. 1911) (remarks of Luther Martin) ("[S]lavery is inconsistent with the genius of republicanism, and has a tendency to destroy those

principles on which it is supported, as it lessens the sense of the equal rights of mankind"); A. Lincoln, Speech at Peoria, Ill. (Oct. 16, 1854), reprinted in 2 The Collected Works of Abraham Lincoln 266 (R. Basler ed. 1953) ("[N]o man is good enough to govern another man, *without that other's consent.* I say this is the leading principle—the sheet anchor of American republicanism. . . . Now the relation of masters and slaves is, *pro tanto*, a total violation of this principle").[68]

Thomas employs his original general meaning approach as a means of constraining judicial discretion and encouraging judicial restraint. In his University of Kansas lecture on "Judging," he declared that "judges should adopt principles of interpretation and methodology that reduce judicial discretion." He explained why this is so important: "Reducing judicial discretion is one of the keys to fostering impartiality among the judiciary. The greater the amount of judicial discretion, the greater the freedom to write one's personal preferences into the law. Narrow judicial discretion, and you reduce the temptation for judges to ignore their duty to be impartial." He noted that constraining discretion and fostering impartiality were especially important for justices on the Supreme Court, for whom "the usual limitations on judicial discretion, such as authority from a superior court or stare decisis, do not exist, or do not exist with the same strength as with other courts."[69]

Thomas continued by observing that "in order to maintain our impartiality, judges must also adopt methodologies and principles that encourage judicial restraint."[70] That methodology for Thomas is original general meaning. As he stated in his concurring opinion in *Lewis v. Casey*, "It is a bedrock principle of judicial restraint that a right be lodged firmly in the text or tradition of a specific constitutional provision before we will recognize it as fundamental. Strict adherence to this approach is essential if we are to fulfill our constitutionally assigned role of giving full effect to the mandate of the Framers without infusing the constitutional fabric with our own political views."[71]

In his lecture on "Judging," Thomas declared that his original general meaning approach "works in several ways to reduce judicial discretion and to maintain judicial impartiality."[72] He mentioned three in particular. To begin with, "it deprives modern judges of the opportunity to write their own preferences into the Constitution by tethering their analysis to the understanding of those who drafted and ratified the text." Additionally, "it places the authority for creating legal rules in the hands of the people and their representatives rather than in the hands of the nonelected, unaccountable federal judiciary."[73] Thomas flatly rejected the famous words of Charles Evans Hughes, the New York governor who later became chief justice of the Supreme Court: "We are under a Constitution, but the

Constitution is what the Court says it is."[74] Thomas instead insisted that "the Constitution means not what the Court says it means, but what the delegates of the Philadelphia and of the state ratifying conventions understood it to mean."[75] Finally, he noted, his original general meaning approach "recognizes the basic principle of a written Constitution. We as a nation adopted a written Constitution precisely because it has a fixed meaning that does not change." He contrasted the U.S. Constitution with "the British approach of an unwritten, evolving constitution. Aside from an amendment adopted pursuant to the procedures set forth in Article V, the Constitution's meaning cannot be updated, or changed, or altered by the Supreme Court, the Congress, or the President."[76]

Thomas also explained how his original general meaning approach not only encourages self-restraint but also discourages the adoption of multipart balancing tests, favored by many of his colleagues. As he observed, his approach lends itself to bright-line rules that find a law or action to be consistent or inconsistent with the original general meaning of the Constitution. He pointed out that "it is always tempting to adopt balancing tests or to rest one's decision on the presence or absence of various factors," for this allows judges to say that "they decided the case on its facts" but also to preserve "some degree of flexibility for future cases." While acknowledging that "this may be appropriate for trial courts," Thomas said it is not appropriate for the Supreme Court or an appellate court, which should, "whenever possible," adopt "clear, bright-line rules that, as I like to say to my clerks, you can explain to the gas station attendant as easily as you can explain to a law professor." Clear, bright-line rules "provide private parties with notice" even as they "limit judicial discretion by narrowing the ability of judges in the future to alter the law to fit their policy preferences."[77]

Thomas's lecture on "Judging" was delivered just a year after he issued an opinion concurring in the judgment in *McIntyre v. Ohio Elections Commission*.[78] In that case, he argued that "the phrase 'freedom of speech, or of the press,' as originally understood, protected anonymous political leafleting."[79] Thomas used that case and his conclusion to make a key point: "If the Court holds broadly today, for example, that all anonymous leafleting is to be given First Amendment protection, then a future Court will not have wiggle room to reverse course to remove that protection for leaflets that turn out to be written by an unpopular group, like the Nazis. Broader rules are more likely to be impartial in their impact on and application to specific parties." Thomas then added to the mix other elements that promote impartiality, stating, "Thus, clear rules along with life tenure and an irreducible salary encourage judges to maintain their impartiality."[80]

The subsequent chapters in this book provide numerous examples of how Thomas's faithful adherence to his original general meaning approach helps him maintain his impartiality and keeps him from writing his own preferences into the Constitution. The list of cases in the following paragraph is not exhaustive but merely illustrative.

Thomas's original general meaning approach led him in *Gonzales v. Raich*,[81] discussed in chapter 2, to vote to uphold California's medical marijuana law. It led him in the negative Commerce Clause cases of *Hillside Dairy v. Lyons*[82] and *United Haulers Association v. Oneida-Herkimer Solid Waste Management Authority*,[83] both also discussed in chapter 2, to uphold economic protectionist measures by states rather than to eliminate undue burdens on the free market. It led to his antibusiness federal preemption opinions in *Pharmaceutical Research and Manufacturers of America v. Walsh*[84] and *Wyeth v. Levine*,[85] discussed in chapter 3. It led to his opinion in *Federal Communications Commission v. Fox*,[86] discussed in chapter 4, to extend full First Amendment protection to indecent broadcast speech. It led him in the partial-birth abortion case of *Gonzales v. Carhart*,[87] also discussed in chapter 4, to question whether Congress had the power to enact a federal law on this subject. And it led him to vote on behalf of a wide range of criminal defendants concerning a wide variety of Bill of Rights guarantees in cases such as *Georgia v. McCollum*,[88] *Wilson v. Arkansas*,[89] *Lynce v. Mathias*,[90] *United States v. Hubbell*,[91] *Apprendi v. New Jersey*,[92] *Harris v. United States*,[93] *Blakely v. Washington*,[94] *United States v. Booker*,[95] and *Shepard v. United States*,[96] all discussed in chapter 5.

As Thomas pursues his original general meaning approach, he rejects past decisions that depart from that meaning. He wants to return to bare wood, and he invites his colleagues to join him by engaging in the hard jurisprudential work of scraping away the excrescence of misguided precedent and restoring the contours of the Constitution as it was generally understood by those who framed and ratified it. He has done so since early in his first year on the High Bench.[97] In *White v. Illinois*,[98] decided on January 15, 1992, Thomas, in an opinion concurring in part and concurring in the judgment, "respectfully suggest[ed] that, in an appropriate case, we reconsider how the phrase 'witness against' in the Confrontation Clause pertains to the admission of hearsay."[99] Likewise, in another early criminal procedure case, *Helling v. McKinney*,[100] he declared:

> To state a claim under the Cruel and Unusual Punishments Clause, a party must prove not only that the challenged conduct was both cruel and unusual, but also that it constitutes punishment. The text and history of the Eighth Amendment, together with pre-*Estelle* [*v. Gamble*[101]] precedent, raise substantial doubts in my mind that the Eighth Amendment proscribes a prison deprivation that is not inflicted as part of a sentence. And *Estelle* itself has not dispelled these doubts. Were the issue squarely presented, therefore, I might vote to overrule *Estelle*.[102]

Thomas wants to remove excrescence as well from the First Amendment. In his concurring opinion in the 2005 Ten Commandments case of *Van Orden v. Perry*,[103] Thomas condemned the "incoherence of the Court decisions" that had rendered "the Establishment Clause impenetrable and incapable of consistent application," called for a "return to the views of the Framers,"[104] and argued for the adoption of physical coercion "as the touchstone for our Establishment Clause inquiry."[105] And, as noted earlier, in his opinion concurring in the judgment in *McIntyre v. Ohio Elections Commission*,[106] he argued that "the phrase 'freedom of speech, or of the press,' as originally understood, protected anonymous political leafleting."[107] Scalia dissented from the Court's invalidation of Ohio's statute prohibiting the distribution of anonymous leaflets on the grounds of "the widespread and longstanding traditions of our people." He pointed out that the earliest statute prohibiting this practice was adopted by Massachusetts in 1890; that by the end of World War I, twenty-four states had such bans; and that in 1995 (the year of the Court's decision), "every State of the Union except California has one, as does the District of Columbia, and as does the Federal Government where advertising relating to candidates for federal office is concerned." Scalia asserted, "A governmental practice that has become general throughout the United States, and particularly one that has the validation of long, accepted usage, bears a strong presumption of constitutionality. And that is what we have before us here."[108] Thomas disagreed.

> While, like Justice Scalia, I am loath to overturn a century of practice shared by almost all of the States, I believe the historical evidence from the framing outweighs recent tradition. When interpreting other provisions of the Constitution, this Court has believed itself bound by the text of the Constitution and by the intent of those who drafted and ratified it. It should hold itself to no less a standard when interpreting the Speech and Press Clauses.[109]

Thomas's dissent in *Kelo v. City of New London*[110] is worthy of mention in this respect as well. In this case involving the Takings Clause of the Fifth Amendment (which reads "nor shall private property be taken for public use without just compensation"), Thomas observed that "something has gone seriously awry with this Court's interpretation of the Constitution. Though citizens are safe from the government in their homes, the homes themselves are not."[111] He regretted that the Court majority relied not on the constitutional text but "almost exclusively on this Court's prior cases to derive today's far-reaching, and dangerous, result." The principles the Court should have employed to dispose of this case, he argued, are not to be found in precedent but rather "in the Public Use Clause itself." And, he concluded, "when faced with a clash of constitutional principle and a line of unreasoned cases wholly divorced from the text, history, and structure of our founding document, we should not hesitate to resolve the tension in favor of the Constitution's original meaning."[112]

Thomas's dissent in *Utah v. Evans*[113] is another superb example of his original general understanding approach to the text of the Constitution itself. The Court in this case approved the use by the 2000 census of "hot-deck imputation"—a way by which the Census Bureau imputed the population of a particular address or unit about which it was uncertain by inferring that it had the same population characteristics as those of a nearby sample address or unit. The result of the Census Bureau's use of this imputation was that North Carolina instead of Utah gained a congressional district. Utah filed suit, claiming that this imputation technique violated the constitutional command of Article I, § 2, cl. 3, requiring the census to apportion congressional seats among the states based on "an actual enumeration." Utah, however, lost before the Supreme Court on a five-to-four decision. Justice Stephen Breyer held for the majority that the Constitution is not violated if all efforts have been made to reach every household, if the methods used consist not of statistical sampling but of inference, if that inference involves a tiny percent of the population, if the alternative is to make a far less accurate assessment of the population, and if manipulation of the method is thus highly unlikely.

Thomas filed a dissent, joined by Justice Anthony Kennedy. He began with a statement that fully articulated his original general meaning approach: "The Constitution apportions power among the States based on their respective populations; consequently, changes in population shift the balance of power among them. Mindful of the importance of calculating the population, the Framers chose their language with precision, requiring an 'actual Enumeration.'" He noted that the framers "opted for this language even though they were well aware that estimation methods and inferences could be used to calculate population." Furthermore, he continued, "if the language of the Census Clause leaves any room for doubt, the historical context, debates accompanying ratification, and subsequent early Census Acts confirm that the use of estimation techniques— such as 'hot-deck imputation,' sampling, and the like—do not comply with the Constitution."[114]

Thomas noted that the Census Bureau referred to hot-deck imputation procedures as "estimation," and he stated, "Whether this 'estimation' technique passes constitutional muster depends on an evaluation of the language of the Census Clause and its original understanding."[115] He began this evaluation by exploring the Clause's original public meaning, which prescribed both "counting the whole numbers of persons" and an "actual Enumeration." He noted that dictionaries of the era inform our understanding. "Actual" was defined at the time of the founding as "really done": T. Sheridan, *A Complete Dictionary of the English Language* (6th ed. 1796) (defining "actual" as "really in act, not merely potential; in act, not purely in speculation"). Sheridan defined "enumeration" as "the act of numbering or counting over" and "to enumerate" as "to reckon up singly; to count over distinctly." See also 1 S. Johnson, *A Dictionary of the English Language* 658 (4th rev. ed. 1773) . . . [and] 1 N. Webster, *An American Dictionary of the English Language* (1828).[116]

Thomas then widened his interpretive focus to include comments in *The Federalist*, debates during the First Congress, and early practice. Thus, he pointed out that population estimates, rather than an "actual enumeration," could be "skewed for political or financial purposes" and lent themselves to "political chicanery" and that Hamilton in *Federalist* No. 36 remarked that the Constitution's Census Clause "effectually shuts the door to partiality and oppression."[117] He noted that in the debate in the First Congress over the first Census Act, Madison drew a sharp distinction between "conjecture" and "estimation" and "an exact number of every division."[118] And he turned to the "early Census Acts" that imposed "a series of requirements for how to accomplish the census; none mention[s] the use of sampling or any other statistical technique or method of estimation."[119]

He concluded: "The text, history, and a review of the original understanding of the Census Clause confirm that an actual enumeration means an actual count, without estimation." Although the framers were well aware of estimation, he said, they "chose to make an 'Actual Enumeration' part of our constitutional structure. Today, the Court undermines their decision, leaving the basis of our representative government vulnerable to political manipulation."[120]

Other illustrative examples of Thomas's original general understanding approach to the text of the Constitution itself come from his Commerce Clause opinions. For instance, in *United States v. Lopez*,[121] Thomas wrote a concurring opinion in which he declared, "Although I join the majority, I write separately to observe that our case law has drifted far from the original understanding of the Commerce Clause. In a future case, we ought to temper our Commerce Clause jurisprudence in a manner that both makes sense of our more recent case law and is more faithful to the original understanding of that Clause."[122] In his concurrence in *United States v. Morrison*,[123] he took a harder line: "The very notion of a 'substantial effects' test under the Commerce Clause is inconsistent with the original understanding of Congress' powers and with this Court's early Commerce Clause cases. . . . Until this Court replaces its existing Commerce Clause jurisprudence with a standard more consistent with the original understanding, we will continue to see Congress appropriating state police powers under the guise of regulating commerce."[124]

In his dissenting opinion in *Camps Newfound/Owatonna v. Town of Harrison*,[125] Thomas urged his colleagues "to abandon th[e] failed jurisprudence" of the negative Commerce Clause;[126] quite interestingly, however, he then offered a thoughtful alternative and invited them "to consider restoring the original Import Export Clause check on discriminatory state taxation to what appears to be its proper role."[127] He intensified his attack on the negative Commerce Clause in his opinion concurring in the judgment in *United Haulers Association v. Oneida-Herkimer Solid Waste Management Authority*:[128] "As the debate between the majority and dissent shows, application of the negative Commerce Clause turns solely on policy considerations, not on the Constitution. Because this Court has no policy role in regulating interstate commerce, I would discard the Court's negative Commerce Clause jurisprudence."[129]

In his concurrence in *United States v. Lara*, Thomas won the begrudging admiration of many Native American tribal leaders. He did so by pointing out that the Indian Commerce Clause did not confer upon Congress plenary power to extinguish tribal sovereignty and by declaring that the Court had to "reexamine the premises and logic of our tribal sovereignty cases."[130]

In his 1998 concurring opinion in *Eastern Enterprises v. Apfel*,[131] Thomas even indicated his willingness to overturn a 200-year-old precedent, the 1798 decision in *Calder v. Bull*[132] that held that the Ex Post Facto Clause of Article I, § 9 applied only to criminal, not civil, matters. He indicated that he was writing "separately to emphasize that the Ex Post Facto Clause of the Constitution, even more clearly reflects the principle that 'retrospective laws are, indeed, generally unjust.'" Since *Calder v. Bull*, however, the Court has considered the Clause to apply only in the criminal context. But, he averred, "I have never been convinced of the soundness of this limitation, which in *Calder* was principally justified because a contrary interpretation would render the Takings Clause unnecessary. In an appropriate case, therefore, I would be willing to reconsider *Calder* and its progeny to determine whether a retroactive civil law that passes muster under our current Takings Clause jurisprudence is nonetheless unconstitutional under the Ex Post Facto Clause."[133]

As mentioned earlier, Thomas employs the original general meaning approach not only to constitutional texts but also to statutory texts.[134] He begins with the text of the statute—as he said in *United States v. Alvarez-Sanchez*, "When interpreting any statute, we look first and foremost to its text."[135] With the assistance of dictionaries and canons of construction,[136] Thomas asks whether the text has an unambiguous meaning. If so, his job is done. In *Connecticut National Bank v. Germain*, he noted that "when the words of a statute are unambiguous, then, the first canon is the last; judicial inquiry is complete."[137] In other words, where the text is clear, he considers it conclusive evidence of legislative intent. In his dissent in *McFarland v. Scott*, he observed that "in any case of statutory interpretation, our primary guide to Congress' intent should be the text of the statute."[138] If, however, the text is ambiguous and it appears likely that Congress had no relevant intent, Thomas will reluctantly turn to legislative history.

Thomas shares much of Scalia's aversion to the use of legislative history in statutory construction and for many of the same reasons. To begin with, consideration of legislative history makes it too easy for the Court to abandon the text as a guide. Thus, in his majority opinion in *Shannon v. United States*, Thomas rejected the petitioner's reliance on a Senate report to support his argument by noting that this "single passage of legislative history . . . is in no way anchored in the text of the statute. On its face, the passage Shannon identifies does not purport to explain or interpret any provision" of the act in question. "Rather, it merely conveys the Committee's 'endorsement' of [a] 'procedure'—a procedure that Congress did not include in the text of the Act. To give effect to this snippet of legislative history, we would have to abandon altogether the text of the statute as a guide in the interpretative process."[139]

Additionally, Thomas opposes using legislative history because doing so grants it the force of law. *United States v. R.L.C.*[140] is a perfect example of how this happens. In his judgment for the Court, Justice David Souter relied on legislative history to construe an ambiguous federal law and, in the process, to bar a juvenile from being sentenced to a prison term longer than a court could impose on a similarly situated adult. In his opinion concurring in part and concurring in the judgment, Thomas began by noting that Souter's "use of legislative history to construe an otherwise ambiguous penal statute against a criminal defendant is difficult to reconcile with the rule of lenity"[141]—that is, a canon of construction that requires a court, when construing an ambiguous criminal statute, to resolve the ambiguity in favor of the defendant.[142] He continued by noting that the Court had "developed innumerable rules of construction powerful enough to make clear an otherwise ambiguous penal statute," and, he added, those rules were far superior to the use of legislative history.[143] But Thomas then proceeded to his main point: "Like Congress' statutes, the decisions of this Court are law, the knowledge of which we have always imputed to the citizenry." At issue in *R.L.C.*, however, was a rule that would also require knowledge by the citizenry "of committee reports and floor statements, which are not law."[144] As Professor H. Brent McKnight has put it so well: "Because the citizenry is presumed to know the law, using legislative history to resolve ambiguity gives a Senate Report or other form of legislative history the force of law, a status never intended. Granting legislative history this status usurps the legislative process."[145]

Nonetheless, there are occasions when Thomas will turn to legislative history; they arise when the text is so ambiguous that there is no legislative intent to discern.[146] He did this, for example, in his dissent in *Commissioner of Internal Revenue v. Lundy*,[147] which addressed the question of whether Congress intended to adopt two different "look-back" periods (two years in Tax Court, three years in federal district court) depending on where the refund petition was filed, during which a refund can be claimed by a delinquent taxpayer for overpayment of federal income taxes after the Internal Revenue Service has mailed a delinquency notice. Justice Sandra Day O'Connor wrote for a seven-member majority concluding that Congress had. Thomas, joined in his dissent by Justice Stevens, concluded to the contrary. He found nothing in the text of the relevant tax code sections to suggest "that Congress intended to *shorten* the look-back period in a proceeding in Tax Court,"[148] especially since the text in question "was meant to be *more* protective of the taxpayer litigating in the Tax Court."[149] In the absence of clear textual language that reflected Congress's intent, he stated that it did not make sense that that body would deliberately adopt a two-year look-back period

> only in Tax Court proceedings—i.e., to punish only the taxpayer whose cash reserves make it impossible for him to provide the Government a still larger loan in any amount it demands while the taxpayer pursues relief in the district court or Court of Federal Claims, the taxpayer who is too unsophisticated to realize that a suit in district court could preserve his right to a refund, and the taxpayer whose expected refund is too small in relation to attorney's fees and other costs to justify a suit in district court. Obviously Congress could constitutionally have adopted such a strange scheme, but I will not simply presume that it has done so.[150]

Thomas was convinced that "Congress quite likely was simply not thinking about the[se] effects on delinquent filers. Or, to put it another way, Congress may have had *no* intent regarding" this issue.[151] And in the absence of any congressional intent, he turned to legislative history. "To my mind, then, the question is whether . . . the statute's legislative history, or other related statutory provisions indicate that Congress meant to prevent a taxpayer from receiving his refund from the Tax Court, even though the other courts could have ordered the refund."[152] To answer that question, he looked to a 1962 Senate report explaining the text in question and quoted the following: "Your committee believes it is desirable to amend the language of present law to make it clear" that the same three-year look-back period applies in all courts.[153] McKnight has argued that *Lundy* "suggests legislative history has a limited 'last resort' role" in Thomas's jurisprudence, observing, "Thomas believes the text is the guide in statutory construction. However, his *Lundy* opinion demonstrates that where the text is ambiguous and it is likely Congress had no relevant intent, rules of construction are powerless, making resort to legislative history necessary. Canons of construction help to discern congressional intent from the text, but they do not apply where there is no intent to discern."[154]

Thomas not only employs the same original general meaning approach to constitutional and statutory texts but also seeks to remove the buildup of precedent in the statutory realm as well. Perhaps his most determined and extensive effort in this regard is his opinion concurring in the judgment in *Holder v. Hall*,[155] in which he harshly criticized the Supreme Court's interpretation of § 2 of the Voting Rights Act in *Thornburgh v. Gingles*.[156] Convinced that the Court's voting rights "jurisprudence has gone awry,"[157] he called for "a systematic reexamination of the Act."[158] He wrote:

> The "inherent tension"—indeed, I would call it an irreconcilable conflict—
> between the standards we have adopted for evaluating vote dilution claims
> and the text of the Voting Rights Act would itself be sufficient in my view
> to warrant overruling the interpretation of § 2 set out in *Gingles*. When
> that obvious conflict is combined with the destructive effects our expansive
> reading of the Act has had in involving the federal judiciary in the project of
> dividing the Nation into racially segregated electoral districts, I can see no
> reasonable alternative to abandoning our current unfortunate understanding
> of the Act.[159]

Thomas has been criticized for his willingness to differ with past decisions that depart from the Constitution's original general meaning and has been charged with "engaging in his own brand of judicial activism." Stephen J. Wermeil, for example, argues that "Thomas is gradually building up, in concurring and dissenting opinions, an impressive array of invitations to litigants to bring cases to the Supreme Court and raise specific Constitutional issues he would like an opportunity to decide."[160] By so doing, Wermeil suggests, "Thomas hardly promotes the image of a classic conservative justice who sticks to the issues raised in the cases before him and does not go roaming over the landscape of the Constitution. . . . It is somewhat surprising to see Thomas profess a form of constitutional restraint . . . and meanwhile, reach out beyond the issues presented to the Supreme Court for opportunities to advance his views of the Constitution."[161]

This criticism is misdirected. As Thomas said in *Lewis v. Casey*, judicial restraint is, for him, fulfilling "our constitutionally assigned role of giving full effect to the mandate of the Framers without infusing the constitutional fabric with our own political views."[162] If past Courts have departed from the original general meaning of the Constitution, Thomas understands that it is his "constitutionally assigned role" and responsibility to argue against these precedents, to refuse to apply them in the instant case, and when appropriate to invite future cases that can overturn them so that the Constitution again means "what the delegates of the Philadelphia and of the state ratifying conventions understood it to mean."[163] For Thomas, judicial restraint does not mean acquiescence in departures from the "mandate of the Framers"; it means actively attempting to restore the Constitution's original general meaning.[164]

Chapters 2 and 3 move from providing an overview of Thomas's original general meaning approach to an examination of how he brings it to bear on questions of constitutional structure as they relate to federalism. Chapter 2 is devoted exclusively to Thomas's extensive writing on and understanding of the Interstate, "negative," and Indian Commerce Clauses. His other federalism opinions are addressed in chapter 3, which concludes with an overall assessment of his federalism jurisprudence.

Chapter Two

Constitutional Structure and Federalism: The Commerce Clause

In his Dwight D. Opperman Lecture delivered at the Drake University Law School on September 24, 1999, Justice Thomas addressed the question of "Why Federalism Matters." His answer was direct: federalism is a "structural safeguard" essential for protecting "individual liberty and the private ordering of our lives."[1] He quoted Madison's words from *Federalist* No. 51 on how federalism and separation of powers together provided a "double security" for "the rights of the people,"[2] and he observed that Madison did not say federalism existed "to protect the states as institutions, although that is its subsidiary effect." Thomas asserted that federalism "exists to protect 'the rights of the people'" — "a theme that has been unnoticed" but that, he proclaimed, "underlies" his federalism jurisprudence.[3]

Thomas told his audience that federalism is a constitutional mechanism that checks and controls governmental power "so that a sphere of private activity and individual freedom can flourish free from state interference." It does so, he argued, in three ways.

First, "it enhances self-government by creating a local decision-making system that is closer to the people, and hence more responsive to their wishes." States, he noted, "still retain jurisdiction over most of the policies that affect the daily lives of their citizens, and so they can play a creative role in defining individual rights." They both "tailor national programs to local conditions and needs" and "provide innovation in recognizing and protecting rights." And at a broader level, "the existence of numerous states . . . creates a beneficial marketplace of sorts. Since people can vote with their feet, by moving to states with whose policies they agree, they force the states into a competition to offer policies that best protect individuals and their rights."[4]

Second, federalism protects individual liberty by "diffusing power among many different political centers" and "creat[ing] independent sovereigns." As Thomas was quick to point out, however, "states do not have sovereignty for sovereignty's sake. Instead, the framers believed that these sovereigns would have an interest in monitoring the activities of the federal government and ensuring that it lives within its enumerated authorities." And though keeping the federal government within the written limits was important for the framers, Thomas observed that it was not "a goal in itself" for them. "Rather, the framers believed that controlling the federal government, through the recognition and protection of independent state sovereigns, was necessary to protect individual liberty itself. These state sovereigns would provide both constitutional and political checks upon the powers of the national government." He invoked the language of James Madison from his June 8, 1789, speech in the First Congress when he introduced what eventually became the Bill of Rights: These protections of individual liberty would be secured by "State Legislatures [that] will jealously and closely watch the operations of this Government, and be able to resist with more effect every assumption of power, than any other power on earth can do . . . [for even] the greatest opponents to a Federal Government admit the State Legislatures to be sure guardians of the people's liberty."[5]

The third "and perhaps most important way that federalism protects individual liberty" is that states "exist as the organizers of resistance to the unwarranted exercise of federal powers." On this point, Thomas quoted Alexander Hamilton from *Federalist* No. 26: "The state legislatures, who will always be not only vigilant, but suspicious and jealous guardians of the rights of the citizens, against encroachments from the federal government, will constantly have their attention awake to the conduct of the national rulers and will be ready enough, if anything improper appears, to sound the alarm to the people and not only be the *voice*, but if necessary the *arm* of their discontent."[6] Thomas argued that the framers understood the nation's leaders "someday might stray from their duty and seek to expand federal powers for their own benefit," and to guard against this possibility, he said, they created "centers of political opposition that could control the excesses of the national government." It is this very sovereignty that Thomas is committed to protecting, for as he announced, "take away that sovereignty and you undermine the ability of the federalist structure to maintain multiple centers of legal and political power."[7]

He concluded his Opperman Lecture by justifying why it is appropriate and necessary for the Supreme Court to engage in an "expanded exercise of judicial review" to protect federalism, especially given the argument that "federalism needs no judicial review, because the 'political safeguards of federalism'—primarily the representation of the states in the Senate—would protect state interests in the making of legislation." Although he conceded that "the Constitution has no clause mandating judicial review at all," he argued that "the original understanding suggests that judicial review, to the extent it was to exist, should apply with equal force to federalism as to any other type of cases." He told his audience that when the Constitution was ratified in 1788, it contained no bill of rights. So, he reasoned, "if judicial review was to exist, it was designed from the beginning to maintain the limits on the powers of the federal government as much as to guard individual rights directly. Ratification of the Bill of Rights in 1791 gave individual rights the same protections that state sovereignty had already received in 1788." And since federalism, no less than the Bill of Rights, exists "to check the powers of the government so as to protect individual rights and a private civil society," judicial review of federalism questions "appears all the more appropriate and justified."[8]

Thomas has written extensively and in depth on questions of federalism. What follows in this chapter is an examination of his federalism jurisprudence in cases dealing with the Interstate Commerce Clause, the negative Commerce Clause, and the Indian Commerce Clause. Chapter 3 continues by examining his federalism jurisprudence in cases dealing with federal preemption of state laws, the Necessary and Proper Clause, the Tenth Amendment, and state sovereign immunity. It concludes with an assessment of how faithful he has been in the cases taken up in these two chapters to his original general meaning approach to constitutional interpretation.

The Interstate Commerce Clause

In cases involving the Interstate Commerce Clause, Thomas is known primarily for his concurring and dissenting opinions.[9] His initial major opinion was his concurring opinion in *United States v. Lopez*.[10] For the first time in almost six decades, the Supreme Court in *Lopez* invalidated a federal law—in this case, the Gun-Free School Zones Act of 1990—for exceeding the scope of the Commerce Clause. Chief Justice William Rehnquist held for a five-member majority that the act (which made it a federal offense "for any individual knowingly to possess a firearm at a place that the individual knows, or has reasonable cause to believe, is a school zone")[11] "neither regulates a commercial activity nor contains a requirement that the possession be connected in any way to interstate commerce"; consequently, it "exceeds the authority of Congress 'to regulate Commerce . . . among the several States.'"[12]

Rehnquist began by answering what prior case law had left as an open question, namely, for an activity to be within Congress's power to regulate under the Commerce Clause, is it enough that it merely "affects" interstate commerce, or must it affect it "substantially"? He concluded for the majority that the "proper test" was that the regulated activity must "substantially affect" interstate commerce.[13] Applying that test, he concluded that "the possession of a gun in a local school zone is in no sense an economic activity that might, through repetition elsewhere, substantially affect any sort of interstate commerce."[14]

Both the federal government in its brief to the Court and Justice Stephen Breyer in his dissent argued that the possession of a gun in a school zone did substantially affect commerce. Rehnquist summarized their argument as follows: "The presence of guns in schools poses a substantial threat to the education process by threatening the learning environment. A handicapped education process, in turn, will result in a less productive citizenry. That, in turn, would have an adverse effect on the Nation's economic well-being."[15] The problem with that argument, the chief justice contended, was that it made it impossible "to posit any activity by an individual that Congress is without power to regulate."[16] In fact, he added, that argument "would bid fair to convert congressional authority under the Commerce Clause to a general police power of the sort retained by the States."[17] He acknowledged that "some of our prior cases have taken long steps down that road," but he declined "to proceed any further."[18]

The dissenters uniformly complained that the majority had abandoned "the practice of deferring to rationally based legislative judgments."[19] For Justice David Souter, the "touchstone of constitutionality" was "rational possibility,"[20] that is, "whether the legislative judgment is within the realm of reason."[21] There was no evidence in the record that Congress had found that the presence of a gun within a school zone substantially affected interstate commerce, but, Souter insisted, "the legislation implies such a finding, and there is no reason to entertain claims that Congress acted *ultra vires* intentionally."[22] Justice Breyer reminded the majority that the Constitution requires the Court to judge "the connection between a regulated activity and interstate commerce, not directly, but at one remove." The Court must therefore give Congress "a degree of leeway" when determining whether there is a sufficiently "significant factual connection" between the two, he said, not only because the Constitution "delegates the commerce power directly to Congress" but also because that determination "requires an empirical judgment of a kind that a legislature is more likely than a court to make with accuracy. The traditional words 'rational basis' capture this leeway."[23]

Interestingly, Breyer was unwilling to give Congress as much "leeway" as Souter was. Whereas Souter inferred a connection between guns in school zones and their effect on interstate commerce from the fact that Congress enacted the measure in question, Breyer felt obliged to prove the "empirical connection" that he claimed Congress could have made with greater "accuracy," when in fact Congress had not bothered to make it at all.[24] Thus, Breyer spent six pages of his dissent (and added a fourteen-page appendix of citations)[25] to justify the leeway he was willing to give Congress in determining that its unstated "empirical judgment" concerning the impact of guns on education and therefore on the economy was rational.

Justice Thomas wrote a separate concurrence to comment on how far the Court's case law had drifted "from the original understanding of the Commerce Clause"[26] and to distance himself from the substantial effects test. "We have said that Congress may regulate not only 'Commerce . . . among the several states,' but also anything that has a 'substantial effect' on such commerce. This test, if taken to its logical extreme, would give Congress a 'police power' over all aspects of American life."[27]

He argued that "we have never come to grips with this implication of our substantial effects formula. Although we have supposedly applied the substantial effects test for the past 60 years, we *always* have rejected readings of the Commerce Clause and the scope of federal power that would permit Congress to exercise a police power; our cases are quite clear that there are real limits to federal power."[28] He noted that "on this crucial point," the majority and Justice Breyer agreed in principle: namely, that "the Federal Government has nothing approaching a police power."[29] However, even though Breyer acknowledged that there were limits to federal power, Thomas observed that his colleague could not "muster even one example" of something Congress could not regulate and that "when asked at oral argument if there were *any* limits to the Commerce Clause, the Government was at a loss for words."[30] Unlike Breyer and U.S. Solicitor General Drew S. Days III, who argued for the government, Thomas was not at a loss for words and mustered several examples: "The power to regulate 'commerce' can by no means encompass authority over mere gun possession, any more than it empowers the Federal Government to regulate marriage, littering, or cruelty to animals, throughout the 50 States. Our Constitution quite properly leaves such matters to the individual States, notwithstanding these activities' effects on interstate commerce. Any interpretation of the Commerce Clause that even suggests that Congress could regulate such matters is in need of reexamination."[31]

Thomas then focused on "the text, structure, and history of the Commerce Clause."[32] He began by turning to dictionaries of the era and found that "at the time the original Constitution was ratified, 'commerce' consisted of selling, buying, and bartering, as well as transporting for these purposes."[33] He cited a variety of Federalist and Anti-Federalist sources to demonstrate that "during the ratification period, they often used trade (in its selling/bartering sense) and commerce interchangeably."[34] He then quoted Hamilton from several numbers of *The Federalist* and delegates from the Massachusetts and New York Ratifying Conventions to support his argument that "the term 'commerce' was used in contradistinction to productive activities such as manufacturing and agriculture."[35]

Earlier in his opinion, Thomas had indicated that a further reconsideration of the Court's substantial effects test should be deferred to some "appropriate case" in the future,[36] but he nonetheless felt compelled to observe that the Commerce Clause does not state that Congress may "regulate matters that substantially affect commerce with foreign Nations, and among the several States, and with the Indian Tribes." In contrast, the Constitution itself temporarily prohibited amendments that would "affect" Congress' lack of authority to prohibit or restrict the slave trade or to enact unproportioned direct taxation. Clearly, the Framers could have drafted a Constitution that contained a "substantially affects interstate commerce" clause had that been their objective.[37]

Thomas then introduced one of the key arguments in his opinion. The Court's substantial effects test combined with its reading of the Necessary and Proper Clause had rendered "wholly superfluous" many of "Congress' other enumerated powers under Article I, § 8." He wrote:

> After all, if Congress may regulate all matters that substantially affect commerce, there is no need for the Constitution to specify that Congress may enact bankruptcy laws, cl. 4, or coin money and fix the standard of weights and measures, cl. 5, or punish counterfeiters of United States coin and securities, cl. 6. Likewise, Congress would not need the separate authority to establish post-offices and post-roads, cl. 7, or to grant patents and copyrights, cl. 8, or to "punish Piracies and Felonies committed on the high Seas," cl. 10. It might not even need the power to raise and support an Army and Navy, cls. 12 and 13, for fewer people would engage in commercial shipping if they thought that a foreign power could expropriate their property with ease. Indeed, if Congress could regulate matters that substantially affect interstate commerce, there would have been no need to specify that Congress can regulate international trade and commerce with the Indians. As the Framers surely understood, these other branches of trade substantially affect interstate commerce.[38]

Thomas insisted that an interpretation of the Interstate Commerce Clause, based on the substantial effects test, "that makes the rest of § 8 superfluous simply cannot be correct." Yet, he continued, this is what both the majority and dissenting opinions had endorsed: "The power we have accorded Congress has swallowed Art. I, § 8, . . . something we can assume the Founding Fathers never intended."[39] He concluded this section by observing that "our construction of the scope of congressional authority has the additional problem of coming close to turning the Tenth Amendment on its head. Our case law could be read to reserve to the United States all powers not expressly *prohibited* by the Constitution. Taken together, these fundamental textual problems should, at the very least, convince us that the 'substantial effects' test should be reexamined."[40]

Up to this point in his *Lopez* concurrence, Thomas was making what might be called an original public meaning interpretation based simply on the text of Article I, § 8 and the original meaning of that text. But he went on to explain the text based on his original general meaning interpretation of "commerce among the several states." He began in this respect by acknowledging that "early Americans understood that commerce, manufacturing, and agriculture, while distinct activities, were intimately related and dependent on each other—that each 'substantially affected' the others." This made perfect sense, he said, for "items produced by farmers and manufacturers were the primary articles of commerce at the time."[41] But, Thomas added, "despite being well aware that agriculture, manufacturing, and other matters substantially affected commerce, the founding generation did not cede authority over all these activities to Congress." He quoted Hamilton in *Federalist* No. 17 as denying that the federal government could regulate agriculture and like concerns: "The administration of private justice between the citizens of the same State, the supervision of agriculture and of other concerns of a similar nature, all those things in short which are proper to be provided for by local legislation, can never be desirable cares of a general jurisdiction." Thomas continued to quote from Hamilton: if the federal government were to attempt to exercise authority over such matters, such an attempt "would be as troublesome as it would be nugatory."[42]

Furthermore, Thomas noted, where the framers intended to grant federal authority over an activity substantially affecting interstate commerce, they specifically enumerated a power over that particular activity. He offered two examples. Madison in *Federalist* No. 42 spoke of the bankruptcy power as being "intimately connected with the regulation of commerce," and Hamilton in *Federalist* No. 24 declared that "if we mean to be a commercial people or even to be secure on our Atlantic side, we must endeavor as soon as possible to have a navy."[43] The framers expressly delegated to Congress in Article I, § 8 both of those powers. They drew the "constitutional line" between those activities that substantially affected interstate commerce that Congress could regulate—because the power to do so was delegated to it—and those it could not, and Thomas insisted that the Court had to respect that line.[44]

In his dissent, Breyer argued that Chief Justice Marshall had established in *Gibbons v. Ogden*[45] that Congress could control all local activities that significantly affected interstate commerce and, further, that Marshall's opinion in *Gibbons* was the traditional method of interpreting the Commerce Clause.[46] Thomas felt obliged to respond. He reviewed *Gibbons* and subsequent case law and concluded: "I am aware of no cases prior to the New Deal that characterized the power flowing from the Commerce Clause as sweepingly as does our substantial effects test."[47] To the contrary, he said, his review of these cases established "a simple point: from the time of the ratification of the Constitution to the mid 1930s, it was widely understood that the Constitution granted Congress only limited powers, notwithstanding the Commerce Clause."[48] As he saw it, the substantial effects test was an "innovation of the 20th century"[49] and a clear departure from "the original understanding of the Constitution."[50]

Lopez was decided in Thomas's fourth year on the Court, and at that point, he was not as bold as he would later become in rejecting precedent and removing excrescence. Thus, he concluded somewhat tentatively: "This extended discussion of the original understanding and our first century and a half of case law does not necessarily require a wholesale abandonment of our more recent opinions."[51] He ended that sentence by dropping a footnote that read: "Although I might be willing to return to the original understanding, I recognize that many believe that it is too late in the day to undertake a fundamental reexamination of the past 60 years. Consideration of *stare decisis* and reliance interests may convince us that we cannot wipe the slate clean."[52] He did assert, however, "We ought to temper our Commerce Clause jurisprudence"[53] so that it would not be "a blank check"[54] to Congress allowing it to regulate everything "under the guise of the Commerce Clause."[55]

In *Printz v. United States*,[56] Thomas built on his *Lopez* concurrence. In *Printz*, the Court considered the constitutionality of those provisions of the Brady Handgun Violence Prevention Act that commanded the chief law enforcement officer (CLEO) of each local jurisdiction to conduct background checks on prospective handgun purchasers on an interim basis until a national instant background check system could become operational. Justice Scalia held for a five-member majority that this congressional command was "fundamentally incompatible with our constitutional system of dual sovereignty" and was, therefore, unconstitutional.[57]

In his concurring opinion, Thomas described his approach as a "revisionist" one in which, as he explained in *Lopez*, "the Federal Government's authority under the Commerce Clause . . . does not extend to the regulation of wholly *intra*state, point of sale transactions."[58] If, as he believed, Congress lacked "the underlying authority to regulate the intrastate transfer of firearms," then "Congress surely lacks the corollary power to impress state law enforcement officers into administering and enforcing such regulations."[59] And even if the Court were to construe Congress's authority to regulate interstate commerce as encompassing those intrastate transactions that substantially affect interstate commerce, he said, he questioned whether Congress had the power to regulate these particular transactions.

The Constitution, he reminded his colleagues, delegated certain enumerated powers to Congress but also placed "whole areas outside the reach of Congress' regulatory authority. The First Amendment, for example, is fittingly celebrated for preventing Congress from 'prohibiting the free exercise' of religion or 'abridging the freedom of speech.'"[60] Interestingly, Thomas went on to anticipate the majority opinion in *District of Columbia v. Heller*[61] when he wrote: "The Second Amendment similarly appears to contain an express limitation on the government's authority." He recognized that the Court had "not had recent occasion to consider the nature of the substantive right safeguarded by the Second Amendment." But, he declared, if "the Second Amendment is read to confer a *personal* right to 'keep and bear arms,' a colorable argument exists that the Federal Government's regulatory scheme, at least as it pertains to the purely intrastate sale or possession of firearms, runs afoul of that Amendment's protections." Since the parties did not raise this argument, he agreed that there was no need to consider it in the present case. Nonetheless, he wondered whether "at some future date, this Court will have the opportunity to determine whether Justice Story was correct when he wrote that the right to bear arms 'has justly been considered, as the palladium of the liberties of a republic.' 3 J. Story, *Commentaries* § 1890, p. 746 (1833)."[62]

By the time of his concurring opinion in *United States v. Morrison*,[63] Thomas had become considerably bolder in articulating his views in *Lopez* and attacking the substantial effects test. In *Morrison*, the Supreme Court held, by a five-to-four vote, that Congress lacked the constitutional authority to enact a key provision of the Violence against Women Act (VAWA) of 1994 under either the Commerce Clause or § 5 of the Fourteenth Amendment, both of which Congress had explicitly identified as sources of its authority to legislate in this area.

In his majority opinion, Chief Justice Rehnquist expressed concern that if the Court were to uphold Congress's authority under the Commerce Clause to enact VAWA, the result would be "to completely obliterate the Constitution's distinction between national and local authority":

> The reasoning that petitioners advance seeks to follow the but-for causal chain from the initial occurrence of violent crime (the suppression of which has always been the prime object of the States' police power) to every attenuated effect upon interstate commerce. If accepted, petitioners' reasoning would allow Congress to regulate any crime as long as the nationwide, aggregated impact of that crime has substantial effects on employment, production, transit, or consumption. Indeed, if Congress may regulate gender-motivated violence, it would be able to regulate murder or any other type of violence since gender-motivated violence, as a subset of all violent crime, is certain to have lesser economic impacts than the larger class of which it is a part.[64]

Rehnquist feared that a Court decision affirming the constitutionality of VAWA would provide Congress with authority to legislate on matters of family law as well:

> Petitioners' reasoning, moreover, will not limit Congress to regulating violence but may . . . be applied equally as well to family law and other areas of traditional state regulation since the aggregate effect of marriage, divorce, and childrearing on the national economy is undoubtedly significant. Congress may have recognized this specter when it expressly precluded [VAWA] from being used in the family law context. Under our written Constitution, however, the limitation of congressional authority is not solely a matter of legislative grace.[65]

Thomas declared in his concurrence that the majority opinion correctly applied *Lopez* and that he joined it in full.[66] He wrote separately, however, to renew his attack on the substantial effects test, which he declared

> is inconsistent with the original understanding of Congress' powers and with this Court's early Commerce Clause cases. By continuing to apply this rootless and malleable standard, however circumscribed, the Court has encouraged the Federal Government to persist in its view that the Commerce Clause has virtually no limits. Until this Court replaces its existing Commerce Clause jurisprudence with a standard more consistent with the original understanding, we will continue to see Congress appropriating state police powers under the guise of regulating commerce.[67]

In *Gonzales v. Raich*,[68] the Court addressed an action by the respondents to seek injunctive and declaratory relief prohibiting the federal government from enforcing the federal Controlled Substances Act (CSA) and preventing them from possessing, obtaining, or growing marijuana for their personal medical use, consistent with California's Compassionate Use Act (passed in 1996 as a ballot initiative). The District Court for the Northern District of California denied their motion for a preliminary injunction, but the Ninth Circuit reversed. It found that the respondents had demonstrated a strong likelihood of success on the claim that the CSA as applied was an unconstitutional exercise of Congress's Commerce Clause power to prohibit the intrastate, noncommercial cultivation and possession of marijuana for personal medical purposes as recommended by a patient's physician pursuant to this valid California state law. The court relied heavily on *Lopez* and *Morrison* to hold that this separate class of purely local activities was beyond the reach of federal power.

Justice Stevens's opinion for a five-member majority overturned the Ninth Circuit and held that the regulation of marijuana under the CSA was squarely within Congress's commerce power because production of marijuana meant for home consumption had a substantial effect on the supply and demand of marijuana in the national market. In light of the enforcement difficulties in distinguishing between marijuana cultivated locally and marijuana grown elsewhere, as well as concerns about diversion of medical marijuana into illicit channels, Stevens concluded that Congress had a rational basis for believing that failure to regulate the intrastate manufacture and possession of marijuana would leave a "gaping hole" in the CSA and that Congress was acting well within its authority under the Commerce Clause.[69]

Surprisingly to many, Justice Scalia concurred in the judgment. He argued that activities that merely substantially affect interstate commerce are not part of interstate commerce, and thus the power to regulate them cannot come from the Commerce Clause alone; that Congress's regulatory authority over intrastate activities that are not part of interstate commerce derives from the Constitution's Necessary and Proper Clause; and that if it is necessary to make a regulation of interstate commerce effective, Congress has the power to regulate even those intrastate activities that do not substantially affect interstate commerce.[70] In the CSA, he declared,

> Congress has undertaken to extinguish the interstate market in Schedule I controlled substances, including marijuana. The Commerce Clause unquestionably permits this. . . . To effectuate its objective, Congress has prohibited almost all intrastate activities related to Schedule I substances—both economic activities (manufacture, distribution, possession with the intent to distribute) and noneconomic activities (simple possession). That simple possession is a noneconomic activity is immaterial to whether it can be prohibited as a necessary part of a larger regulation. Rather, Congress's authority to enact all of these prohibitions of intrastate controlled-substance activities depends only upon whether they are appropriate means of achieving the legitimate end of eradicating Schedule I substances from interstate commerce.[71]

Thomas, in his second major Commerce Clause opinion, felt compelled to dissent on original general meaning grounds. He opened with the following salvo: "Respondents Diane Monson and Angel Raich use marijuana that has never been bought or sold, that has never crossed state lines, and that has had no demonstrable effect on the national market for marijuana. If Congress can regulate this under the Commerce Clause, then it can regulate virtually any-thing—and the Federal Government is no longer one of limited and enumerated powers."[72]

Thomas insisted that the respondents' conduct was "purely intrastate and noncommercial" and therefore beyond Congress's reach: "Monson and Raich neither buy nor sell the marijuana that they consume. They cultivate their can-nabis entirely in the State of California—it never crosses state lines, much less as part of a commercial transaction." Moreover, he pointed out, there was "certainly no evidence from the founding" to suggest that "commerce" included "the mere possession of a good or some purely personal activity that did not involve trade or exchange for value." He made clear how far the *Raich* majority had departed from the original understanding of the Commerce Clause, stating, "In the early days of the Republic, it would have been unthinkable that Congress could pro-hibit the local cultivation, possession, and consumption of marijuana."[73]

Thomas acknowledged that "on its face, a ban on the intrastate cultivation, possession and distribution of marijuana" may be necessary and proper and therefore "plainly adapted to stopping the interstate flow of marijuana. Unregu-lated local growers and users could swell both the supply and the demand sides of the interstate marijuana market, making the market more difficult to regulate." But he noted that the respondents did not challenge the CSA on its face. Instead, they challenged it as applied to their conduct. "The question is thus whether the intrastate ban is 'necessary and proper' as applied to medical marijuana users like respondents"[74]—"seriously ill Californians" subject to the strict regulations of California's Compassionate Use Act and suffering from such diseases as "cancer, AIDS, or arthritis" for whom cannabis can relieve pain.[75] And since "no one argues that permitting use of these drugs under medical supervision has under-mined the CSA's restrictions," Thomas insisted that it was not necessary to apply the CSA to them.[76] "Congress' goal of curtailing the interstate drug trade would not plainly be thwarted if it could not apply the CSA to patients like Monson and Raich. That is, unless Congress' aim is really to exercise police power of the sort reserved to the States in order to eliminate even the intrastate possession and use of marijuana."[77]

As in his concurrences in *Lopez* and *Morrison*, Thomas again criticized the "rootless and malleable" substantial effects test as "not tethered to either the Commerce Clause or the Necessary and Proper Clause."[78] Once Stevens, writ-ing for the majority, had defined economic activity to include "the production, distribution, and consumption of commodities,"[79] the test allowed the Court to hold that the CSA applied to the respondents. But, Thomas complained, that definition of economic activity combined with the substantial effects test carve[d] out a vast swath of activities that are subject to federal regulation. If the majority is to be taken seriously, the Federal Government may now regulate quilting bees, clothes drives, and potluck suppers throughout the 50 States. This makes a mockery of Madison's assurance to the people of New York [in *Federalist* No. 45] that the "powers delegated" to the Federal Government are "few and defined," while those of the States are "numerous and indefinite."[80]

Thomas concluded by insisting that although "Congress is authorized to regulate 'Commerce,'" what Monson and Raich were engaged in did not qualify "under any definition of that term." The majority opinion, he argued, illustrated "the steady drift away from the text of the Commerce Clause." Under the Court's "inexorable expansion" of "commerce," the power of the federal government "expands, but never contracts" because the Court "is not interpreting the Commerce Clause, but rewriting it."[81]

Thomas speculated that this rewriting may have been "rooted in the belief that, unless the Commerce Clause covers the entire web of human activity, Congress will be left powerless to regulate the national economy effectively." But, he added,

the Framers understood what the majority does not appear to fully appreciate: There is a danger to concentrating too much, as well as too little, power in the Federal Government. This Court has carefully avoided stripping Congress of its ability to regulate interstate commerce, but it has casually allowed the Federal Government to strip States of their ability to regulate intrastate commerce—not to mention a host of local activities, like mere drug possession, that are not commercial.[82]

He declared that one would search "in vain" in the majority opinion for "any hint of what aspect of American life is reserved to the States." Until the Court is willing either "to enforce limits on federal power" or "declare the Tenth Amendment a dead letter," he asserted, there will be "no measure of stability to our Commerce Clause jurisprudence." He proposed to remove excrescence and to reestablish stability "by discarding the stand-alone substantial effects test and revisiting our definition of 'Commerce among the several States.'"[83]

Given these arguments, it was not surprising that in *National Federation of Independent Business* [NFIB] *v. Sebelius*,[84] Thomas found unconstitutional the individual mandate in the Affordable Care Act (commonly know as Obamacare) requiring all individuals to purchase health insurance and imposing penalties on those who fail to do so. He wrote a short opinion quoting from his *Morrison* concurrence that the Court's continued use of the substantial effects test "has encouraged the Federal Government to persist in its view that the Commerce Clause has virtually no limits" and pointing out that "the Government's unprecedented claim in this suit that it may regulate not only economic activity but also *inactivity* that substantially affects interstate commerce is a case in point."[85]

Additionally, he joined Antonin Scalia, Anthony Kennedy, and Samuel Alito in a highly unusual joint dissent, holding that Congress's power to regulate commerce does not extend to the power to direct the "creation of commerce" by mandating the purchase of health insurance. "If every person comes within the Commerce Clause power of Congress to regulate by the simple reason that he will one day engage in commerce, the idea of a limited Government power is at an end."[86] In the same joint dissent, he and his colleagues rejected Chief Justice John Roberts's argument for the Court majority that the individual mandate was independently authorized under Congress's taxing power. For the joint dissenters, the issue was not whether Congress had the power to frame the individual mandate as a tax "but whether it *did* so." For them, "the nail in the coffin" of Roberts's "invented and atextual" claim was that the mandate and penalty were located in Title I of the Affordable Care Act, "its operative core, rather than where a tax would be found—in Title IX, containing the Act's 'Revenue Provisions.'" And thus, they concluded, "to say the individual mandate merely imposes a tax is not to interpret the statue but to rewrite it."[87]

Thomas's original understanding approach in *Lopez, Printz, Morrison, Raich,* and *NFIB* is powerful but also somewhat myopic, in that it does not address the question of how adherence to the original understanding of the text is to be secured. Thomas assumes it is the duty and role of the Court to enforce the text as explained.[88] The framers, however, understood that the means to ensure, first, that the Commerce Clause (or any other delegated power, for that matter) would not become a blank check by which Congress could regulate everything and, second, that the reserved powers of the states would be protected was the mode of electing (and, perhaps more important, reelecting) the U.S. Senate.[89] Until the Seventeenth Amendment, senators were elected by state legislatures, and the significance of that structural feature of the Constitution was clear to the members of the founding generation. In fact, it was perfectly captured in a July 1789 letter to John Adams in which Roger Sherman emphasized that "the senators, being eligible by the legislatures of the several states, and dependent on them for reelection, will be vigilant in supporting their rights against infringement by the legislative or executive of the United States."[90]

On May 31, 1787, very early in the Constitutional Convention, the assembled delegates rejected Resolution 5 of the Virginia Plan, which proposed that the "second branch of the National Legislature ought to be elected by those of the first," by a vote of seven states "no" and three states "yes."[91] Instead, on June 7, the delegates unanimously accepted a motion made by John Dickinson and seconded by Roger Sherman providing for the appointment of the Senate by the state legislatures.[92]

The delegates were apparently persuaded by Dickinson's argument that the "sense of the States would be better collected through their Governments than immediately from the people at large"[93] and by George Mason's observation that election of the Senate by state legislatures would provide the states with "some means of defending themselves against encroachments of the National Government. In every other department, we have studiously endeavored to provide for its self-defense. Shall we leave the States alone unprovided with the means for this purpose? And what better means can we provide than giving them some share in, or rather making them a constituent part of, the Nat'l Establishment?"[94]

During the New York Ratifying Convention, Hamilton explicitly connected the mode of electing the Senate with the protection of the interests of the states as states and with ensuring that Congress would not abuse the exercise of its delegated powers:

> When you take a view of all the circumstances which have been recited, you will certainly see that the senators will constantly look up to the state governments with an eye of dependence and affection. If they are ambitious to continue in office, they will make every prudent arrangement for this purpose, and, whatever may be their private sentiments or politics, they will be convinced that the surest means of obtaining reelection will be a uniform attachment to the interests of their several states.[95]

He also declared: "Sir, the senators will constantly be attended with a reflection, that their future existence is absolutely in the power of the states. Will not this form a powerful check?"[96]

The framers favored election of the Senate by state legislatures not simply because it provided, in Hamilton's words from *Federalist* No. 59, incentives for senators to remain vigilant in their protection of the "States in their political capacities."[97] They also favored this mode of election because it helped them sidestep what Madison described in *Federalist* No. 37 as the "arduous" task of "marking the proper line of partition, between the authority of the general, and that of the State Governments."[98]

An episode at the outset of the convention tells it all. On May 31, the convention, meeting as a committee of the whole, had just taken up Resolution 6 of the Virginia Plan, which proposed, inter alia, that "the National Legislature ought to be empowered . . . to legislate in all cases to which the separate States were incompetent." Charles Pinckney and John Rutledge "objected to the vagueness of the term *incompetent*, and said they could not well decide how to vote until they should see an exact enumeration of the powers comprehended by this definition."[99] Edmund Randolph, governor of Virginia and therefore head of the Virginia delegation, quickly "disclaimed any intention to give indefinite powers to the national Legislature,"[100] but Madison took a different tack and explained the reason for the language. He expressed his "doubts concerning [the] practicality" of "an enumeration and definition of the powers necessary to be exercised by the national Legislature." Despite having arrived at the convention with a "strong bias in favor of an enumeration," he owned that during the weeks before a quorum gathered in Philadelphia (during which he and his fellow Virginia delegates drafted the Virginia Plan, including the language in Resolution 6), "his doubts had become stronger." He declared that he would "shrink from nothing," including, he implied, abandoning any attempt to enumerate the specific powers of the national government, "which should be found essential to such a form of Government as would provide for the safety, liberty, and happiness of the community. This being the end of all our deliberations, all the necessary means for attaining it must, however reluctantly, be submitted to."[101] Madison would later elaborate on this same "means-ends" argument in *Federalist* No. 41, when he declared, "It is vain to oppose constitutional barriers to the impulse of self-preservation. It is worse than in vain; because it plants in the Constitution itself necessary usurpations of power, every precedent of which is a germ of unnecessary and multiplied repetitions."[102]

On May 31, Madison merely foreshadowed the argument he would later develop more fully in *Federalist* No. 51, namely, that the power of the new federal government was to be controlled not through an exact enumeration (that is, through the use of "parchment barriers")[103] but by "so contriving the interior structure of the government, as that its several constituent parts may, by their mutual relations, be the means of keeping each other in their proper places."[104] Nonetheless, his words were obviously reassuring, for the convention voted at the conclusion of his speech to accept that portion of Resolution 6 by a vote of nine states "yes," one state "divided."[105]

The convention delegates apparently shared Madison's doubts about the "practicality" of partitioning power between the federal government and the states through an enumeration of the powers of the former. Spending almost no time debating what specific powers the federal government should have, they focused instead and almost exclusively on the question of constitutional structure. Thus, the only resolution pertaining to the powers of the federal government forwarded by the delegates to the Committee of Detail (charged with taking "the proceedings of the Convention for the establishment of a Natl. Govt." and "prepar[ing] and report[ing] a Constitution conformable thereto")[106] stated only that "the Legislature of the United

States ought to possess the legislative Rights vested in Congress by the Articles of Confederation; and moreover to legislate in all Cases for the general Interests of the Union, and also in those Cases to which the States are separately incompetent, or in which the Harmony of the United States may be interrupted by the Exercise of individual Legislation."[107]

Not even when the Committee of Detail created out of whole cloth what ultimately became Article I, § 8 did the convention delegates systematically scrutinize the powers enumerated therein. Thus, for example, on August 16, when the language of the Committee of Detail concerning commerce first came up for discussion, Madison simply reported in his Notes: "Clause for regulating commerce with foreign nations, &c. agreed to nem. con."[108] There was no discussion of Congress's power to regulate commerce "among the several States," and interestingly, Madison did not even allude to that portion of what would become the Interstate Commerce Clause but mentioned only foreign commerce.[109]

The delegates did not even object to the proposed Necessary and Proper Clause. On August 20, when the convention first took up the language proposed by the Committee of Detail that gave Congress the authority "to make all laws necessary and proper for carrying into execution the foregoing powers, and all other powers vested, by this Constitution, in the Government of the U. S. or any department or officer thereof," the only discussion centered on a motion by James Madison and Charles Pinckney "to insert between 'laws' and 'necessary' 'and establish all offices,' it appearing to them liable to cavil that the latter was not included in the former." Madison reported in his Notes that "Mr. Govr. [*sic*] Morris, Mr. Wilson, Mr. Rutlidge [*sic*] and Mr. Elseworth [*sic*] urged that the amendment could not be necessary," and it was defeated by a vote of nine states "no" and two states "yes." With that matter resolved, Madison stated that "the clause as reported was then agreed to nem. con."[110]

The conclusion is clear: rather than rely on precisely drawn lines demarcating the powers of the federal and state governments, the framers preferred instead to rely on such structural arrangements as the election of the Senate by the state legislatures to ensure that the vast powers they provided to the national government would not be abused.

One final point is in order here. The framers relied on the mode of electing (and reelecting) the Senate and on the self-interest of senators—not on the Supreme Court—to prevent Congress from treating the Commerce Clause as a blank check. They clearly did not expect that the Court would protect the reserved powers of the states or interfere with Congress's decision about where to draw the line between federal and state powers. They understood that drawing such a line involved prudential considerations beyond the Court's legal capacity to pass judgment. They also understood that to the extent that the Constitution authorized the

Court to exercise the power of judicial review (and whether it did so was itself a major question),[111] it was only pertinent in those cases in which the popular branches had acted, in the words of *Federalist* No. 78, "contrary to the *manifest tenor* of the Constitution."[112] The Court was not to invalidate congressional measures in close cases. As James Wilson, a vigorous defender of judicial review,[113] acknowledged in the Constitutional Convention: "Laws may be unjust, may be unwise, may be dangerous, may be destructive; and yet may not be *so unconstitutional* as to justify the Judges in refusing to give them effect."[114] Rather, as Hamilton made clear in *Federalist* No. 78, the Court was to invalidate measures only in cases in which Congress's disregard for "certain specified exceptions to the legislative authority" was akin to its passage of a bill of attainder or an ex post facto law.[115] Decisions by Congress regarding where federal power ends and state power begins were of a different character; they did not implicate "specified exceptions" to Congress's legislative authority but merely involved prudential judgments, agreed to by a Senate elected by state legislatures, concerning the outer reaches of the delegated powers of Congress. As a consequence, these decisions could never be held unconstitutional by the Court because they never could be regarded as clearly contrary to the Constitution's "manifest tenor."

Hamilton's discussion in *Federalist* No. 33 of the Necessary and Proper Clause is also instructive in this regard, for in it, he did not so much as allude to the Supreme Court when he answered his own question of who was "to judge the necessity and propriety of the laws to be passed for executing the powers of the Union." For Hamilton, Congress was to judge "in the first instance the proper exercise of its powers; and its constituents [and for the Senate, that meant the state legislatures] in the last." If Congress were to use the Necessary and Proper Clause "to overpass the just bounds of its authority and make a tyrannical use of its powers," Hamilton argued, "the people whose creature it is must appeal to the standard they have formed, and take such measures to redress the injury done to the constitution, as the exigency may suggest and prudence justify."[116] Again, he made no reference to the Supreme Court exercising judicial review to negate such congressional actions.

The adoption and ratification of the Seventeenth Amendment, providing for direct election of the Senate, changed all that. After an eighty-six-year campaign, the amendment was approved by the U.S. Congress in 1912 and ratified by the states in 1913 to make the Constitution more democratic.[117] The consequences of the ratification of the Seventeenth Amendment on what the framers regarded as the crucial constitutional means for ensuring that Congress would not act in ways that exceeded its delegated powers went completely unexplored by those who adopted and ratified it.[118] These consequences may be of little moment to nonoriginalist justices, but they should be troubling to an originalist like Thomas. They raise the question of why it is appropriate to secure the original understanding of the Commerce Clause by means (judicial review) inconsistent with the way in which the framers understood that clause would be secured. This is more of a problem for an original general meaning justice like Thomas than it is for an original public meaning justice like Scalia.

The Negative Commerce Clause

As he began his 2008 Wriston Lecture to the Manhattan Institute, Thomas teased his audience by threatening to talk about the negative Commerce Clause (that is his typical term, but at the lecture he called it "the dormant Commerce Clause").[119] "For years, I have wanted to give a talk on the dormant Commerce Clause," he said, but "they have hidden the audience for that talk someplace with Osama bin Laden." Indicating that the topic was "an intriguing thing" and "pretty fascinating when you think about it," he assured those assembled that he would "reserve that talk for another time" and spoke instead on "Judging in a Government by Consent."[120]

The negative (or dormant) Commerce Clause is a legal doctrine holding that the Commerce Clause of Article I, § 8 not only grants power to Congress to regulate commerce among the states but also confers power on the Court to protect the "right to engage in interstate trade free from restrictive state regulation."[121] It holds that "the very purpose of the Commerce Clause was to create an area of free trade among the several States" and that the Clause "by *its own force* created an area of trade free from interference by the States."[122] Therefore, irrespective of whether Congress has itself acted on the basis of its delegated power to prohibit this interference, it holds that the Court is constitutionally authorized to protect this "area of free trade" and to vindicate this right to engage in interstate commerce free from state interference by weighing the burdens that state regulation of commerce imposes against the benefits it provides and invalidating all discriminatory burdens it concludes are unjustified. On original general meaning grounds, Thomas has become a fierce critic of the negative Commerce Clause, but it was not always so.

In the 1994 case of *Oregon Waste Systems v. Department of Environmental Quality of the State of Oregon*,[123] Thomas wrote the opinion for a seven-member majority holding that Oregon offered no legitimate reason to subject waste generated in other states to a discriminatory surcharge and that its imposition of that surcharge was therefore facially invalid under the negative Commerce Clause. He cited *Chemical Waste Management v. Hunt*,[124] a negative Commerce Clause case he joined during his first year on the High Bench,[125] and declared, "We deem it . . . obvious here that Oregon's $2.25 per ton surcharge is discriminatory on its face. The surcharge subjects waste from other States to a fee almost three times greater than the $0.85 per ton charge imposed on solid in-state waste. The statutory determinant for which fee applies to any particular shipment of solid waste to an Oregon landfill is whether or not the waste was 'generated out of state.' . . . In making that geographic distinction, the surcharge patently discriminates against interstate commerce."[126]

Later that same year, he held in *Associated Industries of Missouri v. Lohman,*[127] for an eight-member majority, that Missouri's use tax violated the negative Commerce Clause in those local jurisdictions in the state where the use tax exceeded the local sales tax. He observed that "although the Commerce Clause is phrased merely as a grant of authority to Congress to 'regulate Commerce . . . among the several States,' it is well established that the Clause also embodies a negative command forbidding the States to discriminate against interstate trade."[128] And also in that year, he complained in his dissent in *Northwest Airlines v. County of Kent, Michigan*[129] that the case should have been remanded so that the lower courts could have been "given the opportunity to consider the merits of petitioners' dormant Commerce Clause challenge."[130] Northwest Airlines and other carriers had argued that because Michigan's Kent County International Airport charged commercial airlines 100 percent of their allocated air operations and terminal/concession costs but general aviation only 20 percent of their allocated costs, the airport discriminated against interstate commerce in favor of primarily local traffic, in violation of the negative Commerce Clause.

In 1995, Thomas took for granted the validity of the negative Commerce Clause in his unanimous opinion for the Court in *National Private Truck Council v. Oklahoma Tax Commission.*[131] And in 1996, he readily joined Justice David Souter's unanimous opinion in *Fulton Corporation v. Faulkner*[132] that North Carolina's intangibles tax discriminated against interstate commerce in violation of the negative Commerce Clause.

But all that changed in 1997 with his dissent in *Camps Newfound/Owatonna v. Town of Harrison.*[133] Justice John Paul Stevens held, in a five-to-four decision, that a Maine statute exempting charitable organizations from real estate and personal property taxes if they operated principally for the benefit of state residents but not if they operated principally for the benefit of nonresidents violated the negative Commerce Clause. In his words, the Commerce Clause "not only granted Congress express authority to override restrictive and conflicting commercial regulations adopted by the States" but also "immediately effected a curtailment of state power" that the Court could enforce.[134]

Thomas experienced an epiphany. He began his dissent by pointing out that "the tax at issue here is a tax on real estate, the quintessential asset that does not move in interstate commerce."[135] By invalidating Maine's tax assessment on the real property of charitable organizations primarily serving nonresidents, he said that the Court majority had worked "a significant, unwarranted, and, in my view, improvident expansion in our 'dormant,' or 'negative,' Commerce Clause jurisprudence"[136] —one that compelled him to "revisit . . . the underlying justifications for our involvement in the negative aspects of the Commerce Clause."[137] Although this expansion found "some support in the morass of our negative Commerce Clause case law," for Thomas that only served "to highlight the need to abandon that failed jurisprudence" and—here, his original general meaning approach was on display—"to consider restoring the original Import Export Clause check on discriminatory state taxation to what appears to be its proper role." Declaring that "the tax (and tax exemption) at issue in this case seems easily to survive Import Export Clause scrutiny; I would therefore, in all likelihood, sustain Maine's tax under that Clause as well, were we to apply it instead of the judicially created negative Commerce Clause."[138]

Thomas asserted what Scalia had argued a decade before in *Tyler Pipe Industries, Inc. v. Washington State Department of Revenue*[139] and *Bendix Autolite Corp. v. Midwesco Enterprises*,[140] namely, that "the negative Commerce Clause has no basis in the text of the Constitution, makes little sense, and has proved virtually unworkable in application."[141] Further, Thomas wrote, it had led the Court to "make policy laden judgments that we are ill equipped and arguably unauthorized to make."[142] Thomas therefore urged the Court to "confine itself to interpreting the text of the Constitution, which itself seems to prohibit in plain terms certain of the most egregious state taxes on interstate commerce," that is, Article I, § 10, cl. 2 of the Constitution, providing that "no State shall, without the Consent of the Congress, lay any Imposts or Duties on Imports and Exports."[143]

Thomas acknowledged that as a result of the Court's decision in the 1869 case of *Woodruff v. Parham*,[144] the Import Export Clause has come to be understood to prohibit states from levying imposts and duties on goods imported from or exported to foreign nations. But he insisted—and went to great lengths to document—that *Woodruff* was "wrongly decided."[145] Citing scores of founding-era sources, Thomas made the compelling case that "for the Constitution's Framers and ratifiers—representatives of States which still viewed themselves as semi-independent sovereigns—the terms 'imports' and 'exports' encompassed not just trade with foreign nations, but trade with *other States* as well."[146]

Thomas noted that because of the wrongly decided *Woodruff* opinion, "much of what the Import Export Clause appears to have been designed to protect against has since been addressed under the negative Commerce Clause." He added that the Court's "rule that state taxes that discriminate against interstate commerce are virtually *per se* invalid under the negative Commerce Clause may well approximate the apparent prohibition of the Import Export Clause itself." Thomas conceded that "were it simply a matter of invalidating state laws under one clause of the Constitution rather than another, I might be inclined to leave well enough alone." But, he insisted, "without the proper textual roots, our negative Commerce Clause has gone far afield of its core—and we have yet to articulate either a coherent rationale for permitting the courts effectively to legislate in this field, or a workable test for assessing which state laws pass negative Commerce Clause muster." Always wanting to remove excrescence and restore the original understanding, he asserted that "precedent as unworkable as our negative Commerce Clause jurisprudence has become is simply not entitled to the weight of *stare decisis.*"[147]

If the Court were to shed itself of its nontextual negative Commerce Clause and simply apply the relevant Import Export Clause, Thomas was convinced that "this would seem to be a fairly straightforward case" and would be decided on behalf of the state of Maine.[148] The Maine property tax at issue was not an impost, he argued, "for, as 18th century usage of the word indicates [and as the several examples Thomas supplied established], an impost was a tax levied on *goods* at the time of *importation.*"[149] And it was not a duty: "The tax at issue here is nothing more than a tax on real property. Such taxes were classified as 'direct' taxes at the time of the Framing, and were not within the class of 'indirect' taxes encompassed by the common understanding of the word duties.'"[150]

Thomas's originalist approach to the negative Commerce Clause differs from Scalia's in two particulars. First, though both Scalia[151] and Thomas[152] stress that the negative Commerce Clause has no basis in the text of the Constitution, the matter ends there for Scalia but does not for Thomas. Given his original public meaning approach, Scalia is content simply to reject the negative Commerce Clause,[153] whereas Thomas, given his original general meaning approach, proceeded in *Camps Newfound* to identify the Import Export Clause as the appropriate "textual mechanism with which to address the more egregious of State actions, discriminating against interstate commerce."[154]

Second, although Scalia is willing on stare decisis grounds to enforce the negative Commerce Clause in cases where the doctrine is not expanded further, Thomas is not. In *Itel Containers International Corporation v. Huddleston,*[155] Scalia announced that "on *stare decisis* grounds," he would "enforce a self-executing, 'negative' Commerce Clause in two circumstances."[156] The first would be "against a state law that facially discriminates against interstate commerce,"[157] and the second would be "against a state law that is indistinguishable from a type of law previously held unconstitutional by this Court."[158]

By contrast, in every case since *Camps Newfound*, Thomas has rejected the negative Commerce Clause and refused to join any opinion that enforces it. In

Hillside Dairy v. Lyons,[159] for example, he concurred in part but dissented in that part of the otherwise unanimous opinion that dealt with the negative Commerce Clause: "Although I agree that the Court of Appeals erred in its statutory analysis, I nevertheless would affirm its judgment on this claim because 'the negative Commerce Clause has no basis in the text of the Constitution, makes little sense, and has proved virtually unworkable in application,' [he cited his dissent in *Camps Newfound*] and, consequently, cannot serve as a basis for striking down a state statute."[160] And in his concurrence in the judgment in *United Haulers Association v. Oneida-Herkimer Solid Waste Management Authority*,[161] Thomas went further. In this case, Chief Justice John Roberts, proceeding on judicial minimalist grounds, attempted to narrow somewhat the reach of the negative Commerce Clause, but for Thomas, no negative Commerce Clause at all was far preferable to a somewhat circumscribed one. He wrote, "As the debate between the majority and dissent shows, application of the negative Commerce Clause turns solely on policy considerations, not on the Constitution. Because this Court has no policy role in regulating interstate commerce, I would discard the Court's negative Commerce Clause jurisprudence."[162] He criticized the Court for its "erroneous assumption" that it had to "choose between economic protectionism and the free market," for the Constitution "vests that fundamentally legislative choice in Congress." Moreover, he said, "to the extent that Congress does not exercise its authority to make that choice, the Constitution does not limit the States' power to regulate commerce." When Congress is silent, the states are free to balance protectionism and the free market as they wish. However, he noted, instead of accepting "this constitutional reality, the Court clings to its negative Commerce Clause jurisprudence which 'gives nine Justices of this Court the power to decide the appropriate balance.'"[163]

As for Roberts's minimalism, Thomas offered the following consideration: rather than acknowledging that its "negative Commerce Clause jurisprudence, created out of whole cloth," is "illegitimate" and "repudiat[ing] that doctrinal error," Roberts "further propagates the error by narrowing the negative Commerce Clause for policy reasons—reasons that later majorities of this Court may find [entirely unpersuasive]." He concluded in frustration, "Today's majority trifles with an unsound and illegitimate jurisprudence yet fails to abandon it."[164]

In every negative Commerce Clause case since *Camps Newfound*, Thomas has denounced the Court's employment of this doctrine in his solo opinions. However, in what Justice Stevens described as "his persuasive and comprehensive dissenting opinion" in the negative Commerce Clause case of *Granholm v. Heald*,[165] Thomas never mentioned *Camps Newfound* and for good reason—he was not dissenting by himself. Since the three justices who joined him in his dissent in this case (Chief Justice Rehnquist and Justices Stevens and O'Connor) all embraced the doctrine, Thomas prudentially made other, albeit equally compelling, arguments.

Michigan and New York regulated the sale and importation of wine through a three-tier system requiring separate licenses for producers, wholesalers, and retailers. This scheme allowed in-state—but not out-of-state—wineries to make direct sales to consumers, which unquestionably violated the negative Commerce Clause because many small wineries did not produce enough wine or have sufficient consumer demand for their wines to make it economical for wholesalers to carry their products. State residents and intervening out-of-state wineries sued the states, claiming that their laws violated the Commerce Clause. The states responded that the direct-shipment ban was a valid exercise of their power under § 2 of the Twenty-First Amendment, which expressly provides that "the transportation or importation into any State, Territory, or possession of the United States for delivery or use therein of intoxicating liquors, in violation of the laws thereof, is hereby prohibited." When the Sixth Circuit found that Michigan's law violated the negative Commerce Clause but the Second Circuit found that New York's law fell within the ambit of the Twenty-First Amendment, the Supreme Court granted certiorari and invalidated both states' laws. Justice Kennedy wrote for a five-member majority (which included Scalia), holding that these laws discriminated against interstate commerce in violation of the negative Commerce Clause and that this discrimination was neither authorized nor permitted by the Twenty-First Amendment.

Stevens filed a short dissent, joined by O'Connor. He had no problem with the negative Commerce Clause and acknowledged that the laws of Michigan and New York "would be patently invalid under well-settled dormant Commerce Clause principles if they regulated sales of an ordinary article of commerce rather than wine. But ever since the adoption of the Eighteenth Amendment and the Twenty-first Amendment, our Constitution has placed commerce in alcoholic beverages in a special category."[166] He added "historical context" by noting that "in the years following the ratification of the Twenty-first Amendment, States adopted manifold laws regulating commerce in alcohol, and many of these laws were discriminatory. So-called 'dry states' entirely prohibited such commerce; others prohibited the sale of alcohol on Sundays; others permitted the sale of beer and wine but not hard liquor; most created either state monopolies or distribution systems that gave discriminatory preferences to local retailers and distributors."[167] He also joined Thomas's opinion in its entirety.

Thomas began by pointing out that "a century ago, this Court repeatedly invalidated, as inconsistent with the negative Commerce Clause, state liquor legislation that prevented out-of-state businesses from shipping liquor directly to a State's residents. The Webb-Kenyon Act and the Twenty-first Amendment cut off this intrusive review, as their text and history make clear and as this Court's early cases on the Twenty-first Amendment recognized." He accused the Court majority of "seiz[ing] back this power. . . . Because I would follow . . . the language of both the statute that Congress enacted and the Amendment that the Nation ratified, rather than the Court's questionable reading of history and the 'negative implications' of the Commerce Clause, I respectfully dissent."[168]

Thomas insisted that the Webb-Kenyon Act of 1913 exempted state liquor laws from judicial scrutiny under the negative Commerce Clause. In relevant part, the act prohibits "the shipment or transportation, in any manner or by any means whatsoever," of alcoholic beverages into any states when those beverages are "intended, by any person interested therein, to be received, possessed, sold, or in any manner used, either in the original package or otherwise, in violation of any law of such State." As he bluntly announced:

> The Michigan and New York direct-shipment laws are within the Webb-Kenyon Act's terms and therefore do not run afoul of the negative Commerce Clause. Those laws restrict out-of-state wineries from shipping and selling wine directly to Michigan and New York consumers. Any winery that ships wine directly to a Michigan or New York consumer in violation of those state-law restrictions is a "person interested therein" "intend[ing]" to "s[ell]" wine "in violation of" Michigan and New York law, and thus comes within the terms of the Webb-Kenyon Act.[169]

Thomas insisted that his construction of Webb-Kenyon was "no innovation"; the Court itself had adopted this reading of the act in 1932 in *McCormick & Co. v. Brown*,[170] and Congress followed suit in 1935 when, with the end of Prohibition, it reenacted the act without alteration.[171] Beyond that, he asserted Webb-Kenyon did not proscribe state laws that regulated in a discriminatory manner the receipt, possession, and use of alcoholic beverages: "It does not mention 'discrimination,' much less discrimination against out-of-state liquor products. Instead, it prohibits the interstate shipment of liquor into a State 'in violation of any law of such State.' 'Any law of such State' means any law, including a 'discriminatory' one."[172]

Thomas noted that although there was "no need to interpret the Twenty-first Amendment because the Webb-Kenyon Act resolves these cases," Michigan's and New York's laws were also "lawful under the plain meaning of § 2 of the Twenty-first Amendment."[173] The amendment's terms were broader than Webb-Kenyon, but they "parallel[ed]" the act's structure. "In particular," he noted, "the Twenty-first Amendment provides that any importation into a State contrary to state law violates the Constitution, just as the Webb-Kenyon Act provides that any such importation contrary to state law violates federal law."[174]

Thomas concluded by remarking that though the Court was convinced of "the evils of state laws that restrict the direct shipment of wine" and sincerely believed that "its decision serves this Nation well," "the Twenty-first Amendment and the Webb-Kenyon Act took those policy choices away from judges and returned them to the States. Whatever the wisdom of that choice, the Court does this Nation no service by ignoring the textual commands of the Constitution and Acts of Congress."[175]

The Indian Commerce Clause

In *United States v. Lara*,[176] Justice Breyer held for the Court that the Indian Commerce Clause (Article I, § 8, cl. 3 delegates to Congress the power "to regulate Commerce . . . with the Indian Tribes") grants Congress "plenary and exclusive" powers to legislate with respect to Indian tribes.[177] He also held that Congress therefore had the power to relax the restrictions on the tribes' inherent sovereignty to enforce their criminal laws against nonmember Indians[178]—restrictions that had previously been imposed by the political branches (through treaties negotiated by the president with the tribes or through congressional enactments). Concurring in the judgment, Thomas declared, "I cannot agree that the Indian Commerce Clause 'provides Congress with plenary power to legislate in the field of Indian affairs.'"[179] He found Breyer's assertion, based on decades of relevant precedent, "implausible," "troubl[ing]," and "very strained," and wishing to restore the original understanding of the Indian Commerce Clause, he indicated that he "would be willing to revisit the question."[180]

Thomas was right when he attributed "the confusion reflected in our precedent" to "two largely incompatible and doubtful assumptions. First, Congress (rather than some other part of the Federal Government) can regulate virtually every aspect of the tribes without rendering tribal sovereignty a nullity. Second, the Indian tribes retain inherent sovereignty to enforce their criminal laws against their own members."[181] He was on target when he described federal Indian policy as "schizophrenic"[182] in that, with regard to the question of whether "the tribes are or are not separate sovereigns, . . . our federal Indian law cases untenably hold both positions simultaneously."[183] And he was correct when he concluded that "until we begin to analyze these questions honestly and rigorously, the confusion that I have identified will continue to haunt our cases."[184] However, he was wrong on the original general meaning of the Indian Commerce Clause.[185]

The original understanding of the Clause begins with Article IX of the Articles of Confederation, which conferred to "the United States in Congress assembled the sole and exclusive right and power of . . . regulating the trade and managing all affairs with the Indians, not members of any of the States, provided that the legislative right of any State within its own limits be not infringed or violated." This language completely muddled the issue. Though it seemed to reserve the power of the states over Indians who were "members of any of the States," it did not define who those "members" were, and though it protected the states' "legislative rights within [their] own limits," it did not define the scope of those rights. As James Madison would observe in *Federalist* No. 42, this provision was "obscure and contradictory":

> What description of Indians are to be deemed members of a State, is not yet settled, and has been a question of frequent perplexity and contention in the federal councils. And how the trade with Indians, though not members of a State, yet residing within its legislative jurisdiction, can be regulated by an external authority, without so far intruding on the internal rights of legislation, is absolutely incomprehensible. This is not the only case in which the articles of Confederation have inconsiderately endeavored to accomplish impossibilities; to reconcile a partial sovereignty in the Union, with complete sovereignty in the States; to subvert a mathematical axiom, by taking away a part, and letting the whole remain.[186]

This confusion was not removed until 1789 when the U.S. Constitution, eliminating all reference to state power with respect to Indian tribes, went into effect. The framers granted to Congress in Article I, § 8, cl. 3 the power "to regulate Commerce with foreign Nations, and among the several States, and with the Indian Tribes." The contrast between the Constitution and the Articles of Confederation could not have been clearer. Compared with the ambiguous language of Article IX of the Articles of Confederation, the Constitution's Article I, § 8 conferred an explicit, broad, and exclusive grant of power to the federal government to deal with Indian tribes. And since its language authorized Congress to regulate trade among various types of sovereigns, it also made clear that the tribes possessed sovereignty of a nature different from that of foreign sovereign nations or the states of the Union.

With the ratification of the Constitution, the ability of the First Congress to set Indian policy, under its various Article I, § 8 powers, was established and on immediate display. But first, a word about the First Congress is needed. David P. Currie has described the First Congress as "a sort of continuing constitutional convention."[187] Many of its members—including James Madison, Oliver Ellsworth, Elbridge Gerry, Rufus King, Robert Morris, Pierce Butler, William Johnson, and William Paterson—helped to draft and ratify the Constitution. And beyond that, the

First Congress was responsible for taking the generalities of the Constitution—what Chief Justice John Marshall would later call its "great outlines"[188]—and translating them into concrete and functioning institutions. As Currie points out, the First Congress accomplished many things: it determined its own procedures; established the great executive departments of war, state, justice, and treasury; set up the federal judiciary; enacted a system of taxation; provided for payment of Revolutionary War debts; created a national bank; provided for national defense; regulated relations with Indian tribes; advised the president on foreign affairs (the Senate); passed statutes regarding naturalization, patents, copyrights, and federal crimes; regulated relations with existing states and admitted new ones; provided for the administration of the territories; established a permanent seat of government; and adopted a bill of rights.[189] Thus, by the time the First Congress adjourned on March 3, 1791, "the country had a much clearer idea of what the Constitution meant than it had had when that body had first met in 1789."[190] It is not surprising that two months into the Second Congress, Fisher Ames, a Massachusetts congressman, lamented in a November 24, 1791, letter to William Tudor, "Congress is not engaged in very interesting work. The first acts were the pillars of the federal edifice. Now we have only to keep the sparks from catching the shavings; we must watch the broom, that it is not set behind the door with fire on it, etc. etc. Nobody cares much for us now, except the enemies of the excise law, who remonstrate and make a noise."[191] The work of the First Congress illustrates how well the members of this "continuing constitutional convention" acted in conformity with the understanding of the delegates to the Philadelphia Convention.

During the first five weeks of the First Congress's initial session, thirteen statutes were passed, four of which dealt in whole or in part with Indian affairs. On August 7, 1789, Congress passed legislation establishing the Department of War and authorized the president to assign to the department responsibility "relative to Indians affairs."[192] On that same day, it reenacted the Northwest Ordinance of 1787,[193] which included in the second sentence of Section 14, Article 3 (immediately after the famous words "Religion, morality, and knowledge, being necessary to good government and the happiness of mankind, schools and the means of education shall forever be encouraged"), the following language:

> The utmost good faith shall always be observed towards the Indians; their lands and property shall never be taken from them without their consent; and, in their property, rights, and liberty, they shall never be invaded or disturbed, unless in just and lawful wars authorized by Congress; but laws founded in justice and humanity, shall from time to time be made for preventing wrongs being done to them, and for preserving peace and friendship with them.

On August 20, the First Congress appropriated $20,000 to defray "the expense of negotiating and treating with the Indian tribes."[194] And on September 11, it set the salary for "the superintendent of Indian affairs in the northern department."[195] In passing these four statutes, Congress used its delegated powers to declare war, govern the territories, and spend money.

Then, on July 22, 1790, Congress exercised for the first time its power to regulate commerce with the Indian tribes. It passed "an Act to regulate trade and intercourse with the Indian tribes."[196] In § 1, it declared "that no person shall be permitted to carry on any trade or intercourse with the Indian tribes without a license for that purpose under the hand and seal of the superintendent of the department, or of such other person as the President of the United States shall appoint for that purpose." In § 2, it provided for the recall of that license for the "transgress[ion of] any of the regulations or restrictions provided." In § 3, it authorized the forfeiture of "all the merchandise" of those trading without that license. In § 4, it forbade the "sale of lands made by Indians, or any nation or tribe of Indians within the United States" to any person or state "unless the same shall be made and duly executed at some public treaty, held under the authority of the United States." And in § 5, it provided for the punishment of non-Indians committing crimes and trespasses against the Indians. This section clearly did not address an issue of commerce or trade, and it read as follows:

> If any citizen or inhabitant of the United States, or of either of the territorial districts of the United States, shall go into any town, settlement or territory belonging to any nation or tribe of Indians, and shall there commit any crime upon, or trespass against, the person or property of any peaceable and friendly Indian or Indians, which, if committed within the jurisdiction of any state, or within the jurisdiction of the said districts, against a citizen or white inhabitant thereof, would be punishable by the laws of such state or district, such offender or offenders shall be subject to the same punishment.

The First Congress's belief that the Indian Commerce Clause delegated to it the power to pass such legislation is significant, for it set in motion the first of many federal laws predicated on the assumption that the federal government had plenary power over Indian tribes.

This first Indian Trade and Intercourse Act was subsequently expanded by the Trade and Intercourse Acts in 1793,[197] 1796,[198] and 1799.[199] All of these measures were temporary and contained language indicating how long they would remain in force. On March 30, 1802, the Seventh Congress enacted the first permanent Trade and Intercourse Act,[200] declaring in § 22 that it "shall be in force" thereafter. It carried forward the policies already adopted and added a new one of particular interest: § 6 provided that "if any such citizen, or other person, shall go into any town, settlement or territory belonging to any nation or tribe of Indians, and shall there commit murder, by killing any Indian or Indians, belonging to any nation or tribe of Indians, in amity with the United States, such offender, on being thereof convicted, shall suffer death" — clearly another example of how broadly the early Congress construed the Indian Commerce Clause. In contrast to Thomas's narrow interpretation of the Indian Commerce Clause in *Lara*, these acts show how expansive the founding generation understood that clause to be.

The Indian Commerce Clause also figured prominently in another respect. In *Cherokee Nation v. Georgia*,[201] the Cherokee Nation of Indians, claiming the status of a foreign nation, brought suit in the U.S. Supreme Court, under its original jurisdiction, against the state of Georgia. It did so under those provisions of Article III, § 2 of the Constitution that (1) give the Supreme Court jurisdiction in cases and controversies in which the parties are a state of the United States or the citizens thereof, on the one hand, and a foreign state, citizens, or subjects thereof, on the other, and (2) give the Supreme Court original jurisdiction in all cases in which a state shall be a party. The Cherokee Nation sought an injunction to prevent the execution of various Georgia laws that sought to assert control over Cherokee lands within the state that were protected by a 1790 U.S. treaty with the Cherokee. The issue for the Court was whether the Cherokee Nation was a foreign nation in the sense in which that term was used in the Constitution (and, therefore, whether the Court had jurisdiction to hear the case). Marshall concluded that it was not.

He noted that the relation of the Indians to the United States "is perhaps unlike that of any other two people in existence"[202] and "is marked by peculiar and cardinal distinctions which exist nowhere else."[203] Foreign nations, he observed, do not owe a "common allegiance to each other."[204] But, he continued, consider the tribes; their territory "[is] part of the United States," and "in any attempt at intercourse between Indians and foreign nations, they are considered as within the jurisdictional limits of the United States." The tribes "acknowledge themselves in their treaties to be under the protection of the United States," and the "right to the lands they occupy" can be "extinguished by a voluntary cession to our government." They cannot, therefore, be "denominated foreign nations." Rather, he insisted, they are "more correctly . . . denominated domestic dependent nations," occupying land to which the United States asserts "a title independent of their will." They are, he declared, in "a state of pupilage. Their relation to the United States resembles that of a ward to his guardian."[205]

After all, he continued, the tribes look to the United States "for protection; rely upon its kindness and its power; appeal to it for relief to their wants; and address the president as their great father." Furthermore, he pointed out, foreign nations consider the tribes as "so completely under the sovereignty and dominion of the United States" that any attempt by them to acquire tribal lands or to form political alliances with the tribes would be regarded as an "invasion" of U.S. territory and a clear "act of hostility."[206]

Marshall found that his conclusion that tribes are not foreign nations— and therefore not authorized to pursue "an action in the courts of the United States"—was strengthened by the text of Article I, § 8, cl. 3 of the Constitution. He noted that the Commerce Clause "clearly contradistinguish[ed]" the Indian tribes from both foreign nations and the several states composing the Union; they were "designated by a distinct appellation." The Constitutional Convention, he concluded, "considered them as entirely distinct."[207]

Based on the tribes' status as "domestic dependent nations" and therefore on what the Supreme Court in *County of Oneida v. Oneida Indian Nation*[208] called "the unique trust relationship between the United States and the Indians,"[209] one major consequence has been the development of a distinctive set of canons of construction for federal Indian law.[210] These canons require that treaties, treaty substitutes, statutes, and executive orders be liberally construed in favor of the Indians; that all ambiguities be resolved in their favor; and that tribal property rights and sovereignty be preserved unless Congress's intent to the contrary is clear and unambiguous. In addition, treaties and treaty substitutes are to be construed as the Indians would have understood them.[211]

These canons were first developed in the context of treaty interpretation. Beginning with the treaties that formed the foundation of *Cherokee Nation v. Georgia*, the Supreme Court read each treaty broadly in favor of the tribes; resolved ambiguous expressions in favor of the tribes; interpreted each treaty and its negotiations as the Indians would have understood it; and considered the history and circumstances behind each treaty in question. The canons were developed because the tribes were regarded as wards of the federal government, their guardian; as the third branch of that federal government, the Court had to act in the tribes' best interests. Additionally, the Court recognized the manner in which treaties were negotiated with tribes—they were initiated by the United States and drafted by the United States, not the tribes, and they were written and explained in English, a language very few Indians spoke and none could read, meaning that the tribes had to rely on the representations and promises of the federal representatives. The canons of construction thus arose from the disadvantaged bargaining position that Indians often occupied during treaty negotiations. As a result, the Supreme Court declared in *United States v. Winans:*[212] "We have said we will construe a treaty with the Indians as 'that unlettered people' understood it, and 'as justice and reason demand, in all cases where power is exerted by the strong over those to whom they owe care and protection.'"[213]

Over time in a series of cases, the Supreme Court consistently extended these canons beyond treaties to treaty substitutes (for example, in *Winters v. United States*);[214] to statutes (for example, in *Bryan v. Itasca County*);[215] and to executive orders (for example, in *Arizona v. California*).[216] It has determined that federal legislation, orders, and regulations relating to Indians are to be given a liberal construction, and doubtful expressions are to be resolved in favor of the interests of the tribes, whose members are wards of the nation and wholly dependent on its protection and good faith. Courts as well as all federal agencies are to follow the general rule that indicates federal statutes passed for the benefit of Indians are to be liberally construed.[217]

Nonetheless, these canons are essentially rules of interpretation that the justices are free to apply or ignore. They have been described by Philip P. Frickey, in his famous article entitled "Marshalling Past and Present: Colonialism, Constitutionalism, and Interpretation in Federal Indian Law," as nothing more than "quasi-constitutional" rules that members of the Court can recognize or reject at their discretion.[218] Few justices have been more inclined to reject these canons than Clarence Thomas.

Cohen's Handbook of Federal Indian Law mentions "a recent Supreme Court case [that] confirms that these canons remain vital"[219]—*Minnesota v. Mille Lacs Band of Chippewa Indians*.[220] In this case, the tribe sued the state of Minnesota to enforce an 1837 treaty in which the tribe had ceded lands to the United States but retained the right to hunt, fish, and gather in those areas. Minnesota claimed, however, that those rights had been extinguished by an 1855 treaty in which the tribe agreed to "fully and entirely relinquish and convey to the United States, any and all right, title, and interest, of whatsoever nature the same may be, which they may now have in, and to any other lands in the Territory of Minnesota or elsewhere." Even though that broad language would seem to have ceded all of the tribe's usufructuary rights, Justice Sandra Day O'Connor relied on the canons and concluded that the tribe's rights were not abrogated. She pointed out that the sentence did not mention the 1837 treaty and did not refer to hunting, fishing, and gathering rights. She wrote, "The entire 1855 Treaty, in fact, is devoid of any language expressly mentioning—much less abrogating—usufructuary rights. Similarly, the Treaty contains no language providing money for the abrogation of previously held rights. These omissions are telling."[221]

O'Connor declared that "to determine whether this language abrogates Chippewa Treaty rights, we look beyond the written words to the larger context that frames the Treaty, including 'the history of the treaty, the negotiations, and

the practical construction adopted by the parties.'" Such an examination of the
historical record would, she insisted, provide "insight into how the parties to the
Treaty understood the terms of the agreement. This insight is especially helpful
to the extent that it sheds light on how the Chippewa signatories to the Treaty
understood the agreement because we interpret Indian treaties to give effect to
the terms as the Indians themselves would have understood them."[222]

Once her historical examination was complete, O'Connor summarized her
findings. The historical record provided no support for the theory that the 1855
treaty was designed to abrogate the usufructuary privileges guaranteed under the
1837 treaty. It merely supported "the theory that the Treaty . . . was designed to
transfer Chippewa land to the United States," she argued; "at the very least," it
"refute[d] the State's assertion that the 1855 Treaty 'unambiguously' abrogated
the 1837 hunting, fishing, and gathering privileges." Again explicitly invoking
the canons, she declared that, "given this plausible ambiguity, we cannot agree
with the State that the 1855 Treaty abrogated Chippewa usufructuary rights. We
have held that Indian treaties are to be interpreted liberally in favor of the Indians
and that any ambiguities are to be resolved in their favor."[223]

Thomas dissented. He was more concerned with how the Court had
"exact[ed] serious federalism costs" by imposing limitations "upon Minnesota's
sovereign authority over its natural resources"[224] than he was with abiding by the
canons. He pointed out that unlike other contemporaneous Indian treaties, the
Chippewa Treaty of 1837 did not reserve "a right to fish, hunt, or gather on ceded
lands" but only "*a privilege*" to do so.[225] He was unwilling to understand these
terms as the Chippewa of the 1830s would have, and he declared that "in the
appropriate case we must explain whether reserved treaty *privileges* limit States'
ability to regulate Indians' off-reservation usufructuary activities in the same way
as a treaty reserving *rights*."[226]

Thomas was in dissent when he rejected the canons in *Mille Lacs Band*,
but he wrote for a seven-member majority when he did so in *South Dakota v.
Bourland*.[227] The Fort Laramie Treaty of 1868 established the Great Sioux Reservation and provided that it be held for the "absolute and undisturbed use and occupation" of Sioux tribes. In 1944, however, Congress passed the Flood Control
Act authorizing the establishment of a comprehensive flood control plan along
the eastern border of the Cheyenne River Sioux Reservation (part of what was
once the Great Sioux Reservation) and mandating that all water project lands be
open for the general public's use and recreational enjoyment. Ten years later in
the Cheyenne River Act, the Cheyenne River Sioux Tribe conveyed all interests
in 104,420 acres of former trust lands to the United States for the Oahe Dam
and Reservoir Project. Among the rights the act reserved to the tribe or tribal
members was a "right of free access [to the taken lands,] including the right to

hunt and fish, subject . . . to regulations governing the corresponding use by other [U.S.] citizens."

Until 1988, the tribe enforced its game and fish regulations against all violators, whereas petitioner South Dakota limited its enforcement to non-Indians. In that year, however, the tribe announced that it would no longer recognize state hunting licenses, prompting South Dakota to file an action in federal district court against tribal officials, seeking to enjoin the tribe from excluding non-Indians from hunting on nontrust lands within the reservation. After the district court permanently enjoined the tribe from exerting such authority, the Court of Appeals for the Eighth Circuit reversed and remanded, ruling that the tribe had authority to regulate non-Indian hunting and fishing on the 104,420 acres because the Cheyenne River Act did not clearly reveal Congress's intent to divest the tribe of its treaty right to do so. The Supreme Court granted certiorari and reversed.

Thomas began his majority opinion with a truism, "Congress has the power to abrogate Indians' treaty rights," but then admitted that "we usually insist that Congress clearly express its intent to do so." Although he acknowledged that "'statutes are to be construed liberally in favor of the Indians, with ambiguous provisions interpreted to their benefit,'" he declared that "our reading of the relevant statutes persuades us that Congress has abrogated the Tribe's rights under the Fort Laramie Treaty to regulate hunting and fishing by non-Indians in the area taken for the Oahe Dam and Reservoir Project." [228]

Thomas not only ignored the canons; he actually reversed them. Instead of finding express congressional intent to abrogate tribal rights, he focused on the lack of express congressional intent to protect them: "If Congress had intended by this provision to grant the Tribe the additional right to regulate hunting and fishing, it would have done so by a similarly explicit statutory command." [229] And even though the Eighth Circuit had concluded that, because the terms of the Cheyenne River Act preserved to the tribe mineral, grazing, and timber rights, Congress had preserved the right of the tribe to regulate use of the land by non-Indians as well and had not abrogated the tribe's preexisting regulatory authority, Thomas declared: "We disagree. Congress' explicit reservation of certain rights in the taken area does not operate as an implicit reservation of all former rights." [230]

Thomas would again reject the canons of federal Indian law in his majority opinion for the Court in *Carcieri v. Salazar.*[231] At issue in this recent case was the language in the Indian Reorganization Act (IRA), enacted in 1934, that authorized the secretary of the interior to acquire land and hold it in trust "for the purpose of providing land for Indians" and that defined Indians to "include all persons of Indian descent who are members of any recognized tribe now under Federal jurisdiction." In a six-to-three decision, Thomas defined the ambiguous word *now* narrowly and held that it applied only to tribes under federal jurisdiction in 1934; he refused to define *now* liberally and in the best interests of the Narragansett Indian Tribe by holding that it also meant tribes currently under federal jurisdiction. Thomas pointed out that "elsewhere in the IRA, Congress expressly drew into the statute contemporaneous and future events by using the phrase 'now or hereafter.'"[232] Employing legislative history, he also noted that "in correspondence with those who would assist him in implementing the IRA," John Collier, the commissioner of Indian affairs and "the principal author of the IRA," explained that the term *Indian* included "all persons of Indian descent who are members of any recognized tribe *that was under Federal jurisdiction at the date of the Act.*"[233]

This prompted Justice Stevens to complain in his dissent that the majority had engaged in a "cramped reading of the statute intended to be 'sweeping' in scope" and had "ignored the principle deeply rooted in [our] Indian jurisprudence" that "'statutes are to be construed liberally in favor of the Indians.'"[234]

Chapter 3 continues the consideration of how Thomas employs his general original meaning approach when confronted with questions concerning federalism not raised by the Commerce Clause. It addresses the topics of federal preemption, the Necessary and Proper Clause, the Tenth Amendment, and state sovereign immunity.

Chapter Three

Constitutional Structure and Federalism: Other Federalism Questions

Chapter 2 examined Thomas's federalism jurisprudence in cases dealing with the Interstate Commerce Clause, the negative Commerce Clause, and the Indian Commerce Clause. This chapter continues an exploration of his federalism jurisprudence by focusing on cases dealing with federal preemption of state laws, the Necessary and Proper Clause, the Tenth Amendment, and state sovereign immunity. It concludes with an assessment of how faithful Thomas has been in all of these cases to his original general meaning approach to constitutional interpretation.

Federal Preemption of State Laws

When Congress enters a field in which it is authorized by the Constitution to act, its legislation supersedes or preempts all incompatible state regulations under the Supremacy Clause. This rule of statutory construction is simple to state but difficult for the Court to apply. Professor Catherine M. Sharkey has put it well:

> Preemption jurisprudence is notably variegated. One dimension of the analysis is akin to statutory interpretation—how best to read and interpret the precise words used or implied by Congress in the statutes it enacts. Another layer consists of federalism-based presumptions, driven by a vision of the appropriate constitutional balance of power and authority between the federal and state governments. Embedded within this doctrinal edifice is another valence of political or policy predilections including affinities for regulation writ large and preferences toward bureaucratic versus common law jury enforced norms. And finally, an oft-overlooked piece of the puzzle is the interpretive and regulatory role assumed by the underlying federal agency. From these various dimensions of preemption analysis one might construct a series of representative matrices of institutional actors along which one could classify judicial philosophies: Congress vs. courts; courts vs. agencies; courts vs. states; agencies vs. states. Something like a rotating

tetrahedron might be necessary to capture variation along each of these dimensions simultaneously.[1]

Sharkey argues that in this complex and variegated field, "Thomas is guided by an overarching principle: a judge should refrain from acting unless constitutionally commanded to do something by Congress or a [federal] agency—in which case, text provides the roadmap for action."[2] She is exactly right.

Sharkey distinguishes between two kinds of preemption and describes Thomas's views toward each. "Where Congress has spoken (express preemption), he follows suit and ousts competing state interests."[3] But "where Congress has only murmured (implied preemption) . . . , he resists any impulse to stray outside the text looking for reasons to displace state law."[4]

In express preemption cases, Thomas is guided in his reading of statutory texts by two principles: express preemption provisions should be read according to their ordinary meaning and without a "presumption against preemption" statutory default canon.

Egelhoff v. Egelhoff[5] provides a good example of a Thomas opinion addressing a straightforward express preemption issue, even though the result is a blow to family law, a field traditionally reserved to the states. While David A. Egelhoff was married to Samantha Egelhoff, he designated her as the beneficiary of a life insurance policy and pension plan provided by his employer and governed by the Employee Retirement Income Security Act of 1974 (ERISA). Six months after the two divorced, David Egelhoff was fatally injured and died intestate. His children by a previous marriage filed separate suits against Samantha Egelhoff in state court to recover the insurance proceeds and pension plan benefits, relying on a Washington statute providing that the designation of a spouse as the beneficiary of a nonprobate asset—defined to include a life insurance policy or employee benefit plan—is revoked automatically upon divorce. The children argued that in the absence of a qualified named beneficiary, the proceeds would pass to them as David Egelhoff's statutory heirs under state law. At the end of state court proceedings, the Washington State Supreme Court held that the statute, although applicable to employee benefit plans, did not "refer to" or have a "connection with" an ERISA plan that would compel preemption under that statute.

Thomas wrote for a seven-member majority and reversed the finding, arguing "[that] the Washington statute falls within the terms of ERISA's express preemption provision and that it is pre-empted by ERISA."[6] ERISA's preemption section states that ERISA "shall supersede any and all State laws insofar as they may now or hereafter relate to any employee benefit plan" covered by ERISA. Thomas pointed out that in *Shaw v. Delta Air Lines*,[7] the Court had defined *relate to* as meaning "connection with" and that, given that definition, "the Washington statute has an impermissible connection with ERISA plans." He noted that "the statute binds ERISA plan administrators to a particular choice of rules for determining beneficiary status. The administrators must pay benefits to the beneficiaries chosen by state law, rather than to those identified in the plan documents. The statute thus implicates an area of core ERISA concern" because it governs the payment of benefits, "a central matter of plan administration."[8] Additionally, the Washington statute interfered with "nationally uniform plan administration" because "uniformity is impossible" when plans are subject to "different legal obligations in different states."[9] He wrote,

> Plan administrators cannot make payments simply by identifying the beneficiary specified by the plan documents. Instead they must familiarize themselves with state statutes so that they can determine whether the named beneficiary's status has been "revoked" by operation of law. And in this context the burden is exacerbated by the choice-of-law problems that may confront an administrator when the employer is located in one State, the plan participant lives in another, and the participant's former spouse lives in a third. In such a situation, administrators might find that plan payments are subject to conflicting legal obligations.[10]

Thomas concluded that "the Washington statute has a 'connection with' ERISA and is therefore preempted."[11]

His dissent in *Altria Group v. Good*[12] is the perfect example of an express preemption case in which he read a statute's preemption provisions according to their ordinary meaning and without a "presumption against preemption." In *Altria Group*, Justice Stevens held for a five-member majority that fraudulent advertising claims made concerning "light cigarettes" (that they, in fact, delivered less tar and nicotine than regular brands)[13] brought under the Maine Unfair Trade Practices Act were neither expressly nor impliedly preempted by the Federal Cigarette Labeling and Advertising Act.

The labeling act in question required that specific health warnings be placed on all cigarette packing and advertising[14] in order to eliminate "diverse, nonuniform, and confusing cigarette labeling and advertising regulations with respect to any relationship between smoking and health."[15] It then expressly preempted state laws in this area: in a section entitled "Preemption," Congress declared at § 1334(b): "State regulations. No requirement or prohibition based on smoking and health shall be imposed under State law with respect to the advertising or promotion of any cigarettes the packages of which are labeled in conformity with the provisions of this chapter." It offered but one exception at § 1334(c): "Exception. Notwithstanding subsection (b), a State or locality may enact statutes and promulgate regulations, based on smoking and health, that take effect after the effective date of the Family Smoking Prevention and Tobacco Control Act, imposing specific bans or restrictions on the time, place, and manner, but not content, of the advertising or promotion of any cigarettes."[16]

Despite what would seem to be a compelling case of express preemption, Stevens rejected Altria's defense. He began by employing the presumption against preemption: "When addressing questions of express or implied pre-emption, we begin our analysis 'with the assumption that the historic police powers of the States [are] not to be superseded by the Federal Act unless that was the clear and manifest purpose of Congress.' That assumption applies with particular force when Congress has legislated in a field traditionally occupied by the States."[17] And though he agreed that the labeling act preempted state law that supplemented the federally prescribed warnings, he asserted that it did not limit "States' authority to prohibit deceptive statements in cigarette advertising."[18] Stevens relied on the plurality opinion in *Cipollone v. Liggett Group*,[19] which had also applied the presumption against preemption in order to hold that the labeling act's phrase *based on smoking and health* did not preempt a state court claim that cigarette manufacturers had fraudulently misrepresented and concealed a material fact because the claim alleged a violation of a duty not to deceive, a duty not based on "smoking and health." Stevens noted that Maine's Unfair Trade Practices Act said "nothing about either 'smoking' or 'health'" and was simply a "general rule that creates a duty not to deceive."[20] He concluded, therefore, that it was not preempted.[21]

Thomas wrote a dissent that was joined by Chief Justice Roberts and Justices Scalia and Alito. Ever ready to reject failed precedent, he began by announcing that "this appeal requires the Court to revisit its decision in *Cipollone*" and its "atextual approach to express preemption."[22] *Cipollone* had created, he said, "an unworkable test for preemption" and "frustrat[ed]" lower courts attempting to apply it. "The Court's fidelity to *Cipollone* is unwise and unnecessary. The Court should instead provide the lower courts with a clear test that advances Congress' stated goals by interpreting § 5(b) to expressly pre-empt any claim that 'imposes an obligation . . . because of the effect of smoking upon health.'"[23]

He began by attacking Stevens's reliance on the presumption against preemption. In the 2005 case of *Bates v. Dow Agrosciences*, Thomas had flatly declared that the "presumption does not apply when Congress has included within a statute an express preemption provision."[24] In *Altria*, he cited a wide range of cases supporting his contention, observing that "since *Cipollone*, the Court's reliance on the presumption against preemption has waned in the express preemption context."[25]

He then turned to the text of the labeling act and argued that, "contrary to the majority's policy arguments, faithful application of the statutory language does not authorize fraudulent advertising with respect to smoking and health." He noted that 15 U.S.C. 1336 provided that any misleading promotional statements for cigarettes remained subject to oversight by the Federal Trade Commission. Thus,

> the relevant question . . . is not whether "petitioners will be prohibited from selling as 'light' or 'low tar' only those cigarettes that are not actually light and do not actually deliver less tar and nicotine." Rather, the issue is whether the Labeling Act allows regulators and juries to decide, on a state-by-state basis, whether petitioners' light and low-tar descriptors were in fact fraudulent, or instead whether [the labeling act] charged the Federal Government with reaching a comprehensive judgment with respect to this question.[26]

Thomas argued that Congress had made clear its goals in the labeling act: "Commerce and the national economy may . . . not [be] impeded by diverse, nonuniform, and confusing cigarette labeling and advertising regulations with respect to any relationship between smoking and health." Stevens's "distorted interpretation defeats this express congressional purpose," he added, "opening the door to an untold number of deceptive-practices lawsuits across the country." Since the question of whether marketing a light cigarette is deceptive would doubtless be answered differently from state to state, the inevitable result would be a nonuniform imposition of liability for the marketing of light and low-tar cigarettes, "the precise problem that Congress intended . . . to remedy."[27]

Thomas concluded: "The Court today elects to convert the *Cipollone* plurality opinion into binding law, notwithstanding its weakened doctrinal foundation, its atextual construction of the statute, and the lower courts' inability to apply its methodology." Additionally, he said, it "will have the perverse effect of increasing the nonuniformity of state regulation of cigarette advertising. . . . Because I believe that respondents' claims are pre-empted under the Labeling Act, I respectfully dissent."[28]

If Congress speaks clearly and expressly preempts state law, Thomas rejects the presumption against preemption and gives the statutory text its "ordinary meaning,"[29] regardless of its impact on federalism.[30] But if Congress only "murmurs," to use Sharkey's wonderfully descriptive word, he refuses to displace state law.[31] From his first days on the Court, Thomas has rejected the doctrine of implied preemption, insisting, as he did in his dissent in *Allied-Bruce Terminix v. Dobson*, that "we should resolve the uncertainty in light of core principles of federalism." He went on, "To the extent that federal statutes are ambiguous, we do not read them to displace state law. Rather, we must be 'absolutely certain' that Congress intended such displacement before we give preemptive effect to a federal statute."[32]

Congress can murmur in different ways. It may enact such a comprehensive, detailed regulatory scheme that it wholly occupies a particular field and withdraws state lawmaking power over that field. In some cases, the Court has indicated that a federal regulatory scheme may be "so pervasive" as to imply "that Congress left no room for the States to supplement it."[33] Likewise, the "federal interest" in the field that a federal statute addresses may be "so dominant" that federal law "will be assumed to preclude enforcement of state laws on the same subject."[34] As Thomas pointed out in his dissent in *Camps Newfound/Owatonna*, the Court's "recent cases have frequently rejected field pre-emption in the absence of statutory language expressly requiring it."[35] Congress can also murmur when it enacts legislation that "actually conflicts" with state law.[36] As Caleb Nelson has noted, conflict preemption impliedly preempts "if either (1) compliance with both the state and federal law is 'a physical impossibility' or (2) state law 'stands as an obstacle to the accomplishment and execution of the full purposes and objectives of Congress.'"[37] Although Nelson notes that "the first part of this test is vanishingly narrow," the second part "is ubiquitous. So-called 'obstacle preemption' potentially covers not only cases in which state and federal law contradict each other, but also all other cases in which courts think that the effects of state law will hinder" the accomplishment of the purposes and objectives behind federal law.[38]

Thomas has opposed the use of implied obstacle preemption since his first year on the Court,[39] but his concurrence in the judgment in the 2009 case of *Wyeth v. Levine*[40] represents his more comprehensive and relentless assault on the Court's obstacle preemption jurisprudence, which he labeled "inherently flawed," "judicially manufactured," "freewheeling," "extratextual," and "inconsistent with the Constitution."[41]

Wyeth manufactures an antinausea drug called Phenergan. A clinician injected Diana Levine with Phenergan by the "IV-push" method, whereby the drug was injected directly into her vein (as opposed to an "IV-drip" method, whereby the drug would have been introduced into a saline solution that would more slowly enter her body through a catheter inserted into her vein). As a result of the IV-push procedure, Levine developed gangrene, and doctors were forced to amputate her forearm. She brought a state-law damages action, alleging that Wyeth had failed to provide an adequate warning about the significant risks of administering Phenergan by the IV-push method. A Vermont jury determined that Levine's injury would not have occurred if Phenergan's label included an adequate warning, and it awarded damages for her pain and suffering, substantial medical expenses, and loss of her livelihood as a professional musician. The trial court refused to overturn the jury's verdict and rejected Wyeth's argument that Levine's failure-to-warn claims were preempted by federal law because Phenergan's labeling had been approved by the federal Food and Drug Administration (FDA). The Vermont Supreme Court affirmed, as did the U.S. Supreme Court in a six-to-three decision.

Justice Stevens wrote for the majority, rejecting Wyeth's argument that it was impossible for the company to comply with both the state-law duties underlying Levine's claims and its federal labeling duties. He argued that although a manufacturer generally may change a drug label only after the FDA approves a supplemental application, the FDA's "changes being effected" regulation permitted certain preapproval labeling changes that added or strengthened a warning to improve drug safety. He also rejected Wyeth's obstacle preemption argument, finding the FDA's assertion that the state law was an obstacle to its ability to achieve its statutory objectives was at odds with the available evidence of Congress's "purposes and objectives"; moreover, he found Wyeth's argument contradicted the FDA's own long-standing position that state law is a complementary form of drug regulation without providing a reasoned explanation.

Thomas broke with his conservative colleagues (Alito wrote a dissent joined by Roberts and Scalia) by writing an opinion that concurred in the judgment. He agreed with Stevens on obstacle preemption grounds,[42] but he did so by providing an interesting insight. Thomas observed that there are circumstances where "it is not 'physically impossible' to comply with both state and federal law, even when the state and federal laws give directly conflicting commands. For example, if federal law gives an individual the right to engage in certain behavior that state law prohibits, the laws would give contradictory commands notwithstanding the fact that an individual could comply with both by electing to refrain from the covered behavior."[43] However, he strenuously objected to the obstacle preemption arguments made by both Stevens for the majority and Alito in dissent.[44]

Thomas began by remarking that he had "become increasingly skeptical of this Court's 'purposes and objectives' pre-emption jurisprudence. Under this approach, the Court routinely invalidates state laws based on perceived conflicts with broad federal policy objectives, legislative history, or generalized notions of congressional purposes that are not embodied within the text of federal law. Because implied pre-emption doctrines that wander far from the statutory text are inconsistent with the Constitution, I concur only in the judgment."[45]

Thomas pointed out that federal law can preempt conflicting state law because of the Supremacy Clause, but, he added, a federal law is supreme only if it is "made in pursuance" of the Constitution. And to be "made in pursuance thereof," federal laws "must comply with two key structural limitations in the Constitution that ensure that the Federal Government does not amass too much power at the expense of the States. The first structural limitation, which the parties have not raised in this case, is 'the Constitution's conferral upon Congress of not all governmental powers, but only discrete, enumerated ones.'" The second structural limitation was central to this case—"the complex set of procedures that Congress and the President must follow to enact 'Laws of the United States.'" For Thomas, the Supremacy Clause "requires that pre-emptive effect be given only to those federal standards and policies that are set forth in, or necessarily follow from, the statutory text that was produced through the constitutionally required bicameral and presentment procedures."[46]

The "vague and 'potentially boundless' doctrine of 'purposes and objectives' preemption," Thomas wrote, "[departs from] these constitutional principles [and allows the Court]" to preempt state law "based on its interpretation of broad federal policy objectives, legislative history, or generalized notions of congressional purposes that are not contained within the text of federal law." For Thomas, that was unacceptable: "Congressional and agency musings . . . do not satisfy the Art. I, § 7 requirements for enactment of federal law and, therefore, do not pre-empt state law under the Supremacy Clause. When analyzing the preemptive effect of federal statutes or regulations validly promulgated thereunder, 'evidence of preemptive purpose [must be] sought in the text and structure of the [provision] at issue' to comply with the Constitution."[47]

Thomas concurred in the Court's judgment because the majority reached "the right conclusion." But he refused to join the majority opinion because its use of "purposes and objectives" preemption required it to inquire into "matters beyond the scope of proper judicial review." He pointed out how Stevens's opinion relied heavily on the fact that Congress did not enact an express preemption provision regarding FDA approval of drug labels during the seventy-year history of the federal Food, Drug, and Cosmetic Act and that this "silence on the issue," coupled with Congress's "certain awareness of the prevalence of state tort litigation," was evidence that Congress did not intend for federal approval of drug labels to preempt state tort judgments.

Thomas granted that the absence of a statutory provision preempting all state tort suits related to approved federal drug labels was "pertinent to a finding that such lawsuits are not pre-empted." However, he insisted, "the relevance is in the fact that no statute explicitly pre-empts the lawsuits, and not in any inferences that the Court may draw from congressional silence about the motivations or policies underlying Congress' failure to act."[48]

Thomas drilled down further, arguing that the majority "concluded from silence" that Congress believed state lawsuits posed no obstacle to federal drug-approval objectives. That was the "required conclusion," he said, but only because it was compelled by the text of the relevant statutory and regulatory provisions, not by "judicial suppositions about Congress' unstated goals. The fact that the Court reaches the proper conclusion does not justify its speculation about the reasons for congressional inaction." The majority had relied on "the perceived congressional policies underlying inaction" to find that state law was not preempted, but Thomas worried that "once the Court shows a willingness to guess at the intent underlying congressional inaction, the Court could just as easily rely on its own perceptions regarding congressional inaction to give unduly broad pre-emptive effect to federal law." He concluded by reiterating that under the Supremacy Clause, "state law is preempted only by federal law 'made in Pursuance' of the Constitution—not by extratextual considerations of the purposes underlying congressional inaction."[49]

Thomas repeated his opposition to the use of obstacle preemption in *Arizona v. United States*.[50] In 2010, the Arizona legislature passed a statute known as S.B. 1070 to address pressing issues related to the large number of illegal aliens in the state. Section 3 of the statute made failure to comply with federal alien-registration requirements a state misdemeanor; § 5(C) made it a misdemeanor for an unauthorized alien to seek or engage in work in the state; § 6 authorized state and local officers to arrest without a warrant a person "the officer has probable cause to believe . . . has committed any public offense that makes the person removable from the United States"; and § 2(B) required officers conducting a stop, detention, or arrest to make efforts, in some circumstances, to verify the person's immigration status with the federal government. A federal district court held that the statute was preempted by federal law, and the Ninth Circuit affirmed, agreeing that the United States had established a likelihood of success on its preemption claims.

Employing obstacle preemption, Kennedy found for the Court that §§ 3, 5(C), and 6 were facially preempted but not § 2(B), which could be implemented, subject to subsequent "as applied" challenges. Thomas concurred in part and dissented in part. He concurred in part because he agreed with the Court's judgment, albeit on other grounds, that § 2(B) was not preempted. He dissented in part because he believed that none of the statute's sections were preempted.

Citing his concurrence in *Wyeth*, he declared that "federal immigration law does not pre-empt any of the challenged provisions of S. B. 1070 . . . for the simple reason that there is no conflict between the 'ordinary meaning' of the rel-

evant federal laws and that of the four provisions of Arizona law at issue here."[51]
He added: "Despite the lack of any conflict between the ordinary meaning of the
Arizona law and that of the federal laws at issue here, the Court holds that various
provisions of the Arizona law are pre-empted because they 'stan[d] as an obstacle
to the accomplishment and execution of the full purposes and objectives of Congress.'"[52] He reiterated his *Wyeth* complaint that "the 'purposes and objectives'
theory of implied pre-emption is inconsistent with the Constitution because it
invites courts to engage in freewheeling speculation about congressional purpose
that roams well beyond the statutory text." In conclusion, he stated that "under
the Supremacy Clause, pre-emptive effect is to be given to congressionally enacted laws, not to judicially divined legislative purposes. Thus, even assuming the
existence of some tension between Arizona's law and the supposed 'purposes and
objectives' of Congress, I would not hold that any of the provisions of the Arizona
law at issue here are pre-empted on that basis."[53]

Sharkey has reiterated Thomas's position on preemption as follows: "A judge
should refrain from acting unless constitutionally commanded to do something
by Congress or a [federal] agency—in which case, text provides the roadmap for
action."[54] But what if the text is ambiguous as to preemption? This is where a
federal agency comes into play because of Thomas's willingness to give what is
called *Chevron* deference to agency interpretations of statutory language.[55] (In
Chevron U.S.A. Inc. v. Natural Resources Defense Council,[56] the Supreme Court
held that it would defer to agency interpretations of statutory language if the statutory language was ambiguous and the agency interpretation was reasonable.)

Thomas has given *Chevron* deference in two preemption cases, one to reject
implied preemption and the other to affirm what he concluded was express preemption.[57] In *Pharmaceutical Research and Manufacturers of America v. Walsh,*
he argued that "*Chevron* imposes a perhaps-insurmountable barrier to a claim of
obstacle preemption" for two reasons: (1) because the Medicaid Act "cannot be
read to unambiguously" preempt Maine Rx (under Maine's Medicaid prescription drug program, if a drug company did not enter into a rebate agreement, its
Medicaid sales would be subjected to a prior authorization procedure), and (2)
because the secretary of health and human services had adopted an interpretation of the Medicaid Act that did not preclude states from negotiating prices and
rebates.[58]

More interesting is his opinion in *Cuomo v. The Clearing House Association,*[59] in which Thomas, joined by Chief Justice Roberts and Justices Kennedy
and Alito, dissented from Scalia's majority opinion. New York Attorney General
Mario Cuomo sought to determine whether various national banks had violated
that state's fair-lending laws by sending them letters in 2005 requesting, in "lieu
of subpoena," that they provide certain nonpublic information about their lend-

ing practices. The banks, the federal Office of the Comptroller of the Currency (OCC), and a banking trade group brought suit to enjoin the information request, claiming that the comptroller's regulation promulgated under the National Bank Act (NBA) prohibited that form of state law enforcement against national banks. Key to the controversy was the following language from the NBA: "No national bank shall be subject to any visitorial powers except as authorized by Federal law, vested in the courts . . . or . . . directed by Congress." The comptroller's regulation implementing these words forbade states to "exercise visitorial powers with respect to national banks, such as conducting examinations, inspecting or requiring the production of books or records," or "prosecuting enforcement actions." Scalia rejected the respondents' arguments. Although he conceded that there was "some ambiguity as to the meaning of the statutory term 'visitorial powers'" and as to the comptroller's power to "give authoritative meaning to the statute within the bounds of that uncertainty," he held that the Court could, nonetheless, "discern the outer limits of the term 'visitorial powers' even through the clouded lens of history" and that those powers "do not include, as the Comptroller's expansive regulation would provide, ordinary enforcement of the law." Scalia pointed out that when the NBA was enacted in 1864, the word *visitation* was understood to refer to a state's supervisory power over the manner in which corporations conducted business but not to its power to use prerogative writs to exercise control if a corporation abused its lawful power, acted adversely to the public, or created a nuisance. For Scalia, text and tradition resolved the ambiguity and established that the NBA's language regarding "visitorial powers" did not preempt state consumer protection laws.[60]

Thomas dissented:

> The Court holds that the term "visitorial powers" as used in the NBA refers only "to a sovereign's supervisory powers over corporations," which are limited to "administrative oversight" including "inspect[ion of] books and records on demand." Based on that definition, the Court concluded the NBA does not preempt a "state attorney general's . . . suit to enforce state law against a national bank." I would affirm the Court of Appeals' determinations that the term "visitorial powers" is ambiguous and that it was reasonable for the Office of the Comptroller of the Currency to interpret the term to encompass state efforts to obtain national bank records and to enforce state fair lending laws against national banks.[61]

Thomas noted that the OCC "did not declare the preemptive scope of the statute; rather, it interpreted the term 'visitorial powers' to encompass state enforcement of state fair lending laws. The preemption of state enforcement authority to which petitioner objects thus follows from the statute itself—not agency action."[62] He continued, "Here, Congress—not the agency—has decided that 'no national bank shall be subject to any visitorial powers except as authorized by Federal law.' . . . As a result, OCC has simply interpreted that term to encompass petitioner's decision to demand national bank records and threaten judicial enforcement of New York fair lending laws as a means of obtaining them."[63] He concluded that the majority's "federalism-based objections to *Chevron* deference ultimately turn on a single proposition: It is doubtful that Congress preempted state enforcement of state laws but not the underlying state laws themselves." However, Thomas insisted, "it is not this Court's task to decide whether the statutory scheme established by Congress is unusual or even 'bizarre.' The Court must decide only whether the construction adopted by the agency is unambiguously foreclosed by the statute's text." For Thomas, the text, structure, and history of "visitorial powers" supported the agency's reasonable interpretation of the NBA. He also noted that the Court had failed to identify "any constitutional principle that would require Congress to take the greater step of preempting all enforcement of state lending laws (including private enforcement) even though its central concern was the allocation of the right to exercise public visitation over national bank activities."[64]

The Necessary and Proper Clause

The Necessary and Proper Clause figured prominently in Thomas's dissent in *Gonzales v. Raich*. But his views on the Clause are nowhere more clearly articulated than in his dissent in the 2010 case of *Comstock v. United States*.[65]

Congress passed a federal civil-commitment law authorizing the Department of Justice to detain a mentally ill, sexually dangerous federal prisoner beyond the date it lawfully could hold the individual on a charge or conviction for a federal crime.[66] The Court had previously examined similar statutes enacted under state law to determine whether they violated the Due Process Clause, and in *Kansas v. Hendricks*,[67] Thomas wrote the majority opinion upholding these state statutes. But *Comstock* presented a different question: did Congress's enactment of a federal civil-commitment regime fall "beyond the reach of a government of enumerated powers"?[68]

In an opinion crafted by Justice Breyer, seven justices agreed that the Necessary and Proper Clause granted Congress sufficient authority to enact this civil-commitment statute. They rejected Graydon Comstock's argument that, when legislating pursuant to the Necessary and Proper Clause, Congress's authority "can be no more than one step removed from a specifically enumerated power."[69]

And they denied that the Court's holding would confer on Congress a "general 'police power, which the Founders denied the National Government and reposed in the States.'"[70] The civil-commitment statute had been applied to only a small fraction of federal prisoners, and its reach was limited to individuals already "in the custody" of the federal government. The justices denied that the statute upset the balance of federalism or invaded the states' reserved powers because it "requires accommodation of state interests" by instructing the attorney general to release committed persons to the state in which they were domiciled or tried if that state wishes to "assume . . . responsibility" for them. Thus, Breyer concluded, the statute was far from exercising a "general police power" and was a reasonably adapted and narrowly tailored means of pursuing the government's legitimate interest as a federal custodian in the responsible administration of its prison system.[71]

Thomas, joined by Scalia for most of his opinion, dissented, arguing that "the Necessary and Proper Clause empowers Congress to enact only those laws that 'carr[y] into Execution' one or more of the federal powers enumerated in the Constitution." Because the federal civil-commitment statute "'execut[es]' no enumerated power," he said, "I must respectfully dissent."[72]

He turned to Chief Justice Marshall's analysis of the Necessary and Proper Clause in *McCulloch v. Maryland*,[73] observing that federal legislation is a valid exercise of Congress's authority under the Clause only if it satisfies a two-part test: "First, the law must be directed toward a 'legitimate' end, which *McCulloch* defines as one 'within the scope of the Constitution'—that is, the powers expressly delegated to the Federal Government by some provision in the Constitution. Second, there must be a necessary and proper fit between the 'means' (the federal law) and the 'end' (the enumerated power or powers) it is designed to serve."[74]

Thomas acknowledged that *McCulloch* accords Congress "a certain amount of discretion in assessing means-end fit under this second inquiry." But, he went on, "unless the end itself is 'legitimate,' the fit between means and end is irrelevant." Making an original general meaning argument, he pointed out that this limitation was of "utmost importance to the Framers." He noted that during the state ratification debates, the Anti-Federalists expressed alarm that the Necessary and Proper Clause would give Congress virtually unlimited power. Yet he observed that "Federalist supporters of the Constitution swiftly refuted that charge, explaining that the Clause did not grant Congress any freestanding authority, but instead made explicit what was already implicit in the grant of each enumerated power." *McCulloch* confirmed this understanding, as he saw it, and "since then, our precedents uniformly have maintained that the Necessary and Proper Clause is not an independent fount of congressional authority, but rather a caveat that

Congress possesses all the means necessary to carry out the specifically granted 'foregoing' powers of § 8 'and all other Powers vested by this Constitution.'"[75]

Thomas pointed out that "no enumerated power in Article I, § 8, expressly delegates to Congress the power to enact a civil-commitment regime for sexually dangerous persons, nor does any other provision in the Constitution vest Congress or the other branches of the Federal Government with such a power." Consequently, the civil-commitment statute would be a valid exercise of congressional authority only if it was "necessary and proper for carrying into Execution" one or more of those federal powers actually enumerated in the Constitution. But, he insisted, the government identified "no specific enumerated power or powers as a constitutional predicate" for the statute, "and none are [*sic*] readily discernable." For Thomas, it was clear that "on the face of the Act and in the Government's arguments urging its constitutionality," the statute was "aimed at protecting society from acts of sexual violence, not toward 'carrying into Execution' any enumerated power or powers of the Federal Government."[76] Thomas agreed that protecting society from violent sexual offenders "is certainly an important end." Nonetheless, he argued, "the Constitution does not vest in Congress the authority to protect society from every bad act that might befall it"; accordingly, the civil-commitment statute did not execute "*any* enumerated power" and was "therefore unconstitutional."[77]

The Court's argument that the civil-commitment statute did not upset the balance of federalism or invade the states' reserved powers because states could assume responsibility for these sexually danger persons was dismissed by Thomas as "mere window dressing."[78] He argued that "once it is determined that Congress has the authority to provide for the civil detention of sexually dangerous persons" and that it "is acting within the powers granted it under the Constitution," it "may impose its will on the States." The civil-commitment statute's "right of first refusal is thus not a matter of constitutional necessity, but an act of legislative grace." He found unconvincing the majority's reliance on the fact that twenty-nine states submitted amici briefs arguing that the statute was constitutional. He wrote, "They tell us that they do not object to Congress retaining custody of 'sexually dangerous persons' after their criminal sentences expire because the cost of detaining such persons is 'expensive'—approximately $64,000 per year—and these States would rather the Federal Government bear this expense." Congress's power, he reminded his colleagues, "is fixed by the Constitution; it does not expand merely to suit the States' policy preferences, or to allow State officials to avoid difficult choices regarding the allocation of state funds. Absent congressional action that is in accordance with, or necessary and proper to, an enumerated power, the duty to protect citizens from violent crime, including acts of sexual violence, belongs solely to the States."[79] And he concluded: "In [today's ruling], the Court endorses the precise abuse of power Article I is designed to prevent—the use of a limited grant of authority as a 'pretext . . . for the accomplishment of objects not intrusted to the government.' I respectfully dissent."[80]

The Tenth Amendment

Thomas has invoked and relied upon the Tenth Amendment in scores of his opinions. However, his sustained and detailed discussion of it in his dissent in *U.S. Terms Limits, Inc. v. Thornton*[81] offers the best insight into his understanding of what is for him a critically important protection of federalism, and it fully displays his general original meaning approach to constitutional interpretation.[82]

At the general election on November 3, 1992, the voters of Arkansas adopted Amendment 73 to their state constitution. Proposed as a "term limitation amendment," it prohibited, in § 3, the name of otherwise eligible candidates for Congress from appearing on the general election ballot if they had already served three terms in the House of Representatives or two terms in the Senate (although they could still run as write-in candidates). Various parties challenged its constitutionality on the ground that it violated the U.S. Constitution by adding an additional qualification to the age, citizenship, and residency requirements for congressional service enumerated in the Qualifications Clauses of Article 1, § 2, cl. 2 and Article I, § 3, cl. 3 of the U.S. Constitution. Both an Arkansas trial court and the Arkansas Supreme Court found the term limits measure unconstitutional, as did the U.S. Supreme Court in a five-to-four decision.

Justice Stevens wrote for the five-member majority. He held that the three qualifications of age, citizenship, and residency are "fixed" (that is, exclusive) and cannot be supplemented by either Congress (the Court's holding in *Powell v. McCormack*)[83] or the states (the Court's holding in the present case). He turned to the Constitution's text, to the records of the Constitutional Convention and state ratifying conventions, to court decisions, to congressional experience dealing with state attempts to impose qualifications, and especially to the "fundamental principle of our representative democracy . . . 'that the people should choose whom they please to govern them.'" He concluded that permitting individual states to impose diverse qualifications for their congressional representatives would result in a patchwork that would be inconsistent with the framers' vision of a uniform national legislature representing the people of the United States.[84] He rejected the argument of U.S. Terms Limits, Inc., an intervener in the case, that there was no additional qualification added because term-limited candidates could still run as write-in candidates, finding it an indirect attempt to "evade" the Qualifications Clauses.[85]

Thomas wrote the dissent, which was joined by Chief Justice Rehnquist and Justices O'Connor and Scalia. It remains Thomas's lengthiest opinion, totaling 27,915 words (covering 81 pages in the *United States Reports*).[86] In it, he insisted that "nothing in the Constitution deprives the people of each State of the power to prescribe eligibility requirements for the candidates who seek to represent them in Congress. The Constitution is simply silent on this question. And where the Constitution is silent, it raises no bar to action by the States or the people."[87]

He started with "first principles" to show how Stevens "fundamentally misunderst[ood] the notion of 'reserved powers'"[88] and thereby placed "an enormous and untenable limitation on the principle expressed by the Tenth Amendment."[89] Though readily acknowledging that the framers "affirmatively deprived the States of certain powers, see, *e.g.*, Art. I, § 10, and . . . affirmatively conferred certain powers upon the Federal Government, see, *e.g.*, Art. I, § 8," he insisted that "the people of the several States are the only true source of power" and that "the Federal Government enjoys no authority beyond what the Constitution confers: the Federal Government's powers are limited and enumerated." Reciting the "basic principles . . . enshrined in the Tenth Amendment," he observed that "in each State, the remainder of the people's powers—'the powers not delegated to the United States by the Constitution, nor prohibited by it to the States,' Amdt. 10—are either delegated to the state government or retained by the people." Further, he noted that the Constitution "does not specify which of these two possibilities obtains; it is up to the various state constitutions to declare which powers the people of each State have delegated to their state government." According to the Constitution, therefore, "the States can exercise all powers that the Constitution does not withhold from them."[90] He declared that "the Federal Government and the States thus face different default rules: where the Constitution is silent about the exercise of a particular power—that is, where the Constitution does not speak either expressly or by necessary implication—the Federal Government lacks that power and the States enjoy it."[91] As Thomas saw it, those default rules meant that "if we are to invalidate Arkansas' Amendment 73, we must point to something in the Federal Constitution that deprives the people of Arkansas of the power to enact such measures."[92]

Stevens, writing for the Court majority, had categorically rejected Thomas's first principles. For him, the Tenth Amendment was irrelevant because the states could not reserve any powers that they did not control at the time the Constitution was drafted, and at that point, they had no power to add qualifications to service in a house and senate that did not then exist.[93] But Thomas insisted, "It was not the state governments that were doing the reserving. The Constitution derives its authority instead from the consent of *the people* of the States. Given the fundamental principle that all governmental powers stem from the people of the States, it would simply be incoherent to assert that the people of the States could not reserve any powers that they had not previously controlled."[94] He gave the following example: "If someone says that the power to use a particular facility is reserved to some group, he is not saying anything about whether that group has previously used the facility. He is merely saying that the people who control the facility have designated that group as the entity with authority to use it." For him, the Tenth Amendment was similar: "The people of the States, from whom all governmental powers stem, have specified that all powers not prohibited to the States by the Federal Constitution are reserved 'to the States respectively, or to the people.'"[95] Thomas turned to the Constitution's treatment of presidential elections to make his point. Though the individual states had no "reserved" power to set qualifications for the office of president, he argued, the Court had long recognized that "they do have the power (as far as the Federal Constitution is concerned) to set qualifications for their Presidential electors—the delegates that each State selects to represent it in the electoral college that actually chooses the Nation's chief executive. Even the respondents agreed that the States have power to establish qualifications for their delegates to the electoral college, as long as those qualifications pass muster under the First and Fourteenth Amendments." And since Stevens was unable to establish how the Constitution affirmatively granted this power to the states, "the power must be one that is 'reserved'" to them. He went on, "It necessarily follows that the majority's understanding of the Tenth Amendment is incorrect, for the position of Presidential elector surely 'spring[s]' out of the existence of the national government.'"[96]

All of this led Thomas to conclude that "the people of Arkansas do enjoy 'reserved' powers over the selection of their representatives in Congress . . . unless something in the Federal Constitution deprives them of the power to enact such measures."[97] Stevens, however, argued that there was "something in the Constitution"—the Qualifications Clauses that he read as "fix[ing]" both a floor and a ceiling on what states could impose.[98]

Thomas strenuously disagreed, asserting that the Clauses were "negative" in formulation and merely established "minimum qualifications."[99] They did not "prohibit the people of a State from establishing additional eligibility requirements for their own representatives," as would, for example "an exclusive formulation such as the following: 'Every Person who shall have attained to the age of twenty five Years, and been seven Years a Citizen of the United States, and who shall, when elected, be an Inhabitant of that State in which he shall be chosen, shall be eligible to be a Representative.'"[100] But, he noted, the framers did not include exclusive formulation clauses; in fact, quite to the contrary, they rejected them. Consistent with his original general meaning approach, Thomas remarked that, though an early draft of the Constitution prepared by the Committee of

Detail (the committee established by the Constitutional Convention to take the resolutions approved by the delegates and transform them into a draft constitution) included exclusive formulation language concerning qualifications for both the House and Senate, these exclusivity provisions were deleted by the committee in later drafts. That action, Thomas said, "indicates that the Committee expected neither list of qualifications to be exclusive."[101] He insisted that the clauses the framers did write should not be read to "mean anything more than what they say,"[102] a conclusion that "is buttressed by our reluctance to read constitutional provisions to preclude state power by negative implication."[103]

Thomas agreed with Stevens that *Powell v. McCormack* correctly held that Congress could not add qualifications for service in the House and Senate. As he put it, "Congressional power over qualifications would have enabled the representatives from some States, acting collectively in the National Legislature, to prevent the people of another State from electing their preferred candidates."[104] However, he insisted, the situation was entirely different when individual states added qualifications for their own representatives and senators: "When the people of a State themselves decide to restrict the field of candidates whom they are willing to send to Washington as their representatives, they simply have not violated the principle that 'the people should choose whom they please to govern them.' See 2 Elliot 257 (remarks of Alexander Hamilton at the New York convention)."[105]

Thomas cited further evidence from the text of the Constitution indicating that the Qualifications Clauses set only minimal qualifications that the states could supplement, namely, the Religious Test Clause of Article VI, cl. 3: "No religious Test shall ever be required as a Qualification for any Office or public Trust under the United States." As Thomas observed, "Both the context and the plain language of the Clause show that it bars the States as well as the Federal Government from imposing religious disqualifications on federal offices. But the only reason for extending the Clause to the States would be to protect Senators and Representatives from state-imposed religious qualifications. . . . The Framers' prohibition on state-imposed religious disqualifications for Members of Congress suggests that other types of state-imposed disqualifications are permissible."[106]

Pursuing his original general meaning approach, Thomas turned as well to the "contemporaneous practical exposition" of the Qualifications Clauses in the states "immediately after the ratification of the Constitution." Instead of understanding these clauses to be exclusive, he argued, "five States supplemented the constitutional disqualifications in their very first election laws," with "the surviving records suggest[ing] that the legislatures of these States considered and rejected the interpretation of the Constitution that the majority adopts today."[107] Thus, he developed in some detail, Virginia's first election law "erected a property qualification for Virginia's contingent in the Federal House of Representatives." In addition, "five of the seven States that divided themselves into districts for House elections added that representatives also had to be inhabitants of the district that elected them," and "three of these States adopt[ed] durational residency requirements too, insisting that representatives have resided within their districts for at least a year (or, in one case, three years) before being elected."[108] This history of state practice, he concluded, "refutes the majority's position that the Qualifications Clauses were generally understood to include an unstated exclusivity provision."[109]

Finally, in addition to denying that the Qualifications Clauses prohibited states from adding additional qualifications, Thomas also denied that Amendment 73 added any qualifications. He noted that the amendment "does not say that covered candidates may not serve any more terms in Congress if reelected, and it does not indirectly achieve the same result by barring those candidates from seeking reelection. It says only that if they are to win reelection, they must do so by write-in votes."[110] Thomas then proceeded to identify various congressional candidates who had won as write-ins, including Representative Dale Alford from Arkansas. He also mentioned Ross Perot's write-in victory in the 1992 North Dakota Democratic presidential primary,[111] and had he been clairvoyant, he would have mentioned Lisa Murkowski's huge and nationally significant 2010 victory in Alaska as a write-in candidate in the general election to retain her seat in the U.S. Senate. Term-limited candidates obviously were handicapped by having to run as write-ins, but, Thomas noted, "laws that allegedly have the purpose and effect of handicapping a particular class of candidates traditionally are reviewed under the First and Fourteenth Amendments rather than the Qualifications Clauses." And then, tweaking his colleagues in the majority, Thomas speculated: "To analyze such laws under the Qualifications Clauses may open up whole new vistas for courts." He noted,

> [If] it can be shown that nonminorities are at a significant disadvantage
> when they seek election in districts dominated by minority voters,
> would the intentional creation of "majority-minority districts" violate
> the Qualifications Clauses even if it were to survive scrutiny under the
> Fourteenth Amendment? More generally, if "district lines are rarely neutral
> phenomena" and if "districting inevitably has and is intended to have
> substantial political consequences," will plausible Qualifications Clause
> challenges greet virtually every redistricting decision?[112]

Although conceding that the majority opinion "may not go so far," he said that it did not "suggest any principled stopping point," which prompted him to say once again, "I would read the Qualifications Clauses to do no more than they say. I respectfully dissent."[113]

Interestingly, Thomas never considered whether the Court should have reversed the Arkansas Supreme Court because the permissibility of using term limits for members of Congress was a "political question" to be resolved by the political branches—in this case, by Congress itself. In *Baker v. Carr*,[114] Justice William Brennan spelled out for a unanimous Supreme Court six criteria for determining whether it was confronted with a nonjusticiable political question. The first and most prominent criterion was "a textually demonstrable constitutional commitment of the issue to a coordinate political department."[115] Article I, § 4 provides a "textually demonstrable constitutional commitment" to Congress to resolve questions concerning the permissibility of term limits for members of Congress. It says: "The Times, Places and Manner of holding Elections for Senators and Representatives, shall be prescribed in each State by the Legislature thereof; but the Congress may at any time by Law make or alter such Regulations, except as to the Place of Chusing Senators." Term limits relate to the manner of holding elections; states are free to prescribe them if they think them wise, and Congress is free to eliminate them if it disagrees.

State Sovereign Immunity

In *Seminole Tribe of Florida v. Florida* (1996),[116] Chief Justice Rehnquist wrote, for a five-member majority, that Congress lacked power under the Commerce Clause to abrogate state sovereign immunity protected by the Eleventh Amendment. In 1988, pursuant to its powers under the Indian Commerce Clause, Congress passed the Indian Gaming Regulatory Act, which allowed Indian tribes to conduct certain gaming activities provided they were in conformity with the terms of a valid compact between the tribe and the state in which the gaming activities were located. Under the act, Congress imposed on states a duty to negotiate in good faith with a tribe toward the formation of a compact, and it authorized the tribes to sue a state in federal court in order to compel performance of that duty. When the Seminole Tribe sued the state of Florida for its refusal to enter into good faith negotiations, Florida moved to dismiss the complaint on the ground that congressional authorization of the suit violated its sovereign immunity from suit in federal court. When the district court denied Florida's motion, the U.S. Court of Appeals for the Eleventh Circuit reversed, concluding that under the Eleventh Amendment, the federal courts had no jurisdiction. The Supreme Court agreed.

In his majority opinion, joined by Thomas, Rehnquist had to overcome a major textual problem. By its terms, the Eleventh Amendment simply does not bar the kind of suit brought by the Seminole Tribe. It reads as follows: "The Judicial power of the United States shall not be construed to extend to any suit in law or equity, commenced or prosecuted against one of the United States by Citizens of another State, or by Citizens or Subjects of any Foreign State." The members of the Seminole Tribe were not "Citizens of another State, or . . . Citizens or Subjects of any Foreign State" bringing suit under the federal court's state-citizen diversity jurisdiction (granted by Article III in the original Constitution but then subsequently repealed by the Eleventh Amendment). Rather, they were bringing suit under the federal court's federal-question (also known as "subject matter" or "arising under") jurisdiction (granted by Article III and left untouched by the Eleventh Amendment).

Although the words of the Eleventh Amendment did not bar the suit filed by the Seminole Tribe, Rehnquist nevertheless proclaimed that a "blind reliance upon the text of the Eleventh Amendment" would be "overly exacting" and would result in a "construction never imagined or dreamed of."[117] The Eleventh Amendment, he insisted, stands "not so much for what it says, as for the presupposition . . . which it confirms." That presupposition, he continued, has two parts: "First, that each State is a sovereign entity in our federal system; and second, that 'it is inherent in the nature of sovereignty not to be amenable to suit without its consent.'"[118]

Rehnquist pointed out that the Eleventh Amendment was a reaction to "the now-discredited decision in *Chisholm v. Georgia*"[119] in which the Supreme Court had held that a state could be sued by a citizen of another state or by an alien. The Eleventh Amendment reversed that decision, and as Rehnquist emphasized, it "dealt in terms only with the problem presented" by *Chisholm*. Because the federal courts in 1793 did not have federal-question jurisdiction (in fact, they would not have it until 1875), Rehnquist concluded that the authors of the Eleventh Amendment did not see a threat to the principle of state sovereign immunity coming from that quarter. Instead, they believed the threat would come from suits brought under the federal courts' diversity jurisdiction, and therefore, they barred only those suits.[120] The goal of these drafters, Rehnquist implied, was to protect the principle of state sovereign immunity from any threat. Their means—which, in retrospect, were less comprehensive than they should have been—were to bar suits under the federal courts' diversity jurisdiction.

In the lead dissent, Justice David Souter argued that *Chisholm* settled the question of whether the states could be sued not only under the federal courts' citizen-state diversity jurisdiction but also, "by implication," under their federal-question jurisdiction. He wrote, "The constitutional text on federal-question jurisdiction, after all, was just as devoid of immunity language as it was on citizen-state diversity."[121] Yet, he pointed out, Congress drafted the Eleventh Amendment to protect the states only from suits brought against them under the federal courts' diversity jurisdiction. As he went on to say: "If the Framers had meant the Amendment to bar federal-question suits as well, they could not only have made their intention clearer very easily, but could simply have adopted the first post-*Chisholm* proposal adopted by Theodore Sedgwick of Massachusetts on instructions from the Legislature of that Commonwealth." That proposal would have covered expressly what Rehnquist asserted the Eleventh Amendment was intended to convey: "No state shall be liable to be made a party defendant, in any of the judicial courts, established, or which shall be established under the authority of the United States, at the suit of any person or persons, whether a citizen or citizens, or a foreigner or foreigners, or any body politic or corporate, whether within or without the United States."[122]

Sedgwick's proposed amendment, with its references to suits by citizens as well as noncitizens, clearly reached beyond the federal courts' state-citizen diversity jurisdiction for a reason that would have been obvious to the people of the time. As Justice Souter pointed out in his dissent, "Sedgwick sought such a broad amendment because many of the States, including his own, owed debts subject to collection under the Treaty of Paris. Suits to collect such debts would 'arise under' that Treaty and thus be subject to federal-question jurisdiction under Article III." Such suits were actually already pending against Massachusetts, including one by "Christopher Vassal, an erstwhile Bostonian whose move to England on the eve of revolutionary hostilities had presented his former neighbors with the irresistible temptation to confiscate his vacant mansion."[123] But Sedgwick's proposed amendment went further still: it would have barred all "arising under" or federal-question suits as well. It declared, after all, that "no state shall be liable to be made a party defendant" in any federal court action brought against it by "any body politic or corporate, whether within or without the United States." It would have conferred on the states complete sovereign immunity that could not be abrogated even by Congress.

Despite the unequivocal text of the Eleventh Amendment and Souter's effective use of legislative history to show the original understanding of its drafters, Thomas joined Rehnquist's majority opinion. He would also join the majority opinions issued by other colleagues in six more state sovereign immunity cases. He joined a Kennedy opinion in *Idaho v. Coeur d'Alene Tribe of Idaho*,[124] holding that a tribe's claims to exclusive use of submerged waters against state officials were barred by the Eleventh Amendment. He joined a Rehnquist opinion in *Florida Prepaid Postsecondary Education Expense Board v. College Savings Bank*,[125] invalidating that provision of the Patent Remedy Act of 1992 expressly abrogating state sovereign immunity from claims of patent infringement. He joined Scalia's opinion in *College Savings Bank v. Florida Prepaid Postsecondary Education Expense Board,*[126] invalidating that provision of the Trademark Remedy Clarification Act of 1992 subjecting states to suits brought under the Trademark Act of 1946 for false and misleading advertising.[127] He joined Kennedy's opinion in *Alden v. Maine,*[128] invalidating the 1974 amendments to the Fair Labor Standards Act authorizing private actions against the states in their own courts without their consent. He joined O'Connor's opinion in *Kimel v. Florida Board of Regents,*[129] invalidating amendments to the Age Discrimination in Employment Act of 1967 abrogating state sovereign immunity for suits charging states with discrimination because of an individual's age.[130] And he joined Rehnquist's opinion in *Trustees of the University of Alabama v. Garrett,*[131] invalidating that provision of the Americans with Disabilities Act of 1990 that abrogated state sovereign immunity and allowed state employees to recover monetary damages by reason of the state's failure to comply with the act's provisions.

Finally, in *Federal Maritime Commission v. South Carolina State Ports Authority,*[132] Thomas wrote the majority opinion that is perhaps the Court's most extraordinary attempt to protect nonconsenting states from legal actions against them. And in the process, he went far beyond any arguments in *Seminole Tribe* or *Alden.* In *Seminole Tribe,* Rehnquist departed from the text of the Eleventh Amendment when it held that its "presupposition" barred suits against the states without their consent—not only under the federal courts' state-citizen diversity jurisdiction but also under their subject matter jurisdiction. In *Alden,* Kennedy departed further still from the text by holding that this presupposition barred Congress from authorizing suits against nonconsenting states both in federal courts and in state courts as well. In *Federal Maritime Commission,* Thomas abandoned the text altogether, holding that this same presupposition barred actions against nonconsenting states not only in courts generally but even in federal regulatory agencies.[133]

A cruise ship operator filed a complaint with the Federal Maritime Commission (FMC), alleging that South Carolina's ports authority had violated the Shipping Act of 1984 by denying the operator permission to berth its ships at Charleston—these ships would depart from port and enter international waters for no other reason than to allow patrons to gamble on board. When an administrative law judge dismissed the complaint on the basis that the ports authority, as an arm of the state, was entitled to sovereign immunity from suits by private parties, litigation was set in motion. Ultimately, the case reached the Supreme Court. Justice Thomas held for the same five-member majority,[134] present in all the previously mentioned state sovereign immunity cases, that "the Eleventh

Amendment does not define the scope of the States' sovereign immunity"; rather, he wrote, "it is but one particular exemplification of that immunity."[135] Declaring that "the preeminent purpose of state-sovereign immunity is to accord States the dignity that is consistent with their status as sovereign entities"[136] and noting the "remarkably strong resemblance" of an FMC administrative proceeding to civil litigation in federal courts (it "walks, talks, and squawks very much like a lawsuit"[137]), he held that

> state sovereign immunity bars the FMC from adjudicating complaints filed
> by a private party against a nonconsenting State. Simply put, if the Framers
> thought it an impermissible affront to a State's dignity to be required
> to answer the complaints of private parties in federal courts, we cannot
> imagine that they would have found it acceptable to compel a State to
> do exactly the same thing before the administrative tribunal of an agency,
> such as the FMC. The affront to a State's dignity does not lessen when
> an adjudication takes place in an administrative tribunal as opposed to an
> Article III court. In both instances, a State is required to defend itself in an
> adversarial proceeding against a private party before an impartial federal
> officer.[138]

Justice Breyer wrote the lead dissent. He began by observing, "The Court holds that a private person cannot bring a complaint against a State to a federal administrative agency where the agency (1) will use an internal adjudicative process to decide if the complaint is well founded, and (2) if so, proceed to court to enforce the law." He then inquired: "Where does the Constitution contain the principle of law that the Court enunciates? I cannot find the answer to this question in any text, in any tradition, or in any relevant purpose." He found the lack of a textual basis especially troubling. He stated, "The Court's principle lacks any firm anchor in the Constitution's text. The Eleventh Amendment cannot help. It says: 'The *Judicial* power of the United States shall not . . . extend to any suit . . . commenced or prosecuted against one of the . . . States by Citizens of another State.'" Breyer pointed out that federal administrative agencies "do not exercise the 'judicial power of the United States.'" And, he continued, though "this Court has read the words 'Citizens of another State' as if they also said 'citizen of the same State,' . . . it has never said that the words 'judicial power of the United States' mean 'the executive power of the United States.' Nor should it."[139]

Thomas must have been stung by these words. After all, in his 1996 Stephenson Lecture at the University of Kansas entitled "Judging," he had asserted that he would turn to his original general meaning approach only in those cases where the "text's meaning is not readily apparent."[140] But here, the meaning of the text of the Eleventh Amendment was, in fact, "readily apparent." Its words clearly bar state-citizen diversity cases in federal courts but say absolutely nothing about barring complaints launched against state entities by federal regulatory agencies. And even if the words were not "readily apparent," a faithful employment of Thomas's original general meaning approach would require that he take seriously Representative Sedgwick's initial formulation of the Eleventh Amendment. Thomas relied on a change in the original formulation of the Qualifications Clauses by the Committee of Detail to conclude in *U.S. Terms Limits* that these clauses were not intended to be exclusive. He should also have relied on a change in Sedgwick's initial formulation of the Eleventh Amendment to conclude that the amendment is limited in its reach simply to state-citizen diversity cases—and to read its words "to do no more than they say."[141]

Interestingly, after Thomas's high-water opinion in *South Carolina State Ports Authority*, the Court suddenly became much more deferential to congressional abrogation of state sovereign immunity, as *Nevada Department of Human Resources v. Hibbs*,[142] *Tennessee v. Lane*,[143] and *Central Virginia Community College v. Katz*[144] make clear.[145] In *Hibbs*, Rehnquist held for a six-member majority that state employees could sue their employers in federal court for violation of the family-care leave provisions of the Family and Medical Leave Act (FMLA) because Congress had validly exercised its § 5 enforcement powers under the Fourteenth Amendment to abrogate the states' Eleventh Amendment immunity to such suits. In *Lane*, Stevens held for a five-member majority that Title II of the Americans with Disabilities Act—guaranteeing, among other things, the right of disabled persons to physical access to state courts and authorizing them to file suits in federal court for money damages when that right is violated—was a valid exercise of Congress's enforcement authority under § 5 of the Fourteenth Amendment. And in *Katz*, Stevens held for a five-member majority that the Bankruptcy Clause, Article I, § 8, cl. 4, empowering Congress to establish "uniform Laws on the subject of Bankruptcies throughout the United States," gives Congress the authority to abrogate states' immunity from private suits. In all three of these cases, Thomas remained committed to his nontextualist and nonoriginalist approach to protecting state sovereign immunity from congressional efforts at abrogation. He joined Scalia's lone dissent in *Hibbs* and both Rehnquist's and Scalia's dissents in *Lane*, and he wrote the dissent in *Katz*.

This and the preceding chapter have addressed Thomas's federalism jurisprudence in cases involving the Interstate Commerce Clause, the negative Commerce Clause, the Indian Commerce Clause, federal preemption of state laws, the Necessary and Proper Clause, the Tenth Amendment, and state sovereign immunity. They have examined how faithful he has been in these cases to his original general meaning approach to constitutional interpretation. The results of this examination can be summarized as follows.

Thomas's definition of commerce in *Lopez* was certainly consistent with its original general meaning, as was his discussion of how the substantial effects test has the capacity to render superfluous all the other enumerated powers in Article I, § 8. And by turning to *The Federalist* and other materials from the founding, he was able to demonstrate that the Court's employment of the substantial effects test was a twentieth-century innovation and a clear departure from the original general meaning of the Constitution. His depiction in *Morrison* of the substantial effects test as "rootless and malleable" and as encouraging the federal government to believe that the Commerce Clause has no limits was compellingly made. So, too, was his call to replace the Court's existing Commerce Clause jurisprudence with a standard more consistent with its original general meaning, a standard that could better withstand Congress's continuing appropriation of the police powers of the states. His conclusion in *Raich* that those who framed and ratified the Constitution would have found it "unthinkable" that Congress could prohibit the local cultivation, possession, and consumption of marijuana, his recognition that the founding generation was concerned about the danger of concentrating either too much or too little power in the federal government, and his call for the Court to discard its substantial effects test were consistent with his originalist understanding that the enumerated powers of Article I, § 8 are "few and defined" whereas the reserved powers of the states are "numerous and indefinite."

As noted earlier, however, Thomas's originalist understanding of what powers were to be exercised by the federal government (and why) does not extend to an equal appreciation that the mode of electing the U.S. Senate was the means the framers employed to ensure (1) that the Commerce Clause would not become a blank check by which Congress could regulate everything, and (2) that the reserved police powers of the states would be protected. To date, Thomas apparently has not given much thought to enforcing the original understanding of the Commerce Clause by relying on nonoriginalist means.

By contrast, he has given considerable thought to the negative Commerce Clause. After initially accepting this legal doctrine in several early opinions, he has, beginning with his dissent in *Camps Newfound*, become its fiercest critic. Finding it to have no basis in the text of the Constitution—and hence "illegitimate"—and also finding it to have thrust justices into the role of policymakers, he argues that it should be discarded and refuses to join any opinion that enforces it. Given his commitment to original general meaning—to connecting means to ends—Thomas explains how the framers drafted the Import Export Clause as the appropriate check on particularly egregious state burdens on interstate commerce that the Court can legitimately apply. This is an impressive illustration of his original general meaning jurisprudence.

Thomas's understanding of the Indian Commerce Clause remains largely inchoate. In *Lara*, he was troubled by the argument that the Clause's language gave Congress plenary and exclusive power over the tribes, and he was perplexed that the Court's case law toward Indian tribes was "schizophrenic," viewing them as sovereign yet completely subject to congressional whim. He therefore invited his colleagues to think through these issues "honestly and rigorously." Thomas appears unwilling to concede that the Indian Commerce Clause gives Congress plenary power over the tribes and the ability to regulate all aspects of life in Indian country because that would seem to suggest that the Interstate Commerce Clause gives Congress an equally blank check to exercise an unlimited police power over the American citizenry. But that apprehension keeps him from appreciating that the original understanding of the Indian Commerce Clause was fully revealed by the actions of the early Congresses when they enacted a whole series of trade and intercourse acts. That same apprehension appears to keep him from accepting what other justices have embraced and made clear in their opinions, namely, that it is "well established that the Interstate Commerce and Indian Commerce Clauses have very different applications."[146] As Justice Stevens has pointed out in *Cotton Petroleum Corp. v. New Mexico*, "while the Interstate Commerce Clause is concerned with maintaining free trade among the States . . . , the central function of the Indian Commerce Clause is to provide Congress with plenary power to legislate in the field of Indian affairs." Further, the Court's case law under the Interstate Commerce Clause is premised, again in Stevens's words, "on a structural understanding of the unique role of the States in our constitutional system that is not readily imported to cases involving the Indian Commerce Clause."[147]

In preemption cases, Thomas places text over states' rights. If Congress expressly preempts, he rejects efforts by his colleagues to apply a presumption against preemption; however, if Congress murmurs an unclear message concerning preemption of state laws, Thomas insists that the Court should refrain from acting. He consistently has held that the Court should uphold the preemption of state laws only when constitutionally commanded to do so by Congress or a federal agency under *Chevron* deference—"in which case, text provides the roadmap for action."[148]

Concerning the Necessary and Proper Clause, Thomas in *Comstock* staunchly and correctly protected federalism, insisting that Marshall's analysis in *McCulloch* was governing and arguing that, although *McCulloch* accorded Congress "a certain amount of discretion" in assessing the fit between ends and means, "unless the end itself is 'legitimate,' the fit between means and end is irrelevant." Making an original general meaning argument, he pointed out that this limitation was of "utmost importance to the Framers" but utterly lacking in *Comstock*, where the end Congress sought to advance was "protecting society from acts of sexual violence, not toward 'carrying into Execution' any enumerated power or powers of the Federal Government."[149]

Thomas's understanding of the Tenth Amendment displays total fidelity to his original general meaning approach. The best statement in his entire lengthy opinion in *U.S. Terms Limits* is the following:

> The majority's essential logic is that the state governments could not "reserve" any powers that they did not control at the time the Constitution was drafted. But it was not the state governments that were doing the reserving. The Constitution derives its authority instead from the consent of the people of the States. Given the fundamental principle that all governmental powers stem from the people of the States, it would simply be incoherent to assert that the people of the States could not reserve any powers that they had not previously controlled.[150]

As Thomas argued in his Opperman Lecture at Drake Law School, federalism, as articulated in part in the Tenth Amendment, "exists to protect 'the rights of the people,'" and this understanding consistently underlies his federalism jurisprudence.[151]

Finally, in the several cases addressing the question of state sovereign immunity, Thomas, like his fellow originalist Scalia, has regrettably drifted far from his originalist moorings. He has agreed to language written by his colleagues that has proclaimed a "blind reliance upon the text of the Eleventh Amendment" to be "overly exacting," and he has concurred in their nontextualist assertions that the Eleventh Amendment stands "not so much for what it says, as for the presupposition . . . which it confirms." If *South Carolina State Ports Authority* (and its holding that the Constitution prohibits the federal government from passing legislation making various arms of the state subject to the administrative proceedings of federal regulatory agencies) was the first Thomas opinion that someone read, that individual would doubtless be astonished to learn that he regards himself as a textualist and as committed to a jurisprudence of original general meaning.

Chapter 4 moves from a consideration of constitutional structure to substantive rights and addresses how Thomas's original general meaning approach informs his understanding of the First, Second, Fifth, and Fourteenth Amendments. It does so by examining in detail his many opinions on the free exercise and establishment of religion, freedom of speech and the press, the Takings Clause, and the Court's abortion jurisprudence.

Chapter Four

Thomas's Original General Meaning Approach to Substantive Rights

In such areas as free exercise and establishment of religion, freedom of speech and press, the Second Amendment, the Takings Clause, and the Court's abortion jurisprudence, Clarence Thomas has consistently employed an original general meaning approach in an effort to apply the constitutional texts in question as their words demand and as they were understood and explained by those who drafted and ratified them. This chapter focuses on the opinions he has written on these matters.

Free Exercise and Establishment of Religion

The First Amendment begins by declaring that "Congress shall make no law respecting an establishment of religion, or prohibiting the free exercise thereof." Interestingly, only two major free exercise cases have come before the Court since Thomas's elevation to the High Bench. The first was *Locke v. Davey*,[1] in which Thomas wrote a brief dissent objecting on free exercise grounds to a provision in the Washington State Constitution barring academically gifted students from using the state's Promise Scholarship Program, established to assist them with postsecondary education expenses, to pursue a degree in theology.[2] He also joined Scalia's longer dissent that argued when a state withholds a benefit to some individuals that is available to others based solely on the fact that their field of study is religion, it violates the Free Exercise Clause.[3]

The second free exercise case was decided eight years later. In *Hosanna-Tabor Evangelical Lutheran Church and School v. Equal Employment Opportunity Commission*, Chief Justice John Roberts held for a unanimous Court that the Religion Clauses bar suits brought on behalf of ministers against their churches claiming termination in violation of employment discrimination laws. Thomas wrote a separate brief concurrence to emphasize that the Free Exercise Clause requires "civil courts to apply the ministerial exception and to defer to a religious organization's good-faith understanding of who qualifies as its minister." A religious organization's right to choose its ministers "would be hollow," he argued, "if secular courts could second-guess the organization's sincere determination that a given employee is a 'minister' under the organization's theological tenets." He noted that "our country's religious landscape includes organizations with different leadership structures and doctrines that influence their conception of ministerial status. The question whether an employee is a minister is itself religious in nature, and the answer will vary widely."[4]

By contrast, Thomas's critique of and efforts to correct the Court's Establishment Clause jurisprudence, which he has rightly characterized as "in shambles" and a "mess," have been considerable.[5] In dissent from the Court's denial of certiorari in *Utah Highway Patrol Association v. American Atheists, Inc.*, Thomas pointed out that the Court's "'*Lemon*/endorsement test,' which asks whether the challenged governmental practice has the actual purpose of endorsing religion or whether it has that effect from the perspective of a 'reasonable observer,'"[6] has been "impenetrable," remains "incapable of coherent explanation," and is the area of law most "in need of clarity."[7] He noted that "a crèche displayed on government property violates the Establishment Clause, except when it doesn't," and cited five cases where federal appellate courts were in disagreement. He noted that "a menorah displayed on government property violates the Establishment Clause, except when it doesn't," and cited three lower court cases taking opposite points of view. He stated that "a display of the Ten Commandments on government property also violates the Establishment Clause, except when it doesn't," and pointed to five cases in conflict. And he declared that "a cross displayed on government property violates the Establishment Cause, . . . except when it doesn't," and mentioned six inconsistent cases. He was compelled to conclude that "such arbitrariness is the product of an Establishment Clause jurisprudence that does nothing to constrain judicial discretion."[8] In a series of opinions, Thomas has thought through and articulated a comprehensive understanding of the Establishment Clause, based on original general meaning.

His first effort to come to grips with the original general meaning of the Establishment Clause was in his concurrence in *Rosenberger v. Rector and Visitors of the University of Virginia*,[9] in which Kennedy held for a five-member majority that the university's refusal to pay for the publication of a Christian student newspaper out of its student activities fund constituted viewpoint discrimination in violation of the organization's First Amendment right of free speech.[10] In his dissent, Souter argued that direct funding of the newspaper would support religious evangelism in violation of the Establishment Clause.

Thomas's concurrence was directed toward refuting Souter's argument. He began by noting that "although the dissent starts down the right path in consulting the original meaning of the Establishment Clause, its misleading application of history yields a principle that is inconsistent with our Nation's long tradition of allowing religious adherents to participate on equal terms in neutral govern-mental programs."[11] He declared that there was "much to commend" the view that "the Framers saw the Establishment Clause simply as a prohibition on gov-ernmental preferences for some religious faiths over others." He then turned to Madison's statements in the First Congress when he was proposing the adoption of a bill of rights as supporting the proposition that the First Amendment was "designed to prohibit the establishment of a national religion, and perhaps to prevent discrimination among sects, but not as requiring neutrality on the part of government between religion and irreligion."[12]

He rejected Souter's claim that the Establishment Clause "permits neutral-ity in the context of access to governmental facilities but requires discrimination in access to government funds" by pointing to "one famous example" in which both houses of the First Congress elected chaplains and enacted legislation pro-viding for their salaries. "Madison himself was a member of the committee that recommended the chaplain system in the House," he noted.[13] He also found "overwhelming" the historical evidence of government support for religious in-stitutions through property tax exemptions. He wrote, "A tax exemptions in many cases is economically and functionally indistinguishable from a direct monetary subsidy. . . . Whether the benefit is provided at the front or the back end of the taxation process, the financial aid to religious groups is undeniable."[14]

Thomas's next opportunity to elaborate on his understanding of the Estab-lishment Clause came in his judgment for the Court in *Mitchell v. Helms*,[15] in which he held that direct and nonincidental governmental aid to religious schools by the federal government was permissible under the Establishment Clause where such aid was made available neutrally to both religious and secu-lar beneficiaries on a nondiscriminatory basis. He argued, "The religious nature of a recipient should not matter to the constitutional analysis, so long as the re-cipient adequately furthers the government's secular purpose. If a program offers permissible aid to the religious, the a-religious, and the irreligious, it is a mystery which view of religion the government has established, and thus a mystery what the constitutional violation would be."[16] He declared that nothing in the Estab-lishment Clause required the exclusion of religious schools from an otherwise permissible aid program, and he stated that any doctrine to the contrary, "born of bigotry, should be buried now."[17]

Thomas's breakthrough opinion on his understanding of the Establishment Clause, however, came in *Zelman v. Simmons-Harris*,[18] which he further refined in his subsequent concurring opinions in *Elk Grove Unified School District v. Newdow*[19] and *Van Orden v. Perry*.[20] In *Zelman*, the Court addressed the question of whether the Establishment Clause was violated by an Ohio program that pro-vided vouchers for students residing in Cleveland's failing public school system (many of them black) to attend participating public or private schools of their parents' choosing, even though they frequently chose private schools that had a religious affiliation. Chief Justice Rehnquist held for a five-member majority that it did not. He cited *Mitchell v. Helms* and argued that the program was entirely neutral with respect to religion. Thomas fully joined Rehnquist's opinion and added a concurring opinion to articulate his emerging thoughts on the Establishment Clause.

He began his opinion by quoting the words of Frederick Douglass: "'Education means emancipation. It means light and liberty. It means the uplifting of the soul of man into the glorious light of truth, the light by which men can be made free.'" Thomas then added, "Today many of our inner-city public schools deny emancipation to urban minority students."[21] He ended his opinion by again quoting Douglass: "'No greater benefit can be bestowed upon a long benighted people, than giving them, as we are earnestly this day endeavoring to do, the means of an education.'"[22]

Between the bracketed passages quoting the celebrated former slave, social reformer, orator, writer, and statesman, Thomas laid out a bold new understanding of the Establishment Clause and how it applies to the states. "I agree with the Court that Ohio's program easily passes muster under our stringent [*Mitchell*] test," he wrote, "but, as a matter of first principles, I question whether this test should be applied to the states."[23] Although the Establishment Clause "originally protected States—and by extension their citizens—from the imposition of an established religion by the Federal Government," he found that it was a "more difficult question" whether and how it constrained state action under the Fourteenth Amendment, understood by the Court since Justice Hugo Black's majority opinion in *Everson v. Board of Education*[24] to incorporate the Establishment Clause to apply to the states.

Thomas accepted the idea, expressed by the first Justice John Marshall Harlan in his dissenting opinion in *Plessy v. Ferguson*,[25] that the Fourteenth Amendment "added greatly to the dignity and glory of American citizenship, and to the security of personal liberty."[26] But he then made an obvious point that no previous justice had expressed so emphatically: "When rights are incorporated against the States through the Fourteenth Amendment, they should advance, not constrain individual liberty."[27] He continued,

> While the Federal Government may "make no law respecting an establishment of religion," the States may pass laws that include or touch on religious matters so long as these laws do not impede free exercise rights or any other individual religious liberty interest. By considering the particular religious liberty right alleged to be invaded by the State, federal courts can

strike a proper balance between the demands of the Fourteenth Amendment on the one hand and the federalism prerogatives of States on the other.[28]

Although he readily accepted that the Fourteenth Amendment "protects religious liberty rights," he rejected "its use to oppose neutral programs of school choice through the incorporation of the Fourteenth Amendment. There would be a tragic irony in converting the Fourteenth Amendment's guarantee of individual liberty into a prohibition on the exercise of educational choice."[29]

Thomas continued his "rethinking"[30] of the Establishment Clause in the *Newdow* case, where the question before the Court was whether a school district's policy of having students recite each day the Pledge of Allegiance (with its words *under God*) violated the Establishment Clause. Thomas dissented from the Court's conclusion that Michael Newdow lacked standing to bring suit and thus its refusal to address the merits of the case; finding unpersuasive the Court's prudential prohibition of third-party standing, he reached the merits and used the occasion to argue that the Establishment Clause "is a federalism provision which . . . resists incorporation" and that "the Pledge policy is not implicated by any sensible incorporation of the Establishment Clause, which would probably cover little more than the Free Exercise Clause."[31]

Newdow had argued that the school's policy of reciting the pledge violated the Court's decision in *Lee v. Weisman*, which held that invocations and benedictions given at public school graduation ceremonies violated the Establishment Clause because students were subjected to "peer pressure" to attend these ceremonies and to stand or maintain a respectful silence during such prayers.[32] Thomas argued that if *Lee* had been correctly decided, the pledge policy should be struck down because it posed "more serious difficulties" than were present in *Lee*: "A prayer at graduation is a one-time event [whereas the students were] exposed to the Pledge each and every day."[33] But, he insisted, *Lee* "adopted an expansive definition of coercion that cannot be defended" and was, therefore, "wrongly decided" because "peer pressure, unpleasant as it may be, is not coercion."[34]

Thomas elaborated. He readily conceded that the Free Exercise Clause "clearly protects an individual right" and "applies to the States through the Fourteenth Amendment," but he stressed that "the Establishment Clause is another matter. The text and history of the Establishment Clause strongly suggest that it is a federalism provision intended to prevent Congress from interfering with state establishments." Its incorporation has led to "a peculiar outcome: It would prohibit precisely what the Establishment Clause was intended to protect—state establishments of religion."[35]

Nonetheless, he continued, even if he were to accept Black's argument in *Everson* that the Fourteenth Amendment incorporated the Establishment

Clause, "the traditional 'establishments of religion' to which the Establishment Clause is addressed necessarily involve actual legal coercion."[36] He quoted from the preeminent historian of the founding era, Leonard Levy, who had written: "The coercion that was the hallmark of historical establishments of religion was coercion of religious orthodoxy and of financial support by force of law and threat of penalty. Typically, attendance at the state church was required; only clergy of the official church could lawfully perform sacraments; and dissenters, if tolerated, faced an array of civil disabilities."[37] In the end, Thomas concluded that the school district's pledge policy did not "expose anyone to the legal coercion associated with an established religion." Consequently, he found that it "fully comports with the Constitution."[38]

In his *Van Orden* concurrence, Thomas further explained his understanding of "actual legal coercion." This case addressed whether the presence of a 6-foot monolith inscribed with the Ten Commandments and located among twenty-one historical markers and seventeen monuments surrounding the Texas State Capitol violated the Establishment Clause. Chief Justice Rehnquist, for a five-member majority, held it did not. Thomas joined that majority and in a concurring opinion elaborated on what he meant by actual legal coercion: "There is no question that, based on the original meaning of the Establishment Clause, the Ten Commandments display at issue here is constitutional. In no sense does Texas compel petitioner Van Orden to do anything. The only injury to him is that he takes offense at seeing the monument as he passes it on this way to the Texas Supreme Court library." But, Thomas continued, "he need not stop to read it or even look at it, let alone to express support for it or adopt the Commandments as guides for his life. The mere presence of the monument along his path involves no coercion and thus does not violate the Establishment Clause."[39] He concluded powerfully by asserting, "Much, if not all, of this [confusion on the Court's part] would be avoided if the Court would return to the views of the Framers and adopt coercion as the touchstone of our Establishment Clause inquiry. Every acknowledgment of religion would not give rise to an Establishment Clause claim. Courts would not act as theological commissions, judging the meaning of religious matters." Though he applauded Rehnquist's majority opinion, he was convinced that "a more fundamental rethinking of our Establishment Clause jurisprudence remains in order."[40]

Freedom of Speech and Press

In his very first free speech opinion, in *McIntyre v. Ohio Elections Commission*,[41] Thomas laid out his original general meaning approach to the First Amendment's prohibition against abridgments of the freedom of speech or press. He wrote, "When interpreting the Free Speech and Press Clauses, we must be guided by their original meaning, for 'the Constitution is a written instrument. As such its meaning does not alter. That which it meant when adopted, it means now.' We should seek the original understanding when we interpret the Speech and Press Clauses, just as we do when we read the Religion Clauses of the First Amendment." He continued, "When the Framers did not discuss the precise question at issue," the Court must turn to "what history reveals was the contemporaneous understanding" of the Clauses: "The line we must draw between the permissible and the impermissible is one which accords with history and faithfully reflects the understanding of the Founding Fathers."[42] Thomas has assiduously followed that approach in his many and significant free speech and press opinions,[43] which can usefully be clustered under the following rubrics: commercial speech, regulation of campaign finance, obscenity and the electronic media, cross burning, and free speech rights for minors.

Commercial Speech

Clarence Thomas has emerged as the Court's staunchest defender of commercial speech. His commercial speech jurisprudence, however, began inauspiciously.[44] In his second year on the bench, he joined a dissent by Chief Justice Rehnquist in *City of Cincinnati v. Discovery Network, Inc.*,[45] holding that commercial speech deserves less First Amendment protection because it relates to economic self-interest and is, therefore, more durable; because it is less important than political speech; and because granting it more protection would "erode the First Amendment protection accorded noncommercial speech."

By the time Thomas wrote his first opinion in a commercial speech case, he had considered these questions more deeply. In *Rubin v. Coors Brewing Company*,[46] his first opinion for the Court on free speech—handed down the same day as his concurrence in the judgment in *McIntyre*—Thomas held for a unanimous Court that a federal law prohibiting beer labels from displaying alcohol content in an effort to suppress the threat of "strength wars" among brewers violated the First Amendment's protection of commercial speech. He noted that even though "we once took the position that the First Amendment does not protect commercial speech"[47] (and he cited *Valentine v. Chrestensen*[48] to that effect), "we repudiated that position in *Virginia Board of Pharmacy v. Virginia Citizens Consumer Council*"[49] and now apply the multifactor balancing test set out in *Central Hudson Gas & Electric Corporation v. Public Service Commission of New York*: "For commercial speech to come within the First Amendment, it at least must concern lawful activity and not be misleading. Next, we ask whether the asserted government interest is substantial. If both inquiries yield positive answers, we must determine whether the regulation directly advances the governmental interest asserted, and whether it is not more extensive than is necessary to serve that interest."[50] Methodically applying that conventional test, Thomas concluded that "the ban infringes respondent's freedom of speech."[51]

The federal government had argued that legislatures should have more latitude to regulate speech that promotes socially harmful activities, such as alcohol consumption or gambling, than they have to regulate other types of speech. Thomas rejected that argument in a footnote, distinguishing the precedents on which the federal government had relied. Interestingly, however, six years later in his concurring opinion in *Lorillard Tobacco Company v. Reilly*,[52] he offered this fulsome explanation for doing so:

> No legislature has ever sought to restrict speech about an activity it regarded as harmless and inoffensive. Calls for limits on expression always are made when the specter of some threatened harm is looming. The identity of the harm may vary. People will be inspired by totalitarian dogmas and subvert the Republic. They will be inflamed by racial demagoguery and embrace hatred and bigotry. Or they will be enticed by cigarette advertisements and choose to smoke, risking disease. It is therefore no answer for the State to say that the makers of cigarettes are doing harm: perhaps they are. But in that respect they are no different from the purveyors of other harmful products, or the advocates of harmful ideas. When the State seeks to silence them, they are all entitled to the protection of the First Amendment.[53]

Just a year after *Rubin*, in a concurrence in *44 Liquormart v. Rhode Island*,[54] Thomas "fired his first real shot" in the commercial speech revolution.[55] A Rhode Island liquor retailer was fined $400 for violating a state law banning the advertisement of the prices of alcoholic beverages except at the place of sale. After paying the fine, company officials took their case to federal district court and successfully obtained a declaratory judgment that Rhode Island's law violated the First Amendment. The Court of Appeals for the First Circuit reversed, finding "inherent merit" in Rhode Island's claim that competitive price competition would ultimately increase sales, to the detriment of the state's asserted interest in promoting temperance. Justice Stevens routinely applied the *Central Hudson* test and invalidated the law.

In his concurrence, Thomas displayed a matured understanding of the issue of commercial speech. He rejected the *Central Hudson* test that he himself had applied the year before in *Rubin* and concluded that continuing to apply it "makes no sense to me when the asserted state interest is of the type involved here."[56] He repudiated the test for three reasons.

First, he noted, "the courts, including this Court, have found the *Central Hudson* 'test' to be, as a general matter, very difficult to apply with any uniformity." Picking up on a theme he had developed in his lecture on "Judging," which he delivered at the University of Kansas School of Law just one month earlier,[57] Thomas attributed this difficulty to the "inherently nondeterminative nature of a case-by-case balancing 'test' unaccompanied by any categorical rules, and the consequent likelihood that individual judicial preferences will govern application of the test."[58]

Second, he observed that *Central Hudson* "requires judges to delineate those situations in which citizens cannot be trusted with information, and invites judges to decide whether they themselves think that consumption of a product is harmful enough that it *should* be discouraged. In my view, the *Central Hudson* test asks the courts to weigh incommensurables—the value of knowledge versus the value of ignorance—and to apply contradictory premises—that informed adults are the best judges of their own interests, and that they are not."[59]

The third and by far the most compelling reason that Thomas cited for repudiating the *Central Hudson* test was because he had come to reject the Court's long-standing assumption (which he had shared as recently as four years earlier in *Discovery Network*) that commercial speech occupied a "subordinate position in the scale of First Amendment values" and thus was of "less constitutional moment." He forthrightly proclaimed: "I do not see a philosophical or historical basis for asserting that 'commercial' speech is of 'lower value' than 'noncommercial speech."[60] Therefore, "in cases such as this, in which the government's asserted interest is to keep legal users of a product or service ignorant in order to manipulate their choices in the marketplace, the balancing test adopted in *Central Hudson* should not be applied. . . . Rather, such an 'interest' is *per se* illegitimate and can no more justify regulation of 'commercial' speech than it can justify regulation of 'noncommercial' speech."[61]

Thomas argued that the *Central Hudson* test failed to give sufficient recognition to "the importance of free dissemination of information about commercial choices in a market economy; the anti-paternalistic premises of the First Amendment; the impropriety of manipulating consumer choices or public opinion through the suppression of accurate 'commercial' information; the near impossibility of severing 'commercial' speech from speech necessary to democratic decision-making; and the dangers of permitting the government to do covertly what it might not have been able to muster the political support to do openly."[62] As a consequence, he rejected *Central Hudson* as a controlling precedent in *44 Liquormart*, and he has subsequently refused to join opinions that employ it. Thus, in *Glickman v. Wileman Brothers & Elliott*,[63] he joined a Souter dissent except for the part that applied *Central Hudson*, stating, "I continue to disagree with the use of the *Central Hudson* balancing test and the discounted weight given to commercial speech generally." He has made similar remarks in his separate concurring opinions in *Greater New Orleans Broadcasting Association v. United States*[64] and *Thompson v. Western States Medical Center*.[65]

Glickman raised an issue regarding commercial speech quite apart from its application of the *Central Hudson* test. *Glickman* upheld a federal marketing program that forced agricultural producers to pay for generic fruit advertising. Wileman Brothers & Elliott, California growers of peaches, nectarines, pears, and plums, challenged a provision of the American Marketing Agreement Act of 1937 and its generic advertising regulations, claiming that they violated the company's First Amendment right to free speech because they compelled the growers to provide financial aid to support commercial speech to which they objected. Justice Stevens, for a five-member majority, held that this coerced funding of advertising did not fall within the ambit of the First Amendment at all but was simply "a species of economic regulation that should enjoy the same strong presumption of validity that we accord to other policy judgments made by Congress."[66]

Thomas was outraged.[67] "It is one thing to differ about whether a particular regulation involves an 'abridgment' of the freedom of speech," he declared, "but it is entirely another matter—and a complete repudiation of our precedent—for the majority to deny that 'speech' is even at issue in this case."[68] He pointed out that in "numerous cases, this Court has recognized that paying money for the purposes of advertising involves speech" and "that compelling speech raises a First Amendment issue just as much as restricting speech." "Given these two elemental principles of our First Amendment jurisprudence," he went on, "it is incongruous to suggest that forcing fruit-growers to contribute to a collective advertising campaign does not even *involve* speech, while at the same time effectively conceding that forbidding a fruit-grower from making those same contributions voluntarily would violate the First Amendment." Yet, he complained, "that is precisely what the majority opinion does."[69]

Expressing bafflement, he declared that accepting "at face value" Stevens's opinion led to two "disturbing consequences: Either (1) paying for advertising is not speech at all, while such activities as draft card burning, flag burning, armband wearing, public sleeping, and nude dancing are, or (2) compelling payment for third party communication does not implicate speech, and thus the Government would be free to force payment for a whole variety of expressive conduct that it could not restrict. In either case, surely we have lost our way."[70]

Campaign Finance Regulations and Free Speech

In regard to commercial speech, Thomas initially accepted the Court's traditional understanding that it was not entitled to full First Amendment protection and applied the *Central Hudson* test before thinking the matter through for himself and announcing his full-throated defense of commercial speech in *44 Liquormart*. By contrast, in regard to the relationship of free speech and campaign finance reform regulations, Thomas has articulated a very clear and consistent understanding from the outset. It can be summarized in Thomas's remarks on the Supreme Court's landmark precedent in this area, *Buckley v. Valeo*,[71] which upheld caps on financial contributions to candidates and parties. Thomas stated that this ruling "was in error, and I would overrule it";[72] that both campaign contributions and expenditures "involve core First Amendment expression";[73] and that any efforts by the federal government or the states to impose limitations on these contributions and expenditures must be subjected to "strict scrutiny," under which "broad prophylactic caps on both spending and giving in the political process . . . are unconstitutional."[74]

In *Nixon v. Shrink Missouri Government PAC*, in which the Court ratified what Thomas described in dissent as "Missouri's sweeping repression of political speech" by upholding the state's extremely low limits on campaign contributions, he began with "a proposition that ought to be unassailable: Political speech is the primary object of First Amendment protection."[75] He continued: "The Founders sought to protect the rights of individuals to engage in political speech because a self-governing people depends upon the free exchange of political information. And that free exchange should receive the most protection when it matters the most—during campaigns for elective office." He said he started with these "foundational principles" because "the Court today abandons them."[76] He noted that in a series of cases over the prior half century, the Court had extended free speech protections on "making false defamatory statements, filing lawsuits, dancing nude, exhibiting drive-in movies with nudity, burning flags, and wearing military uniforms." In light of these cases, he observed, "today's decision is a most curious anomaly. Whatever the proper status of such activities under the First Amendment, I am confident that they are less integral to the functioning of our Republic than campaign contributions. Yet the majority today, rather than going out of its way to *protect* political speech, goes out of its way to *avoid* protecting it." Thomas insisted that campaign contributions "generate essential political speech." He added, "Contribution caps, which place a direct and substantial limit on core speech, should be met with the utmost skepticism and should receive the strictest scrutiny."[77]

Shrink Missouri allowed Thomas to elaborate upon the basic themes he had introduced four years earlier in *Colorado Republican Federal Campaign Committee v. Federal Election Commission* [FEC], the first of his opinions on campaign finance regulations. In it, he spelled out in detail his fully developed understanding of this issue. He began by pointing out the flaws in *Buckley*, in which

the Court invalidated on free speech grounds expenditure limitations on candidates but upheld limitations on the amounts that individuals or groups could
contribute to a candidate or political committee. The Court majority justified
this decision based on two assertions about the nature of contributions: "First,
though contributions may result in speech, that speech is by the candidate and
not by the contributor; and second, contributions express only general support
for the candidate but do not communicate the reasons for that support." Since
Buckley, Thomas argued, "our campaign finance jurisprudence has been based
in large part on this distinction between contributions and expenditures." In his
view, however, "the distinction lacks constitutional significance, and I would not
adhere to it, [because] . . . contributions and expenditures are two sides of the
same First Amendment coin."[78]

He explained why: "Contributions and expenditures both involve core First
Amendment expression because they further the 'discussion of public issues and
debate on the qualifications of candidates . . . integral to the operation of the system of government established by our Constitution.'" He pointed out that when
an individual donates money to a candidate or to a partisan organization, "he
enhances the donee's ability to communicate a message and thereby adds to political debate, just as when that individual communicates the message himself.
Indeed, the individual may add more to political discourse by giving rather than
spending, if the donee is able to put the funds to more productive use than can
the individual."[79] (Thomas elaborated on this point in *Shrink Missouri*: "The
decision of individuals to speak through contributions rather than through independent expenditures is entirely reasonable. Political campaigns are largely candidate focused and candidate driven. Citizens recognize that the best advocate
for a candidate [and the policy positions he supports] tends to be the candidate
himself.")[80] Thomas was led to conclude that "the contribution of funds to a
candidate or to a political group thus fosters the 'free discussion of governmental
affairs,' just as an expenditure does."[81]

From Thomas's perspective, "giving and spending in the electoral process"
involves not only free speech rights but also "associational rights under the First
Amendment." He reminded his colleagues that, in *FEC v. National Conservative
Political Action Committee*,[82] the Court had affirmed that political associations
allowing citizens to pool their resources and make their advocacy more effective
were fully protected by the First Amendment. He then proceeded to make the
obvious point that "if an individual is limited in the amount of resources he can
contribute to the pool, he is most certainly limited in his ability to associate for
purposes of effective advocacy."[83]

Thomas also rejected *Buckley*'s assertion that contribution caps only marginally restrict speech and are therefore constitutionally permissible because a

contribution signals only general support, not the reasons for that support. He thereby essentially defended the free speech rights of those who may be inarticulate:

> Assuming the assertion is descriptively accurate (which is certainly questionable), it still cannot mean that giving is less important than spending in terms of the First Amendment. A campaign poster that reads simply "We support candidate Smith" does not seem to me any less deserving of constitutional protection than one that reads "We support candidate Smith because we like his position on agriculture subsidies." Both express a political opinion. Even a pure message of support, unadorned with reasons, is valuable to the democratic process.[84]

Finally, he announced that all curbs on free speech, including limitations on campaign contributions and expenditures, "must be strictly scrutinized," that is, there must be both a "compelling governmental interest" justifying the curb and "legislative means narrowly tailored to serve that interest."[85] He acknowledged that the Court had found the governmental interest in preventing corruption or the appearance of corruption to be "compelling,"[86] but he insisted that "wholesale limitations that cover contributions having nothing to do with bribery—but with speech central to the First Amendment—are not narrowly tailored" and cannot stand.[87]

Thomas consistently held to these views in subsequent campaign finance cases, as in his dissents in *FEC v. Colorado Republican Federal Campaign Committee*[88] and *FEC v. Beaumont*[89] and his concurrence in the judgment in *Randall v. Sorrell*.[90] In *McConnell v. Federal Election Commission*,[91] in which the Court upheld the constitutionality of the Bipartisan Campaign Reform Act (BCRA)—popularly known as McCain-Feingold—Thomas repeated many of his previous arguments, but he added two others wholly consistent with his past opinions.

First, he attacked the Court majority's reliance on *Austin v. Michigan Chamber of Commerce*, a 1990 decision in which the Court upheld restrictions on corporate speech because "corporate wealth can unfairly influence elections."[92] Thomas derisively observed that *Austin* held corporations should not be allowed, "on behalf of their shareholders, . . . to convince voters of the correctness of their ideas. Apparently, winning in the marketplace of ideas is no longer a sign that 'the ultimate good' has been 'reached by free trade in ideas,' or that the speaker has survived 'the best test of truth' by having 'the thought . . . get accepted in the competition of the market.'" Rather, he went on, "it is now evidence of 'corruption.' This conclusion is antithetical to everything for which the First Amendment stands." In typical Thomas fashion, he declared that he "would overturn *Austin* and hold that the potential for corporations and unions to influence voters, via independent expenditures aimed at convincing these voters to adopt particular views, is not a form of corruption justifying any state regulation or suppression."[93]

He expanded on the dangers of *Austin* and why the Court's reliance on it to uphold BCRA was such a threat to the First Amendment. The five-member *McConnell* majority upheld the key provisions of BCRA, including both its "electioneering communication provisions" (requiring the disclosure of and prohibiting the use of corporate and union treasury funds to pay for broadcast, cable, and satellite ads clearly identifying a federal candidate targeted to the candidate's electorate within thirty days of a primary or sixty days of a general election) and its "soft money" ban (prohibiting federal parties, candidates, and officeholders from raising or spending funds not in compliance with contribution restrictions and prohibiting state parties from using such soft money in connection with federal elections). By so doing, the Court majority gave legitimacy to what Thomas called "the most significant abridgment of the freedoms of speech and association since the Civil War."[94] What really alarmed Thomas, however, was the "chilling endpoint" of the majority's reasoning—"outright regulation of the press."[95] He explained:

> None of the rationales offered by the defendants, and none of the reasoning employed by the Court, exempts the press. . . . Media companies can run procandidate editorials as easily as nonmedia corporations can pay for advertisements. Candidates can be just as grateful to media companies as they can be to corporations and unions. In terms of "the corrosive and distorting effects" of wealth accumulated by corporations that has "little or no correlation to the public's support for the corporation's political ideas," *Austin v. Michigan Chamber of Commerce*, there is no distinction between a media corporation and a nonmedia corporation. Media corporations are influential. There is little doubt that the editorials and commentary they run can affect elections. Nor is there any doubt that media companies often wish to influence elections. One would think that the *New York Times* fervently hopes that its endorsement of Presidential candidates will actually influence people. What is to stop a future Congress from determining that the press is "too influential," and that the "appearance of corruption" is significant when media organizations endorse candidates or run "slanted" or "biased" news stories in favor of candidates or parties? Or, even easier, what is to stop a future Congress from concluding that the availability of unregulated media corporations creates a loophole that allows for easy "circumvention" of the limitations of the current campaign finance laws?[96]

Thomas quoted from Elliot's *Debates* in noting that freedom of the press is "one of the greatest bulwarks of liberty," and though he acknowledged that the majority's opinion did not "expressly strip the press of First Amendment protection, there is no principle of law or logic that would prevent the application of the Court's reasoning in that setting. The press now operates at the whim of Congress."[97]

His fears were fully vindicated six years later during the oral argument in *Citizens United v. FEC*.[98] Citizens United, a nonprofit corporation, sought to run television commercials to promote its latest political documentary, *Hillary: The Movie*, and to air the movie on DirecTV. The movie was highly critical of then-Senator Hillary Clinton. When in January 2008 a federal district court judge agreed with the FEC that the television advertisements for *Hillary: The Movie* violated BCRA's restrictions on corporations engaging in "electioneering communications" within thirty days of the 2008 Democratic primaries, the Supreme Court noted probable jurisdiction and scheduled oral argument for March 24, 2009.

During that oral argument, Deputy Solicitor General Malcolm L. Stewart, representing the FEC, argued that, based on the *Austin* ruling, the government would have the power under BCRA to ban the publication of a 500-page book if it contained even one line expressly advocating the election or defeat of a candidate and if it was published or distributed by a corporation or union. When pressed by the justices, Stewart further argued that under *Austin*, the government could ban the digital distribution of political books through Amazon's Kindle reader or prevent a union from hiring a writer to author a political book. At the conclusion of this colloquy, Justice Samuel Alito was prompted to remark: "That's pretty incredible."[99]

Citizens United was reargued on September 9, 2009, and decided on January 21, 2010. In his opinion for a five-member majority, Kennedy did what Thomas had called for in *McConnell*. After repeated references to Thomas's concern about "outright regulation of the press," he declared that "*Austin* should be and now is overruled,"[100] and he proceeded to overrule *McConnell* in part by declaring unconstitutional BCRA's restrictions on independent political expenditures by corporations and unions.

In addition to his attack on *Austin*, Thomas added a second argument in *McConnell* to those he had already made in his previous campaign finance opinions—the unconstitutionality of the disclosure provisions in BCRA. He had argued in *McIntyre v. Ohio Elections Commission*, his initial opinion addressing the First Amendment, that "the phrase 'freedom of speech, or the press,' as originally understood, protected anonymous political leafletting."[101]

As mentioned earlier, in *McIntyre* Thomas argued that "when interpreting the Free Speech and Press Clauses, we must be guided by their original meaning, for 'the Constitution is a written instrument. As such, its meaning does not alter. That which it meant when adopted, it means now.'" Invoking his original general meaning approach, he declared that "the meaning of the Constitution 'must necessarily depend on the words of the Constitution and the meaning and intention of the convention which framed and proposed it for adoption and ratification to the conventions . . . in the several states.'" If the framers did not discuss the precise question at issue, he argued that "we . . . must turn to what history reveals was the contemporaneous understanding" of the rights in question.[102] And since "we have no record of discussion of anonymous political expression either in the First Congress, which drafted the Bill of Rights, or in the state ratifying conventions," he turned to "the practices and beliefs held by the Founders concerning anonymous political articles and pamphlets." What he found was an extensive record of eighteenth-century Americans engaging in anonymous political writing. He pointed to *The Federalist Papers*, published under the pseudonym of Publius, as "only the most famous example of the outpouring of anonymous political writing that occurred during the ratification of the Constitution."[103] He recalled that "the earliest and most famous American experience with freedom of the press, the 1735 Zenger trial, centered around anonymous political pamphlets."[104] He then added nine pages to the *United States Reports* with additional historical examples of anonymous writing during the founding era, culminating in the debate between Pacificus (Alexander Hamilton) and Helvidius (James Madison) over President George Washington's Proclamation of Neutrality in the war between England and France.[105] All of this historical evidence led him to conclude that "Founding-era Americans opposed attempts to require that anonymous authors reveal their identities on the ground that forced disclosure violated the 'freedom of the press.'"[106]

Thomas applied this conclusion from *McIntyre* to *McConnell*, stating, "The 'historical evidence indicates that Founding-era Americans opposed attempts to require that anonymous authors reveal their identities on the ground that forced disclosure violated the freedom of the press.'" Further, he noted that even the Court majority in *McIntyre* "explicitly recognized that 'the interest in having anonymous works enter the marketplace of ideas unquestionably outweighs any public interest in requiring disclosure'"; thus, a "decision to remain anonymous . . . is an aspect of the freedom of speech protected by the First Amendment." He worried, however, that all eight of his colleagues backed away from this principle, "allowing the established right to anonymous speech to be stripped away based on the flimsiest of justifications."[107] As he saw it, "the only reading of *McIntyre* that remains consistent with the principles it contains is that it overturned *Buck-*

ley to the extent that *Buckley* upheld a disclosure requirement solely based on the governmental interest in providing information to the voters." He concluded, with no support from any of his colleagues, "The right to anonymous speech cannot be abridged based on the interests asserted by the defendants. I would thus hold that the disclosure requirements of BCRA . . . are unconstitutional."[108]

In *Citizens United*, Thomas readily joined the majority opinion except for its conclusion that BCRA's disclosure provisions were constitutional. He dissented from its conclusion that the disclosure requirements "impose no ceiling on campaign-related activities" and prevent no one "from speaking."[109] Thomas insisted that "Congress may not abridge the 'right to anonymous speech' based on the simple interest in providing voters with additional relevant information."

He pointed to Proposition 8, a California ballot measure that successfully amended the state's constitution to provide that "only marriage between a man and a woman is valid or recognized in California." State law required the disclosure of the full name, address, occupation, and employer of any donor who gave more than $100 to a committee supporting or opposing any measure and further required the posting of this information on the Internet by the California secretary of state. Thomas stated that as a result of these disclosure requirements, "some opponents of Proposition 8 compiled this information and created Web sites with maps showing the locations of homes or businesses of Proposition 8 supporters. Many supporters (or their customers) suffered property damage, or threats of physical violence or death, as a result." Becoming more specific, he cited articles in the *Wall Street Journal* discussing how the director of the non-profit California Musical Theater, who gave $1,000 to support the initiative, was forced to resign after artists complained to his employer and how the director of the Los Angeles Film Festival had to resign after giving $1,500 because opponents threatened to boycott and picket the next film festival. Thomas also cited articles in the *Los Angeles Times* about how a woman who had managed her popular, family-owned restaurant for twenty-six years was forced to resign after she gave the Proposition 8 effort $100 "because 'throngs of angry protesters' repeatedly arrived at the restaurant and 'shouted shame on you' at customers. The police even had to 'arrive in riot gear one night to quell the angry mob' at the restaurant."[110]

After offering a half dozen more examples, Thomas made clear that it was not his point "to express any view on the merits of the political controversies I describe. Rather, it is to demonstrate—using real-world, recent examples—the fallacy in the Court's conclusion that 'disclosure requirements impose no ceiling on campaign-related activities, and do not prevent anyone from speaking.' Of course they do." BCRA's disclosure requirements, he insisted, "enable private citizens and elected officials to implement political strategies *specifically calculated* to curtail campaign-related activity and prevent the lawful, peaceful exercise of

First Amendment rights."[111] He concluded powerfully: "I cannot endorse a view of the First Amendment that subjects citizens of this Nation to death threats, ruined careers, damaged or defaced property, or pre-emptive and threatening warning letters as the price for engaging in 'core political speech, the primary object of First Amendment protection.'"[112]

Obscenity and the Electronic Media

Thomas's main contribution to the Court's efforts to grapple with the presence of obscene materials in the electronic media has been to argue that broadcast, cable, and Internet companies should enjoy the same First Amendment protections as the print media.

His first major opinion on this topic was *Denver Area Educational Telecommunications Consortium [Denver AETC] v. Federal Communications Commission [FCC]*,[113] in which he dissented from the Court's conclusion that two sections of the Cable Television Consumer Protection and Competition Act of 1992 violated the First Amendment. One permitted a cable system operator to prohibit the broadcasting on leased access channels (those channels that federal law required a cable system operator to reserve for commercial lease by unaffiliated third parties) of programming that the operator reasonably believed described or depicted sexual or excretory activities or organs in a patently offensive manner. If a cable operator decided to permit such "patently offensive" programming, the operator was required to segregate that programming on a single channel and block the channel from viewer access unless the viewer requested access in advance and in writing.

The other section permitted a cable system operator to prohibit the broadcasting of such programming on public access channels (those channels that local governments required cable system operators to set aside for public, educational, or governmental purposes). A badly fractured Court found these sections unconstitutional because by permitting the cable operator to exercise editorial discretion as to what would be shown, the sections restricted the free speech rights (1) of the leased and public access programmers to transmit their indecent but constitutionally protected programming, and (2) of the viewers to receive this programming. Thomas considered both sections to be constitutional because his concern focused on the free speech rights of the cable operators. For him, the first section merely restored part of the editorial discretion that a cable operator would have had absent the federal government's "forced speech" regulations, and the second section was narrowly tailored to satisfying the government's compelling state interest in protecting children.

Thomas began with a theme that pervades his opinions in this field, asserting, "The text of the First Amendment makes no distinctions among print, broadcast, and cable media, but we have done so."[114] The Court did this, he said, in *Red Lion Broadcasting v. FCC*,[115] in which it upheld the "fairness doctrine," requiring "that discussion of public issues be presented on broadcast stations, and that each side of those issues must be given fair coverage." *Red Lion* held that the federal government may require a broadcast licensee "to share his frequency with others and to conduct himself as a proxy or fiduciary with obligations to present those views and voices which are representative of his community and which would otherwise, by necessity, be barred from the airwaves."[116] As Thomas noted, the Court thereby permitted a level of "governmental interference" with regard to the broadcast media that it had never permitted with regard to the print media. But what about cable, he asked? Thomas noted that the Court's First Amendment distinctions among media, "dubious from their infancy," initially placed cable in "a doctrinal wasteland in which regulators and cable operators alike could not be sure whether cable was entitled to the substantial First Amendment protections afforded the print media or was subject to the more onerous obligations shouldered by the broadcast media." Over time, however, he was pleased to see that the Court was drawing closer to recognizing that "cable operators should enjoy the same First Amendment rights as the nonbroadcast media," and he used his dissent to push the Court even closer.[117]

He did so by noting that two years earlier, in *Turner Broadcasting System v. FCC*,[118] the Court "stated expressly" that *Red Lion* did not apply to cable operators. That decision had powerful ramifications. *Red Lion* "legitimized consideration of the public interest" and declared that "it is the right of viewers and listeners, not the right of the broadcasters, which is paramount."[119] And as Thomas made clear, after *Turner* that "view can no longer be given any credence in the cable context. It is the operator's right that is preeminent." Thus, "when there is a conflict, a programmer's asserted right to transmit over an operator's cable system must give way to the operator's editorial discretion." He drew the following analogies to the print media: "The author of a book is protected in writing the book, but has no right to have the book sold in a particular bookstore without the store owner's consent. Nor can government force the editor of a collection of essays to print other essays on the same subject."[120] He summed up his argument by saying the federal access requirements "as a whole" infringed the free speech rights of the cable operator, not the access programmer. To illustrate this conclusion, he suggested that "if Congress passed a law forcing bookstores to sell all books published on the subject of congressional politics, we would undoubtedly entertain a claim by bookstores that this law violated the First Amendment." Yet he doubted that "we would similarly find merit in a claim by publishers of gardening books that the law violated their First Amendment rights." He indicated that to the extent he was right, then the leased and public access programmers and their viewers could not "reasonably assert" that the Court should interpret the provisions at issue in a way "that maximizes their ability to speak over leased and public access channels and, by necessity, minimizes the operators' discretion."[121]

Most of Thomas's dissent in *Denver AETC* was devoted to explaining why the section of the act that permitted cable operators to prohibit lease and public access operators from transmitting indecent materials over their cable systems was constitutional. But he also briefly addressed why the section of the act that required cable operators to segregate and block indecent programming that the operators had agreed to carry was also constitutional when subjected to strict scrutiny: "The parties agree that Congress has a 'compelling interest in protecting the physical and psychological well-being of minors' and that its interest extends to shielding minors from the influence of indecent speech that is not obscene by adult standards." Because he found that section "narrowly tailored to achieve that well-established compelling interest," he declared that he would "uphold it," and he dissented from "the Court's decision to the contrary."[122]

What Thomas attempted to do for cable operators in *Denver AETC*, he also sought to do for Internet providers in *Ashcroft v. American Civil Liberties Union*,[123] namely, secure the same free speech protections for these electronic media as the Court had secured in past decisions for the print media. In his opinion for the Court in *Ashcroft*, he rejected a facial challenge to the Child Online Protection Act (COPA) of 1998 that sought to protect children from exposure to pornography on the Internet by restricting materials that are "harmful to minors," defined as materials that failed the three-part obscenity test set forth in *Miller v. California*.[124] The Court had applied this test to movies and the print media, and Thomas, rejecting the argument that new technology requires new rules, saw no reason why it should not be applied equally to the Internet. As Steven B. Lichtman has put it: "There was essentially nothing so distinctive about the Internet that required treating it differently [in this case, more leniently] under the First Amendment than other communicative media."[125]

What Thomas attempted to do for cable operators and Internet providers he also attempted to do for the broadcast media in *FCC v. Fox Television [Fox I]*.[126] In his concurring opinion, he agreed that as a matter of administrative law, Scalia, writing for a five-member majority, had correctly upheld an FCC policy with respect to indecent broadcast speech. But he also wrote separately "to note the questionable viability"[127] of the two cases the FCC cited in support of its assertion of constitutional authority to regulate the programming in question—*Red Lion*, upholding the fairness doctrine, and *FCC v. Pacifica Foundation*,[128] upholding the FCC's authority to impose sanctions for broadcasting indecent speech. He declared that both were "unconvincing when they were issued, and the passage of time has only increased doubt regarding their continued validity." He then repeated his words from *Denver AETC v. FCC:* "The text of the First Amendment makes no distinctions among print, broadcast, and cable media, but we have done so."[129]

The Court in *Red Lion* relied on the scarcity of available broadcast frequencies to conclude that the broadcast spectrum could be regulated by the federal government, and in *Pacifica*, it relied on *Red Lion.* Thomas found "this deep intrusion" into the free speech rights of broadcasters, which the Court justified based only "on the nature of the medium," to be "problematic on two levels."

It was problematic, first and foremost, because the Court failed to look to "first principles" to evaluate the constitutional question and instead relied on "a set of transitory facts, *e.g.,* the 'scarcity of radio frequencies,' to determine the applicable First Amendment standard." Bringing his original general meaning approach to bear, he insisted that the original meaning of the Constitution "cannot turn on modern necessity: 'Constitutional rights are enshrined with the scope they were understood to have when the people adopted them, whether or not future legislatures . . . think that scope too broad.'" The Court in *Red Lion* adopted and in *Pacifica* reaffirmed a legal rule that breached this principle and lacked any textual basis in the Constitution.[130]

"This deep intrusion" into the free speech rights of broadcasters was also problematic, according to Thomas, because "dramatic technological advances have eviscerated the factual assumptions underlying those decisions." To begin with, he pointed out that broadcast spectrum is significantly less scarce than it was when *Red Lion* was decided, with the number of over-the-air broadcast stations doubling since then. Thomas was confident that the trend would continue with broadcast television stations' "imminent switch from analog to digital transmission," allowing the FCC to stack broadcast channels closer together along the spectrum.[131]

More important, however, he noted that traditional over-the-air broadcasting is no longer the "uniquely pervasive medium it once was." Traditional broadcast media programming is "now bundled with cable or satellite services," is "widely available over the Internet," and can be accessed "by portable computer, cell phones, and other wireless devices." Thomas concluded: "The extant facts that drove this Court to subject broadcasters to unique disfavor under the First Amendment simply do not exist today." Ever ready to scrape away past precedent and get back to bare wood, that is, to the original general meaning of the Constitution, he argued that "these dramatic changes in factual circumstances might well support a departure from precedent under the prevailing approach to *stare decisis*. For all these reasons, I am open to reconsideration of *Red Lion* and *Pacifica* in the proper case."[132] Interestingly, three years later in *FCC v. Fox Television*,[133] in which eight members of the Court (including Thomas) concluded that the FCC violated the Fifth Amendment's Due Process Clause when it failed to give Fox fair notice prior to the broadcasts in question that fleeting expletives and momentary nudity could be found actionably indecent, Justice Ruth Bader Ginsburg concurred only in the judgment; she saw this case as a free speech case, cited Thomas's concurring opinion in *Fox I*, and agreed with him that *Pacifica* "bears reconsideration."[134]

Free Speech, the Ku Klux Klan, and the Cross

In *R. A. V. v. City of St. Paul*, a unanimous Court struck down the Bias-Motivated Crime Ordinance in St. Paul, Minnesota, and in the process overturned the conviction of R. A. V., a teenager, for burning a cross on the lawn of a black family.[135] In his majority opinion, Scalia held that the First Amendment protected from criminal prosecution those who engage in even "constitutionally proscribable" speech (for example, cross burning or "fighting words") if the government's efforts to regulate that speech are "based on hostility toward the underlying message expressed."[136] He insisted that even speech subject to content regulation (the total banning of all fighting words or all cross burning) cannot be subjected to viewpoint discrimination. Thomas, serving in his first year on the Court, joined Scalia's majority opinion.

Three years later, Thomas wrote his first opinion concerning free speech and the cross in *Capitol Square v. Pinette*.[137] In that case, he also joined Scalia's opinion for the Court in holding that the Ku Klux Klan's placement of an unattended cross on Ohio's statehouse plaza, a forum for the discussion of public questions and for public activities, did not implicate the Establishment Clause but rather was a display of private religious speech that was fully protected under the Freedom of Speech Clause as secular private expression. But Thomas also wrote a concurring opinion, arguing that no one should "think that a cross erected by the Ku Klux Klan [KKK] is a purely religious symbol. The erection of such a cross is a political act, not a Christian one." In his view, there was little doubt that for the Klan, "the cross is a symbol of white supremacy and a tool for the intimidation and harassment of racial minorities, Catholics, Jews, Communists, and any other groups hated by the Klan. The cross is associated with the Klan not because of religious worship, but because of the Klan's practice of cross burning."[138] Thomas was convinced that "the Klan had a primarily nonreligious purpose in erecting the cross. The Klan simply has appropriated one of the most sacred of religious symbols as a symbol of hate. In my mind, this suggests that this case may not have truly involved the Establishment Clause, although I agree with the Court's disposition because of the manner in which the case has come before us."[139]

Thomas's most spirited discussion of the Klan and cross burning came in his dissent in *Virginia v. Black*.[140] In this case, three individuals were convicted in separate cases of cross burning in violation of Virginia law: one burned a cross during a Klan rally; the other two burned a cross in the yard of a black neighbor who had complained about their use of his backyard as a firing range. The Supreme Court overturned their convictions. In her opinion for a plurality of the Court, O'Connor argued that although it was not unconstitutional to prohibit cross burning with the intent to intimidate because it was conduct rather than expression, cross burning could also constitute expressive conduct and therefore could not be proscribed unless it was done with the intent to intimidate. Since a section of the Virginia law provided that any cross burning was prima facie evidence of intent to intimidate, that section was unconstitutional on its face for it created an unacceptable risk of suppressing ideas in violation of the First Amendment. It blurred the distinction between proscribable threats of intimidation and the Klan's protected "messages of shared ideology."[141]

Thomas agreed with O'Connor that it was constitutionally permissible to ban cross burning carried out with the intent to intimidate. But he insisted that she erred when she inferred "an expressive component to the activity in question. In my view, whatever expressive value cross burning has, the legislature simply wrote it out by banning only intimidating conduct undertaken by a particular means." He found her conclusion that the statute prohibiting cross burning with intent to intimidate went beyond a prohibition on certain conduct and entered "the zone of expression" to overlook "not only the words of the statute but also reality."[142]

Thomas called the Klan the "world's oldest and most persistent terrorist organization," committed "to intimidate, or even eliminate those it dislikes, us[ing] the most brutal of methods . . . typically includ[ing] cross burning."[143] Of course, he knew whereof he wrote. In his memoir, *My Grandfather's Son*, he recalled how intimidating the Klan was for him and his family when he was a child in Savannah, Georgia:

> In the Fifties and Sixties, blacks steered clear of many parts of Savannah, which clung fiercely to racial segregation for as long as it could. The Ku Klux Klan held a convention there in 1960, and 250 of its white-robed members paraded down the city's main street one Saturday afternoon. No matter how curious you might be about the way white people lived, you didn't go where you didn't belong. That was a recipe for jail, or worse."[144]

As he continued in his dissent, "In our culture, cross burning has almost invariably meant lawlessness and understandably instills in its victims well-grounded fear of physical violence."[145]

Thomas rejected out of hand the suggestion that the Virginia statute was intended to squelch the message of shared ideology, that is, support of segregation. He pointed out that the statute in question was passed by a racist Virginia legislature in 1952 that was simultaneously passing laws requiring racial segregation in prisons, separation of "white" and "colored" at any place of entertainment or other public assemblage, separate waiting rooms for "whites" and "colored races," and separate personal property tax books for "whites" and "colored."[146] In light of these other segregationist laws, Thomas declared that it "strains credulity" to suggest that a state legislature that adopted this litany of segregationist laws "self-contradictorily intended to squelch the segregationist message. Even for segregationists, violent and terroristic conduct, the Siamese twin of cross burning, was intolerable. The ban on cross burning with intent to intimidate demonstrates that even segregationists understood the difference between intimidating and terroristic conduct and racist expression." From his perspective, it was "simply beyond belief that, in passing the statute now under review, the Virginia legislature was concerned with anything but penalizing conduct it must have viewed as particularly vicious."

Thomas insisted that Virginia's statute prohibited only conduct, not expression. He added, "Just as one cannot burn down someone's house to make a political point and then seek refuge in the First Amendment, those who hate cannot terrorize and intimidate to make their point." Because he saw the statute in question as addressing only conduct, he concluded that there was no need to analyze it under any of the Court's First Amendment tests.[147]

However, since O'Connor had implicated the First Amendment in her plurality opinion, Thomas felt obliged to continue and to deny that the statute's provision that any cross burning was prima facie evidence of intent to intimidate rendered it unconstitutional. Its prima facie clause was, he insisted, an "inference, not an irrebuttable presumption," and therefore consistent with "our Due Process precedents." "As the jury instructions given in this case demonstrate," he wrote, "Virginia law still requires the jury to find the existence of each element, including intent to intimidate, beyond a reasonable doubt."[148]

Thomas concluded his opinion with a rhetorical flourish on behalf of his race. He found it remarkable that according to the Court plurality, "whether a governmental interest is sufficiently compelling depends not on the harm a regulation in question seeks to prevent, but on the area of society at which it aims." He pointed out, for instance, that in *Hill v. Colorado*,[149] the same Justice O'Connor joined a majority opinion that upheld a restriction on protests near abortion clinics because the state had a legitimate interest, which was sufficiently narrowly tailored, in protecting those seeking the services of such establishments from "unwanted advice" and "unwanted communication." The Court majority upheld the restriction because it was concerned about the "vulnerable physical and emotional conditions" of the patients. Thomas sarcastically observed that when it came to the rights of those seeking abortions, the Court deemed restrictions on "'unwanted advice,' which, notably, can be given only from a distance of at least 8 feet from a prospective patient, justified by the countervailing interest in obtaining abortion. Yet, here [in *Virginia v. Black*], the plurality strikes down the statute because one day an individual might wish to burn a cross, but might do so without an intent to intimidate anyone." Barely constraining himself, he declared that even though "cross burning subjects its targets, and, sometimes, an unintended audience to extreme emotional distress, and is virtually never viewed merely as 'unwanted communication,' but rather, as a physical threat," this was of "no concern to the plurality. Henceforth, under the plurality's view, the physical safety [of blacks] will be valued less than the right [of women seeking an abortion] to be free from unwanted communications."[150] His anger was palpable.

Free Speech for Minors

In *Morse v. Frederick*,[151] Thomas brought to bear his original general meaning approach to the question of whether students have free speech rights in public schools, and on that basis, he called for the overturning of what he regarded as another misguided precedent: *Tinker v. Des Moines Independent Community School District*.[152] In January 2002, Deborah Morse, a high school principal in Juneau, Alaska, suspended eighteen-year-old Joseph Frederick for ten days after he displayed a 14-foot-long, pro–drug use banner reading BONG HITS 4 JESUS at a school event she had arranged so her students could watch the 2002 Olympic torch relay. Frederick sued, claiming his constitutional rights to free speech were violated. His suit was dismissed by the federal district court, but on appeal, the Ninth Circuit reversed, holding that Morse had punished Frederick without demonstrating that his speech gave rise to the risk of a substantial disruption. Chief Justice Roberts, for a five-member majority, reversed the Ninth Circuit and concluded a school principal may, consistent with the First Amendment, restrict student speech at a school event when the speech is reasonably viewed as promoting illegal drug use.

The foundational decision concerning student speech was *Tinker*, in which the Court made clear that "First Amendment rights, applied in light of the special characteristics of the school environment, are available to teachers and students."[153] *Tinker* involved a group of high school students who decided to protest the Vietnam War by wearing black armbands. After school officials learned of this plan, they adopted a policy that prohibited the students from doing so. When several students violated the policy and wore armbands to school nonetheless, they were suspended. The students sued, claiming that their First Amendment rights had been violated, and the Supreme Court agreed, holding that student expression may not be suppressed unless school officials reasonably conclude that it will "materially and substantially disrupt the work and discipline of the school."[154]

Roberts acknowledged the precedential value of *Tinker* but observed that it had been qualified in two subsequent cases. In *Bethel School District No. 403 v. Fraser*,[155] the Court upheld the suspension of a student for delivering a speech before a high school assembly in which he employed what the Court called "an elaborate, graphic, and explicit sexual metaphor"; the Court declared that "the constitutional rights of students in public school are not automatically coextensive with the rights of adults in other settings."[156] And in *Hazelwood School District v. Kuhlmeier*,[157] the Court held that school officials do not offend the free speech rights of students by exercising editorial control over the style and content of student speech in a school-sponsored student newspaper as long as their actions are reasonably related to "legitimate pedagogical concerns."[158]

To these two qualifications, Roberts now added a third: "The 'special characteristics of the school environment,' and the governmental interest in stopping student drug abuse—reflected in the policies of Congress and myriad school boards—allow schools to restrict student expression that they reasonably regard as promoting illegal drug use." Although *Tinker* warned that schools "may not prohibit student speech because of 'undifferentiated fear or apprehension of disturbance' or 'a mere desire to avoid the discomfort and unpleasantness that always accompany an unpopular viewpoint,'" Roberts insisted that "the danger here is far more serious and palpable. The particular concern to prevent student drug abuse at issue here, embodied in established school policy, extends well beyond an abstract desire to avoid controversy."[159]

Thomas joined Roberts's opinion "in full" but wrote a separate concurring opinion to express his view that the standard set forth in *Tinker* "is without basis in the Constitution." That was because "the history of public education suggests that the First Amendment, as originally understood, does not protect student speech in public schools."[160]

Schools at the time of the ratification of the First Amendment were "exclusively private," but Thomas noted that by the early 1800s, public schools were rapidly proliferating, and by the time of the ratification of the Fourteenth Amendment (held by the Court to incorporate the First Amendment to apply to the states), public schools were relatively common. "If students in public schools were originally understood as having free-speech rights, one would have expected 19th century public schools to have respected those rights and courts to have enforced them." However, he observed, "they did not."[161] After presenting evidence to support his argument, he concluded: "In the earliest public schools, teachers taught, and students listened. Teachers commanded, and students obeyed.

Teachers did not rely solely on the power of ideas to persuade; they relied on discipline to maintain order."[162]

Through the doctrine of *in loco parentis*, courts upheld the right of schools to discipline students and to regulate their speech, as his review of nineteenth-century state case law showed. However, Thomas noted, *Tinker* changed all that and altered "the traditional understanding of the judiciary's role in relation to public schooling, a role limited by *in loco parentis*." He speculated that it was for that reason that the Court has subsequently introduced exceptions to the *Tinker* standard, "or rather set the standard aside on an *ad hoc* basis."[163] Roberts, he pointed out, created still a third exception and by so doing continued to distance the Court from *Tinker*—but without overruling it or offering an explanation for when it should be applied. "I am afraid," he wrote, "that our jurisprudence now says that students have a right to speak in schools except when they do not—a standard continuously developed through litigation against local schools and their administrators. In my view, petitioners could prevail for a much simpler reason. As originally understood, the Constitution does not afford students a right to free speech in public schools."[164]

Thomas acknowledged that schools today face different administrative and pedagogical challenges than schools well over a century ago, and "the idea of treating children as though it were still the 19th century would find little favor today." But, he insisted, there is no "constitutional imperative requiring public schools to allow all student speech." If today's parents, in fact, want their children to have free speech rights in their schools, they can challenge rules denying these rights in the political process and elect school boards that will change these rules.[165]

As mentioned earlier, one of the reasons Thomas pursues an original general meaning jurisprudence is because it constrains judicial discretion. His concurrence here perfectly encapsulates that reasoning. "In place of that democratic regime," he wrote, "*Tinker* [by departing from the original understanding of the First Amendment and holding that public schools must secure the free speech rights of students] substituted judicial oversight of the day-to-day affairs of public schools." It imposed a new and malleable standard that schools could not inhibit student speech unless "it substantially interfered with the requirements of appropriate discipline in the operation of the school." Applying that standard involves "judgment calls" that "historically courts reasoned only local school districts were entitled and competent to make." *Tinker* "usurped that traditional authority for the judiciary."[166] He concluded characteristically: "I join the Court's opinion because it erodes *Tinker*'s hold in the realm of student speech, even though it does so by adding to the patchwork of exceptions to the *Tinker* standard. I think the better approach is to dispense with *Tinker* altogether, and given the opportunity, I would do so."[167]

In his dissent in *Brown v. Entertainment Merchants Association*,[168] Thomas expanded on his *Morse* concurrence. When California passed a law prohibiting the sale or rental of "violent video games" to minors and requiring that such games be placed in packaging that was labeled "18," an association that represented the video game and software industries filed a preenforcement action against the governor of California, claiming that the statute violated the First Amendment. A federal district court agreed, permanently enjoining enforcement of the statute, and the Ninth Circuit affirmed. Once the case reached the Supreme Court, Scalia held for a seven-member majority that video games qualify for First Amendment protection because, like protected books, plays, and movies, they communicate ideas through familiar literary devices and features distinctive to the medium. California's law, he held, imposed a restriction on the content of protected speech and was invalid under the Court's strict scrutiny test. In particular, the law was not narrowly tailored: its video game regulations were wildly underinclusive because they did not restrict other violent media, such as Saturday morning cartoons, and they were also greatly overinclusive as a means of assisting parents because not all of the children who were prohibited from purchasing violent video games had parents who disapproved of their doing so.

In a solo dissent, Thomas again brought his original general meaning approach to bear on his consideration of the First Amendment:

> The Court's decision today does not comport with the original public understanding of the First Amendment. . . . The practices and beliefs of the founding generation establish that "the freedom of speech," as originally understood, does not include a right to speak to minors (or a right of minors to access speech) without going through the minors' parents or guardians. I would hold that the law at issue is not facially unconstitutional under the First Amendment and reverse and remand for further proceedings.[169]

Thomas invoked his *McIntyre* concurrence as he spelled out his originalist approach: "When interpreting a constitutional provision, 'the goal is to discern the most likely public understanding of [that] provision at the time it was adopted.' Because the Constitution is a written instrument, 'its meaning does not alter.' 'That which it meant when adopted, it means now.'" As originally understood, the Free Speech Clause did not extend to all speech; there were "certain well-defined and narrowly limited classes of speech, the prevention and punishment of which have never been thought to raise any Constitutional problem," for example, fighting words. And in Thomas's view, the "practices and beliefs held by the Founders" revealed another category of excluded speech — "speech to minor children bypassing their parents."

Thomas then devoted 8,000 words in his opinion to providing evidence from the Puritan experience, the writings of John Locke and Jean-Jacques Rousseau, the writings of John Adams and Thomas Jefferson, the reflections of other members of the founding generation such as Noah Webster, William Blackstone's *Commentaries on the Laws of England* and James Kent's *Commentaries on American Law*, and late eighteenth-century and early nineteenth-century case law. His aim was to establish the "historical evidence show[ing] that the founding generation believed parents had absolute authority over their minor children and expected parents to use that authority to direct the proper development of their children. It would be absurd to suggest that such a society understood 'the freedom of speech' to include a right to speak to minors (or a corresponding right of minors to access speech) without going through the minors' parents." He contended that the founding generation "would not have considered it an abridgment of 'the freedom of speech' to support parental authority by restricting speech that bypasses minors' parents."[170]

Thomas acknowledged that "the original public understanding of a constitutional provision does not always comport with modern sensibilities." He was untroubled by this prospect; if the people wanted modern sensibilities to prevail, all they had to do was have the California legislature pass a law allowing minors access, against their parents' wishes, to violent video games. But until and unless the public did so, Thomas was content to act in conformity with the original public understanding, especially when "the notion that parents have authority over their children and that the law can support that authority persists today." He gave several examples: at least in some states, it remains a crime to lure or entice a minor away from the minor's parent; in every state, there is still a minimum age for marriage without parental or judicial consent; and under federal law, minors cannot enlist in the military without parental consent.[171]

The Second Amendment

The Second Amendment reads: "A well regulated Militia, being necessary to the security of a free State, the right of the people to keep and bear Arms, shall not be infringed." In *Heller v. District of Columbia*,[172] the Court's seminal interpretation of this Clause, Justice Scalia held, for a five-member majority, that it secured to individuals the personal right to possess a firearm unconnected with service in a militia and to use that weapon for purposes of self-defense. Thomas joined Scalia's majority opinion — a classic expression of Scalia's textualist jurisprudence in which he systematically explored the original meaning of the words in the text of the Second Amendment and what its words meant to the society that adopted it.[173]

Two years later, in *McDonald v. Chicago*,[174] the Court confronted the question of whether the Second Amendment as understood in *Heller* should be incorporated by the Fourteenth Amendment to apply to the states. For a five-member majority, Justice Alito delivered the opinion of the Court and held that it was. Chief Justice Roberts and Justices Scalia and Kennedy joined him as to the reason: "The Due Process Clause of the Fourteenth Amendment [substantive due process] incorporates the Second Amendment right recognized in *Heller*."[175] The critical fifth vote to incorporate the Second Amendment came from Thomas—but for an entirely different reason. As he wrote in his opinion concurring in part and concurring in the judgment:

> I agree with the Court that the Fourteenth Amendment makes the
> right to keep and bear arms set forth in the Second Amendment "fully
> applicable to the States." I write separately because I believe there is a
> more straightforward path to this conclusion, one that is more faithful
> to the Fourteenth Amendment's text and history. . . . I cannot agree that
> it is enforceable against the States through a clause that speaks only of
> "process." Instead, the right to keep and bear arms is a privilege of American
> citizenship that applies to the States through the Fourteenth Amendment's
> Privileges and Immunities Clause.[176]

The Fourteenth Amendment declares that "no state shall make or enforce any law which shall abridge the privileges or immunities of citizens of the United States; nor shall any State deprive any person of life, liberty, or property, without due process of law; nor deny to any person within its jurisdiction the equal protection of the laws." Out of an acrimonious debate over the specific intentions of the members of the Thirty-Ninth Congress who framed this amendment, a general agreement has emerged regarding what overall ends the amendment was intended to advance and how its three major clauses were to meet these ends. As a group, the Privileges or Immunities, Due Process, and Equal Protection Clauses were intended to place economic and civil liberties on the safe and secure foundation of federal protection. The Privileges or Immunities Clause was to protect substantive rights (for instance, freedom of speech, religious freedom, the right to engage in lawful occupations, and freedom from improper police violence), and the Due Process and Equal Protection Clauses were to protect procedural rights, with the former guaranteeing procedural safeguards and judicial regularity in the enforcement of those rights and the latter barring legislative and executive discrimination with respect to those substantive rights.[177]

However, as Thomas pointed out in *Saenz v. Roe*,[178] the Court's 1873 decision in *The Slaughter-House Cases*,[179] decided just five years after the ratification of the Fourteenth Amendment, "sapped the Privileges and Immunities Clause of any meaning."[180] Speaking for the majority, Justice Samuel F. Miller drew a distinction between state citizenship and national citizenship and, hence, between those privileges or immunities that accrued to an individual by virtue of state citizenship and those that stemmed from national citizenship. Only the latter, he insisted, were protected by the Fourteenth Amendment. And in distinguishing the privileges or immunities of state citizenship from those of national citizenship, Justice Miller quoted earlier decisions in an effort to demonstrate that the whole body of commonly accepted civil and economic rights—including the right to pursue lawful employment in a lawful manner, which lay at the heart of *The Slaughter-House Cases*—fell within the privileges or immunities of state citizenship. Such rights included "protection by the government, with the right to acquire and possess property of every kind, and to pursue and obtain happiness and safety, subject, nevertheless, to such restraints as the [state] government may prescribe for the general good of the whole." Miller contended that the framers of the Fourteenth Amendment had not intended to transfer this whole body of rights to the protection of the federal government. To interpret the amendment otherwise, he argued, would be to accept consequences "so serious, so far-reaching and pervading" that they would alter radically "the whole theory of the relations of the state and Federal governments to each other." This the Court refused to do, "in the absence of language which expresses such a purpose too clearly to admit of doubt."[181]

Miller and the majority did not argue that national citizenship conferred no privileges or immunities. Although declining to define them precisely, they did suggest that such privileges or immunities included the right of a citizen "to come to the seat of the government to assert any claim he may have upon that government"; the "right of free access to its seaports"; and the right "to demand the care and protection of the Federal government over his life, liberty, and property when on the high seas, or within the jurisdiction of a foreign government."[182] This list, however, left the whole body of traditional economic and civil rights solely under the protection of the states. As far as the federal Constitution was concerned, therefore, the privileges or immunities of the citizens of the separate states remained exactly as they had been before the Fourteenth Amendment was adopted.

Justice Miller's argument prompted a frustrated Justice Stephen B. Field to complain in his dissent that if that was all the Privileges or Immunities Clause meant, "it was a vain and idle enactment, which accomplished nothing, and most unnecessarily excited Congress and the people on its passage." For Justice Field, the Clause was intended to have a "profound significance and consequence."[183] He argued that what the Privileges and Immunities Clause of Article IV, § 2 "did for the protection of the citizens of one State against hostile and discriminating legislation of other States, the Fourteenth Amendment does for the protection of every citizen of the United States against hostile and discriminating legislation against him in favor of others, whether they reside in the same or in different states."[184]

The *Slaughter-House* decision knocked out the only substantive (and thus the most important) clause of the Fourteenth Amendment designed by its framers to protect economic and civil liberties. This was, in the words of Michael Kent Curtis, "one of the signal disasters of American judicial history."[185] In 1935, the Court made a feeble effort to prop up this substantive leg and to restore the Privileges or Immunities Clause, holding in *Colgate* v. *Harvey*[186] that the right of a U.S. citizen to do business and place a loan in a state other than that in which he resided was a privilege of national citizenship. However, just five years later in *Madden v. Kentucky*,[187] the Court expressly overturned that decision and returned to the old interpretation that "the right to carry out an incident of a trade, business, or calling such as the deposit of money in banks is not a privilege of national citizenship." And four years later in *Snowden v. Hughes*,[188] it again reaffirmed its narrow *Slaughter-House* interpretation when it held that the right to become a candidate for and be elected to a state office was an attribute of state citizenship, not a privilege of national citizenship. Those who had been denied this right, the Court declared, had to look to their own state constitutions and laws for redress.

Until 1999, it was altogether accurate to say that with respect to the Privileges or Immunities Clause, the Court's decision in *The Slaughter-House Cases* remained good law. However, that year, in *Saenz v. Roe*, Justice John Paul Stevens once again launched a campaign to restore the Privileges or Immunities Clause, invoking its language to strike down a durational residency requirement in California's welfare statute as an impermissible infringement on the right to travel and holding further that congressional approval of such a requirement did not resuscitate its constitutionality. Justice Stevens held for a seven-member majority that a privilege and immunity of national citizenship is the right of travelers who elect to become permanent residents of a state "to be treated like other citizens of that State." Thomas dissented, arguing that Stevens attributed a meaning to the Clause that was unintended when the Fourteenth Amendment was ratified.[189] He faulted Stevens for failing to address the Clause's "historical underpinnings." Yet, he boldly declared, "because I believe that the demise of the Privileges or Immunities Clause has contributed in no small part to the current disarray of our Fourteenth Amendment jurisprudence, I would be open to reevaluating its meaning in an appropriate case." "Before invoking the Clause," he added, "we should endeavor to understand what the framers of the Fourteenth Amendment thought it meant." And he went further: "We should also consider whether the Clause should displace, rather than augment, portions of our equal protection and substantive due process jurisprudence." He concluded by expressing his apprehension about the Court's sudden invocation of the Privileges or Immunities Clause. Because Stevens used it to protect a right not expressly mentioned in the Constitution, he worried that it would become "yet another convenient tool for inventing new rights, limited solely by the 'predilections of those who happen at the time to be Members of this Court.'"[190]

Interestingly, Thomas's dissent in *Saenz* gave great encouragement to Alan Gura, the brash young attorney who successfully argued the *Heller* case before the Supreme Court and who was retained to represent Otis McDonald, the petitioner in *McDonald v. Chicago*. Gura gambled, devoting fifty-six of his sixty-three pages of argument in his initial brief to the Privileges or Immunities Clause argument. He so alarmed the National Rifle Association (NRA) that it filed a brief making the case for selective incorporation under the Due Process Clause much more forcefully and at much greater length than did Gura's brief. In addition, the NRA asked for (and was granted) some of Gura's time during oral argument, and it hired former solicitor general Paul Clement (who argued the federal government's case in *Heller*) to participate in the oral argument.[191] The NRA's action proved wise, as Gura's efforts to rely on the Privileges or Immunities Clause were immediately challenged during oral argument; Chief Justice Roberts quickly questioned his reliance on Privileges or Immunities, noting that *The Slaughter-House Cases* had been good law for 140 years and adding that "it's a heavy burden for you to carry to suggest that we ought to overrule that decision."[192] Soon thereafter, Scalia challenged his argument in the following colloquy:

JUSTICE SCALIA: Mr. Gura, do you think it is at all easier to bring the Second Amendment under the Privileges or Immunities Clause than it is to bring it under our established law of substantive due?

MR. GURA: It's—

JUSTICE SCALIA: Is it easier to do it under privileges and immunities than it is under substantive due process?

MR. GURA: It is easier in terms, perhaps, of the text and history of the original public understanding of—

JUSTICE SCALIA: No, no. I'm not talking about whether—whether the *Slaughter-House Cases* were right or wrong. I'm saying, assuming we give, you know, the Privileges or Immunities Clause your definition, does that make it any easier to get the Second Amendment adopted with respect to the States?

MR. GURA: Justice Scalia, I suppose the answer to that would be no, because—

JUSTICE SCALIA: Then if the answer is no, why are you asking us to overrule 150, 140 years of prior law, when you can reach your result under substantive due [process]—I mean, you know, unless you are bucking for a—a place on some law school faculty—

(Laughter.)

MR. GURA: No. No. I have left law school some time ago and this is not an attempt to return.

JUSTICE SCALIA: What you argue is the darling of the professoriate, for sure, but it's also contrary to 140 years of our jurisprudence. Why do you want to undertake that burden instead of just arguing substantive due process, which as much as I think its wrong, . . . even I have acquiesced in it?

(Laughter.)[193]

Despite the questions posed by Roberts and Scalia—and the laughter they elicited—Thomas was unfazed. He insisted that the proper basis for incorporating the Second Amendment was the Privileges or Immunities Clause. He did so based both on his understanding of what the Clause originally meant and on his outrage at—and passionate desire to sweep into the ash heap of history—the Court's notorious decision in *United States v. Cruikshank*,[194] on which the Seventh Circuit had relied to uphold Chicago's draconian law banning its citizens from possessing handguns. In *Cruikshank*, the Court had relied on *The Slaughter-House Cases*, handed down a mere three years before, to overturn the conviction of "members of a white militia who had brutally murdered as many as 165 black Louisianans congregating outside a courthouse," arguing that they had not "deprived the victims of their privileges as American citizens to peaceably assemble or keep and bear arms." In a 20,000-word solo opinion, Thomas insisted that the right to keep and bear arms was an "inalienable right that pre-existed the

Constitution's adoption" and a privilege and immunity that could be enforced against the states under the Fourteenth Amendment.[195]

McDonald provided the first occasion for Thomas to address the question of whether and how the rights found in the Bill of Rights should be incorporated to apply to the states. Rather than simply applying past precedents, as Scalia was willing to do,[196] he wanted to scrape them away and return to bare wood. He branded as "a legal fiction" the Court's use of substantive due process to incorporate rights found in the Bill of Rights as well as rights "that are not mentioned in the Constitution at all," that is, abortion and homosexual sodomy: "The notion that a constitutional provision that guarantees only 'process' before a person is deprived of life, liberty, or property could define the substance of those rights strains credulity for even the most casual user of words." Moreover, Thomas stated, it was a "dangerous" legal fiction, for the Court's substantive due process precedents lacked "a guiding principle to distinguish 'fundamental' rights that warrant protection from nonfundamental rights that do not." He pointed to Alito's plurality opinion and the dissenting opinions by Stevens and Breyer to illustrate his point. The dissenters "laud[ed] the 'flexibility' in this Court's substantive due process doctrine," he said, allowing them to contend that the right to keep and bear arms was not a fundamental right, whereas Alito made "yet another effort to impose principled restraints on its exercise." But, he insisted, "neither side argues that the meaning they attribute to the Due Process Clause" was consistent with public understanding at the time of its ratification. He added, "I cannot accept a theory of constitutional interpretation that rests on such tenuous footing" and that is so "devoid of a guiding principle." Rather, he urged his colleagues to "return" to the original meaning of the Fourteenth Amendment as "a superior alternative," and he argued that a return to that meaning would allow the Court to enforce the rights it was "designed to protect with greater clarity and predictability than the substantive due process framework has so far managed."[197]

He acknowledged "the volume of precedents" that has been built upon the substantive due process framework and the "importance of *stare decisis*" to the stability of the legal system. But, he insisted, "*stare decisis* is only an 'adjunct' of our duty as judges to decide by our best lights what the Constitution means." He reminded his colleagues that "as judges, we interpret the Constitution one case or controversy at a time." He was not asking the Court to consider whether its entire Fourteenth Amendment jurisprudence should be "preserved or revised, but only whether, and to what extent, a particular clause in the Constitution protects the particular right at issue here. With the inquiry appropriately narrowed, I believe this case presents an opportunity to reexamine, and begin the process of restoring, the meaning" of the Privileges or Immunities Clause.[198]

And so he seized that opportunity, initially by scraping away all of the Court's precedents in this area. He quoted Chief Justice Marshall in *Marbury v. Madison*—"It cannot be presumed that any clause in the constitution is intended to be without effect"[199]—and he continued by declaring that "because the Court's Privileges or Immunities Clause precedents have presumed just that, I set them aside for the moment and begin with the text" and with the objective of discerning what "ordinary citizens" at the time of the ratification of the Fourteenth Amendment understood that Clause to mean.[200]

He began by providing pages of evidence showing that when the Thirty-Ninth Congress was drafting the Fourteenth Amendment, "the terms 'privileges' and 'immunities' had an established meaning as synonyms for 'rights.' The two words, standing alone or paired together, were used interchangeably with the words 'rights,' 'liberties,' and 'freedoms,' and had been since the time of Blackstone."[201] Moreover, these rights were not understood as "entitlements, but as inalienable rights of all men, given legal effect by their codification in the Constitution's text."[202] He then provided extensive documentation demonstrating that privileges and immunities were understood to include the "individual rights enumerated in the Constitution, including the right to keep and bear arms."[203]

Thomas next turned to the legislative history of the Fourteenth Amendment's drafting and adoption. Given his original general meaning approach, he declared that when interpreting a constitutional text, "the goal is to discern the most likely public understanding of a particular provision at the time it was adopted." To that end, "statements by legislators can assist in this process to the extent they demonstrate the manner in which the public used or understood a particular word or phrase." They "can further assist to the extent there is evidence that these statements were disseminated to the public." For Thomas, this evidence is useful "not because it demonstrates what the draftsmen of the text may have been thinking, but only insofar as it illuminates what the public understood the words chosen by the draftsmen to mean."[204] With that thought in mind, he focused in particular on three major speeches given on the floor of the House of Representatives by John Bingham, the principal draftsman of § 1 of the Fourteenth Amendment, including its Privileges or Immunities Clause, because they were also printed in pamphlet form and "broadly distributed." Based on "these well-circulated speeches," the public understood that § 1 would "enforce the constitutionally declared rights against the States" and that the Privileges or Immunities Clause "would accomplish that task."[205]

Thomas also turned to "interpretations of the Fourteenth Amendment in the period immediately following its ratification" to help establish the public understanding of the text at the time of its adoption. He gave numerous examples of public understanding but found one especially compelling due to its racial element. In an 1871 Ku Klux Klan prosecution, U.S. Attorney Daniel Corbin declared:

> The Fourteenth Amendment changes all that theory, and lays the same restriction upon the States that before lay upon the Congress of the United States—that, as Congress heretofore could not interfere with the right of the citizen to keep and bear arms, now, after the adoption of the Fourteenth Amendment, the State cannot interfere with the right of the citizen to keep and bear arms. The right to keep and bear arms is included in the Fourteenth Amendment under "privileges and immunities." Proceedings in the Ku Klux Trials at Columbia, S. C., in the United States Circuit Court, November Term, 1871, p. 147 (1872).[206]

Thomas believed this evidence plainly showed that the ratifying public understood the Privileges or Immunities Clause to protect constitutionally enumerated rights, including the right to keep and bear arms.[207] And so, though the Court was correct when it held that § 1 was understood to enforce the Second Amendment against the states, the reason was not substantive due process but "because the right to keep and bear arms was understood to be a privilege of American citizenship guaranteed by the Privileges and Immunities Clause."[208]

At this point, Thomas, who had previously set the Court's precedents "aside for the moment," returned to precedents. He "rejected" *The Slaughter-House Cases'* narrow understanding of the Privileges or Immunities Clause as inconsistent with its original general meaning.[209] Then he turned to *Cruikshank* and its holding, based on *The Slaughter-House Cases*, that the right to keep and bear arms was not a privilege of American citizenship, "thereby overturning the convictions of militia members responsible for the brutal Colfax Massacre. *Cruikshank* is not a precedent entitled to any respect." The flaws in its interpretation of the Privilege or Immunities Clause had been revealed by the preceding evidence of its original meaning that Thomas had presented, and so, he declared, "I would reject the holding on that basis alone. But, the consequences of *Cruikshank* warrant mention as well."[210] Its holding that "blacks could look only to state governments for protection of their right to keep and bear arms enabled private forces, often with the assistance of local governments, to subjugate the newly freed slaves and their descendants through a wave of private violence designed to drive blacks from the voting booth and force them into peonage, an effective return to slavery." Its holding barred "federal enforcement of the inalienable right to keep and bear arms" and tragically allowed these militias and mobs to wage "a campaign of terror against the very people the Fourteenth Amendment had just made citizens."[211]

Despite congressional legislation to suppress these activities, he noted, "there were at least 3,446 reported lynchings of blacks in the South. They were tortured and killed for a wide array of alleged crimes, without even the slightest hint of due process." In the face of this mob violence, "the use of firearms for self-defense was often the only way black citizens could protect themselves." Thomas quoted Eli Cooper, "one target of such violence": "The Negro has been run over for fifty years, but it must stop now, and pistols and shotguns are the only weapons to stop a mob." "Sometimes, as in Cooper's case," Thomas regretted, "self-defense did not succeed. He was dragged from his home by a mob and killed as his wife looked on." "At other times," he added, "the use of firearms allowed targets of mob violence to survive. One man recalled the night during his childhood when his father stood armed at a jail until morning to ward off lynchers."[212]

Thomas concluded:

> In my view, the record makes plain that the Framers of the Privileges or Immunities Clause and the ratifying-era public understood—just as the Framers of the Second Amendment did—that the right to keep and bear arms was essential to the preservation of liberty. The record makes equally plain that they deemed this right necessary to include in the minimum baseline of federal rights that the Privileges or Immunities Clause established in the wake of the War over slavery.

Given the human tragedy that followed in its wake, he contended, "there is nothing about *Cruikshank's* contrary holding that warrants its retention."[213] And unlike Alito and the Court plurality who never addressed what to do about *Cruikshank*, Thomas wanted this blight on the Court's history to be expressly overturned because of the grievous harm it had caused his race.

The Takings Clause

The Fifth Amendment includes the Takings Clause, declaring that private property shall not "be taken for public use without just compensation." Thomas's insistence that the plain understanding of that text should apply was initially apparent when he provided the decisive fifth vote for Scalia's 1992 majority opinion in *Lucas v. South Carolina Coastal Council*[214] and for Chief Justice Rehnquist's 1994 majority opinion in *Dolan v. City of Tigard*.[215] *Lucas* held that when a state seeks to sustain a regulation that deprives land of all economically beneficial use, it must pay just compensation to the landowner unless it can show that its proscribed use of the property was part of the owner's title when the property was purchased. *Dolan* held that it was impermissible for a city to require a property owner, as a condition for obtaining a building permit to expand her hardware store, to dedicate a portion of the property to the city in furtherance of its land use plan unless it was roughly proportionate to the expanded building's projected impact on that plan.

In 1995, Thomas wrote his first opinion on the Takings Clause in his dissent from the Court's denial of certiorari in *Parking Association of Georgia v. Atlanta*.[216] Seeking to improve the appearance of its downtown area, the Atlanta City Council passed an ordinance requiring 350 existing surface parking lots to include landscaped areas equal to at least 10 percent of the paved area and to have at least one tree for every eight parking spaces. The parking lot owners estimated that compliance with the landscaping requirements would cost approximately $12,500 per lot, for a total of $4,375,000. Additionally, they would lose revenue because the number of parking spaces would be reduced and because they would forfeit advertising contracts worth $1,636,000, since the trees would obscure existing advertising signs. The parking lot owners sought injunctive and declaratory relief on the ground that the Atlanta ordinance was an uncompensated taking of property in violation of the Fifth Amendment. A state trial court ruled in favor of the city, as did a divided Georgia Supreme Court, holding that the ordinance was neither a physical nor a regulatory taking because it left the owners with an economically viable use in their property. The court distinguished *Dolan*, which required a showing of rough proportionality between the conditions imposed and the impact of the owner's development, because the city of Tigard had failed to make an individualized determination that the required dedication was related in both nature and extent to the impact of the development, whereas the city of Atlanta had made a legislative determination with regard to many landowners, thus placing the parking lot owners' case outside the reach of *Dolan*.

Thomas pointed out that the lower courts were in conflict concerning *Dolan's* applicability to cases where the alleged taking occurred through the action of the legislature. But he wondered why the existence of a taking should "turn on the type of governmental entity responsible for the taking. A city council can take property just as well as a planning commission can." Had Atlanta seized hundreds of homes to build a highway, "there would be no doubt that Atlanta had taken private property. The distinction between sweeping legislative takings and particularized administrative takings appears to be a distinction without a constitutional difference." Because the parking lot owners' petition "posed a substantial federal question concerning regulatory takings" and because of "confusion in the lowers courts," Thomas declared that he would grant certiorari.[217]

Three years later, he filed a "fascinating concurrence"[218] in *Eastern Enterprises v. Apfel*.[219] Eastern Enterprises, an energy company, had been in the coal-mining business from 1947 until 1965, when it sold its coal-mining operation. While in the business, it paid medical benefits under a defined contribution program for its employees, as required by law. Twenty-seven years later, Congress passed the Coal Industry Health Benefits Act of 1992, requiring the company to pay $100 million in additional medical benefits not previously required to help support health care for coal industry retirees. The company filed suit seeking a declaratory judgment that the law was both an unconstitutional taking and a violation of substantive due process. A federal district court and the Court of Appeals for the First Circuit denied the company's claims, but the Supreme Court, in a five-to-four decision, reversed. O'Connor held for a four-member plurality that the law's imposition of retroactive liability constituted a regulatory taking in violation of the Fifth Amendment. Kennedy provided the critical fifth vote, but he concurred only in the judgment, finding the law to violate well-established principles of due process.

Thomas joined the plurality but then suggested that the provision might well have violated the Ex Post Facto Clause of Article I, § 9 as well. His concurrence was short, although it fully displayed his insistence that the Court proceed on the basis of an original general meaning jurisprudence and his commitment to scrape off misguided precedent, however venerable. He said he wrote separately to emphasize that the Ex Post Facto Clause "even more clearly reflects the principle that 'retrospective laws are, indeed, generally unjust.'" Since 1798 and its decision in *Calder v. Bull*,[220] the Court had held that the Ex Post Facto Clause applied only in the criminal context, but Thomas confessed that he had "never been convinced of the soundness of this limitation," which in *Calder* was principally justified because of the belief that a contrary interpretation would render the Takings Clause unnecessary.[221] But since more recent Courts had taken the "starch"[222] out of the Takings Clause, Thomas indicated that "in an appropriate case, I would be willing to reconsider [*Calder*] and its progeny to determine whether a retroactive civil law that passes muster under our current Takings Clause jurisprudence is nonetheless unconstitutional under the Ex Post Facto Clause. Today's case, however, does present an unconstitutional taking, and I join Justice O'Connor's well-reasoned opinion in full."[223]

Thomas wrote a brief dissent in *Tahoe-Sierra Preservation Council v. Tahoe Regional Planning Agency*,[224] in which the Court held that no compensation was due to property owners who were temporarily deprived of all economically viable use of their land through, as in this case, the imposition of a moratorium on development imposed by governmental agencies during the process of drafting a comprehensive land use plan. He wrote, "A taking is exactly what occurred in this case. No one seriously doubts that the land use regulations at issue rendered petitioners' land unsusceptible of *any* economically beneficial use. This was true at the inception of the moratorium, and it remains true today." The landown-ers were deprived of the opportunity to build permanent, retirement, or vaca-tion residences on land "upon which such construction was authorized when purchased." Thomas argued that "regulations prohibiting all productive uses of property are subject to *Lucas' per se* rule, regardless of whether the property so burdened retains theoretical useful life and value if, and when, the 'temporary' moratorium is lifted." "To my mind," he added, "such potential future value bears on the amount of compensation due and has nothing to do with the ques-tion whether there was a taking in the first place. It is regrettable that the Court has charted a markedly different path today."[225]

Thomas's most significant opinion on the Takings Clause was rendered in *Kelo v. City of New London*.[226] When Pfizer, the giant pharmaceutical company, announced that it would build a $300 million research facility near New Lon-don's waterfront area, the city was elated. The facility was projected to create over 1,000 jobs, increase tax revenues, and revitalize an economically distressed city — provided the city helped it acquire the land on which the facility would be built through eminent domain. But when the city, through its development agency, sought to use the power of eminent domain to acquire some of the property for the facility, nine owners of privately owned properties in the area, none of which were alleged to be blighted or otherwise in poor condition, brought an action in the New London Superior Court, claiming that the taking of their properties would violate the Fifth Amendment's requirement that private property can be taken only for "public use." After the superior court granted a permanent restrain-ing order prohibiting the taking of the properties, the Connecticut Supreme Court reversed, arguing that the economic development in question qualified as a valid public use. Justice Stevens, for a five-member majority, affirmed. Thomas joined O'Connor's principal dissent, in which she argued that the majority had replaced the "Public Use Clause" with a "Public Purpose Clause,"[227] but he also filed a powerful solo dissent on originalist grounds.

Thomas began by regretting that Stevens's opinion was "simply the latest in a string of our cases construing the Public Use Clause to be a virtual nullity, with-out the slightest nod to its original meaning. In my view, the Public Use Clause, originally understood, is a meaningful limit on the government's eminent do-main power. Our cases have strayed from the Clause's original meaning, and I would reconsider them."[228]

He then turned to the text and argued that "the most natural reading" of the Clause is that "it allows the government to take property only if the government owns, or the public has a legal right to use, the property, as opposed to taking it for any public purpose or necessity whatsoever." He bulwarked his argument by citing Samuel Johnson's definition of the word *use* in his 1773 dictionary and the word's appearance in two of the original Constitution's provisions.[229] He next turned to the "Constitution's common-law background" and demonstrated that the Public Use Clause "embodied the Framers' understanding that property is a natural, fundamental right, prohibiting the government from taking property from A and giving it to B."[230] Finally, since the federal government did not begin to use the power of eminent domain until the late nineteenth century, he turned to how comparable public use provisions in state constitutions were interpreted before and into the twentieth century and found that the occasional efforts by states to redefine public use as public purpose were "hotly contested."[231]

He pointed out that the Court "blindly" adopted its modern reading that public use means public purpose and that legislative bodies should be given great deference by courts concerning their judgments regarding what constitutes a public use—both of which came together in Stevens's majority opinion—based on dicta in two opinions by Justice Rufus Peckham. Peckham, of course, is most famous (Thomas might say notorious) for his decision in *Lochner v. New York*,[232] an opinion in which he employed substantive due process to strike down a New York labor law for the number of hours that bakers could work based on a liberty to contract—an opinion that Thomas has repeatedly defamed.[233]

In *Fallbrook Irrigation District v. Bradley*,[234] Peckham held that a taking of land for purposes of constructing an irrigation ditch was for a public use because "to irrigate and thus to bring into possible cultivation these large masses of otherwise worthless lands would seem to be a public purpose and a matter of public interest, not confined to landowners, or even to any one section of the State." But Thomas pointed out that Peckham's "broad statement was dictum, for the law under review also provided that 'all landowners in the district have the right to a proportionate share of the water. Thus, the 'public' did have the right to use the irrigation ditch because all similarly situated members of the public—those who owned lands irrigated by the ditch—had a right to use it." Nonetheless, subsequent Courts simply followed *Bradley* "with little analysis." [235]

Once again, in *United States v. Gettysburg Electric Railway Company*,[236] Peckham held that "when the legislature has declared the use or purpose to be a public one, its judgment will be respected by the courts, unless the use be palpably without reasonable foundation." And again, Thomas pointed out that this, too, was dictum, for Congress's decision to condemn certain private land for the purpose of building battlefield memorials at Gettysburg, Pennsylvania, was unquestionably "for a public use."[237]

Because of the Court's "blind" reliance on dicta, Thomas declared that he "would revisit our Public Use Clause cases and consider returning to the original meaning of the Public Use Clause: that the government may take property only if it actually uses or gives the public a legal right to use the property."[238]

Thomas then pointed out, as he had in other areas of law, that *Kelo* had a devastating impact on people of his race due to its departure from an original general meaning interpretation of the Constitution. Though New London would be required to provide some compensation for the properties it would take, "no compensation is possible for the subjective value of these lands to the individuals displaced and the indignity inflicted by uprooting them from their homes." And though allowing the government to take property solely for public use is "bad enough," Thomas claimed, extending it to public purpose encompassing any economically beneficial goal "guarantees that these losses will fall disproportionately on poor communities. Those communities are not only systematically less likely to put their lands to the highest and best social use, but are also the least politically powerful. If ever there were justification for intrusive judicial review of constitutional provisions that protect 'discrete and insular minorities,' surely that principle would apply with great force to the powerless groups and individuals the Public Use Clause protects." He reminded his colleagues of the regrettable consequences of "urban renewal" in the 1950s and 1960s:

> Of all the families displaced by urban renewal from 1949 through 1963, 63 percent of those whose race was known were nonwhite, and of these families, 56 percent of nonwhites and 38 percent of whites had incomes low enough to qualify for public housing, which, however, was seldom available to them. Urban renewal projects have long been associated with the displacement of blacks; "in cities across the country, urban renewal came to be known as 'Negro removal.'"

For him, the "predictable consequence" of Stevens's decision was clear: it would "exacerbate these effects."[239]

Thomas concluded by observing that the *Kelo* majority could have avoided these "far-reaching, and dangerous, result[s]" had it employed the principles "found in the Public Use Clause itself" rather than those in Justice Peckham's dicta. "When faced with a clash of constitutional principle and a line of unreasoned cases wholly divorced from the text, history, and structure of our founding document," he advised, "we should not hesitate to resolve the tension in favor of the Constitution's original meaning."[240]

The Court's Abortion Jurisprudence

Most of the Court's major abortion cases were decided before Thomas's elevation to the Supreme Court. Although *Planned Parenthood v. Casey*[241] was decided in his first year on the Court and although he joined Scalia's scathing dissent in this case, it was not until the partial-birth abortion cases that he had the opportunity to weigh in and personally explain why "the Court's abortion jurisprudence, including *Casey* and *Roe v. Wade*, [242] has no basis in the Constitution."[243]

As a result of the Court's decision in *Stenberg v. Carhart*,[244] Thomas was led to brand the Court's abortion jurisprudence as "a particularly virulent strain of constitutional exegesis."[245] In the decision, Breyer, writing for a five-member majority, found that a Nebraska statute criminalizing the performance of any "partial birth abortion" that was not necessary to save the life of the mother violated the U.S. Constitution as interpreted in *Roe* and *Casey*. The statute defined *partial birth abortion* as a procedure in which one "partially delivers vaginally a living unborn child before killing the unborn child and completing the delivery," and it defined the phrase *partially delivers vaginally a living unborn child* as intentionally delivering into the vagina a living unborn child or a substantial portion thereof. Breyer held the statute imposed "an undue burden" on a woman's ability to choose an abortion and lacked any exception to preserve the health of the woman.

Thomas dissented and was joined in his 15,500-word, 40-page opinion by Rehnquist and Scalia. He began by calling *Roe* "grievously wrong." Abortion, he asserted, "is a unique act, in which a woman's exercise of control over her own body ends, depending on one's view, human life or potential human life." He insisted that nothing in the Constitution "deprives the people of this country of the right to determine whether the consequences of abortion to the fetus and to society outweigh the burden of an unwanted pregnancy on the mother." Further, he averred, "although a State *may* permit abortion, nothing in the Constitution dictates that a State *must* do so."[246]

He then turned to *Casey*, declaring that the ruling in that case was created "out of whole cloth" and was devoid of any "historical or doctrinal pedigree"; he denounced its "undue burden" standard as the product of "its authors' own philosophical views about abortion." But, he continued, even if he assumed (as he said he would for the remainder of his dissent) that *Casey*'s "fabricated" undue burden standard merited adherence, the majority's decision was still "extraordinary," for it "inexplicably" held that the states "cannot constitutionally prohibit a method of abortion that millions find hard to distinguish from infanticide and that the Court hesitates even to describe."[247]

Thomas pointed out that in the thirty years since *Roe*, the Court had never described in detail the various methods for aborting a second- or third-trimester fetus but rather had "sanitized" those methods that are "so gruesome" that their use can be "traumatic even for the physicians and medical staff" who perform them. So, Thomas declared, "I begin with a discussion of these methods." The primary form is "dilation and evacuation [D&E]," in which a physician dilates the woman's cervix and then "extract[s] the fetus from her uterus with forceps . . . [by] dismembering the fetus one piece at a time." "At the end of the procedure, the physician is left . . . with a tray full of pieces."[248] But as Thomas pointed out, this procedure was not banned by Nebraska's statute. Neither was another method of abortion called induction, in which the "the amniotic sac is injected with an abortifacient such as a saline solution or a solution known as a prostaglandin. Uterine contractions typically follow, causing the fetus to be expelled."

What Nebraska banned was what medical professionals called "intact D&E" and what the statute called "partial birth abortion." Thomas described the procedure as follows:

> After dilating the cervix, the physician will grab the fetus by its feet and pull the fetal body out of the uterus into the vaginal cavity. . . . Assuming the physician has performed the dilation procedure correctly, the head will be held inside the uterus by the woman's cervix. While the fetus is stuck in this position, dangling partly out of the woman's body, and just a few inches from a completed birth, the physician uses an instrument such as a pair of scissors to tear or perforate the skull. The physician will then either crush the skull or will use a vacuum to remove the brain and other intracranial contents from the fetal skull, collapse the fetus' head, and pull the fetus from the uterus.[249]

For Thomas, there was no question that Nebraska had a valid interest in preventing this procedure: "*Casey* itself noted that States may 'express profound respect for the life of the unborn.' States may, without a doubt, express this profound respect by prohibiting a procedure that approaches infanticide, and thereby dehumanizes the fetus and trivializes human life." In his view, it required no "additional authority. In a civilized society, the answer is too obvious, and the contrary arguments too offensive to merit further discussion."[250]

Seven years later, with Alito having replaced O'Connor after her retirement, the Court again took up the question of the constitutionality of a ban on partial-birth abortion, this time one enacted by Congress. In a five-to-four decision in *Gonzales v. Carhart*, Kennedy rejected a facial challenge to the Partial-Birth Abortion Ban Act of 2003, concluding that the respondents had failed to demonstrate that it was void for vagueness or that it imposed an undue burden on a woman's right to an abortion based on its lack of a health exception. Thomas wrote a brief concurring opinion, reiterating his view that the Court's abortion jurisprudence has no basis in the Constitution but then, true to his federalist principles, posing the question of whether the act "constitutes a permissible exercise of Congress's power under the Commerce Clause." He recognized that "the parties did not raise or brief that issue; it is outside the question presented; and the lower courts did not address it," but he asked it nonetheless.[251]

This chapter has examined Thomas's original general meaning approach to the various substantive rights secured by the Bill of Rights and the Fourteenth Amendment. That approach has led him to reject the Court precedents that have incorporated the Establishment Clause to apply to the states because it prohibited precisely what the Clause was originally intended to protect—state establishments of religion; it also has led him to assert that much of the lower federal judiciary's confusion could be avoided were the Court to return to the views of the framers and adopt legal coercion as the touchstone of its Establishment Clause inquiry.

Regarding free speech and press, his original general meaning approach has led him to reject precedents that treated commercial speech as having less value than noncommercial speech; to spearhead the attack on campaign financial regulations through his rejection of *Buckley v. Valeo*, his insistence that both campaign contributions and expenditures "involve core First Amendment expression," and his argument that the First Amendment fully protects anonymous speech and therefore prohibits financial disclosure requirements; to argue consistently that broadcast, cable, and Internet companies should enjoy the same First Amendment protections as the print media; and to deny that minors have free speech rights in public schools or that the video game industry has a right to have access to minors to sell or rent to them its violent video games without their parents' consent. Interestingly, he did not employ his original general meaning approach in *Virginia v. Black*, arguing instead that cross burning was simply an act of intimidation and terror and rhetorically noting that the Court seemed more interested in protecting women seeking an abortion from the "unwanted communications" of right-to-life protesters than protecting the "physical safety" of blacks from KKK hoodlums.

Thomas's original general meaning approach was again on display in his argument in his lengthy concurrence in *McDonald*, stating that *The Slaughter-House Cases* should be overturned and the right to keep and bear arms should be understood to be a fundamental right of American citizenship that applies to the states through the Fourteenth Amendment's Privileges or Immunities Clause; in his refusal in *Kelo* to join the Court as it converted the "Public Use" Clause into a "Public Purpose" Clause; and in his insistence that the Court's abortion jurisprudence has no basis in the Constitution.

What is striking in a number of the cases reviewed in this chapter is how Thomas combines his originalism with a passionate concern for the members of his race.[252] His *McDonald* concurrence is animated by his loathing of the Court's decision in *Cruikshank* and its holding that barred federal enforcement of the inalienable right to keep and bear arms—a holding that tragically allowed the Klan and others to launch a campaign of terror against the very people the Fourteenth Amendment had just made citizens, individuals it was intended to protect. His *Kelo* dissent concluded that the "predictable consequence" of allowing local governments to use the power of eminent domain for purposes of economic development would fall disproportionately on poor black communities. An analysis of Thomas's combined focus on originalism and race is continued in chapter 6.

But first, chapter 5 will move from substantive rights to procedural rights. Specifically, it will consider how Thomas applies his original general meaning approach to the Constitution's various criminal procedural provisions.

Chapter Five

Thomas's Original General Meaning Approach to Criminal Procedural Rights

Early in his first year on the Supreme Court, Thomas wrote a dissent in *Hudson v. McMillian*[1] that earned him the epithet from the editorial board of the *New York Times* as the Court's "cruelest justice."[2] Keith Hudson, a Louisiana inmate, brought a § 1983 action against Jack McMillian and two other prison guards, claiming that they, acting under color of law, had violated his Eighth Amendment right to be free from cruel and unusual punishment by using excessive physical force against him when there was no need to do so. After a district court judge ruled in Hudson's favor and awarded him $800 in damages, the Fifth Circuit reversed, noting that the injuries inflicted on Hudson were minor and required no medical attention. The Supreme Court granted certiorari and, by a seven-to-two vote, held for Hudson. In her opinion for the Court, Justice O'Connor reminded her colleagues that the Eighth Amendment's prohibition of cruel and unusual punishments "draw[s] its meaning from the evolving standards of decency that mark the progress of a maturing society," and she concluded that "contemporary standards of decency always are violated" when prison officials "maliciously and sadistically use force to cause harm," regardless of whether or not it results in significant injury.[3]

Thomas filed a dissent, joined by Scalia: "In my view, a use of force that causes only insignificant harm to a prisoner may be immoral, it may be tortious, it may be criminal, and it may even be remediable under other provisions of the Federal Constitution, but it is not 'cruel and unusual punishment.'"[4] This statement was a pure expression of his original general meaning approach to the Constitution's criminal procedural provisions. He pointed out that until 1976 when the Court in *Estelle v. Gamble*[5] held for the first time that the Eighth Amendment applied to conditions of confinement, "the Cruel and Unusual Punishment Clause was not deemed to apply at all to deprivations that were not inflicted as part of the sentence for a crime. For generations, judges and commentators regarded the Eighth Amendment as applying only to torturous punishments meted out by statutes or sentencing judges, and not generally to any hardship that might befall a prisoner during incarceration." He relied on the Court's 1910 decision in *Weems v. United*

States,[6] which he declared had "extensively chronicled" the amendment's English antecedents, its adoption by the First Congress, and the contemporaneous "interpretation of analogous provisions by state courts," and he concluded that it only "govern[ed] punishments that were part of the sentence."[7] He described the majority opinion as "yet another manifestation of the pervasive view that the Federal Constitution must address all ills in our society. Abusive behavior by prison guards is deplorable conduct that properly evokes outrage and contempt. But that does not mean that it is invariably unconstitutional." And to the extent this abusive behavior was unconstitutional, Thomas argued that it was because it violated the Due Process Clause of the Fourteenth Amendment, a provision that Hudson's attorneys "concede[d]" was available to him but that they did not pursue. Since he considered the possible denial of due process to be "the appropriate, and appropriately limited, federal constitutional inquiry in this case," Thomas was loath to see the Eighth Amendment—originally intended by its drafters and understood by its ratifiers to be simply a limitation on the sentences that legislatures and judges could impose—"turned into a National Code of Prison Regulation."[8] And for that stance he won the enmity of the *New York Times*.

Despite the bad press he received, Thomas held to his convictions, and the next year, he again filed a dissent (once more joined by Scalia) in another case involving conditions of confinement. In *Helling v. McKinney*,[9] Justice Byron White built on *Hudson* and held for a seven-member majority that the Eighth Amendment applies not only to minor injuries to inmates but also to what Thomas described as the "mere risk of injury"[10] (in this case, the dangers associated with secondhand smoke—what the Court called "environmental tobacco smoke"). In this longer dissent, Thomas was able to display at length his jurisprudence of constitutional restoration.

He began with the amendment's original public meaning, citing dictionaries of the era.

> At the time the Eighth Amendment was ratified, the word "punishment" referred to the penalty imposed for the commission of a crime. See 2 T. Cunningham, *A New and Complete Law-Dictionary* (1771) ("the penalty of transgressing the laws"); 2 T. Sheridan, *A General Dictionary of the English Language* (1780) ("[a]ny infliction imposed in vengeance of a crime"); J. Walker, *A Critical Pronouncing Dictionary* (1791) (same); 4 G. Jacob, *The Law-Dictionary: Explaining the Rise, Progress, and Present State, of the English Law* 343 (1811) ("[t]he penalty for transgressing the Law"); 2 N. Webster, *American Dictionary of the English Language* (1828) ("[a]ny pain or suffering inflicted on a person for a crime or offense").[11]

He then cited the most recent (1990) edition of *Black's Law Dictionary* to show that a court's imposition of a sentence was "also the primary definition of the word today"—a definition that "does not encompass a prisoner's injuries that bear no relation to his sentence."[12]

Thomas then moved to an original intent and original understanding approach to the Eighth Amendment: "Nor, as far as I know, is there any historical evidence indicating that the framers and ratifiers of the Eighth Amendment had anything other than this common understanding of 'punishment' in mind." Calling the English Declaration of Rights of 1689 the "antecedent of our constitutional text," he observed that "the best historical evidence" suggests the "cruell and unusuall Punishments" provision of the Declaration of Rights was "a response to *sentencing* abuses of the King's Bench."[13] There was "no suggestion in English constitutional history that harsh prison conditions might constitute cruel and unusual (or otherwise illegal) punishment." Thomas continued:

> The debates surrounding the framing and ratification of our own
> Constitution and Bill of Rights were silent regarding this possibility. See 2
> J. Elliot, *Debates on the Federal Constitution* 111 (2d ed. 1854) (Congress
> should be prevented from "inventing the most cruel and unheard-of
> punishments, and annexing them to crimes") (emphasis added); 1 *Annals
> of Cong.* 753–754 (1789). The same can be said of the early commentaries.
> See 3 J. Story, *Commentaries on the Constitution of the United States* 750–
> 751 (1833); T. Cooley, *Constitutional Limitations* 694 (8th ed. 1927).[14]

Interestingly, Thomas then noted that "to the extent that there is any affirmative historical evidence as to whether injuries sustained in prison might constitute 'punishment' for Eighth Amendment purposes," that evidence was "consistent with the ordinary meaning of the word." He pointed out, for example, that the Declaration of Rights in the Delaware Constitution of 1792 contained an "analogue of the Eighth Amendment" in that it provided that "excessive bail shall not be required, nor excessive fines imposed, nor cruel or unusual punishments inflicted"; however, he noted, it then went on to add the following: "*and in the construction of jails a proper regard shall be had to the health of prisoners.*"[15] For him, this was evidence that when "members of the founding generation wished to make prison conditions a matter of constitutional guarantee, they knew how to do so."[16]

Thomas reminded his colleagues that the Supreme Court's interpretations of the Cruel and Unusual Punishments Clause were, for the first 185 years of the provision's existence, consistent with its text and history. The Court "did not so much as intimate that the Cruel and Unusual Punishments Clause might reach prison conditions"[17] until the *Estelle* decision in 1976, in which it held that "deliberate indifference to serious medical needs of prisoners"[18] violated the Eighth Amendment. Though he had only suggested as much in his dissent in *Hudson*, Thomas now forthrightly declared that he "seriously doubt[ed] that *Estelle* was correctly decided,"[19] not because the medical needs of inmates were of no constitutional concern to him but because those needs were much more appropriately addressed by the Due Process Clauses of the Fifth and Fourteenth Amendments.

He concluded by calling *Estelle* a "dubious precedent."[20] He stated, "The text and history of the Eighth Amendment, together with pre-*Estelle* precedent, raise substantial doubts in my mind that the Eighth Amendment proscribes a prison deprivation that is not inflicted as part of a sentence. And *Estelle* itself has not dispelled these doubts." He announced, "Were the issue squarely presented, therefore, I might vote to overrule *Estelle*." He acknowledged that "*stare decisis* may call for hesitation in overruling a dubious precedent," but "it does not demand that such a precedent be expanded to its outer limits." Rather, it demands "draw[ing] the line at actual, serious injuries and reject[ing] the claim that exposure to the *risk* of injury can violate the Eighth Amendment."[21]

Thomas's early opinions on the original general meaning of the Cruel and Unusual Punishments Clause provide a window into his approach to the other criminal procedural rights found in the original Constitution, the Bill of Rights, and the Fourteenth Amendment. He consistently wants to apply the constitutional text as its words demand and as it was explained by those who drafted and ratified them.

The Ex Post Facto Clauses

The Ex Post Facto Clauses of Article I, §§ 9 and 10, which prohibit Congress and state legislatures from passing ex post facto laws, have been understood by the Supreme Court since 1798 in *Calder v. Bull*[22] to apply solely to criminal laws, not civil laws. However, as mentioned in chapters 1 and 4, Thomas indicated in his 1998 concurrence in *Eastern Enterprises v. Apfel*[23] that he had never "been convinced of the soundness of this limitation" and that, "in an appropriate case," he "would be willing to reconsider *Calder* and its progeny to determine whether a retroactive civil law" is also unconstitutional under the Ex Post Facto Clauses.[24] When Thomas expresses a willingness to reconsider a controlling precedent he thinks unsound, he almost invariably prefaces his willingness to do so with a detailed original general meaning assessment of what the text in question actually means. Curiously, however, he did not do so in *Apfel*. Moreover, since his original general meaning approach includes a consideration of the text's original public meaning (what it meant to the society that adopted it), it is striking that he failed to explain why a 1798 decision, handed down only a decade after the Constitution was ratified, did not reflect that original public meaning.

Ex post facto cases are relatively rare, but when they do arise, Thomas employs his original general meaning approach to resolve them. In *California Department of Corrections v. Morales*,[25] he wrote for a seven-member majority and reversed a Ninth Circuit decision that held the Ex Post Facto Clause of Article I, § 10 was violated when a 1981 California statute was passed allowing the Board of Prison Terms the discretion to decrease the frequency of parole suitability hearings (from annually to once every two or three years) for those who were convicted of committing their crimes prior to the statute's enactment.[26]

Thomas began by reaffirming that the Ex Post Facto Clause incorporated "a term of art with an established meaning at the time of the framing of the Constitution." And, he continued, "in accordance with this original understanding, we have held that the Clause is aimed at laws that 'retroactively alter the definition of crimes or increase the punishment for criminal acts.'"[27] Since California had not changed the definition of Jose Ramon Morales's crime, "the question before us is whether the 1981 [statute] . . . increases the 'punishment' attached to respondent's crime."[28] His answer was no.

Both before and after the 1981 statute, California punished the offense of second-degree murder, of which Morales was convicted, with an indeterminate sentence of "confinement in the state prison for a term of 15 years to life." Thomas noted that the 1981 statute "made only one change"—it allowed the Board of Prison Terms, after the initial parole hearing, to deny another hearing the next year or the year after that if it found no reasonable probability that the prisoner would be deemed suitable for parole in the interim period.[29] At the time of the 1981 statute's enactment, the board was already finding 90 percent of all prisoners unsuitable for parole at the initial hearing and 85 percent unsuitable at the second and subsequent hearings. Therefore, he found persuasive the California Supreme Court's conclusion that the statute "was a means to 'relieve the Board from the costly and time-consuming responsibility of scheduling parole hearings for prisoners who have no chance of being released.'"[30]

Moreover, Thomas argued, even if the board were to postpone the time until a prisoner's next suitability hearing, "there is no reason to think that such postponement would extend any prisoner's actual period of confinement." The California Supreme Court had declared the possibility of immediate release after a finding of suitability for parole to be largely "theoretica[l]," with a prisoner's parole release date coming at least several years after a finding of suitability—the board being bound by statute to consider "any sentencing information relevant to the setting of parole release dates" with an eye toward establishing "uniform terms for offenses of similar gravity and magnitude in respect to their threat to the public." Under these standards, "a prisoner's ultimate date of release would be entirely unaffected by the change in the timing of suitability hearings."[31] Given these circumstances, Thomas concluded that the California legislation at issue created "only the most speculative and attenuated risk of increasing the measure of punishment attached to the covered crimes" and thus did not violate the Ex Post Facto Clause.[32]

By contrast, two years later in *Lynce v. Mathis*,[33] he found a petitioner's punishment to be "neither 'speculative' nor 'attenuated'" and therefore concurred in part with Justice Stevens's majority in finding an ex post facto violation.[34] While serving his sentence for attempted murder, Kenneth Lynce accumulated release credits, under a Florida statute adopted in response to prison overcrowding, that enabled him to be released from prison early. Shortly before he secured his release, however, the Florida legislature enacted a statute preventing certain categories of offenders from taking advantage of these release credits. Although Lynce's offense placed him in one of those categories, the statute was not applied retroactively, and he was thus released. However, the state attorney general subsequently issued an opinion giving the statute retroactive effect, leading to Lynce's rearrest and return to custody. As Thomas noted, the case involved "not merely an effect on the availability of *future* release credits, but the retroactive elimination of credits already earned and used."[35] Because Florida's law as interpreted by its attorney general retroactively canceled Lynce's release credits after he had used them to gain his freedom, it "violate[d] the Ex Post Facto Clause."[36]

A major question in ex post facto cases is whether the law in question is civil or criminal in nature. This was the central question in *Kansas v. Hendricks*,[37] in which Thomas, writing for a five-member majority, rejected the claim that Kansas had violated the Constitution's ban on ex post facto lawmaking when it passed its Sexually Violent Predator Act, establishing procedures for the civil commitment of persons who, due to a "mental abnormality" or a "personality disorder," are likely to engage in "predatory acts of sexual violence." Kansas filed a petition under the act in state court to have Leroy Hendricks, who had a long history of sexually molesting children, civilly committed upon his scheduled release from prison. After a jury determined that he was a sexually violent predator, the court ordered him committed.

Thomas argued that the act does not establish a criminal proceeding and that involuntary confinement under it is not punishment. Whether a particular proceeding is civil or criminal is, he insisted, a question of statutory construction. Accordingly, he argued that "we must initially ascertain whether the legislature meant the statute to establish 'civil' proceedings. If so, we ordinarily defer to the legislature's stated intent. Here, Kansas' objective to create a civil proceeding is evidenced by its placement of the Act within the Kansas probate code, instead of the criminal code, as well as its description of the Act as creating a '*civil commitment procedure.*'"[38] Thomas saw nothing on the face of the act to suggest that the Kansas legislature sought to create anything other than a civil-commitment scheme.

Additionally, he insisted, commitment under the act did not implicate either of the two primary objectives of criminal punishment: retribution or deterrence. Its purpose was not retributive; it did not affix culpability for prior criminal conduct but rather used such conduct solely for evidentiary purposes. It did not make criminal conviction a prerequisite for commitment, and it lacked a scienter requirement, an important element in distinguishing criminal and civil statutes.[39] Nor, he argued, could the act be said to serve as a deterrent, since persons with a mental abnormality or personality disorder were unlikely to be deterred by the threat of confinement. The conditions surrounding confinement, which were essentially the same as conditions for any civilly committed patient, did not suggest a punitive purpose. Although the state's commitment scheme involved an affirmative restraint, such restraint of the dangerously mentally ill had been historically regarded as a legitimate nonpunitive objective. "If detention for the purpose of protecting the community from harm *necessarily* constituted punishment, then all involuntary civil commitments would have to be considered punishment. But we have never so held."[40]

Thomas found the potential for indefinite confinement to be linked not to any punitive objective but to the purpose of holding a person until his mental abnormality no longer caused him to be a threat to others. If, at any time, the confined person was adjudged "safe to be at large," he was statutorily entitled to immediate release. Furthermore, "commitment under the Act is only *potentially* indefinite. The maximum amount of time an individual can be incapacitated pursuant to a single judicial proceeding is one year. If Kansas seeks to continue the detention beyond that year, a court must once again determine beyond a reasonable doubt that the detainee satisfies the same standards as required for the initial confinement."[41] All of this led Thomas to conclude:

> Where the State has "disavowed any punitive intent"; limited confinement to a small segment of particularly dangerous individuals; provided strict procedural safeguards; directed that confined persons be segregated from the general prison population and afforded the same status as others who have been civilly committed; recommended treatment if such is possible; and permitted immediate release upon a showing that the individual is no longer dangerous or mentally impaired, we cannot say that it acted with punitive intent. We therefore hold that the Act does not establish

criminal proceedings and that involuntary confinement pursuant to the Act is not punitive. . . . [And] because the Act does not criminalize conduct legal before its enactment, nor deprive Hendricks of any defense that was available to him at the time of his crimes, the Act does not violate the Ex Post Facto Clause.[42]

Thomas built on his *Hendricks* majority opinion in *Selling v. Young*.[43] Washington passed a statute similar to Kansas's Sexually Violent Predator Act. After Andre Brigham Young, who was convicted of six rapes over three decades, was civilly committed at the end of his prison term as a sexually violent predator and was confined at a special commitment center, he appealed his commitment, alleging that the actual confinement conditions he experienced divested a facially valid statute of its civil label upon a showing by the clearest proof that the statutory scheme was punitive in effect and therefore in violation of the Ex Post Facto Clause. In an eight-to-one decision, the Supreme Court rejected Young's contentions. Thomas concurred in the Court's judgment. Taking a more forceful line than Justice O'Connor's majority opinion, he argued that actions by an administrative agency can never convert a civil law to a criminal one. His argument was reminiscent of his dissent in *Hudson v. McMillian*, where he argued that brutal behavior by prison guards did not constitute punishment and could not convert those actions into a violation of the Eighth Amendment.

Thomas noted that the Court had granted certiorari to decide whether "an *otherwise* valid civil statute can be divested of its civil nature" simply because of an administrative agency's failure to implement the statute according to its terms.[44] He then chided his colleagues, "The majority declines to answer this question . . . [and] expressly reserves judgment on whether the manner of implementation should affect a court's assessment of a statute as civil in the 'first instance.'" He declared that he was writing separately "to express my view, first, that a statute which is civil on its face cannot be divested of its civil nature simply because of the manner in which it is implemented, and second, that the distinction between a challenge in the 'first instance' and a subsequent challenge is one without a difference."[45] For Thomas, an implementation-based challenge to a facially civil statute was "inappropriate" "because the actual conditions of confinement may change over time and may vary from facility to facility." In his view, "an implementation-based challenge, if successful, would serve to invalidate a statute that may be implemented without any constitutional infirmities at a future time or in a separate facility."[46]

Thomas reiterated his objections to implementation-based challenges in his concurring opinion in *Smith v. Doe*.[47] Many states, including Alaska, enacted statutes that were versions of New Jersey's Megan's Law, named for a child victim who had been sexually assaulted and murdered by a neighbor who, unknown to the victim's family, had prior convictions for sex offenses against children. Alaska's statute required that persons convicted of sex or child-kidnapping offenses had to register with state or local law enforcement authorities and that information, including the offenders' names and addresses, had to be made public. Though the statute did not specify the means of notifying the public, Alaska chose to make most of this information available on the Internet. Two individuals who had been convicted of sexually abusing a minor before the Alaska statute's enactment sought a declaration that its provisions violated the Constitution's ban on ex post facto laws. They argued, in part, that the decision by Alaskan officials to post this information on the Internet was punitive, therefore making it a criminal law prohibited by Article I, § 10.

Thomas joined the Court majority but again wrote a separate concurrence; he cited *Selling* to reiterate that "'there is no place for an implementation-based challenge' in our ex post facto jurisprudence."[48] He insisted that the determination of whether a scheme is criminal or civil must be limited to the analysis of the obligations actually created by statute. In this case, the Alaska statute did not specify the means of making information related to sexual offenders available to the public. The decision to use the Internet to make this information available came from the Department of Public Safety, not the Alaska legislature. By even considering whether Internet dissemination might render the statute punitive, Thomas accused the Court of "stray[ing] from the statute," prompting him only to concur.[49]

The Fourth Amendment

In *Florida v. White*,[50] Thomas delivered the opinion for a seven-member majority and held that the Fourth Amendment does not require the police to obtain a warrant before seizing an automobile from a public place when they have probable cause to believe that the vehicle is forfeitable contraband. Proceeding in an original general meaning manner, he declared that "in deciding whether a governmental action violates the Amendment," the Court must "inquire whether the action was regarded as an unlawful search and seizure when the Amendment was framed."[51] He noted that in *United States v. Carroll*,[52] the Court had held that when federal officers have probable cause to believe that an automobile contains contraband, the Fourth Amendment does not require them to obtain a warrant prior to searching the car for and seizing the contraband. He argued that the "holding was rooted in federal law enforcement practice at the time of the adoption of the Fourth Amendment," for it specifically considered laws passed by the First, Second, and Fourth Congresses authorizing federal officers to conduct warrantless searches of ships and to seize concealed goods subject to duties. These enactments, "contemporaneous with the adoption of the Fourth Amendment," showed that Congress clearly distinguished between goods subject to forfeiture concealed in a building and "like goods in course of transportation and concealed in a movable vessel where they readily could be put out of reach of a search warrant."[53]

For Thomas, the principles laid out in *Carroll* and the acts of the initial Congresses upon which they were based "fully support[ed]" the Court's conclusion that the warrantless seizure of Tyvessel Tyvorus White's car did not violate the Fourth Amendment. And though the police lacked probable cause to believe that his car contained contraband, "they certainly had probable cause to believe that the vehicle *itself* was contraband under Florida law." The "founding era statutes" recognized the need to seize readily movable contraband before it could be spirited away, he said, and "this need is equally weighty when the *automobile*, as opposed to its contents, is the contraband that the police seek to secure." Furthermore, those early federal statutes, like the Florida Contraband Forfeiture Act at issue in the instant case, "authorized the warrantless seizure of *both* goods subject to duties *and* the ships upon which those goods were concealed." Thomas then cited three statutes passed by the First Congress—"See, *e.g.*, 1 Stat. 43, 46; 1 Stat. 170, 174; 1 Stat. 677, 678, 692."[54]

White focused on whether there was a need for a warrant, but as Thomas elaborated in *Groh v. Ramirez*,[55] there is no "precise relationship" between the Fourth Amendment's Warrant Clause ("No Warrants shall issue, but upon probable cause, supported by Oath or affirmation, and particularly describing the place to be searched, and the persons or things to be seized") and its Unreasonableness Clause ("The right of the people to be secure in their persons, houses, papers, and effects, against unreasonable searches and seizures, shall not be violated"). Neither Clause, he argued, "explicitly requires" a warrant.[56] The text of the Fourth Amendment "certainly does not mandate this result." And even though the amendment's history makes clear that its principal target was general warrants, it is far less "clear with respect to when warrants were required, if ever." Thomas, in fact, conceded that "because of the very different nature and scope of federal authority and ability to conduct searches and arrests at the founding, it is possible that neither the history of the Fourth Amendment nor the common law provides much guidance."[57]

However, he pointed out that, over time, the Court has recognized "a plethora of exceptions" to the presumptive unreasonableness of a warrantless search: searches incident to arrest, automobile searches, searches of "pervasively regulated business," administrative searches, exigent circumstances, mobile home searches, inventory searches, and border searches. He wrote, "Our cases stand for the illuminating proposition that warrantless searches are *per se* unreasonable, except, of course, when they are not." Instead of adding to this "confusing jurisprudence," he invited his colleagues to "turn to first principles in order to determine the relationship between the Warrant Clause and the Unreasonableness Clause." Rather than adding to "the sheer number of exceptions to the Court's categorical warrant requirement," Thomas would simply ask in all cases "whether the search was unreasonable."[58]

Thomas asked that question in *Wilson v. Arkansas.*[59] Sharlene Wilson was convicted on state-law drug charges after the Arkansas trial court denied her evidence-suppression motion, in which she asserted that the search of her home was invalid because the police had violated the common-law principle requiring them to announce their presence and authority before entering. The state supreme court affirmed, rejecting her argument that the common-law "knock and announce" principle was required by the Fourth Amendment. For a unanimous Court, Thomas held that at the time of the ratification of the Fourth Amendment in 1791, the common law of search and seizure recognized a law enforcement officer's authority to break open the doors of a dwelling but only if he first announced his presence and authority. And because this common-law knock and announce principle was recognized when the amendment was ratified, it formed a part of the reasonableness inquiry under the Fourth Amendment.[60] He elaborated:

> Our own cases have acknowledged that the common-law principle of announcement is "embedded in Anglo-American law," but we have never squarely held that this principle is an element of the reasonableness inquiry under the Fourth Amendment. We now so hold. Given the longstanding common-law endorsement of the practice of announcement, we have little doubt that the Framers of the Fourth Amendment thought that the method of an officer's entry into a dwelling was among the factors to be considered in assessing the reasonableness of a search or seizure.[61]

Thomas asked that question in *City of Indianapolis v. Edmond.*"[62] In writing the majority opinion in this case, Justice O'Connor distinguished between, on the one hand, suspicionless searches at fixed checkpoints designed to intercept illegal aliens, upheld by the Court in *United States v. Martinez-Fuerte,*[63] and sobriety checkpoints aimed at removing drunk drivers from the road, upheld by the Court in *Michigan Department of State Police v. Sitz,*[64] and, on the other hand, Indianapolis's use of checkpoints on its roads in an effort to interdict unlawful drugs. The former, she argued, were designed to serve purposes closely related to the problems of policing the border or the necessity of ensuring roadway safety. By contrast, the latter was indistinguishable from a general interest in crime control. Thomas, in dissent, wanted to scrape away past precedents and go back to bare wood—to the original general meaning of the Fourth Amendment. He declared: "I am not convinced that *Sitz* and *Martinez-Fuerte* were correctly decided. Indeed, I rather doubt that the Framers of the Fourth Amendment would have considered 'reasonable' a program of indiscriminate stops of individuals not suspected of wrongdoing." However, since James Edmond did not argue for the overruling of these decisions, Thomas yielded, announcing, "I am reluctant to consider such a step without the benefit of briefing and argument."[65]

He asked that question again in *Board of Education of Independent School District No. 92 of Pottawatomie County v. Earls.*[66] He held for a five-member majority that a school's policy of requiring all students who participated in competitive extracurricular activities to submit to suspicionless drug testing was "a reasonable means of furthering the school district's important interest in preventing and deterring drug use among its schoolchildren"[67] and, therefore, did not violate the Fourth Amendment.

He confronted this question once again in *Georgia v. Randolph.*[68] When a police officer arrived at a married couple's home in Georgia as a result of the estranged wife's call to the police concerning a domestic dispute, the wife, in the presence of the husband, volunteered to the officer that there was evidence in the house of her husband's illegal drug use. Although the husband unequivocally refused the officer's request for permission to conduct a warrantless search of the house, the wife nonetheless consented to a search and led the officer to a stash of cocaine, which the policeman seized; after obtaining a search warrant, the officer returned to seize further evidence of drug use. The husband was indicted under state law for cocaine possession but moved to suppress the evidence in question on grounds that it had been obtained as the result of an illegal search. After he was convicted, the husband appealed all the way to the Supreme Court, where Souter, for a five-member majority, held that a physically present co-occupant's stated refusal to permit entry rendered the warrantless entry and search unreasonable and invalid. Thomas dissented. He pointed out that the Supreme Court had long recognized that it is an act of responsible citizenship for individuals to give whatever information they may have to aid in law enforcement and that, as a consequence, no unreasonable search in violation of the Fourth Amendment occurs when a spouse of an accused voluntarily leads the police to potential evidence of wrongdoing by the accused.[69]

Thomas once again confronted the question of when a search is reasonable in *Samson v. California,*[70] where he held for a five-member majority that it was reasonable under the Fourth Amendment for a police officer to conduct a suspicionless search of a parolee. He began by noting California law provides that every prisoner eligible for release on state parole "shall agree in writing to be subject to search or seizure by a parole officer or other peace officer at any time of the day or night, with or without a search warrant and with or without cause."[71] He next cited *United States v. Knights*,[72] which upheld a similar California law pertaining to probationers. Thomas then placed probationers and parolees on a "continuum" and found that on "this continuum, parolees have fewer expectations of privacy than probationers, because parole is more akin to imprisonment than probation is to imprisonment.[73] Thus, if warrantless searches were reasonable for probationers, they were even more so for parolees.

Thomas asked the question of when a search is reasonable once again in *Missouri v. McNeely*,[74] when he filed a lone dissent from Justice Sonia Sotomayor's opinion that in drunk-driving investigations, the natural dissipation of alcohol in the bloodstream does not constitute an exigency in every case sufficient to justify conducting a blood test without a warrant. Because he was convinced that "the body's natural metabolization of alcohol inevitably destroys evidence of the crime, it constitutes an exigent circumstance. As a result, I would hold that a warrantless blood draw does not violate the Fourth Amendment."[75]

Fourth Amendment jurisprudence requires the Court to ask not only whether a particular search or seizure is constitutional but also what to do with evidence that has been unconstitutionally obtained. The Supreme Court's general answer since *Weeks v. United States*[76] in federal cases and *Mapp v. Ohio*[77] in state cases has been to apply the exclusionary rule — evidence seized in violation of the Fourth Amendment must be excluded from introduction at criminal trials. The Court has defended the exclusionary rule as necessary to deter law enforcement personnel from violating the Fourth Amendment rights of criminal defendants.[78]

In *Pennsylvania Board of Probation and Parole v. Scott*,[79] Thomas held for a five-member majority that the exclusionary rule does not apply in parole revocation proceedings. He pointed out that in a series of prior cases, the Court had "repeatedly declined to extend the exclusionary rule to proceedings other than criminal trials"; thus, the rule does not apply to grand jury proceedings, civil tax proceedings, or civil deportation proceedings. Thomas noted that the exclusionary rule "imposes significant costs" by "preclud[ing] consideration of reliable, probative evidence" and by "undeniably detract[ing] from the truthfinding process."[80] These costs are "particularly high" with regard to parole, for they "hinder the functioning of state parole systems."[81] He continued:

> Parole is a "variation on imprisonment of convicted criminals," in which the State accords a limited degree of freedom in return for the parolee's assurance that he will comply with the often strict terms and conditions of

his release. In most cases, the State is willing to extend parole only because it is able to condition it upon compliance with certain requirements. The State thus has an "overwhelming interest" in ensuring that a parolee complies with those requirements and is returned to prison if he fails to do so. The exclusion of evidence establishing a parole violation, however, hampers the State's ability to ensure compliance with these conditions by permitting the parolee to avoid the consequences of his noncompliance. The costs of allowing a parolee to avoid the consequences of his violation are compounded by the fact that parolees (particularly those who have already committed parole violations) are more likely to commit future criminal offenses than are average citizens. Indeed, this is the very premise behind the system of close parole supervision.[82]

Since the exclusionary rule would also "severely disrupt the traditionally informal, administrative process of parole revocation," Thomas concluded that "parole boards are not required by federal law to exclude evidence obtained in violation of the Fourth Amendment."[83]

The Meaning of "Witness" in the Fifth and Sixth Amendments

The Fifth Amendment contains the Self-Incrimination Clause: "No person . . . shall be compelled in any criminal case to be a witness against himself." The Sixth Amendment contains the Compulsory Process Clause: "In all criminal prosecutions, the accused shall enjoy the right . . . to have compulsory process for obtaining witnesses in his favor"; it also contains the Confrontation Clause: "In all criminal prosecutions, the accused shall enjoy the right . . . to be confronted with witnesses against him." Thomas has brought his original general meaning approach to these three provisions in ways that have both expanded and constricted the rights of the accused.

In 1965 in *Griffin v. California*,[84] the Supreme Court held that the Self-Incrimination Clause of the Fifth Amendment, as incorporated by the Fourteenth Amendment to apply to the states, prohibited prosecutors and judges from commenting adversely on criminal defendants' refusal to testify on their own behalf. Thirty-four years later in *Mitchell v. United States*,[85] Justice Kennedy expanded on *Griffin* and, in a five-to-four decision, held that a guilty plea does not waive the privilege against self-incrimination at sentencing. In particular, he announced that despite the defendant's guilty plea to conspiring to distribute and distributing cocaine, she preserved her right to remain silent about the details of her crimes and that as a consequence the sentencing judge could not draw any adverse inferences from her silence—in this case, noting that her failure to testify at her sentencing hearing was a factor in persuading the court to rely on her codefendant's testimony that she had distributed over 5 kilograms of cocaine, requiring her to receive a mandatory minimum sentence of ten years.

Thomas dissented, as did Scalia. Scalia's dissent was more comprehensive and was joined by Rehnquist, O'Connor, and Thomas. He began by noting that as "an original matter, it would seem to me that the threat of an adverse inference does not 'compel' anyone to testify. It is one of the natural (and not governmentally imposed) consequences of failing to testify—as is the factfinder's increased readiness to believe the incriminating testimony that the defendant chooses not to contradict."[86] But, he noted, the Court's decision in *Griffin* "did not even pretend to be rooted in a historical understanding of the Fifth Amendment. Rather, in a breathtaking act of sorcery it simply transformed legislative policy into constitutional command." He declared that "*Griffin* was a wrong turn—which is not cause enough to overrule it, but is cause enough to resist its extension."[87]

Dissenting separately, Thomas built on Scalia's arguments, finding that Scalia had "persuasively" demonstrated that *Griffin* lacked "foundation in the Constitution's text, history, or logic."[88] *Griffin* relied on the premise that comments about a defendant's silence penalized the exercise of his Fifth Amendment privilege, but, as Thomas pointed out, "this so-called 'penalty' lacks any constitutional significance, since the explicit constitutional guarantee has been fully honored— a defendant is not 'compelled . . . to be a witness against himself' merely because the jury has been told that it may draw an adverse inference from his failure to testify." Thomas asserted that "at bottom, *Griffin* constitutionalizes a policy choice that a majority of the Court found desirable at the time. . . . This sort of undertaking is not an exercise in constitutional interpretation but an act of judicial willfulness that has no logical stopping point."[89] Even though he was ready to overturn what he considered bad law, Thomas acknowledged that since the case "asks only whether the principle established in *Griffin* should be extended," he could not succeed on that front, so he simply "agree[d] that the Fifth Amendment does not prohibit a sentencer from drawing an adverse inference from a defendant's failure to testify and, therefore, join[ed] Justice Scalia's dissent."[90]

Thomas's originalism led him to limit the reach of the Self-Incrimination Clause in *Mitchell* but to expand it significantly in another dimension just one year later in *United States v. Hubbell*.[91] The facts in this case are complicated. In 1994, upon the request of the U.S. attorney general, Kenneth Starr was appointed an independent counsel to investigate possible criminal violations relating to, among other matters, President Bill Clinton's relationships with various business entities. In the course of this investigation, Webster Hubbell, a former U.S. associate attorney general, was charged with mail fraud and tax evasion arising out of his billing practices as a member of an Arkansas law firm from 1989 to 1992. In a guilty-plea agreement, Hubbell promised to provide Starr with information about matters relating to the investigation.

In 1996, Starr obtained a subpoena *duces tecum* that called on Hubbell to produce documents before a federal grand jury sitting in Little Rock, Arkansas. Hubbell appeared before the grand jury and invoked his Fifth Amendment privilege against self-incrimination. However, Starr obtained a federal court order directing Hubbell to respond to the subpoena, granting him immunity against the use and derivative use of this compelled testimony. Hubbell delivered the specified documents but was subsequently indicted by a federal grand jury in the District of Columbia, charging him with various tax-related crimes and mail and wire fraud.

The U.S. District Court for the District of Columbia dismissed the indictment, concluding that all of the evidence that would have been offered against Hubbell at trial derived either directly or indirectly from the testimonial aspects of his immunized act of producing those documents. After the U.S. Court of Appeals for the District of Columbia Circuit vacated the district court's judgment and remanded it for further proceedings, the Supreme Court granted certiorari and held that Hubbell's indictment had to be dismissed because the federal government could not prove that the evidence it used to obtain the indictment was derived from legitimate sources that were entirely independent of the testimonial aspect of Hubbell's immunized conduct in producing the subpoenaed documents.

Thomas, joined by Scalia, concurred in the Court's opinion. He agreed that the Supreme Court had properly applied the act-of-production doctrine, which provides that persons compelled to turn over incriminating papers or other physical evidence pursuant to a subpoena *duces tecum* may invoke the Fifth Amendment privilege against self-incrimination as a bar to production only when the act of producing the evidence would contain "testimonial" features. But he wrote separately (1) to express the view that the doctrine was very likely inconsistent with the original meaning of the Fifth Amendment's Self-Incrimination Clause, which understood the privilege to protect against the compelled production not only of incriminating testimony but also of any incriminating evidence, and (2) to indicate that in a future case, he would be willing to reconsider the scope and meaning of the Self-Incrimination Clause.[92]

It was a classic Thomas opinion, employing all the elements of his original general meaning jurisprudence. As he observed, "The key word at issue in this case is 'witness.'" The Court, relying on prior cases, had essentially defined a *witness* as a person who provides testimony, thus restricting the Fifth Amendment's ban to only those communications that were "testimonial" in character.

However, he noted, none of these cases had undertaken "an analysis of the meaning of the term at the time of the founding." His review of that period "revealed
substantial support for the view that the term 'witness' meant a person who gives
or furnishes evidence, a broader meaning than that which our case law currently
ascribes to the term." Consequently, he asserted, "a person who responds to a
subpoena *duces tecum* would be just as much a 'witness' as a person who responds
to a subpoena *ad testificandum.*"[93]

He found that support, first of all, in both law and general dictionaries "published around the time of the founding," including Jacob, A *New Law-Dictionary* (1762); Cunningham, *New and Complete Law-Dictionary* (1771); Potts, *A
Compendious Law Dictionary* (1803); Jacob, *The Law-Dictionary* (1811); Kersey,
A New English Dictionary (1702), and Webster, *An American Dictionary of the
English Language* (1828).[94] They all defined the term *witness* as a person who
gives or furnishes evidence.

Thomas then turned to English case law on the privilege against self-
incrimination, citing several cases that explicitly expressed the eighteenth-
century common-law understanding that it protected against the compelled
production of incriminating physical evidence such as papers and documents.[95]
He noted that it was "against this common-law backdrop" that the privilege was
enshrined in the Virginia Declaration of Rights in 1776, stating that no one may
"be compelled to give evidence against himself." He pointed out that "following
Virginia's lead," seven of the other original states included specific provisions in
their constitutions granting a right against compulsion "to give evidence" or "to
furnish evidence" and that during the debates in the state conventions over the
ratification of the federal Constitution, the four states that offered specific constitutional amendments for the First Congress to adopt all included proposals to
protect individuals from being compelled to give evidence against themselves.[96]

Thomas acknowledged that when James Madison responded to these calls
and proposed what would become the Bill of Rights, he departed from the proposed language of *to give evidence* or *to furnish evidence* and substituted in its
place the phrase *to be a witness*. But, he insisted, it seems likely that Madison's
phrasing was "synonymous" with that of the proposals because the word *witness*
and the background history of the privilege against self-incrimination, which he
had discussed, "support this view." That explains "why Madison's unique phrasing—phrasing that none of the proposals had suggested—apparently attracted no
attention, much less opposition, in Congress, the state legislatures that ratified
the Bill of Rights, or anywhere else." Turning again to the *Annals of Congress* to
buttress his original general meaning argument, Thomas pointed out that only
one member of the First Congress addressed self-incrimination during the debates on the Bill of Rights and that person, John Laurance, "treated the phrases

as synonymous, restating Madison's formulation as a ban on forcing one 'to give evidence against himself.'"[97]

Thomas drew further support for his argument that a witness is one who gives evidence from the language of the Sixth Amendment's Compulsory Process Clause and its early interpretation by Chief Justice John Marshall when he was presiding over the treason trial of Aaron Burr in 1807. Marshall, over the government's objection, granted Burr's motion for the issuance of a subpoena *duces tecum* to obtain a letter from President Thomas Jefferson important to his defense, "holding that the right to compulsory process includes the right to secure papers—in addition to testimony—material to the defense."[98] The contemporary Court's narrow definition of the term *witness* as simply one who testifies seemed, for Thomas, to be "incompatible" with Marshall's opinion in *United States v. Burr.*[99] And, he continued, if the term *witnesses* in the Compulsory Process Clause has "an encompassing meaning, this provides reason to believe that the term 'witness' in the Self-Incrimination Clause has the same broad meaning. Yet this Court's recent Fifth Amendment act-of-production cases implicitly rest upon an assumption that this term has different meanings in adjoining provisions of the Bill of Rights."[100]

Thomas reminded his colleagues that the Court had always understood that a witness is one who gives evidence until *Fisher v. United States*[101] in 1976, when for the first time it limited the privilege to incriminating testimony and permitted the government to force a person to furnish incriminating physical evidence. He concluded in typical Thomas fashion: "None of the parties in this case has asked us to depart from *Fisher*, but in light of the historical evidence that the Self-Incrimination Clause may have a broader reach than *Fisher* holds, I remain open to a reconsideration of that decision and its progeny in a proper case."[102]

Thomas's major exploration of the meaning of *witness* has come not only through his opinions on the self-incrimination and compulsory process clauses but also through his efforts to grapple with what he called in *White v. Illinois*[103] the "complicated and confused" relationship[104] between the constitutional right of the accused to be "confronted with witnesses against him" and the hearsay rules of evidence. *White* was Thomas's first Confrontation Clause case and was argued just two weeks after he took the oath of office.

At Randal D. White's trial on charges that he had sexually assaulted a child, the child never testified—though the state of Illinois attempted on two occasions to call her as a witness, the child experienced emotional difficulty at both times and left without testifying. (The trial court neither made nor was asked to make a specific finding that the child was unavailable to testify.) Over White's objections, however, the trial court, based on Illinois's hearsay exceptions for spontaneous declarations and for statements made in the course of securing medical treatment, permitted testimony by the child's babysitter, her mother, an investigating officer, an emergency room nurse, and a doctor regarding prior, out-of-court statements made by the child to these individuals about the alleged assault, after which White was found guilty of aggravated criminal sexual assault. Having lost in Illinois's appellate courts, he sought Supreme Court review, only to be told by a unanimous Court that the child's hearsay statements did not violate the Confrontation Clause.

Chief Justice Rehnquist held that given the evidentiary value of spontaneous declarations and statements made in the course of medical treatment, their inherent reliability, and the Court's past precedents on these matters, there was no reason to exclude in this case evidence obtained as a result of these two exceptions to the hearsay rule. Thomas, in an opinion in which Scalia joined, concurred in part and concurred in the judgment.

He agreed that the Supreme Court had reached the correct result under its precedents, but he then proceeded to argue that the constitutional right of confrontation directly applies solely to any witness who actually testifies at trial or is implicated by extrajudicial statements only insofar as they are contained in "formalized testimonial materials, such as affidavits, depositions, prior testimony, or confessions." In his view, it was "this discrete category of testimonial materials" that had been "historically abused by prosecutors as a means of depriving criminal defendants of the benefit of the adversary process"; under the approach he proposed, "the Confrontation Clause would not be construed to extend beyond the historical evil to which it was directed."[105] He observed that his reading of the Clause would "greatly simplify" the hearsay rule, and again in characteristic fashion, he suggested that "in an appropriate case, we reconsider how the phrase 'witness against' in the Confrontation Clause pertains to the admission of hearsay."[106]

Thomas employed the formulation he first announced in *White* once more in *Davis v. Washington*, in which he dissented in part from Scalia's majority opinion and concluded that neither a wife's statements in her 911 call concerning domestic battery by her husband nor her answers to questions by the police once they arrived at her home were "a formalized dialogue" such as the Confrontation Clause was adopted to prohibit.[107] He employed the formulation again in *Giles v. California*,[108] when he concurred in Scalia's majority opinion rejecting the defendant's contention that the introduction at trial of the murder victim's statements to the police responding to her domestic violence call deprived him of the right to cross-examine witnesses who gave testimony against him. Thomas wrote, "Here, the police questioning was not 'a formalized dialogue,' because 'the statements were neither Mirandized nor custodial, nor accompanied by any similar indicia of formality'; and 'there is no suggestion that the prosecution attempted to offer [from the victim of domestic violence who was subsequently murdered] hearsay evidence at trial in order to evade confrontation.'"[109] He employed the formulation yet again in *Melendez-Diaz v. Massachusetts*,[110] concurring in Scalia's majority opinion holding that the state laboratory analyst who signed the certificate stating the material seized by the police from the defendant was cocaine of a certain quality had to testify in person and be subject to cross-examination. As Thomas said, "The documents at issue in this case are 'quite plainly affidavits,' [and] as such, they 'fall within the core class of testimonial statements' governed by the Confrontation Clause."[111] In *Michigan v. Bryant*,[112] he concurred in the judgment of Justice Sonia Sotomayor's majority opinion holding that the Confrontation Clause was not violated by the introduction at trial of a police officer's account of what he was told by a dying murder victim regarding the identification and description of the shooter and the location of the shooting. The victim, Thomas wrote, "interacted with the police under highly informal circumstances, while he bled from a fatal gunshot wound. The police questioning was not 'a formalized dialogue,' did not result in 'formalized testimonial materials' such as a deposition or affidavit, and bore no 'indicia of solemnity,'" and as such, it "bears little if any resemblance to the historical practices the Confrontation Clause aimed to eliminate."[113]

Trial by Jury

Article 3, § 2 of the Constitution and the Sixth Amendment both guarantee criminal defendants the right to trial by jury. Since Thomas's elevation to the Supreme Court, a recurring question for him and his colleagues has been whether, at sentencing, every element (or, to use a different word, fact) of the crime for which a convicted defendant is to be punished must be proved beyond a reasonable doubt to the jury.

Thomas first addressed this question in his lengthy concurrence in *Apprendi v. New Jersey*.[114] In this case, Charles Apprendi was charged with firing several shots into the home of an African American family. He had made a statement (which he later retracted) that he did not want the family in his neighborhood because of their race. He pleaded guilty to one count of second-degree possession of a firearm for an unlawful purpose, which carried a prison term of five to ten years. The count did not refer to the state's hate crime statute, which provided for an enhanced sentence if a trial judge found, by a preponderance of the evidence, that the defendant committed the crime with a purpose to intimidate a person or group because of race. After Apprendi pleaded guilty, the prosecutor filed a motion to enhance the sentence, and the trial judge found by a preponderance of the evidence that the shooting was racially motivated and sentenced Apprendi to a twelve-year term on the firearms count. In upholding the sentence, the appeals court rejected Apprendi's claim that the Sixth Amendment, incorporated by the Fourteenth Amendment to apply to the states, requires that a bias finding be proved to a jury beyond a reasonable doubt. When the New Jersey Supreme Court affirmed, Apprendi petitioned for a writ of certiorari to the U.S. Supreme Court. And there, he prevailed when Justice Stevens held for a five-member majority that the Sixth Amendment requires any fact that increases the penalty for a crime beyond the prescribed statutory maximum (other than the fact of a prior conviction) must be submitted to a jury and proved beyond a reasonable doubt. Thomas wrote a concurring opinion that joined the Court's opinion "in full" but that explained why he believed "the Constitution requires a broader rule than the Court adopts."[115]

Thomas spent eighteen heavily documented and closely reasoned pages in the *United States Reports* supporting his conclusion that "a long line of essentially uniform authority addressing accusations, and stretching from the earliest reported cases after the founding until well into the 20th century, establishes that the original understanding of which facts are elements was even broader than the rule that the Court adopts today."[116] This "broader rule" requires the jury to find beyond a reasonable doubt every element that increases the penalty for a crime not only beyond the prescribed statutory maximum (which was Stevens's holding for the majority—more on his part would simply have been dicta) but also beyond the prescribed statutory mandatory minimum.[117] From Thomas's perspective, any element that increases the length of the sentence a convicted defendant can receive (the minimum time to be served no less than the maximum time) must be submitted to the jury and found beyond a reasonable doubt. What "matter[s]" for him is "simply the overall increase in the punishment provided by the law."[118] He harshly criticized *McMillan v. Pennsylvania*,[119] a 1986 case that "spawned a special sort of fact known as a sentencing enhancement"—that is, a "fact [that] increases a defendant's punishment but is not subject to the constitutional protections to which elements are subject"[120]—and thereby "began a revolution in the law regarding the definition of crime."[121]

In his dissent two years later in *Harris v. United States*,[122] joined by Stevens, Souter, and Ginsburg, Thomas criticized the Court for its refusal to "overrule *McMillan*" and for its reliance on that case to uphold an enhancement of the defendant's mandatory minimum sentence for "brandish[ing]" a gun during a drug-trafficking crime—a sentencing factor found not by the jury but by the judge following the trial.[123] Kennedy, for the Court majority, emphasized that *Apprendi* only addressed an increased penalty for a crime beyond its prescribed statutory maximum. But Thomas argued that "the principles upon which it relied apply with equal force to those facts that expose the defendant to a higher mandatory minimum: When a fact exposes a defendant to greater punishment than what is otherwise legally prescribed, that fact is by definition an 'element' of a separate legal offense. Whether one raises the floor or raises the ceiling it is impossible to dispute that the defendant is exposed to greater punishment than is otherwise prescribed."[124]

Thomas finally prevailed on this issue in 2013. In *Alleyne v. United States*,[125] he was joined by Justices Ruth Bader Ginsburg, Stephen Breyer, Sonia Soto-mayor, and Elena Kagan in his opinion holding that because mandatory mini-mum sentences increase the penalty for a crime, any fact that increases the man-datory minimum is an "element" that must be submitted to the jury. Because there was "no basis in principle or logic to distinguish facts that raise the maxi-mum from those that increase the minimum," Thomas concluded that "*Harris* was inconsistent with *Apprendi*. It is, accordingly, overruled."[126]

In his 2005 concurrence in *Shepard v. United States*,[127] Thomas attacked the Court's opinion in *Almendarez-Torres v. United States*.[128] That case constituted "an exception to the *Apprendi* line of cases" in that it held that a defendant's prior convictions (1) are not elements of the current offense, (2) need not be included in the indictment, and (3) allow the judge to enhance the defendant's sentence beyond the sentence that could have lawfully been imposed by reference to facts found by the jury or admitted by the defendant.[129] *Almendarez-Torres*, he wrote, had been "eroded by this Court's subsequent Sixth Amendment jurisprudence, and a majority of the Court now recognizes that *Almendarez-Torres* was wrongly decided." And once again in typical Thomas fashion, he called for its rever-sal: "The parties do not request it here, but in an appropriate case, this Court should consider *Almendarez-Torres'* continuing viability. Innumerable criminal defendants have been unconstitutionally sentenced under the flawed rule of *Almendarez-Torres*, despite the fundamental 'imperative that the Court maintain absolute fidelity to the protections of the individual afforded by the notice, trial by jury, and beyond-a-reasonable-doubt requirements.'"[130]

In *Blakely v. Washington*,[131] Thomas joined Scalia's opinion for a five-mem-ber majority holding that Washington State's determinate sentencing scheme was unconstitutional to the extent it allowed the judge to enhance a defendant's sentence based on elements not found in the jury verdict or admitted by the defendant but based on sentencing factors found simply by the judge. "Our prec-edents make clear . . . that the 'statutory maximum' for *Apprendi* purposes is the maximum sentence a judge may impose *solely on the basis of the facts reflected in the jury verdict or admitted by the defendant*." For Scalia, "the relevant 'statutory maximum' is not the maximum sentence a judge may impose after finding ad-ditional facts, but the maximum he may impose *without* any additional findings.

When a judge inflicts punishment that the jury's verdict alone does not allow, the jury has not found all the facts 'which the law makes essential to the punishment and the judge exceeds his proper authority.'"[132] The dissenters in *Blakely* were alarmed by this decision, fearing it would lead the Court to conclude that the federal sentencing guidelines were also unconstitutional.[133]

That question was addressed the next year in *United States v. Booker*.[134] Stevens wrote for a five-member majority including Thomas that the Sixth Amendment right to trial by jury, as construed in *Blakely*, applied to the guidelines and required that any fact (other than a prior conviction) necessary to enhance a sentence beyond the maximum authorized by the facts established by a plea of guilty or a jury verdict had to be admitted by the defendant or proved to a jury beyond a reasonable doubt.

Ginsburg joined the majority opinion on the question of the application of *Blakely* to the guidelines, but she then switched sides and joined the four members in dissent to form a new majority on the question of how to remedy the conflict between the guidelines and the Sixth Amendment. She joined Breyer's majority opinion on the remedial question that held the section of the Federal Sentencing Act that made the guidelines mandatory was to be severed and excised, converting the guidelines from a mandatory system to a discretionary one.[135] Breyer applied the principles of severability as he understood them and concluded that Congress would likely have preferred the excision of some of the act, namely, its mandatory language, to the invalidation of the entire act.

Stevens dissented from Breyer's remedial opinion and was joined by Scalia and Souter. He insisted that the act's mandatory language was not facially unconstitutional but only unconstitutional as applied in Freddie J. Booker's case. Further, he noted, "I would simply allow the Government to continue doing what it has done since this Court handed down *Blakely*—prove any fact that is required to increase a defendant's sentence under the Guidelines to a jury beyond a reasonable doubt."[136] Thomas filed a solo dissent from Breyer's remedial opinion. He agreed with Stevens that "Booker's case presents an as-applied challenge,"[137] but he then went his own way, arguing that Breyer's excision of the act's mandatory language was "at once too narrow and too broad."[138]

He asserted that it was too narrow because Booker's unconstitutional enhancements stemmed not simply from the act's mandatory language but from a combination of the mandatory language, the guidelines themselves, and the guidelines policy manual; the latter provided instructions for applying the guidelines (including allowing judges to find facts that enhanced the sentence by a mere preponderance of evidence). Taken together, these factors "resulted in unconstitutional factfinding" by the judge.[139] At the same time, Thomas argued that Breyer's remedial opinion was also too broad, as "we have before us only a single unconstitutional application of the mandatory Guidelines. In such a case, facial invalidation is unprecedented. It is particularly inappropriate here, where it is evident [the mandatory language] is entirely constitutional in numerous other applications."[140] As he succinctly concluded,

> The Constitution does not prohibit what the Act's mandatory language accomplishes: binding district courts to the Guidelines. It prohibits allowing a judge alone to make a finding that raises the sentence beyond the sentence that could have lawfully been imposed by reference to facts found by the jury or admitted by the defendant. Many applications of [the mandatory language] suffer from no such vice. Yet the majority, by facially invalidating the statute, also invalidates these unobjectionable applications of the statute and thereby ignores the longstanding distinction between as-applied and facial challenges.[141]

The right to trial by jury raises other constitutional questions as well, including questions about what the Sixth Amendment means when it requires that juries must be "impartial." In *Taylor v. Louisana*[142] in 1975, Justice Byron White held for an eight-member majority that for a jury to be "impartial," it had to be drawn from a "fair cross-section" of the community. He wrote:

> We accept the fair-cross-section requirement as fundamental to the jury trial guaranteed by the Sixth Amendment. . . . The purpose of a jury is to guard against the exercise of arbitrary power—to make available the commonsense judgment of the community as a hedge against the overzealous or mistaken prosecutor and in preference to the professional or perhaps over-conditioned or biased response of a judge. This prophylactic vehicle is not provided if the jury pool is made up of only special segments of the populace or if large, distinctive groups are excluded from the pool.[143]

In *Berghuis v. Smith*,[144] Thomas brought his original general meaning approach to this issue. Although Ginsburg delivered the unanimous opinion of the Court that concluded *Taylor's* fair-cross-section requirement had not been violated in this case, Thomas wrote a concurrence that questioned how *Taylor* could be "square[d] with the Sixth Amendment's text and history." The text, he reminded his colleagues, speaks only of an "impartial jury," and "historically, juries did not include a sampling of persons from all levels of society or even from both sexes." As he noted, "In 1791, every state limited jury service to men; every state except Vermont restricted jury service to property owners or taxpayers; three states permitted only whites to serve; and one state, Maryland, disqualified atheists." In an another effort on his part to scrape away past precedents and get back to bare wood, Thomas indicated that "in an appropriate case I would be willing to reconsider our precedents articulating the 'fair cross section' requirements. But neither party asks us to do so here, and the only question before us is whether the state court's disposition was contrary to, or an unreasonable application of, our precedents. I concur in the Court's answer to that question."[145]

So long as *Taylor* remains good law, an "impartial jury" must be drawn from a fair cross section of the community. Additionally, its jurors must be unbiased, that is, willing to decide the case on the basis of the evidence presented, and they must not be exposed to prejudicial materials or demeanor in the courtroom.[146] On his first year on the High Bench, Thomas dissented from O'Connor's opinion for a seven-member majority in *Riggins v. Nevada*[147] that concluded the defendant had been denied his Sixth Amendment rights when, during his trial for murder and robbery at which he was offering an insanity defense, he was administered Mellaril, an antipsychotic medication, depriving him of the opportunity to show his true mental state as it existed at the time of the crime. Thomas, joined by Scalia, saw no prejudice in David Riggins's forced medication. "Even if Mellaril noticeably affected Riggins' demeanor," he said, "the Court fails to explain why the medication's effects rendered Riggins' trial fundamentally unfair." As Thomas noted, "The trial court offered Riggins the opportunity to prove his mental condition as it existed at the time of the crime through testimony instead of his appearance in court in an unmedicated condition. Riggins took advantage of this offer by explaining to the jury the history of his mental health, his usage of Mellaril, and the possible effects of Mellaril on his demeanor." Thomas further noted that Riggins also called a psychiatrist, who testified about Riggins's condition after his arrest and his likely mental state at the time of the crime and explained Riggins's use of Mellaril and how it might be affecting him.[148]

In *Carey v. Musladin*,[149] Thomas addressed a different kind of prejudicial demeanor question, but this time, he wrote for a unanimous Court. At this murder trial, members of the victim's family sat in the front row of the spectators' gallery wearing buttons displaying the victim's image. Mathew Musladin sought a motion to order the family members not to wear the buttons on the ground that they were inherently prejudicial, which the trial court judge denied. The California Court of Appeal upheld Musladin's conviction, stating that he had to show actual or inherent prejudice to succeed on the buttons claim and ruling that he had not satisfied that test. On habeas, the Ninth Circuit reversed and remanded, finding that the state court's decision was contrary to or involved an unreasonable application of clearly established federal law—in particular, *Estelle v. Williams*,[150] addressing state compulsion of a defendant to stand trial in prison clothes, and *Holbrook v. Flynn*,[151] addressing the state seating state troopers in the courtroom immediately behind the defendant. Thomas reversed the Ninth Circuit, holding that *Williams* and *Flynn* were not controlling because both "dealt with government-sponsored practices." Since the Court had never before addressed a claim that "private-actor conduct was so inherently prejudicial that it deprived a defendant of a fair trial,"[152] he wrote, the state court's decision "was not contrary to or an unreasonable application of clearly established federal law."[153]

Thomas pointed out that buttons did not brand the defendant in the eyes of the jury "with an unmistakable mark of guilt" because they displayed only a photograph of the victim and were "unlikely to have been taken as a sign of anything other than the normal grief occasioned by the loss of a family member." Nonetheless, his opinion was unsatisfying. He acknowledged that as a result of a "lack of guidance from this Court, lower courts have diverged widely in their treatment of defendants' spectator-conduct claims." But by the end of his opinion, he offered no guidance in what he acknowledged was, for the Court, a case of first impression. Because Thomas was silent on the matter, it was left to Kennedy in his concurring opinion to point the way forward:

> The instant case does present the issue whether as a preventative measure, or as a general rule to preserve the calm and dignity of a court, buttons proclaiming a message relevant to the case ought to be prohibited as a matter of course. That rule has not been clearly established by our cases to date. . . . In all events, it seems to me the case as presented to us here does call for a new rule, perhaps justified as much as a preventative measure as by the urgent needs of the situation. That rule should be explored in the court system, and then established in this Court before it can be grounds for relief in the procedural posture of this case.[154]

Another means to ensure that juries are impartial, available in all jurisdictions in the United States, involves some use of peremptory challenges, by which the defense and prosecution can reject a certain number of potential jurors who appear to have an unfavorable bias without cause, that is, without having to give a reason. (Other potential jurors may be challenged for cause by giving a reason why they might be unable to reach a fair verdict.) Peremptory challenges are an important safeguard because they allow attorneys to use their training and experience to dismiss jurors who, even though their statements during the voir dire were unexceptionable, might nonetheless harbor prejudices that could infringe the rights of the defendant to a fair trial.

In *Strauder v. West Viriginia*[155] in 1880, the Court invalidated a state law that allowed only white men to serve as jurors. In the opinion, the Court observed that the racial composition of a jury may affect the outcome of a criminal case:

"It is well known that prejudices often exist against particular classes in the community, which sway the judgment of jurors, and which, therefore, operate in some cases to deny to persons of those classes the full enjoyment of that protection which others enjoy."[156] In 1965 in *Swain v. Alabama*,[157] the Court held that black defendants could challenge on equal protection grounds a state's exercise of peremptory challenges to exclude members of their race from their petit juries. To do so, however, they could not rely simply on the pattern of jury strikes in their own particular cases; rather, they would have to introduce evidence of a systematic exclusion of blacks through the use of peremptories over a period of time. In 1986 in *Batson v. Kentucky*,[158] the Court relaxed the evidentiary requirements of *Swain* and held that a black defendant could establish a prima facie case of purposeful discrimination in the selection of jurors based solely on the prosecutor's exercise of peremptory challenges at the defendant's trial. Justice Lewis Powell declared for the *Batson* majority that "the harm from discriminatory jury selection extends beyond that inflicted on the defendant and the excluded juror to touch the entire community. Selection procedures that purposefully exclude black persons from juries undermine public confidence in the fairness of our system of justice."[159]

In 1991, the Court carried *Batson* to new heights. In *Powers v. Ohio*,[160] it held that a prosecutor in a trial of a white criminal defendant is prohibited from excluding black jurors on the basis of race. And that same year in *Edmonson v. Leesville Concrete Company*,[161] the Court held that even private litigants in civil actions cannot exercise their peremptory challenges in a racially discriminatory manner because they are "state actors" operating on a stage created by the government.

Once *Batson* and *Edmonson* had established that neither prosecutors nor private litigants in civil cases could use their peremptory challenges in a racially discriminatory manner, the next and only remaining question for the Court concerning peremptory strikes came in 1992 in *Georgia v. McCollum*.[162] In *McCollum*, the Court had to decide whether defendants in criminal cases were likewise prohibited from engaging in racial discrimination in their use of peremptories. Justice Blackmun held for a seven-member majority that they were. He began by noting ominously that "as a preliminary matter, it is important to recall that peremptory challenges are not constitutionally protected fundamental rights; rather, they are but one state-created means to the constitutional end of an impartial jury and a fair trial. This Court repeatedly has stated that the right to a peremptory challenge may be withheld altogether without impairing the constitutional guarantee of an impartial jury and a fair trial." After stressing that it "is an affront to justice to argue that a fair trial includes the right to discriminate against a group of citizens based upon their race,"[163] he concluded by stating:

there is a distinction between exercising a peremptory challenge to discriminate invidiously against jurors on account of race and exercising a peremptory challenge to remove an individual juror who harbors racial prejudice. This Court firmly has rejected the view that assumptions of partiality based on race provide a legitimate basis for disqualifying a person as an impartial juror. . . . We therefore reaffirm today that the exercise of a peremptory challenge must not be based on either the race of the juror or the racial stereotypes held by the party . . . , [and] hold that the Constitution prohibits a criminal defendant from engaging in purposeful discrimination on the ground of race in the exercise of peremptory challenges.[164]

In dissent, Justice Scalia commented on the "sheer inanity" of the proposition that "a criminal defendant, in the process of defending himself against the state, is held to be acting on behalf of the state."[165] Chief Rehnquist concurred, noting that he was in dissent in *Edmonson* and that he continued "to believe that case to have been wrongly decided. But so long as it remains the law, I believe that it controls the disposition of this case on the issue of 'state action' under the Fourteenth Amendment. I therefore join the opinion of the Court."[166]

McCollum was decided during Thomas's first year on the Court, so he did not participate in *Edmonson*. At this early stage, he took his guidance from Rehnquist and also concurred, although with clear reservations:

As a matter of first impression, I think that I would have shared the view of the dissenting opinions: A criminal defendant's use of peremptory strikes cannot violate the Fourteenth Amendment because it does not involve state action. Yet, I agree with the Court and the Chief Justice that our decision last Term in Edmonson governs this case and requires the opposite conclusion. Because the respondents do not question *Edmonson*, I believe that we must accept its consequences. I therefore concur in the judgment reversing the Georgia Supreme Court.

Thomas worried that "by restricting a criminal defendant's use of such challenges, this case takes us further from the reasoning and the result of *Strauder*. I doubt that this departure will produce favorable consequences. On the contrary, I am certain that black criminal defendants will rue the day that this Court ventured down this road that inexorably will lead to the elimination of peremptory strikes."[167]

In *Batson*, Thomas argued, the Court departed from *Strauder* by holding that absent an actual showing, an assumption or intuitive judgment about the possibility that a particular juror may harbor racial prejudice has no legitimacy.

But, he noted, "*Strauder* rested on precisely such an 'assumption' or 'intuition.' We reasonably surmised, without direct evidence in any particular case, that all-white juries might judge black defendants unfairly."[168]

Thomas identified two negative consequences resulting from the Court's departure from *Strauder*. First, he saw it as producing "a serious misordering of our priorities. In *Strauder*, we put the rights of defendants foremost. Today's decision, while protecting jurors, leaves defendants with less means of protecting themselves." He believed the Court was exalting the right of citizens to sit on juries over the rights of the criminal defendant, even though, as he pointed out, "it is the defendant, not the jurors, who faces imprisonment or even death." Second, he saw it as taking the Court down "a slope of inquiry that had no clear stopping point." He wondered whether black defendants would be able to strike white veniremen and "whether defendants may exercise peremptories on the basis of sex."[169] He concluded that whatever benefits the Court in *Strauder* perceived to accrue to criminal defendants from having members of their class on the jury, "they have evaporated."[170]

A different but related form of racial discrimination was addressed by the Court in 1998 in *Campbell v. Louisiana*.[171] After Terry Campbell, a white defendant, was indicted by an Evangeline Parish grand jury and was subsequently convicted by a petit jury of second-degree murder, he appealed his conviction on that ground that no black had served as grand jury chairman in that parish for at least the preceding seventeen years, even though more than 20 percent of the registered voters were black.

The trial court denied the motion because Campbell was white and was accused of killing another white. At trial, Campbell was convicted by a petit jury. When this case finally reached the Supreme Court, Justice Kennedy wrote for a seven-member majority, concluding that Campbell had standing to assert the equal protection rights of black persons not to be excluded from grand jury service on the basis of their race. Kennedy cited as precedent *Powers v. Ohio*, in which the Court concluded that a white defendant had standing to challenge discrimination against black persons in the use of peremptory challenges, and Campbell's own claim that his conviction had been procured by means or procedures that contravened his due process rights. Thomas, joined by Scalia, concurred in part (he agreed Campbell had standing to assert his own due process rights) and dissented in part (he denied that Campbell had standing to raise the equal protection rights of black members of the grand jury venire excluded from serving as forepersons because *Powers* was not only "incorrect as an initial matter" but also "inapposite to the case at hand").[172]

Thomas began by indicating that he failed to "understand how the rights of blacks excluded from jury service can be vindicated by letting a white murderer go free."[173] He identified himself with those black veniremen who "would be dismayed to learn" that a white defendant used their constitutional rights as a means to overturn his conviction.[174] Yet, he insisted, this is what the Court held in *Powers*. He was convinced that *Powers* had distorted standing principles and equal protection law and "should be overruled."[175] In any event, he contended that even if *Powers* was "persuasive," it was "wholly inapplicable to this case" because it involved neither peremptory strikes nor discrimination in the selection of the petit jury but rather the selection by the judge of one member of the grand jury venire to serve as foreman, with the remaining members of the grand jury selected at random. He denied that the judge's selection ("rather than exclusion") of a single member of the grand jury was an "'overt' wrong that would affect the remainder of the grand jury proceedings." He also denied that the properly constituted petit jury's verdict of guilt beyond a reasonable doubt was in any way affected by the composition of the grand jury. He concluded by revealing his true sentiments about why Campbell's arguments were hypocritical and contemptible: "Indeed, to the extent that race played any part in the composition of petitioner's petit jury, it was by petitioner's own actions, as petitioner used 5 of his 12 peremptory strikes to eliminate blacks from the petit jury venire. Petitioner's attempt to assert that he was injured by the alleged exclusion of blacks at the grand jury stage is belied by his own use of peremptory strikes against blacks at the petit jury stage."[176]

The Sixth Amendment also requires jury trials to be speedy and public. Thomas addressed the Speedy Trial Clause in his dissent, joined by Rehnquist and Scalia, in *Doggett v. United States*.[177] The facts are important here. In February 1980, Marc Doggett was indicted on federal drug charges, but he left the country before the Drug Enforcement Agency (DEA) could secure his arrest. The DEA knew that he was later imprisoned in Panama, but after requesting that he be extradited back to the United States, the agency never followed up on his status. Once the DEA discovered that he had left Panama for Colombia, it made no further attempt to locate him. It was unaware that he subsequently reentered the United States in 1982, married, earned a college degree, found steady employment, lived openly under his own name, and stayed within the law. The Marshal's Service eventually located him during a simple credit check on individuals with outstanding warrants, and he was arrested in September 1988, eight and a half years after his indictment. Doggett moved to dismiss the indictment on the ground that the government's failure to prosecute him earlier violated his Sixth Amendment right to a speedy trial. When the district court denied his motion, he entered a conditional guilty plea, and the court of appeals affirmed. For a five-member majority, Souter reversed; he applied the four criteria for what constitutes a denial of a speedy trial as spelled out in the Court's decision in *Barker v.*

Wingo,[178] focusing in particular on the long delay between Doggett's indictment and arrest. For Souter,

> the Government's egregious persistence in failing to prosecute Doggett is clearly sufficient. The lag between Doggett's indictment and arrest was 8 ½ years, and he would have faced trial 6 years earlier than he did but for the Government's inexcusable oversights. . . . When the Government's negligence thus causes delay six times as long as that generally sufficient to trigger judicial review and when the presumption of prejudice, albeit unspecified, is neither extenuated, as by the defendant's acquiescence, nor persuasively rebutted, the defendant is entitled to relief.[179]

Thomas began his dissent by observing, "Just as 'bad facts make bad law,' so too odd facts make odd law." He found "extraordinary" Doggett's "8 1/2-year odyssey from youthful drug dealing in the tobacco country of North Carolina, through stints in a Panamanian jail and in Colombia, to life as a computer operations manager, homeowner, and registered voter in suburban Virginia." But, he continued, "even more extraordinary is the Court's conclusion that the Government denied Doggett his Sixth Amendment right to a speedy trial despite the fact that he has suffered none of the harms that the right was designed to prevent. I respectfully dissent."[180]

Thomas argued that the Speedy Trial Clause was directed against "two major evils": undue and oppressive incarceration and the anxiety and concern accompanying public accusation. After noting that the majority did not dispute his claim, he observed that "neither concern is implicated here." Doggett was not in U.S. custody or subject to bail during the entire eight-and-a-half-year period at issue; "as this case comes to us, we must assume that he was blissfully unaware of his indictment all the while, and thus was not subject to the anxiety or humiliation that typically accompanies a known criminal charge."[181]

He rejected Doggett's contention that the long delay between his indictment and arrest deprived him of his right to "repose," a value independently protected by the Speedy Trial Clause. He acknowledged that Doggett has been "leading a normal, productive and law-abiding life" and that his "arrest and prosecution at this late date interrupted his life as a productive member of society and forced him to answer for actions taken in the distant past." Nonetheless, he insisted that "however uplifting this tale of personal redemption, our task is to illuminate the protections of the Speedy Trial Clause, not to take the measure of one man's life."[182] He pointed out that "had Doggett been indicted shortly before his 1988 arrest rather than shortly after his 1980 crime, his repose would have been equally shattered—but he would not have even a colorable speedy trial claim. To recognize a constitutional right to repose is to recognize a right to be tried speed-ily *after the offense*. That would, of course, convert the Speedy Trial Clause into a constitutional statute of limitations—a result with no basis in the text or history of the Clause or in our precedents."[183]

He concluded by noting that

today's opinion, I fear, will transform the courts of the land into boards of law enforcement supervision. For the Court compels dismissal of the charges against Doggett not because he was harmed in any way by the delay between his indictment and arrest, but simply because the Government's efforts to catch him are found wanting. . . . By divorcing the Speedy Trial Clause from all considerations of prejudice to an accused, the Court positively invites the Nation's judges to indulge in ad hoc and result-driven second-guessing of the government's investigatory efforts. Our Constitution neither contemplates nor tolerates such a role.[184]

His final footnote was particularly illuminating and raised the question of why the Court granted certiorari in this case:

It is quite likely, in fact, that the delay benefited Doggett. At the time of his arrest, he had been living an apparently normal, law-abiding life for some five years—a point not lost on the District Court Judge, who, instead of imposing a prison term, sentenced him to three years' probation and a $1,000 fine. Thus, the delay gave Doggett the opportunity to prove what most defendants can only promise: that he no longer posed a threat to society. There can be little doubt that, had he been tried immediately after his cocaine-importation activities, he would have received a harsher sentence.[185]

Jury trials must also be public. Although the right to a public trial is not absolute, it has been strictly enforced by the Court. Before a request for closure will be honored, the Court held in *Press-Enterprise v. Superior Court*[186] that there must be "specific findings . . . demonstrating that first, there is a substantial prob-ability that the defendant's right to a fair trial will be prejudiced by publicity that closure would prevent, and second, reasonable alternatives to closure cannot ad-equately protect the defendant's fair trial rights." *Presley v. Georgia*[187] was a case of first impression, raising the question of whether the selection of a jury is part of a public trial. On summary judgment, a per curiam opinion of the Court cited, inter alia, *Press-Enterprise* and held that it was. Thomas, in dissent with Scalia, argued that he was "unwilling to decide this important question summarily without benefit of full briefing and argument."[188] He acknowledged that "the Court might well be right that a trial court violates the Sixth Amendment if it closes the courtroom without *sua sponte* considering reasonable alternatives to closure." But, he added, "I would not decide the issue summarily" and certainly would not conclude as the Court did that the point was settled with no room for doubt.[189]

The Eighth Amendment

In his 2008 concurrence in the judgment in *Baze v. Rees*,[190] Thomas spelled out what he considered to be the "original understanding of the Cruel and Unusual Punishments Clause." Based on "the historical practices that led the Framers to include it in the Bill of Rights," he concluded that "it is clear that the Eighth Amendment does not prohibit the death penalty." The evidence for this was "the ubiquity of the death penalty in the founding era" and "the Constitution's express provision for capital punishment"—he cited the Fifth Amendment's requirement of an indictment or presentment of a grand jury to hold a person for a capital crime and its prohibition of depriving a person of life without due process of law.[191] All that the Cruel and Unusual Punishments Clause prohibited, he said, were methods of "intensifying a death sentence," that is, "ways of producing a punishment worse than death." One such way was burning at the stake because "burning, unlike hanging, was always painful and destroyed the body." Other methods that Thomas mentioned were "gibbeting," in which the condemned were hanged in iron cages so that their bodies would decompose in public view, and the punishment for high treason—"emboweling alive, beheading, and quartering."[192]

Thomas turned to dictionaries of the founding era to support his contentions, first, that "embellishments upon the death penalty designed to inflict pain for pain's sake would have fallen comfortably within the ordinary meaning of the word 'cruel'" and, second, that "by the late 18th century, the more violent modes of execution had 'dwindled away,' and would for that reason have been 'unusual' in the sense that they were no longer 'regularly or customarily employed.'"[193] He reviewed the debates in the state conventions that ratified the Constitution and found a Massachusetts delegate complaining that Congress was "nowhere restrained from inventing the most cruel and unheard-of punishments, and annexing them to crimes; and there is no constitutional check on them, but that *racks* and *gibbets* may be amongst the most mild instruments of their discipline." He also quoted Patrick Henry in the Virginia convention objecting to the lack of a bill of rights, in part because there was nothing to prevent Congress from inflicting "tortures, or cruel and barbarous punishments."[194]

He invoked Joseph Story's *Commentaries*, noting that "so barbaric were the punishments prohibited by the Eighth Amendment that Joseph Story thought the provision 'wholly unnecessary in a free government, since it is scarcely possible, that any department of such a government should authorize, or justify such atrocious conduct.'"[195] He pointed out that this original understanding had been so consistently adopted by the Court over time that in 1977, even Hugo Bedau, the ardent death penalty abolitionist, was forced to acknowledge "an unbroken line of interpreters has held that it was the original understanding and intent of the framers of the Eighth Amendment . . . to proscribe as 'cruel and unusual' only such modes of execution as compound the simple infliction of death with added cruelties or indignities."[196]

Thomas's original understanding of the Eighth Amendment, most fully developed in *Baze*, explains why he declared fifteen years earlier in *Graham v. Collins*, his first death penalty opinion, that the Cruel and Unusual Punishments Clause "was intended to place only substantive limitations on punishments, not procedural requirements on sentencing."[197] And since it places no "procedural requirements" on the states that impose the death penalty, he has dissented when the Court has found wanting jury instructions at the sentencing stage concerning what is meant by life imprisonment: "It is not this Court's role to micromanage state sentencing proceedings or to develop model jury instructions. I would decline to interfere further with matters that the Constitution leaves to the States."[198] He also wrote for the majority in *Kansas v. Marsh*[199] that Kansas could, consistent with the Constitution, direct imposition of the death penalty when it had proved to the jury beyond a reasonable doubt that mitigators did not outweigh aggravators, including where the aggravating circumstances and mitigating circumstances were in equipoise. He spoke for a five-member majority when he declared that "a State enjoys a range of discretion in imposing the death penalty, including the manner in which aggravating and mitigating circumstances are to be weighed."[200] And though Thomas acknowledged in his *Graham v. Collins* concurrence that the Court was correct to condemn unguided jury discretion in the imposition of the death penalty in *Furman v. Georgia*[201] because beyond it "lay the specter of racial prejudice—the paradigmatic capricious and irrational sentencing factor," he insisted that a mandatory death penalty scheme was a "perfectly reasonable" means of "eliminating explicit jury discretion and treating all defendants equally."[202]

In *Graham v. Collins*, the Court held that *Penry v. Lynaugh*[203] was not to be applied retroactively under the principles of *Teague v. Lane*.[204] Thomas concurred because he "believe[d] *Penry* was wrong decided."[205] He argued that *Penry* imposed "as a constitutional imperative a scheme that simply dumps before the jury all sympathetic factors bearing upon the defendant's background and character, and the circumstances of the offense, so that the jury may decide without further guidance whether the defendant deserves death"; thereby, it threw "open the back door to arbitrary and irrational sentencing."[206] It reintroduced the opportunity for racial prejudice to play the ugly role *Furman* had sought to prohibit. As Thomas put it, "To withhold the death penalty out of sympathy for a defendant who is a member of a favored group is no different from a decision to impose the penalty on the basis of negative bias, and it matters not how narrow the class of death-eligible defendants or crimes."[207]

Thomas also employed his original general meaning approach to the Eighth Amendment to his dissent in *Graham v. Florida*,[208] in which Kennedy, for a six-member majority, held that the imposition of a sentence of life without the possibility of parole for a juvenile offender who did not commit homicide was cruel and unusual punishment.

> The Court holds today that it is "grossly disproportionate" and hence unconstitutional for any judge or jury to impose a sentence of life without parole on an offender less than 18 years old, unless he has committed a homicide. Although the text of the Constitution is silent regarding the permissibility of this sentencing practice, and although it would not have offended the standards that prevailed at the founding, the Court insists that the standards of American society have evolved such that the Constitution now requires its prohibition.[209]

Thomas repeated his argument from *Baze* that the Cruel and Unusual Punishments Clause "was originally understood" as simply prohibiting torturous methods of punishment, and therefore, he continued, it had nothing to do with whether punishment was proportionate to the crime—an interpretation employed in many previous rulings that "is entirely the Court's creation."[210] He cited a penal statute, adopted by the First Congress (the same Congress that proposed the Eighth Amendment), that prescribed capital punishment for offenses ranging from "run[ning] away with . . . goods or merchandise to the value of fifty dollars" to "murder on the high seas" in order to indicate that proportionality in sentencing was not understood to be a "constitutional command."[211]

Having found that the Court's many proportionality rulings lacked "a principled foundation" and intruded "upon areas that the Constitution reserves to other (state and federal) organs of government," Thomas nonetheless felt compelled to address the issue of proportionality on its own terms because the Court's decision in *Graham* "remarkably expand[ed] its reach. For the first time in its history, the Court declares an entire class of offenders immune from a noncapital sentence using the categorical approach it previously reserved for death penalty cases alone."[212]

Until *Graham*, the Court's proportionality rulings had been based on the need to give capital defendants special protection because death was "a uniquely severe punishment" to be reserved only for those "most deserving of execution." And although the Eighth Amendment made no distinction between capital and noncapital sentencing, Thomas suggested that the Court drew a "bright line" between the two kinds of sentencing to justify "the Court's willingness to reject democratic choices regarding the death penalty." But, he noted, *Graham* "eviscerate[d] that distinction. 'Death is different' no longer. The Court now claims not only the power categorically to reserve the 'most severe punishment' for those the Court thinks are 'the most deserving of execution,' *but also* to declare that 'less culpable' persons are categorically exempt from the '*second* most severe penalty.'" And, he commented, it announced no "reliable limiting principle" to prevent it "from immunizing any class of offenders from the law's third, fourth, fifth, or fiftieth most severe penalties as well."[213] He further objected that the Court banned life-without-parole sentences "not just in this case, but in *every* case involving a juvenile non-homicide offender, no matter what the circumstances."[214] Given that thirty-seven of the fifty states allowed for nonhomicide juvenile offenders to receive a sentence of life without the possibility of parole and given that the majority conceded that the Eighth Amendment does not mandate the adoption of "any one penological theory,"[215] he insisted that "neither objective evidence of national consensus nor the notions of culpability on which the Court's 'independent judgment'" relied could justify its decision.[216] He concluded by observing that "the ultimate question in this case is not whether a life-without-parole sentence 'fits' the crime at issue here or the crimes of juvenile nonhomicide offenders more generally, but to whom the Constitution assigns that decision." For Thomas, the answer was clear: this is a matter for "the people and their representatives," not for the Court and "its own sense of morality and retributive justice."[217]

Thomas repeated many of these same arguments in his 2012 dissent in *Miller v. Alabama*,[218] in which Justice Kagan held in a five-to-four decision that the Eighth Amendment forbids a state sentencing scheme that imposes a mandatory sentence of life without the possibility of parole for juvenile homicide offenders. Before this case, the Court had held that individualized sentencing was required only in capital punishment cases and that mandatory sentences imposing life without the possibility of parole were constitutionally authorized in all other cases. One such example was *Harmelin v. Michigan*,[219] in which the Court upheld Michigan's law mandatorily imposing a sentence of life in prison without the possibility of parole for anyone convicted of possessing over 650 grams of cocaine. *Miller,* however, changed that, and Thomas objected:

> Nothing about our Constitution, or about the qualitative difference between any term of imprisonment and death, has changed since *Harmelin* was decided 21 years ago. What has changed (or, better yet, "evolved") is this Court's ever-expanding line of categorical proportionality cases. The Court now uses *Roper* and *Graham* to jettison *Harmelin's* clear distinction between capital and noncapital cases and to apply the former to noncapital juvenile offenders. The Court's decision to do so is even less supportable than the precedents used to reach it.[220]

This chapter has assessed Thomas's employment of his original general meaning approach to various criminal procedural provisions in the original Constitution, the Bill of Rights, and the Fourteenth Amendment. He strives to interpret these provisions as their words demand and as they were understood by those who drafted and ratified them. His approach led him in *Hudson v. McMillian* and *Helling v. McKinney* to reject claims under the Cruel and Unusual Punishments Clause based on conditions of confinement; he found such claims contrary to the original general meaning of the Clause, which framed it simply as a limitation on the sentences that legislatures and judges can impose. It led him to conclude that the Ex Post Facto Clauses were certainly (if not exclusively) aimed at laws that retroactively altered the definition of crimes or increased their punishment; consequently, he denied the relief a defendant sought in *California Department of Corrections v. Morales* but granted relief in *Lynce v. Mathis* and found no ex post facto issue present in *Kansas v. Hendricks* or *Smith v. Doe* because they involved civil, not criminal, matters.

Thomas's original general meaning approach to the Fourth Amendment led him to conclude in *Florida v. White* that, under the Fourth Amendment, warrants are not always necessary and that the Court's focus must be on the reasonableness of the search or seizure; to hold in *Wilson v. Arkansas* that "knock and announce" was a constitutional requirement because it was a common-law principle embedded in Anglo-American law; to doubt in *Indianapolis v. Edmond* whether the framers would have considered reasonable the use of checkpoints indiscriminately to stop individuals not suspected of wrongdoing; and to assert in *Samson v. California* that it was reasonable to subject parolees and probationers to suspicionless searches. His original general meaning approach led him to conclude in *Mitchell v. United States* that the adverse comment rule was not rooted in a historical understanding of the Self-Incrimination Clause; to insist in

United States v. Hubbell that the term *witness* refers to one who gives or furnishes evidence and that, therefore, one who responds to a *subpoena duces tecum* is as much a witness as one who responds to a *subpoena ad testificandum*; and to argue in *White v. Illinois* that the right to confrontation applies only to witnesses who actually testify at trial or provide formalized testimonial materials.

His approach also led him to contend in *Apprendi v. New Jersey* that the Sixth Amendment right to trial by jury requires that a jury find beyond a reasonable doubt every element that increases the penalty for a crime not only beyond the prescribed statutory maximum but also beyond the prescribed statutory mandatory minimum; to deny in *Berghuis v. Taylor* that the right to an impartial jury requires a fair cross section of the community; and to assert in *Doggett v. United States* that the text or history of the Speedy Trial Clause makes clear it was directed against undue and oppressive incarceration and the anxiety and concern accompanying public accusation and that nothing in the petitioner's case implicated either concern. Finally, his original general meaning approach led him in *Baze v. Rees* to conclude that the Cruel and Unusual Punishments Clause prohibits only torturous methods of punishment; to assert in *Graham v. Collins* that it places no procedural requirements on the states that impose the death penalty; and to deny in *Graham v. Florida* and *Miller v. Alabama* that it requires that the punishment be proportionate to the crime.

Thomas's original general meaning approach leads him to rule both for and against criminal defendants. He cannot be characterized as either simply proprosecution or prodefense. As he declared in his lecture on "Judging" at the University of Kansas Law School, he employs an approach that reduces his judicial discretion and fosters judicial impartiality. Whatever his personal preferences toward those charged with and/or convicted of crime might be, it is apparent he has adopted an approach that tethers his analysis to the understanding held by those who drafted and ratified the criminal procedural provisions he is called upon to interpret.

This chapter and the previous one have addressed in passing Thomas's concern for how the Court's interpretation of the Constitution's various provisions can adversely affect members of his race. Chapter 6 puts these concerns front and center. It explores at length Thomas's original general meaning approach to questions of race, equality, and civil rights.

Chapter Six

Thomas's Original General Meaning Approach to Questions of Race and Equality

In no area of constitutional law have Thomas's opinions generated more controversy and debate than in matters relating to race and equality. Thomas replaced Thurgood Marshall, the first black to serve on the Supreme Court. As chief counsel for the National Association for the Advancement of Colored People (NAACP), Marshall led a successful decade-and-a-half legal attack on racial segregation, culminating in his victory in *Brown v. Board of Education.* In that ruling, the Court struck down "separate but equal" public schools on the ground that they were inherently unequal because they "generate[d] a feeling of inferiority" in minority students "in a way unlikely ever to be undone."[1] Over his twenty-four years on the Supreme Court, Marshall provided reliably liberal votes on virtually all issues and was most closely identified with his opinions on race. He supported aggressive efforts to integrate public schools, including the use of interdistrict busing of students;[2] he defended the use of racial quotas in university admissions and government contracting;[3] and he interpreted the Voting Rights Act of 1965 broadly to cover claims of vote dilution and to authorize proportional representation based on race.[4]

Before Clarence Thomas was nominated to the Court, he was already on record criticizing affirmative action because the Constitution protects individual rights, not group rights,[5] and insisting that, based on the principles of the Declaration of Independence, the Constitution is color blind.[6] He had also criticized the Warren Court in *Brown* for basing its decision in that historic case on the dubious findings of social science (Kenneth Clark's controversial doll studies, mentioned in footnote 11 of the Court's unanimous opinion)[7] that showed segregation generated feelings of inferiority. Thomas argued that the decision should have been based instead on the famous words of the first Justice John Marshall Harlan, who in his powerful dissent in *Plessy v. Ferguson* had declared: "In view of the Constitution, in the eye of the law, there is in this country no superior, dominant, ruling class of citizens. There is no caste here. Our Constitution is color-blind, and neither knows nor tolerates classes among citizens."[8]

Thomas's nomination to become an associate justice of the Supreme Court, made by President George Herbert Walker Bush, elevated him from his position as a judge on the Court of Appeals for the District of Columbia. It also unleashed a torrent of harsh personal attacks. Because of Thomas's belief in a color-blind Constitution and his opposition to affirmative action, the NAACP and other leading civil rights organizations opposed his confirmation.[9] And when Anita Hill added fuel to the fire with her allegations of sexual impropriety on his part, Thomas was obliged to assert that from his standpoint, the Senate hearing on his nomination had become "a high-tech lynching for uppity blacks who in any way deign to think for themselves, to do for themselves, to have different ideas."[10]

The assault continued after his narrow confirmation vote when, just three months later, A. Leon Higginbotham, Jr., a black chief judge emeritus of the Third Circuit Court of Appeals, wrote a condescending 10,000-word "Open Letter to Justice Clarence Thomas" that was published in the *University of Pennsylvania Law Review*.[11] Higginbotham began by instructing Thomas that when President Bush elevated him to the Supreme Court, he "suddenly vested in you the option to preserve or dilute the gains this country has made in the struggle for equality. This is a grave responsibility indeed." He then invited Thomas to consider his future legacy: "Forty years from now, when your grandchildren and other Americans measure your performance on the Supreme Court, . . . history will determine whether you fulfilled your responsibility with the vision and grace of the Justice whose seat you have been appointed to fill: Thurgood Marshall."[12]

Claiming to have read "every article you have published, every speech you have given, and virtually every public comment you have made during the past decade," Higginbotham complained, "I could not find one shred of evidence suggesting an insightful understanding on your part of how the evolutionary movement of the Constitution and the work of civil rights organizations have benefitted you." In his view, there was no evidence that Thomas had anything but a "stunted knowledge of history and an unformed judicial philosophy."[13] To correct Thomas's deficiencies, he proposed to educate him on four matters.

First, Higginbotham explained "the impact of the work of the civil rights lawyers and civil rights organization" on Thomas's life. "During the time when civil rights organizations were challenging the Reagan Administration, I was frankly dismayed by some of your responses to and denigrations of these organizations." Higginbotham pointed to a 1984 article in the *Washington Post* in which Thomas had criticized traditional civil rights leaders for going to the news media to "bitch, bitch, bitch, moan and moan, whine and whine" about Reagan administration policies. "If that is still your assessment of these civil rights organizations or their leaders," he continued, "I suggest, Justice Thomas, that you should ask yourself every day what would have happened to you if there had never been a Charles

Hamilton Houston, a William Henry Hastie, a Thurgood Marshall, and that small cadre of other lawyers associated with them, who laid the groundwork for success in the twentieth-century racial civil rights cases?" Higginbotham wondered whether they could not "have been similarly charged with, as you phrased it, bitching and moaning and whining when they challenged the racism in the administrations of prior presidents, governors, and public officials? If there had never been an effective NAACP, isn't it highly probable that you might still be in Pin Point, Georgia, working as a laborer as some of your relatives did for decades?"[14]

Second, Higginbotham was puzzled that Thomas described himself as a black conservative: "I must confess that, other than their own self-advancement, I am at a loss to understand what is it that the so-called black conservatives are so anxious to conserve." Mentioning specifically Presidents Reagan and Bush, he disparagingly asserted that "at every turn, the[se] conservatives, either by tacit approbation or by active complicity, tried to derail the struggle for equal rights in this country."[15]

Third, he wanted Thomas to know that his confirmation, which Higginbotham personally opposed, occurred only because of black voters. He stated, "Of the fifty-two senators who voted in favor of your confirmation, some thirteen hailed from nine southern states. Some may have voted for you because they agreed with President Bush's assessment that you were 'the best person for the position.' But, candidly, Justice Thomas, I do not believe that you were indeed the most competent person to be on the Supreme Court." Asserting that none of the senators who voted to confirm him would have hired him as their lawyer, Higginbotham lectured Thomas that

> many senators probably did not think that you were the most qualified
> person available. Rather, they were acting solely as politicians, weighing
> the potential backlash in their states of the black vote that favored you for
> emotional reasons and the conservative white vote that favored you for
> ideological reasons. The black voting constituency is important in many
> states, and today it could make a difference as to whether many senators are
> or are not re-elected. So here, too, you benefitted from civil rights progress.[16]

Fourth and finally, Higginbotham reminded Thomas of the impact on his life of civil rights victories in the areas of housing and privacy. He suggested that Thomas could live in his middle-class home in northern Virginia and be married to his white wife only because of civil rights victories. "If the Virginia courts [upholding a ban on miscegenation] had been sustained by the United States Supreme Court in 1966," he remarked, "and if, after your marriage, you and your wife had . . . defied the Virginia statute by continuing to live in your present residence, you could have been in the penitentiary today rather than serving as an Associate Justice of the United States Supreme Court."[17]

Admitting that he was "very concerned" about Thomas's appointment and "skeptical" as to what his performance on the Court would be, Higginbotham took comfort in the fact that Hugo Black, an Alabama senator who was once a member of the Ku Klux Klan, was able to repudiate his past and, after being appointed to the Supreme Court, remake himself as a liberal icon. Implicitly suggesting that Thomas's current views on race and equality were as offensive as Black's early views, Higginbotham concluded by inviting Thomas to become the new Thurgood Marshall: "I wonder whether (and how far) the majority of the [Rehnquist] Supreme Court will continue to retreat from protecting the rights of the poor, women, the disadvantaged, minorities, and the powerless. And if, tragically, a majority of the Court continues to retreat, I wonder whether you, Justice Thomas, an African-American, will be part of that majority."[18]

Higginbotham's "Open Letter" was followed by a decade of unrelievedly hostile law review articles on Thomas, focusing especially on his confirmation hearing. Scott Douglas Gerber reports that there were "seventeen law review articles about the Thomas-Hill confirmation battle as well as two symposia. The sheer number of law review articles about the hearings is not surprising; the vitriolic tone of the overwhelming majority of them is."[19] Mark Tushnet, a self-described "radical" law professor then at Georgetown University and later at Harvard Law School and a onetime law clerk to Thurgood Marshall, preposterously suggested that Thomas's confirmation was such a mistake that any five-to-four Supreme Court decision in which Thomas was in the majority should be regarded as nonbinding.[20] An unsigned note in the *Harvard Law Review* went so far as to argue that Thomas "structured his jurisprudence to define himself as separate from— and often in direct opposition to—Justice Marshall."[21]

Thomas has been unfazed by these attacks. He has resolutely refused to abandon his original general meaning approach to the Constitution and vote as Thurgood Marshall would have. In 1998, Thomas was invited to address the annual convention of the National Bar Association, the largest organization of black lawyers and judges. His invitation was met with howls of outrage. Judge Higginbotham led the charge to rescind the invitation, arguing that "it makes no more sense to invite Clarence Thomas than it would have for the National Bar Association to invite George Wallace for dinner the day after he stood in the schoolhouse door and shouted 'Segregation today and segregation forever.'"[22] Higginbotham's efforts failed, and Thomas spoke to the convention delegates and directly addressed this personal affront:

It pains me deeply—more deeply than any of you can imagine—to be perceived by so many members of my race as doing them harm, all the sacrifice, all the long hours of preparation were to help, not hurt. . . . I have come here today not in anger or to anger, though my mere presence has been sufficient, obviously, to anger some, nor have I come to defend my views, but rather to assert my right to think for myself, to refuse to have my ideas assigned to me, as though I was an intellectual slave.[23]

In the pages ahead, Thomas's opinions and other writings on questions concerning desegregation, racial preference, and voting rights are explored. Collectively, they are an extended meditation on several recurring themes in his jurisprudence concerning race and equality.

The first theme is his original general meaning approach to constitutional interpretation, which understands the Declaration of Independence and its "self evident" truth that "all men are created equal" as "preceding and underlying the Constitution."[24] Because all men are created equal, they have the "unalienable rights" to life, liberty, and the pursuit of happiness. Because all men are created equal, no one can take those rights from another without violating the "laws of nature and nature's God." And because all men are created equal, "government must proceed by consent."[25] Thomas reflected on these ideas—these "higher law" principles, as he called them[26]—in an article entitled "An Afro-American Perspective: Toward a 'Plain Reading' of the Constitution—The Declaration of Independence in Constitutional Interpretation." He stressed that the "original intention" of the Constitution was to be "the fulfillment of the ideas of the Declaration of Independence, as Lincoln, Frederick Douglass, and the Founders understood it."[27]

Thomas is fond of referencing and quoting from Lincoln. In the same article, he wrote that "for Lincoln and for the Declaration, equality led to the principle of government by consent, limited government, majority rule, and separation of powers."[28] And in his Opperman Lecture at Drake Law School, he reminded his audience that Lincoln called equality "the great fundamental principle upon which our free institutions rest" and that "the Reverend Martin Luther King, Jr. described it as the 'promissory note to which every American was to fall heir.'"[29]

Lincoln's most memorable language connecting the Declaration's principle of equality to the Constitution invoked Proverbs 25:11: "A word fitly spoken is like an apple of gold in a frame of silver." Lincoln used the proverb to show the relation of the Declaration to the Constitution. The Declaration's self-evident truth of equality was the "word fitly spoken"; it was the "apple of gold," and the Constitution was its "frame of silver" intended "to *adorn*, and *preserve* it." And as Lincoln made clear, the frame was made for the apple—not the apple for the frame.[30] Thomas has invoked this powerful imagery and argued that his original general meaning approach "puts the fitly spoken words of the Declaration of Independence in the center of the frame formed by the Constitution."[31]

Like Lincoln, Thomas knows that men are not "equal in physical and intellectual attributes. Such would be a self-evident delusion rather than a self-evident truth."[32] On June 26, 1857, in Springfield, Illinois, Abraham Lincoln was responding to Chief Justice Roger Taney's assertion in the *Dred Scott* decision that blacks were not included in the words of the Declaration when he proclaimed: "I think the authors of that notable instrument intended to include all men, but they did not intend to declare all men equal in all respects. They did not mean to say all were equal in color, size, intellect, moral developments, or social capacity." Rather, they "defined with tolerable distinctness, in what respects they did consider all men created equal—'equal in certain inalienable rights, among which are life, liberty and the pursuit of happiness.' This they said, and this they meant."[33] Thomas is in full agreement with Lincoln's claim that the authors of the Declaration "did not mean to assert the obvious untruth, that all were then actually enjoying that equality, nor yet, that they were about to confer it immediately upon them. In fact they had no power to confer such a boon. They meant simply to declare the right, so that the enforcement of it might follow as fast as circumstances should permit." As Thomas has written, "With the Declaration as a backdrop, we can understand the Constitution as the Founders understood it—to point toward the eventual abolition of slavery. Nonetheless, emancipation had to be made explicit" through the Civil War Amendments.[34] And even then, Thomas continued, those amendments were not fully able to "assist" black Americans to throw off the chains of slavery and to lay claim to the full rights and dignity of citizenship until they were finally "understood as extensions of the founding principles of equality and liberty."[35]

Continuing his commentary on the *Dred Scott* decision, Lincoln declared that the Declaration's promise of equality "set up a standard maxim for free society, which should be familiar to all, and revered by all; constantly looked to, constantly labored for, and even though never perfectly attained, constantly approximated, and thereby constantly spreading and deepening its influence, and augmenting the happiness and value of life to all people of all colors everywhere." For Thomas, that "standard maxim" found embodiment in the Civil War Amendments and their eventual "proper" interpretation by Justice John Marshall Harlan in his dissent in *Plessy*.[36]

For Lincoln, that promise of equality applied to all men of all races and nationalities. On July 10, 1858, in Chicago, Illinois, he gave a speech in which he reflected on the Fourth of July and the meaning of the Declaration; in it, he indicated that the Americans of his day had among them, in addition to those who were descended from the blood of the founders, perhaps half "who are not

descendants at all of these men, they are men who have come from Europe—
German, Irish, French, Scandinavian—men who have come from Europe themselves or whose ancestors have come thither and settled here, finding themselves
our equals in all things." They have, he said, "no connection by blood" to those
who wrote the Declaration, but they nonetheless can "carry themselves back to
that glorious epic, the time of the drafting of the Constitution and the Declaration, and make themselves feel that they are a part of us." They can do so when
they "look through that old Declaration of Independence" and read those words:
"We hold these truths to be self evident, that all men are created equal." They
then "feel that moral sentiment taught in that day evidences their relation to
those men that it is the father of all moral principles in them and that they have
a right to claim it as though they were blood of the blood and flesh of the flesh of
the men who wrote that Declaration, and so they are."[37]

Thomas understands this, as did Frederick Douglass, who in his Fourth of
July oration in 1852, could declare that the Constitution's "principles and purposes," grounded as they were in the Declaration, were "entirely hostile to the
existence of slavery."[38] Thomas quoted this passage from Douglass before insisting that all black Americans are also blood of the blood and flesh of the flesh of
the men who wrote that Declaration and inviting them to join him in allowing its
"first principles of equality and liberty" to "inspire our political and constitutional
thinking" and to "lead us above petty squabbling over 'quotas,' 'affirmative action,' and race-conscious remedies for social ills. Such a principled jurisprudence
would pose a major alternative to the cynical rejection of 'the laws of nature and
nature's God' from jurisprudence, and esoteric hermeneutics rationalizing expansive powers for the government, especially the judiciary."[39]

Thomas asserts that a constitution based on and infused with the principles of
the Declaration of Independence is necessarily a color-blind constitution.[40] He
adopts as his own the first Justice Harlan's "splendid exegesis" in his *Plessy* dissent
"of the 'original intention' of the Civil War Amendments (not just the Equal Protection Clause), which is rooted in a profound understanding of the founding."[41]
Regarding Harlan's dissent, Thomas has written that "in order to appreciate the
subtleties" of his argument, "one must read it in light of the 'higher law' background of the Constitution" and appreciate that "Justice Harlan understood, as
did Lincoln, that his task was to bring out the best of the Founders' arguments
regarding the universal principles of equality and liberty." Thus, Justice Harlan
argued against segregation by first contending that the Thirteenth Amendment
struck down "badges of slavery or servitude" in addition to the actual institution
of slavery and "decreed universal civil freedom in this country." He then maintained that "segregation constituted an unreasonable infringement of personal
freedom." Harlan finished, Thomas stated, by presenting "arguments which help

us to prevent the term 'color-blind Constitution' from being a bromide, by refer-ring to the Founders' work."[42]

As Thomas asserted, a color-blind constitution in turn emphasizes individual rights, not group rights.[43] When he was serving as chairman of the U.S. Equal Employment Opportunity Commission, he wrote an article in the *Yale Law and Policy Review* that was highly critical of his agency's past use of affirmative action, with its emphasis on "goals and timetables," to address racial discrimination in the workplace; he labeled it "a sideshow in the war on discrimination."[44] Thomas wrote that one of the first things he noticed when he arrived at the EEOC was that it was often employers "who pushed for the use of numerical goals in a settle-ment agreement," even before the commission had identified actual victims. For him, the reason was obvious: "In those cases where numerical relief is possible — this is, where there has been a pattern or practice of discrimination affecting a large class — every identified victim had the right to 'make whole' relief. Giving back pay to each actual victim can be quite expensive, but the cost of agreeing to hire a certain number of blacks or women is generally *de minimus*."[45] Goals and timetables focused on the group, not the individual, and therefore an employer who hired a new black or a woman against whom it had not previously discrimi-nated was relieved of the obligation to make whole the black or the woman who had actually been subject to its discrimination. Thomas was deeply offended by this: "The use of affirmative action, rather than a victim-specific form of remedy, effectively allows employers to shift the cost of the remedy from themselves to the actual victims of their past discrimination, who never receive the back pay and jobs to which they are entitled, and to the qualified persons who will be deprived of the employment opportunity because someone else was given a preference under the remedial plan."[46]

Thomas concluded his article by writing that "goals and timetables are easy on employers who want to avoid back pay liability and easy on interest groups that are more concerned with advancing group interests than the rights of par-ticular individuals." Acknowledging that "the temptation to do things the easy way is always great," he insisted that before "we succumb, we should remember these victims" and choose "the tougher course that promises to yield genuine and lasting equal opportunities."[47]

Thomas's emphasis on individual rights over group rights leads inexorably to his insistence on "personal responsibility" and hard work.[48] In an address entitled "Victims and Heroes in the 'Benevolent State,'" which he delivered to the Eighth Annual Federalist Society Lawyers Convention at which the theme was "Group Rights, Victim Status, and the Law," he declared that "it says something about the current state of affairs in our society that a conference on victims — that is, a conference on the rise of the practice of blaming circumstances for one's situation rather than taking responsibility for changing things for the better—is even necessary." Recalling his impoverished youth in Savannah, he announced that "the very notion of submitting to one's circumstances was unthinkable" in the household where he and his brother were raised. "The mere suggestion that difficult circumstances could prevail over individual effort would evoke a response" from his proudly self-reliant grandfather, Myers Anderson, "that my brother and I could lip-sync on cue: 'Old man can't is dead; I helped bury him.'" Though conceding that it "may have seemed harsh at the time to be told that failure was one's own fault," he insisted that his family preached the message of "self-determination and self-worth, thereby inoculating us against the victim plague that was highly contagious in the hot, humid climate of segregation" and instilling in him and his brother the "more positive message to be gained from adversity: success (as well as failure) is the result of one's own talents, morals, decision, and actions."[49] He proclaimed personal responsibility for both victory and defeat to be "liberating and empowering. . . . Overcoming adversity not only gives us our measure as individuals, but it also reinforces those basic principles and rules without which a society based upon freedom and liberty cannot function."[50]

In his address, he worried that "our culture today discourages, and even at times stifles, heroic virtues—fortitude, character, courage, a sense of self-worth." He regretted that "today's society do[es] not expect the less fortunate to accept responsibility for (and overcome) their present circumstances. Because they are given no chance to overcome their circumstances, they will not have the chance to savor the triumph over adversity." Then, Thomas again recalled his grandfather. "One of my favorite memories of my grandfather is how he would walk slowly by the corn field, admiring the fruits of his labor. I have often thought that just the sight of a tall stand of corn must have been more nourishing to his spirit than the corn itself was to his body."[51] A former seminarian, Thomas concluded his remarks by quoting from Saint Thomas à Kempis: "Take care to ensure that in every place, action, and outward occupation you remain inwardly free and your own master. Control circumstances, and do not allow them to control you. Only so can you be master and ruler of your actions, not their servant or slave; a free man."[52]

Personal responsibility, as Thomas made clear in his address on "Victims and Heroes," requires hard work. In 1998, he elaborated on this matter in his address to the faculty and students at the Thurgood Marshall School of Law at Texas Southern University, a historically black university located in Houston. He reflected with them on his own years at Yale Law School, where he was considered "a bit of a grind." He added, "I spent a lot of time in the stacks" because "it was important to me not to let this opportunity slip away." And then he admonished them: "You don't get from point 'A' to point 'B' by being upset or by being angry or by just listening to speeches. Most of learning is lonely work. Most of great work is lonely work. You are by yourself. So you have to get used to it."[53] And this hard, lonely work is great work, he informed them, if it is based on "preparation, preparation, preparation."

He gave a personal example: "I am Geechie. And we spoke Gulla or a version of it and it is closely related to English and perhaps some of you have another native tongue." He confessed that "it was hard to get rid of the Gulla in my language" and explained that this is why when he attended Holy Cross, "I majored in English literature. I did not necessarily want to be a literature major but I had to learn to speak English." And so, he continued,

> I majored in something that I found extremely difficult in order to be able to function in a difficult society. I give you that as an example, that it isn't easy and perhaps it will require us to swallow a bitter pill of some sort or another. I had a problem with writing English. Do you have the same problem? It was hard for me to write complete paragraphs, but I think having written over and over and over, it finally worked. Now, you can say, "Well, that's mundane." But learning is mundane.[54]

For Thomas, a constitution based on and infused with the principles of the Declaration of Independence also necessarily rejects "racial paternalism"[55] and the idea of black inferiority on which that paternalism is based. In *Missouri v. Jenkins*, he began his concurrence declaring, "It never ceases to amaze me that the courts are so willing to assume that anything that is predominantly black must be inferior"[56] and by indignantly rejecting the idea that black students could learn better if they sat between white students. In Jeffery Rosen's account of the Court's conference after oral argument in *Jenkins*, Thomas "spoke fervently" of his own youthful struggles with the reality of Jim Crow, declaring, "I am the only one at this table who attended a segregated school." Moreover, he continued, the problem with his segregated school was not that "we didn't have white people in our class. The problem was that we didn't have equal facilities. We didn't have heating, we didn't have books, and we had rickety chairs. All society owed us was equal resources and an equal opportunity to make something of ourselves." Rosen reports that Thomas then added: "The evil of segregation was that black students had inferior facilities, not that they were denied the chance to go to school with white students. . . . All my classmates and I wanted was the choice to attend a mostly black or a mostly white school, and to have the same resources in whatever school we choose."[57]

He elaborated on his conviction that because blacks are not inferior, there is no need for forced integration so that they can benefit from their proximity to superior white students. There is no reason to regard "racial imbalance" (or "racial isolation"—two terms Thomas uses interchangeably) as a constitutional problem in need of a remedy.[58] In his view, the Constitution bars taking race into account either to separate the races (segregation) or to mix and therefore balance the races (integration).

And again, because blacks are not inferior, there is no need for affirmative action for blacks in general but only a need for equitable remedies for those individual blacks who have experienced racial discrimination. Affirmative action for blacks in general subtlely undermines a sense of self-worth in those it is intended to benefit.[59] It also generates feelings of racial antipathy among those who believe they were unfairly denied opportunities that their objective measures of worthiness would otherwise have provided them, and it reinforces racial stereotypes and animosity.

And finally, according to Thomas, because the Declaration declares that all men are created equal and because the rights it proclaims are individual rights, not group rights, all blacks have the right to think for themselves. The idea that all blacks think alike is, for Thomas, utterly repugnant. As he argued in *Holder v. Hall*, the "basic premise" that all blacks "must think alike" is "a divisive force" that could not be more effective at "exacerbate[ing] racial tensions."[60]

School Desegregation

Thomas has written major opinions—all of them concurring opinions—in the three major school desegregation cases that have come before the Court during his tenure. His first opinion came in *United States v. Fordice*,[61] a decision handed down during his initial year on the Court. In *Fordice*, Justice Bryon White concluded for an eight-member majority that even though the state of Mississippi had ended the *de jure* segregation of its dual public university system, composed of five historically white and three historically black universities, and had implemented race-neutral admissions policies, those actions alone did not suffice to demonstrate that the state had completely dismantled its dual system of higher education; that if policies traceable to the prior dual system were still in force and had discriminatory effects, those policies had to be reformed to the extent practicable and consistent with sound educational practices; and on remand to the federal district court, the state would have to justify or eliminate several remaining suspect policies with respect to admissions standards, program duplication, institutional mission assignments, and the continued operation of all eight universities.

Thomas concurred in White's opinion but wrote separately to defend the continued operation of the state's historically black universities. As in several other of his opinions, he began by quoting a prominent black civil rights leader; this time it was W. E. B. DuBois: "We must rally to the defense of our schools. We must repudiate this unbearable assumption of the right to kill institutions unless they conform to one narrow standard."[62] He then supported the Court's conclusion that Mississippi had not satisfied its obligation to dismantle its dual system of higher education merely by adopting race-neutral policies for the future administration of that system; endorsed the Court's statement that "if policies traceable to the *de jure* system are still in force and have discriminatory effects, those policies too must be reformed to the extent practicable and consistent with sound educational practices";[63] and agreed with the Court that this statement defined "the appropriate standard to apply in the higher education context." He explained that he was writing separately "to emphasize that this standard is far different from the one adopted to govern the grade-school context" and to underscore that it did not "compel the elimination of all observed racial imbalance," "portend . . . the destruction of historically black colleges," or "sever . . . those institutions from their distinctive histories and traditions."[64]

In the grade school context, the Court employed "remedies as 'radical' as student assignment." The Court in *Fordice* had rejected the use of such remedies in the higher education context and for an obvious reason (postsecondary students are free to choose whether to pursue an advanced education and which of many universities to attend). It concentrated, instead, on "the specific policies alleged to produce racial imbalance, rather than on the imbalance itself." Although Thomas deemed these remarks encouraging, he found "most encouraging the Court's emphasis on *'sound educational practices.'*"[65] And, he added, "one compelling need to be considered" by the federal district court on remand "is the *educational* need of the present and future *students* in the Mississippi university system, for whose benefit the remedies will be crafted." Offering direct advice to that federal district court, Thomas stressed that "in particular, we do not foreclose the possibility that there exists 'sound educational justification' for maintaining historically black colleges *as such*."[66] He wrote of how these institutions "have survived and flourished" despite "the shameful history of state-enforced segregation." He found it "undisputable" that they did so because of "their distinctive histories and traditions." And he insisted there was no equal protection bar to Mississippi "operat[ing] a diverse assortment of institutions—including historically black institutions—open to all on a race-neutral basis, but with established traditions and programs that might disproportionately appeal to one race or another."[67] No one, he told the federal district court that would hear the case on remand, should argue that "such institutional *diversity* is without 'sound educational justification.'" And even as he acknowledged that Mississippi was not "constitutionally required to maintain its historically black institutions," he also insisted that nothing in the Court opinion he joined required the federal distinct court to hold that it was "*forbidden* to do so. It would be ironic, to say the least, if the institutions that sustained blacks during segregation were themselves destroyed in an effort to combat it vestiges."[68]

Thomas's second major concurring opinion was in the Court's 1995 decision in *Missouri v. Jenkins*.[69] In a 1990 decision,[70] decided one year before Thomas's nomination, the Court considered a ruling by Federal District Court Judge Russell Clark, who found that the Kansas City, Missouri, School District (KCMSD) and the state of Missouri were guilty of operating a segregated school system and issued an order detailing a desegregation remedy and the financing necessary to implement it. His remedy was comprehensive and extraordinarily expensive. Among other things, he mandated that every high school, every middle school, and half of the elementary schools in KCMSD had to become magnet schools in order to draw nonminority students from private schools and suburban schools into the school district's system. The cost of implementing his remedial plan was placed between $500 million and $700 million. Justice Kennedy would describe Judge Clark's capital improvement plan as follows:

> High schools in which every classroom will have air conditioning, an alarm system, and 15 microcomputers; a 2,000-square-foot planetarium; greenhouses and vivariums; a 25-acre farm with an air-conditioned meeting room for 104 people; a Model United Nations wired for language translation; broadcast-capable radio and television studios with an editing and animation lab; a temperature-controlled art gallery; movie editing and screening rooms; a 3,500-square-foot, dust-free diesel mechanics room; 1,875-square-foot elementary school animal rooms for use in a Zoo Project; swimming pools; and numerous other facilities.[71]

To pay for this remedy, Judge Clark ordered the state of Missouri to cover 75 percent of the costs, with the school district contributing the rest. When it became clear that state tax limitation laws prohibited the school district from raising property tax rates sufficiently to meet its 25 percent obligation, he enjoined the operation of these state laws and ordered that the district property tax levy be increased from $2.05 to $4.00 per $100 of assessed valuation. When his decree reached the Supreme Court, the justices unanimously concluded that Judge Clark had abused his discretion; however, Justice White wrote for just a five-member majority when he held that Judge Clark had abused it only by specifying the tax levy, not by demanding of the school district that it fully fund his remedy.[72]

When minority student achievement levels in KCMSD continued to remain below "national norms" despite court-ordered spending of what by that point was over $940 million to eliminate the past effects of racial segregation, Judge Clark in 1993 ordered Missouri to fund salary increases for virtually all instructional and noninstructional staff members in the school district and to continue to fund reme-dial "quality education" programs. He reasoned that these increases would elimi-nate the vestiges of state-imposed segregation by improving the "desegregative at-tractiveness" of the city's schools and by reversing "white flight" to the suburbs.

The Supreme Court granted certiorari and in 1995 reversed, holding that Judge Clark's order was "simply too far removed from an acceptable implemen-tation of a permissible means to remedy previous legally mandated segregation." Chief Justice Rehnquist declared that

> just as demographic changes independent of *de jure* segregation will affect the racial composition of student assignments, so too will numerous external factors beyond the control of the KCMSD and the State affect minority student achievement. So long as these external factors are not the result of segregation, they do not figure in the remedial calculus. Insistence upon academic goals unrelated to the effects of legal segregation unwarrantably postpones the day when the . . . school district will be able to operate on its own.[73]

In a lengthy and powerful concurring opinion, Justice Thomas harshly criticized Clark for assuming that if "a school district today is black, it must be educa-tionally inferior" and for exercising his "virtually unlimited equitable powers" to "trample upon principles of federalism and separation of powers" as he pursued "other agendas unrelated to the narrow purpose of precisely remedying a consti-tutional harm."[74]

Thomas began his concurrence with words freighted equally with sadness and anger: "It never ceases to amaze me that the courts are so willing to assume that anything that is predominantly black must be inferior." He was appalled that "instead of focusing on remedying the harm done to those black schoolchildren injured by segregation, the District Court here sought to convert KCMSD into a 'magnet district' that would reverse the 'white flight' caused by desegregation." He did not, however, blame Clark personally; he saw him as faithfully applying the Court's jurisprudence, "two threads" of which were responsible for producing "this unfortunate situation." The first was the Court's embrace of the view, since *Brown v. Board of Education*, that "black students suffer an unspecified psycho-

logical harm from segregation that retards their mental and educational development. This approach not only relies upon questionable social science research
rather than constitutional principle, but it also rests on an assumption of black
inferiority." The second was the Court's willingness to allow the lower federal
courts "to exercise virtually unlimited equitable powers" to remedy problems and
impose policy solutions well outside "our Article III competence."[75]

Concerning the first thread, Thomas asserted, "The mere fact that a school is
black does not mean that it is the product of a constitutional violation" and "the
existence of one-race schools is not by itself an indication that the State is practic-
ing segregation."[76] He remarked that although racial imbalance may result in an
all-black school, that "may well reflect voluntary housing choices or other private
decisions." He also noted that the fact "that certain schools are overwhelmingly
black in a district that is now more than two-thirds black is hardly a sure sign of
intentional state action."[77] Yet Judge Clark found that racial imbalances "constituted an ongoing constitutional violation that continued to inflict harm on black
students. This position appears to rest upon the idea that any school that is black
is inferior, and that blacks cannot succeed without the benefit of the company
of whites."[78]

Thomas traced this idea to *Brown v. Board of Education*, which

> did not need to rely upon any psychological or social-science research in
> order to announce the simple, yet fundamental, truth that the government
> cannot discriminate among its citizens on the basis of race. . . . At the heart
> of this interpretation of the Equal Protection Clause lies the principle that
> the government must treat citizens as individuals, and not as members of
> racial, ethnic, or religious groups. It is for this reason that we must subject
> all racial classifications to the strictest of scrutiny, which . . . has proven
> automatically fatal.[79]

Segregation, Thomas argued, "was not unconstitutional because it might
have caused psychological feelings of inferiority. Public school systems that sepa-
rated blacks and provided them with superior educational resources—making
blacks 'feel' superior to whites sent to lesser schools—would violate the Fourteenth Amendment, whether or not the white students felt stigmatized, just as
do school systems in which the positions of the races are reversed." Thomas
perceived no need for courts to rely on "the unnecessary and misleading assistance of the social sciences" to conclude that segregation violated the Fourteenth
Amendment; "segregation violated the Constitution because the state classified
students based on their race. Of course, segregation additionally harmed black
students by relegating them to schools with substandard facilities and resources.
But neutral policies, such as local school assignments, do not offend the Con-

stitution when individual private choices concerning work or residence produce schools with high black populations."[80]

He concluded his consideration of the first thread by asserting that racial imbalance "itself is not a harm; only state-enforced segregation is." After all, if racial imbalance in schools is itself a harm and if integration is the only way that blacks can receive a proper education, "then there must be something inferior about blacks. Under this theory, segregation injures blacks because blacks, when left on their own, cannot achieve. To my way of thinking, that conclusion is the result of a jurisprudence based upon a theory of black inferiority." The Equal Protection Clause, properly understood, does not require "race mixing," but it does demand that "blacks and whites are treated equally by the State without regard to their skin color." Offering advice to the lower courts, Thomas admonished them not to be "swayed by the easy answers of social science" and to refuse to "accept the findings, and the assumptions, of sociology and psychology at the price of constitutional principle."[81]

Concerning the second thread, Thomas regretted that Judge Clark not only "subscribed to a theory of injury that was predicated on black inferiority" but also "married this concept of liability to our expansive approach to remedial powers." He criticized Clark for ordering "massive expenditures by local and state authorities, without congressional or executive authorization and without any indication that such measures would attract whites back to KCMSD or raise KCMSD test scores. The time has come for us to put the genie back in the bottle."[82] Thomas then spent seven pages reviewing the history and original general meaning of the federal courts' equity power as embodied in Article III, § 2 and found Clark's use of it "at odds" with "the Framers' design," based as it was on federalism and separation of powers.[83]

Judge Clark's orders violated federalism because "when district courts seize complete control over the schools, they strip state and local governments of one of their most important governmental responsibilities, and thus deny their existence as independent governmental entities."[84] And by "presum[ing] to have the institutional ability to set effective, educational, budgetary, or administrative policy," Judge Clark violated the separation of powers by helping to "transform the least dangerous branch into the most dangerous one." Thomas had no doubt that "there are certain things that courts, in order to remain courts, cannot and should not do. There is no difference between courts running school systems or prisons and courts running Executive Branch agencies."[85]

Thomas concluded that Judge Clark's orders were all the more egregious because they were not "precisely designed to benefit only those who have been victims of segregation."[86] He argued that "raising the test scores of the *entire* district is a goal that is not sufficiently tailored to restoring the *victims* of segregation to a position they would have occupied absent discrimination." He faulted Clark for having ordered "broad remedies that indiscriminately benefit[ed] a school district as a whole, rather than the individual students who suffered from discrimination." And he said in summation: "Although I do not doubt that all KCMSD students benefit from many of the initiatives ordered by the courts below, it is for the democratically accountable state and local officials to decide whether they are to be made available even to those who were never harmed by segregation."[87]

Thomas's third major concurring opinion was in *Parents Involved in Community Schools v. Seattle School District No. 1.*[88] In this case, the Court reviewed lower federal court decisions coming out of Seattle and Louisville that had employed *Grutter v. Bollinger*[89] (about which there will be much more later) to affirm voluntary student assignment plans by school districts that relied on race to determine which schools certain children could attend. These courts held such plans survived strict scrutiny because they were narrowly tailored to serve the compelling governmental interests of achieving racial diversity and avoiding racial isolation. Five members of the Court found these plans unconstitutional. Chief Justice Roberts held that the school district plans "are not governed by *Grutter.*"[90] In *Grutter*, he stated, "this Court relied upon considerations unique to institutions of higher education," noting that in light of "'the expansive freedoms of speech and thought associated with the university environment, universities occupy a special niche in our constitutional tradition.' It explained that 'context matters' in applying strict scrutiny, and repeatedly noted that it was addressing the use of race 'in the context of higher education.'"[91] Justice Kennedy supplied the fifth vote to invalidate these plans, but he found unacceptable Chief Justice Roberts's "all-too-unyielding insistence that race cannot be a factor in instances when, in my view, it may be taken into account."[92]

Justice Breyer dissented, lamenting that Roberts's opinion broke "the "promise of *Brown*," which he described as "the promise of true racial equality."[93] Roberts shot back, saying that the promise of *Brown* was "to achieve a system of determining admission to the public schools on a nonracial basis." Furthermore, he said, that promise was what the Court's decision in *Parents Involved* was keeping: "The way to stop discrimination on the basis of race is to stop discriminating on the basis of race." Justice Thomas agreed in his concurrence and developed at length a theme he introduced in this sentence: "Disfavoring a color-blind interpretation of the Constitution, the dissent would give school boards a free hand to make decisions on the basis of race—an approach reminiscent of that advocated by the segregationists in *Brown*."[94]

Breyer argued that purportedly benign racial-based decision making was less constitutionally offensive than invidious race-based decision making, but Thomas rejected this out of hand, remarking, "Every time the government uses racial criteria to 'bring the races together,' someone gets excluded, and the person excluded suffers an injury solely because of his or her race." He continued, "This type of exclusion, solely on the basis of race, is precisely the sort of governmental action that pits the races against one another, exacerbates racial tension, . . . 'provokes resentment among those who believe that they have been wronged by the government's use of race,'"[95] and demands that its use be subjected to strict scrutiny.

Breyer also asserted that the social science evidence showing the ameliorative effects of integration, that is, race mixing, was "strong enough to permit a democratically elected school board reasonably to determine that this interest is a compelling one."[96] Thomas found this assertion "inexplicable. It is not up to the school boards—the very government entities whose race-based practices we must strictly scrutinize—to determine what interests qualify as compelling under the Fourteenth Amendment." To do so would leave the Court's equal protection jurisprudence "at the mercy of elected government officials evaluating the evanescent views of a handful of social scientists."[97]

Thomas attributed Breyer's criticisms of the Court's decision to his "rejection of the color-blind Constitution. The dissent attempts to marginalize the notion of a color-blind Constitution by consigning it to me and the Members of today's plurality." Thomas was not cowed. "I am quite comfortable in the company I keep. My view of the Constitution is Justice Harlan's view in *Plessy*: 'Our Constitution is color blind, and neither knows nor tolerates classes among citizens.' And my view was the rallying cry for the lawyers who litigated *Brown*."[98]

These were points that Thomas had made before. But he then introduced what were, for him, a new set of arguments. He attacked Breyer for replicating, "to a distressing extent," the arguments of "the segregationists in *Brown*." Breyer contended both the Seattle and the Louisville plans embodied "the results of local experience and community consultation," Thomas said, an argument similar to the "repeated appeals to societal practice and expectation" made by segregationists in *Brown*. Further, he noted that Breyer argued that "weight must be given to a local school board's knowledge, expertise, and concerns," a claim also "made and with equal vigor by the segregationists in *Brown* who argued for deference to local authorities." Breyer contended, as well, that the Court's decision "threatens to substitute for present calm a disruptive round of race-related litigation" and "risks serious harm to the law and for the Nation," just like "the segregationists also relied upon the likely practical consequences of ending the state-imposed system of racial separation." And finally, "foreshadowing [Breyer's] dissent," Thomas stated that "the segregationists most heavily relied upon judicial precedent"—*Plessy* for the segregationists, *Grutter* for Breyer.[99] But, he insisted, "the similarities between [Breyer's] dissent and the segregationists' arguments do not stop there." Like Breyer, "the segregationalists repeatedly cautioned the Court to consider practicalities and not to embrace too theoretical a view of the

Fourteenth Amendment." And just as Breyer argued that "the need for these programs will lessen over time, the segregationists claimed that reliance on segregation was lessening and might eventually end."[100]

Thomas would have none of this. "What was wrong in 1954 cannot be right today," he stated. "Whatever else the Court's rejection of the segregationists' arguments in *Brown* might have established, it certainly made clear that state and local governments cannot take from the Constitution a right to make decisions on the basis of race by adverse possession." Thomas noted that "the fact that state and local governments had been discriminating on the basis of race for a long time was irrelevant to the *Brown* Court." Likewise, "the fact that racial discrimination was preferable to the relevant communities was irrelevant to the *Brown* Court." And "the fact that the state and local governments had relied on statements in this Court's opinions was irrelevant to the *Brown* Court. The same principles guide today's decision. None of the considerations trumpeted by the dissent is relevant to the constitutionality of the school boards' race-based plans because no contextual detail—or collection of contextual details—can 'provide refuge from the principle that under our Constitution, the government may not make distinctions on the basis of race.'"[101]

Contrary to the principles of a color-blind Constitution, Thomas noted in summary, Breyer would "permit" measures to keep races together and "proscribe" measures to keep races apart and thereby "constitutionalize today's faddish social theories that embrace" forced race mixing. Then Thomas thundered, "The Constitution is not that malleable." It "enshrines principles independent of social theories," he said, whereupon he again quoted Harlan's words that the Constitution is color blind: "Indeed, if our history has taught us anything, it has taught us to beware of elites bearing racial theories. Can we really be sure that the racial theories that motivated *Dred Scott* and *Plessy* are a relic of the past or that future theories will be nothing but beneficent and progressive? That is a gamble I am unwilling to take, and it is one the Constitution does not allow."[102] Thomas then dropped a powerful and final footnote: "Justice Breyer's good intentions, which I do not doubt, have the shelf life of Justice Breyer's tenure. Unlike the dissenters, I am unwilling to delegate my constitutional responsibilities to local school boards and allow them to experiment with race-based decision-making on the assumption that their intentions will forever remain as good as Justice Breyer's."[103]

Racial Preference

In *Adarand Constructors v. Pena*,[104] the Court held that all governmental classifications based on race had to be subjected to strict scrutiny and, therefore, that a federal subcontractor compensation program providing prime contractors with financial incentives to hire minority business enterprises had to be assessed to determine if it served a compelling government interest and was narrowly tailored to further that interest. Thomas agreed and wrote a short concurrence to disagree with the underlying premise of the dissenters that "there is a racial paternalism exception to the principle of equal protection." He found it "irrelevant whether a government's racial classifications are drawn by those who wish to oppress a race or by those who have a sincere desire to help those thought to be disadvantaged. There can be no doubt that the paternalism that appears to lie at the heart of this program is at war with the principle of inherent equality that underlies and infuses our Constitution. See Declaration of Independence."[105]

Racial paternalism (Thomas also called it "benign prejudice") undermines "the moral basis of the equal protection principle," he said, "purchased at the price of immeasurable human suffering." It is "as poisonous and pernicious as any other form of discrimination," for it "teaches many that because of chronic and apparently immutable handicaps, minorities cannot compete with them without their patronizing indulgence." It engenders in them "attitudes of superiority, or alternatively, provoke[s] resentment among those who believe they have been wronged by the government's use of race." It "stamp[s] minorities with a badge of inferiority," encourages "dependencies," and fosters an attitude of entitlement. It is "just as noxious as discrimination inspired by malicious prejudice."[106]

Thomas's most extensive critique of the use of racial preference came in his opinion in *Grutter v. Bollinger*.[107] In *Grutter*, Justice O'Connor held for a five-member majority that diversity constitutes "a compelling interest that can justify the narrowly tailored use of race in selecting applicants for admission to public universities."[108] She found that the University of Michigan Law School had "a compelling interest in attaining a diverse student body"[109] and that its desire to "enroll a 'critical mass' of minority students" to enhance the educational experience for all of its students survived strict scrutiny.[110] Additionally, she argued that the Law School's admission program was "narrowly tailored" in that it used race in a "flexible, non-mechanical way,"[111] evaluating each applicant "as an individual and not in a way that makes an applicant's race or ethnicity the defining feature of his or her application."[112]

Until *Grutter*, the only governmental use of race that a majority of the Court had held could survive strict scrutiny was remedying the effects of past discrimination. This was a very narrow exception to the rule that all race-based classifications are unconstitutional, and it was also time bound—once the injury to the actual victims of discrimination was remedied, the justification to classify by race ended. In *Grutter*, however, the Court added a broad and open-ended justification for governmental use of race—diversity. O'Connor praised the benefits of diversity not only in educational settings but also in business ("the skills needed in today's increasingly global marketplace can only be developed through expo- sure to widely diverse people, cultures, ideas, and viewpoints"),[113] the military ("a highly qualified, racially diverse officer corps is essential to the military's ability to fulfill its principle [sic] mission to provide national security"),[114] and politics ("in order to cultivate a set of leaders with legitimacy in the eyes of the citizenry, it is necessary that the path to leadership be visibly open to talented and qualified individuals of every race and ethnicity)."[115] And this justification, in principle, is not time bound; the benefits of diversity will continue indefinitely. O'Connor was clearly troubled by the prospect of the perpetual use of Court-approved racial classifications, and so she arbitrarily introduced her own "sunset" provision. "We expect that 25 years from now, the use of racial preferences will no longer be necessary to further the interest approved today."[116]

Thomas filed an impassioned dissent. As in his concurrence in *Zelman v. Simmons-Harris*,[117] the voucher case, he began with a powerful quotation from Frederick Douglass. He prefaced the quote by stating that Douglass, "speaking to a group of abolitionists almost 140 years ago, delivered a message lost on today's majority." He then let Douglass's words speak for themselves:

> What I ask for the negro is not benevolence, not pity, not sympathy,
> but simply *justice*. The American people have always been anxious to
> know what they shall do with us. . . . I have had but one answer from the
> beginning. Do nothing with us! Your doing with us has already played
> the mischief with us. Do nothing with us! If the apples will not remain
> on the tree of their own strength, if they are worm-eaten at the core, if they
> are early ripe and disposed to fall, let them fall! . . . And if the negro cannot
> stand on his own legs, let him fall also. All I ask is, give him a chance to
> stand on his own legs! Let him alone! . . . Your interference is doing him
> positive injury.[118]

Thomas heartily embraced Douglass's proposition, declaring, "I believe blacks can achieve in every avenue of American life without the meddling of university administrators." He added that the Constitution neither "tolerate[s] institutional devotion to the status quo in admissions policies when such devotion ripens into racial discrimination" nor "countenance[s] the unprecedented deference the Court gives to the Law School, an approach inconsistent with the very concept of 'strict scrutiny.'"[119] He was outraged that the Court upheld "the Law School's ra- cial discrimination not by interpreting the people's Constitution, but by respond- ing to the faddish slogan of the cognoscenti." He agreed with O'Connor's opinion in only one detail—when she said that racial discrimination in higher education admissions would be illegal in twenty-five years—but he insisted that "the Law School's current use of race violates the Equal Protection Clause and that the Constitution means the same thing today as it will in 300 months."[120]

Thomas sought to define "with precision" this public law school's interest that was so compelling it justified the use of racial discrimination. Although the school emphasized the educational benefits that flow from student body diversity and the presence of a "critical mass" of "underrepresented minority students," he pointed out that those benefits could be achieved if the school changed its admissions policies, something it was unwilling to do because it would negatively affect its status as an elite law school.[121] Thomas distilled the Law School's argument to its essence: "Classroom esthetics [which he had just defined as "a certain appearance, from the shape of the desks and tables to the color of the students sitting in them"][122] yields educational benefits, racially discriminatory policies are required to achieve the right racial mix, and therefore these policies are required to achieve the educational benefits."[123] Thomas cut through the Law School's rhetoric and O'Connor's assertions: "The preferred interest that the majority vindicates today . . . is not 'diversity.' Instead the Court upholds the use of racial discrimination as a tool to advance the Law School's interest in offering a marginally superior education while maintaining an elite institution. Unless each constituent part of this state interest is a pressing necessity, the Law School's use of race is unconstitutional. I find each of them to fall far short of this standard."[124]

Thomas began by pointing out that the state of Michigan had no compelling interest in having a law school at all. He noted that Alaska, Delaware, Massachusetts, New Hampshire, and Rhode Island all got by quite well with no publicly supported law schools, and it therefore followed that Michigan had no compelling interest in having an "elite one."[125] The Law School, he continued, could have all the diversity it sought by lowering its admission standards for all applicants; that, however, would hurt its "elite status." For Thomas, the Equal Protection Clause required the school to choose between diversity and high admission standards, that is, between "its classroom aesthetic and its exclusionary admissions system—it cannot have it both ways."[126]

Thomas was also astonished at the Court's "unprecedented deference—a deference antithetical to strict scrutiny—on the idea of 'educational autonomy' grounded on the First Amendment."[127] He was nonplussed that instead of "being given license to use racial discrimination," the Law School was not required to "radically reshape its admissions process, even to the point of sacrificing some elements of its character." The Court had demanded this of an institution of higher education in the recent past. In *United States v. Virginia*,[128] "a majority of the Court, without a word about academic freedom, accepted the all-male Virginia Military Institute's (VMI) representation that some changes in its 'adversative' method of education would be required with the admission of women, but did not defer to VMI's judgment that these changes would be too great." Rather, it concluded that they "were 'manageable.'" That case, he reminded his colleagues, involved sex discrimination, which is subjected only to intermediate scrutiny, not to the much more demanding standards of strict scrutiny. Returning to his common theme of rejecting elite opinion, he declared, "So in *Virginia,* where the standard of review dictated that greater flexibility be granted to VMI's educational policies than the Law School deserves here, this Court gave no deference. Apparently where the status quo being defended is that of the elite establishment—here the Law School—rather than a less fashionable Southern military institution, the Court will defer without serious inquiry and without regard to the applicable legal standard."[129]

He also faulted O'Connor and the Court majority for "ignoring the experience of those institutions that have been forced to abandon explicit racial discrimination in admissions." California voters adopted Proposition 209 in 1996, which barred racial preference on the basis of race in the operation of public education, but "the sky has not fallen at Boalt Hall at the University of California, Berkeley. Total underrepresented minority student enrollment at Boalt Hall now exceeds 1996 levels," when it was still engaging in racial preference. "The Court is willfully blind to the very real experience in California and elsewhere, which raises the inference that institutions with 'reputations for excellence' rivaling the Law School's have satisfied their sense of mission without resorting to prohibited racial discrimination."[130]

Thomas then focused on the Law School Admissions Test (LSAT), noting that no law school could "claim ignorance of the poor performance of blacks, relatively speaking," on the LSAT. Yet many law schools, including the University of Michigan's, "continue to use the test and then attempt to 'correct' for black underperformance by using racial discrimination in admissions so as to obtain their aesthetic student body." Thomas found that unacceptable. "Having decided to use the LSAT," he said, "the Law School must accept the constitutional burdens that come with this decision." Thomas had no objection to the Law School freely employing the LSAT and other "allegedly merit-based standards" in whatever fashion it thought best. However, he insisted, "what the Equal Protection Clause forbids, but the Court today allows, is the use of these standards hand-in-hand with racial discrimination." There were, he averred, "an infinite variety of admission methods" available for the Law School to employ that would not include the use of racial discrimination. Yet the Court majority "did not even deign to make the Law School try" any of these other methods but instead granted it "a 25-year license to violate the Constitution." Thomas contrasted the intrepidity of the Court in *Brown* to the pusillanimity of the *Grutter* majority: "The same Court that had the courage to order the desegregation of all public schools in the South now fears, on the basis of platitudes rather than principle, to force the Law School to abandon a decidedly imperfect admissions regime that provides the basis for racial discrimination."[131]

Thomas "contest[ed]" the "benighted notion" in O'Connor's majority opinion that the Court could determine "when racial discrimination benefits (rather than hurts) minority groups."[132] It benefited the Law School for aesthetic reasons: "The Law School seeks only a façade—it is sufficient that the class looks right, even if it does not perform right." He accused the school of cynically "tantaliz[ing] unprepared students with the promise of a University of Michigan degree and all the opportunities that it offers. These overmatched students take the bait, only to find that they cannot succeed in the cauldron of competition."[133] Moreover, the Law School's policy stigmatized those students who were properly prepared and capable of being admitted in the absence of racial preference, raising questions "when blacks take positions in the highest places of government, industry, and academia" about "whether their skin color played a part in their advancement." And, as he had argued in *Adarand*, he stated that the Law School's policy, as others like it, "engenders attitudes of superiority" and "provokes resentment" among those not eligible for similar preferences.[134]

In conclusion, he accused the Court majority of placing "its imprimatur on a practice that can only weaken the principle of equality embodied in the Declaration of Independence and the Equal Protection Clause." His frustration was heartfelt: "Now we must wait another 25 years to see the principle of equality vindicated."[135]

In the 2013 case of *Fisher v. University of Texas at Austin*,[136] the Supreme Court considered a Fifth Circuit Court of Appeals opinion upholding the university's explicit consideration of race in its admissions decisions to determine whether it was consistent with its past decisions "interpreting the Equal Protection Clause of the Fourteenth Amendment, including *Grutter v. Bollinger*." In a seven-to-one decision (Justice Ginsburg dissented and Justice Kagan did not participate), Justice Kennedy held for the majority that the court of appeals did not hold the university to the demanding burden of strict scrutiny articulated in *Grutter*. He wrote, "Because the Court of Appeals did not apply the correct standard of strict scrutiny, its decision affirming the District Court's grant of summary judgment to the University was incorrect. That decision is vacated, and the case is remanded for further proceedings."[137] Thomas not only joined Kennedy's opinion but also added a concurrence on his own. He noted that he wrote separately to explain that "I would overrule *Grutter v. Bollinger* and hold that a State's use of race in higher education admissions decisions is categorically prohibited by the Equal Protection Clause."[138]

As expected, he amplified on arguments that he had already made in *Grutter*. But then he added a new theme, one that he had first introduced in *Parents Involved*: the arguments made by the supporters of racial diversity at the University of Texas–Austin were eerily reminiscent of the arguments made by the proponents of racial segregation in *Brown*. According to Thomas, "The argument that educational benefits justify racial discrimination was advanced in support of racial segregation in the 1950's, but emphatically rejected by this Court. And just as the alleged educational benefits of segregation were insufficient to justify racial discrimination then, see *Brown v. Board of Education*, the alleged educational benefits of diversity cannot justify racial discrimination today."[139]

Thomas found it "noteworthy that, in our desegregation cases, we rejected arguments that are virtually identical to those advanced by the University today." Thus, for example, the university argued that "the diversity obtained through its discriminatory admissions program prepares its students to become leaders in a diverse society. The segregationists likewise defended segregation on the ground that it provided more leadership opportunities for blacks." Similarly, the university insisted that "student body diversity improves interracial relations." Here, too, he said, "the University repeats arguments once marshaled in support of segregation. 'Virginia has established segregation in certain fields as a part of her public policy to prevent violence and reduce resentment. The result, in the view of an overwhelming Virginia majority, has been to improve the relationship between the different races.'"[140] Finally, he stated, when the university admitted that "racial discrimination in admissions is not ideal, it assert[ed] that it is a temporary necessity because of the enduring race consciousness of our society," and it was simply echoing "the hollow justifications advanced by the segregationists. 'We grant that segregation may not be the ethical or political ideal. At the same time we recognize that practical considerations may prevent realization of the ideal.'" As Thomas observed, just as these arguments were "unavailing" in *Brown*—because the Fourteenth Amendment "views racial bigotry as an evil to be stamped out, not as an excuse for perpetual racial tinkering by the State"—so too were "the University's arguments to this effect," for they were "similarly insufficient to justify discrimination."[141]

Thomas continued to draw parallels between the defenders of diversity and the defenders of segregation. He suspected that the university's use of race had "little to do with the alleged educational benefits of diversity and a lot to do with the benighted notion that it is possible to tell when discrimination helps, rather than hurts, racial minorities." For Thomas, "the worst forms of racial discrimination in this Nation have always been accompanied by straight-faced representations that discrimination helped minorities." Citing many sources to support his argument, he reminded his readers that "slaveholders argued that slavery was a 'positive good' that civilized blacks and elevated them in every dimension of life" and that, a century later, "segregationists similarly asserted that segregation was not only benign, but good for black students. They argued, for example, that separate schools protected black children from racist white students and teachers." And now the University of Texas, he complained, "following in these inauspicious footsteps . . . would have us believe that its discrimination is likewise benign." But, Thomas insisted, "I think the lesson of history is clear enough: Racial discrimination is never benign," and for that reason, "the Court has repeatedly held that strict scrutiny applies to all racial classifications, regardless of whether the government has benevolent motives."[142] He concluded: "For the foregoing reasons, I would overrule *Grutter*. However, because the Court correctly concludes that the Court of Appeals did not apply strict scrutiny, I join its opinion."[143]

Voting Rights

Thomas's consistent views in a wide variety of voting rights cases can be summed up in three statements. First, the text of the Voting Rights Act of 1965 does not address questions of vote dilution, and it has been wrong for the Court to read its provisions to regulate, ration, and apportion political power among racial and ethnic groups based on principles of proportional representation.[144] Second, all laws that classify citizens based on race, including racially gerrymandered schemes, are constitutionally suspect and must be strictly scrutinized.[145] And third, federal regulation of state voting practices under the Fifteenth Amendment is constitutional only when there is current evidence of intentional racial discrimination by the states.[146]

By far, Thomas's most important opinion (and also his first) in the area of voting rights came in concurrence in *Holder v. Hall* in 1994.[147] In this case, Kennedy held for a sharply divided Court that the size of a governing body (in this instance, a county commission) was not subject to a vote dilution challenge under § 2 of the Voting Rights Act. Thomas concurred in the judgment but not in the "reasons for reaching that conclusion."[148] He insisted on "anchor[ing]" his analysis in this case in the statutory text, which explicitly states that "only a 'voting qualification or prerequisite to voting, or standard, practice, or procedure,' [related thereto] can be challenged under § 2." And on that basis, he held that neither "the size of a governing body" nor "allegedly dilutive methods that we have considered within the scope of the Act in the past" is a "'standard, practice, or procedure' within the terms of the Act" because "those terms reach only state enactments that limit citizens' access to the ballot."[149] He then introduced the larger points he would make thereafter. He stated that the "broad reach" the Court had given

§ 2 "might suggest that the size of a governing body, like an election method that has the potential for diluting the vote of a minority group, should come within the terms of the Act." But, he insisted, "the gloss we have placed on the words 'standard, practice, or procedure' in cases alleging dilution is at odds with the terms of the statute and has proved utterly unworkable in practice." By construing the act to cover vote dilution, "we have immersed the federal courts in a hopeless project of weighing questions of political theory — questions judges must confront to establish a benchmark concept of an 'undiluted' vote." Even worse, Thomas argued, "in pursuing the ideal measure of voting strength, we have devised a remedial mechanism that encourages federal courts to segregate voters into racially designated districts to ensure minority electoral success. In doing so, we have collaborated in what may aptly be termed the racial 'balkanization' of the Nation." These unfortunate consequences led Thomas to conclude that "a systematic reassessment of our interpretation of § 2 is required in this case."[150]

Initially, he observed, the Voting Rights Act was understood as simply "eliminating literacy tests and similar devices that had been used to prevent black voter registration in the segregated South," and it "was immediately and notably successful" in doing so, "removing barriers to registration and ensuring access to the ballot."[151] But four years later in *Allen v. State Board of Elections*,[152] the Court "fundamental[ly] shift[ed] . . . the focus point of the Act" and held that it applied "not only to changes in electoral laws that pertain to registration and access to the ballot, but to provisions that might 'dilute' the force of minority votes that were duly cast and counted." It thereby "ensured that the terms 'standard, practice, or procedure' would extend to encompass a wide array of electoral practices or voting systems that might be challenged for reducing the potential impact of minority votes."[153] Chief among them was the use of multimember districting as opposed to single-member districting: "It has been the objective of voting rights plaintiffs to use the Act to attack multi-member districting schemes and to replace them with single-member districting systems drawn with majority-minority districts to ensure minority control of seats."[154]

Thomas did not deny that single-member districting would ensure minority control of a certain number of seats. But, he asked, should a minority group's votes be considered more diluted because they "provide *influence* over a great number of seats" as opposed to "*control* over a lesser number of seats"?[155] For Thomas, that was a question of "political theory . . . beyond the ordinary sphere of federal judges."[156] As he pointed out three years later in a concurring opinion in *Reno v. Bossier Parish School Board*,[157] a consequence of increasing majority-minority districts is that it "*necessarily decreases* the level of minority influence in surrounding districts, and to that extent 'dilutes' the vote of minority voters in those other districts, and perhaps dilutes the influence of the minority group as a whole." So, state officials attempting to comply with the Court's interpretation of the Voting Rights Act find themselves in an impossible situation: "A court could strike down *any* reappointment plan, either because it did not include enough majority-minority districts or because it did (and thereby diluted the minority vote in the remaining districts)." Thomas believed the Court had converted the Voting Rights Act from "primarily a prophylactic tool in the important war against discrimination in voting" into "the means whereby the Federal Government . . . usurps the legitimate political judgments of the States."[158]

In his *Holder* concurrence, Thomas pointed to another problem with the Court's focus on vote dilution and its emphasis on single-member districts. "Single-member districting tells a court 'how' members of a minority are to control seats, but not 'how many' seats they should be allowed to control." Yet "'how many' is the critical issue." The Court answered this question in *Thornburg v. Gingles*,[159] the controlling precedent construing the Voting Rights Act. Its answer to the question of how many seats they should control entailed proportional representation—minorities should control the number of seats in a governing body equal to their proportion of the population. Thomas acknowledged that proportional representation "may strike us intuitively as the fairest and most just rule to apply," but he insisted that the Court's "opting for proportionality is still a political choice, not a result required by any principle of law"—and, in fact, it was an option that Congress had "explicitly" rejected.[160]

Thomas cautioned that there was an even "wors[e] aspect of our vote dilution jurisprudence" than the Court's "dabbling in political theory": "Far more pernicious has been the Court's willingness to accept the one underlying premise that must inform every minority vote dilution claim: the assumption that the group asserting dilution is not merely a racial or ethnic group, but a group having distinct political interests as well." Totally rejecting the idea that all blacks think alike, he was deeply offended by the Court's "implicit assumption that members of racial and ethnic groups must all think alike on important matters of public policy and must have their own 'minority preferred' representatives holding seats in elected bodies if they are to be considered represented at all."[161] That pernicious assumption, he observed with regret, has "involved the federal courts, and indeed the Nation, in the enterprise of systematically dividing the country into electoral districts along racial lines—an enterprise of segregating the races into political homelands that amounts, in truth, to nothing short of a system of 'political apartheid.'" It was an assumption that "should have been repugnant to any nation that strives for the ideal of a color-blind Constitution." And it was an assumption that because it led to "the consciously segregated districting system currently being constructed in the name of the Voting Rights Act," contributed greatly to the exacerbation of racial tensions.[162]

All of this led Thomas to declare that "something in our jurisprudence has gone awry" and that "a systematic re-examination of our interpretation of the Act is required."[163] The Court's interpretation of § 2 of the Voting Rights Act in *Gingles* regarding how to evaluate vote dilution claims was in such "irreconcilable conflict" with the text of that section that it warranted the Court's immediate overruling of *Gingles*. Given that *Gingles*'s "disastrous implications" for harmonious race relations were so grave, its "dissembling" approach to the act so damaging to the credibility of the federal judiciary, and its division of the nation into "racially segregated electoral districts" so "destructive" of the country's representative democracy, Thomas declared, "In my view, [*Gingles*] . . . should not continue. Not for another Term, not until the next case, not for another day."[164]

In addition to his criticisms of the Court's interpretation of the Voting Rights Act beginning in *Allen* and culminating in *Gingles*, Thomas has also argued a second major point, namely, that all racial gerrymanders—that is, all intentional legislative attempts to create majority-minority districts—are constitutionally suspect and must be strictly scrutinized. His first major opinion on a racial gerrymandering case came during his fifth year on the Court in his concurrence in the judgment in *Bush v. Vera*.[165]

After the 1990 census, the Texas legislature gerrymandered the lines of the three new congressional districts it received to create two new black districts and one new Hispanic district. A three-judge federal district court panel declared them unconstitutional under the Fourteenth Amendment, and the Supreme Court agreed. However, in her judgment for the Court, O'Connor expressed the view that strict scrutiny would not be invoked when a state creates racially gerrymandered districts in order to comply with the requirement of the Voting Rights Act that minority voters have the right to elect representatives of their choice. Thomas wanted to make clear that "I cannot agree . . . that strict scrutiny is not invoked by the intentional creation of majority-minority districts."[166] It "applies to all governmental classifications based on race, and . . . we have never suggested that a racial gerrymander is subject to anything less than strict scrutiny."[167] He noted Texas readily admitted that "these districts would not have existed but for its affirmative use of racial demographics," and he concluded, "I am content to reaffirm our holding in *Adarand* that all racial classifications by government must be strictly scrutinized and, even in the sensitive area of state legislative redistricting, I would make no exceptions."[168]

However, as *Hunt v. Cromartie* makes clear, Thomas will not strictly scrutinize an alleged racial gerrymander when the lower court record fails to establish that race was the state's predominant motive. In his opinion for the Court, he upheld a plan, developed by the Democrats who controlled the North Carolina legislature, for making a 160-mile-long district that "for much of its length [is] no wider than the Interstate 85 corridor," and that "winds in a snakelike fashion through tobacco country, financial centers, and manufacturing areas 'until it gobbles in enough enclaves of black neighborhoods' to create a minority-majority district."[169] This district was clearly a political gerrymander, but as he noted, the Court had held in *Davis v. Bandemer*[170] that political gerrymanders do not offend the Constitution. "A jurisdiction may engage in constitutional political gerrymandering," the Court ruled, "even if it so happens that the most loyal Democrats happen to be black Democrats and even if the State were *conscious* of that fact."[171] *Cromartie* came before the Court as it was reviewing a summary judgment by the federal district court that North Carolina had engaged in racial gerrymandering; that conclusion was, Thomas held, "inappropriate when the evidence is susceptible of different interpretations or inferences by the trier of fact." On remand, he directed the district court to ascertain whether "race was the State's predominant motive," a question he and his colleagues were in no position to answer based on the facts before them.[172]

Finally, in *Northwest Austin Municipal Utility District Number One* [NAMUDNO] *v. Holder*, Thomas introduced his third major point, concluding that when Congress in 2006 renewed § 5 of the Voting Rights Act without doing so on the basis of "current evidence of intentional discrimination with respect to voting," it exceeded its power to enforce the Fifteenth Amendment.[173]

Most of the Court's opinions on the Voting Rights Act have focused on § 2 and the questions it poses concerning the opportunity for minority voters to elect "representatives of their choice." But § 5 is also of critical importance; it requires, for certain designated states, that all changes to state election law, however insignificant (for example, going to punch-card ballots from voting machines), must be precleared by federal authorities in Washington, D.C. — either by the Department of Justice or by a three-judge panel of federal district court judges — before they can go into effect. Justice Hugo Black found this section unconstitutional in his dissent in *South Carolina v. Katzenbach*: "Section 5, by providing that some of the States cannot pass state laws or adopt state constitutional amendments without first being compelled to beg federal authorities to approve their policies, so distorts our constitutional structure of government as to render any distinction drawn in the Constitution between state and federal power almost meaningless."[174] Black's objections were unavailing, but echoes of his dissent are present in Thomas's solo opinion in *NAMUDNO*, in which he concurred in the judgment in part and dissented in part.

NAMUDNO was a small utility district with an elected board. Because it is located in Texas, it was required under § 5 to seek federal preclearance before it could change anything about its elections, even though there was no evidence it had ever discriminated on the basis of race in those elections. The utility district filed suit in federal district court seeking relief under the "bailout" provision in § 4(a) of the Voting Rights Act, which allows a "political subdivision" to be released from the preclearance requirements if certain conditions are met. The utility argued in the alternative that if § 5 was interpreted to render it ineligible for bailout, § 5 was unconstitutional. The district court rejected both claims, concluding that bailout under § 4(a) is available only to counties, parishes, and subunits that register voters, not to an entity like the district that did not register its own voters. It also concluded that a 2006 congressional amendment extending § 5 for twenty-five years was constitutional. Chief Justice Roberts, for an eight-member majority, declined to rule on the constitutionality of that provision, citing the principle of constitutional avoidance; he did conclude, however, that the district was eligible to apply for a bailout from this section because the definition of *political subdivision* included a district of this nature. This decision was consistent with Roberts's embrace of "judicial minimalism," whereby he attempts to avoid invalidation of federal law or rejection of past judicial precedent unless absolutely necessary.

Thomas, however, is no judicial minimalist, and he dissented in part because he did not believe that "the doctrine of constitutional avoidance is applicable here. The ultimate relief sought in this case is not bailout eligibility—it is bailout itself." Thomas agreed that the Court properly declined to give NAMUDNO bailout because it had not yet proved to the lower courts its compliance with the statutory requirements for such relief. But, he continued, because the Court was not in a position to award NAMUDNO bailout, "adjudication of the constitutionality of § 5, in my view, cannot be avoided."[175] And though he noted that the Court majority "quite properly alerts Congress that § 5 tests the outer boundaries of its Fifteenth Amendment enforcement authority and may not be constitutional," Thomas insisted that it is "necessary to definitively resolve that important question" and conclude that it "can no longer be justified as an appropriate mechanism for enforcement of the Fifteenth Amendment."[176]

Thomas then turned to the same federalism argument Justice Black had invoked in *Katzenbach*. He reminded his colleagues that "in the specific area of voting rights, this Court has consistently recognized that the Constitution gives the States primary authority over the structuring of electoral systems. State autonomy with respect to the machinery of self-government defines the States as sovereign entities rather than mere provincial outposts subject to every dictate of a central governing authority." Further, he invoked the Tenth Amendment. "In the main, the Framers of the Constitution intended the States to keep for themselves, as provided in the Tenth Amendment, the power to regulate elections." He acknowledged that "state authority over local elections is not absolute under the Constitution. The Fifteenth Amendment guarantees that the 'right of citizens of the United States to vote shall not be denied or abridged by the United States or by any State on account of race, color, or previous condition of servitude,' § 1, and it grants Congress the authority to 'enforce' these rights 'by appropriate legislation,' § 2." But, he added, "because States still retain sovereign authority over their election systems, any measure enacted in furtherance of the Fifteenth Amendment must be closely examined to ensure that its encroachment on state authority in this area is limited to the appropriate enforcement of this ban on discrimination."[177]

The Court in *Katzenbach* held that § 5 withstood constitutional scrutiny because, when it was enacted, it was an appropriate and necessary response to a well-documented common practice in some states of staying one step ahead of the federal courts by passing new discriminatory voting laws as soon as the old ones had been struck down. That practice was made possible because each new law remained in effect until the Justice Department or private plaintiffs were able to sustain the burden of proving that the new law, too, was discriminatory. But, Thomas insisted, "to accommodate the tension between the constitutional imperatives of the Fifteenth and Tenth Amendments—a balance between allowing the Federal Government to patrol state voting practices for discrimination and preserving the States' significant interest in self-determination," the continued constitutionality of § 5 must depend on the proven existence of intentional racial discrimination so extensive that it would be impossible to eliminate it through case-by-case enforcement."[178]

Thomas insisted that "for § 5 to withstand renewed constitutional scrutiny, there must be a demonstrated connection between the 'remedial measures' chosen and the 'evil presented' in the record made by Congress when it renewed the [Voting Rights] Act. 'Strong measures appropriate to address one harm may be an unwarranted response to another, lesser one.'" However, he averred, Congress presented no evidence that the covered jurisdictions were currently engaging in the type of discrimination that underlay the initial enactment of § 5: "Punishment for long past sins is not a legitimate basis for imposing a forward-looking preventative measure that has already served its purpose." He pointed out that the supporters of the reenactment of § 5 argued that, without it, these jurisdictions would resume their racially discriminatory practices of thirty and forty years earlier. But, Thomas observed, "there is no evidence that public officials stand ready, if given the chance, to again engage in concerted acts of violence, terror, and subterfuge in order to keep minorities from voting." Without such evidence, the supporters of § 5 premised its reenactment simply "on outdated assumptions about racial attitudes in the covered jurisdictions." He concluded by offering them some reassurance: "Admitting that a prophylactic law as broad as § 5 is no longer constitutionally justified based on current evidence of discrimination is not a sign of defeat. It is an acknowledgment of victory."[179]

Chapter 4 showed Thomas coming to the defense of his race when he angrily charged his colleagues with being more interested in protecting women seeking an abortion from the "unwanted communications" of right-to-life protesters than in protecting the "physical safety" of blacks from the terror and intimidation of KKK cross burnings in *Virginia v. Black*, asserting the right of black citizens to keep and bear arms as protected by the Privileges or Immunities Clause in *McDonald v City of Chicago*, and condemning the harm that blacks suffer (urban renewal as "Negro removal") when the Court in *Kelo v. City of New London* replaced "public use" with "public purpose." Chapter 5 likewise addressed Thomas's concern in *Graham v. Collins* that the Court's requirement in death penalty cases that juries consider every sympathetic factor bearing upon the defendant's background and character actually reintroduced the opportunity for racial prejudice against blacks to play a role in the sentences they impose. What motivated him in those cases, as in the cases considered in this chapter, was the principle of equality—the Declaration of Independence's claim that all men are created equal and are to receive equal justice as individuals before the law.

Nonetheless, a frequent complaint made by critics of Thomas's opinions on race and equality is that they are not impartial or principled but rather are "passionately inflamed with personal experience" and "racial familiarity."[180] Thomas has been described as wearing "his racial identity on his sleeve,"[181] and he has been labeled a consistent practitioner of "'first-person' jurisprudence." As one remarked, "Although Clarence Thomas may believe that our Constitution is color-blind, he has consistently made the case for this color-blind vision in terms that are fully (and unapologetically) race-conscious."[182] His critics are fond of quoting a passage from Thomas's lecture on "Judging," where he stated: "In my mind, impartiality is the very essence of judging and being a judge. A judge does not look to his or her sex or racial, social, or religious background when deciding a case. It is exactly these factors that a judge must push to one side in order to render a fair, reasoned judgment on the meaning of the law."[183] As one critic has trenchantly put it, "Labeling success that comes from affirmative action as 'stigmatized' or marked by a 'badge of inferiority' is a very personalized evaluation and conclusion, and a conclusion clearly not shared by all individuals who have benefitted historically from affirmative action. This is a Thomas-specific life experience which leaks, waterfall like, into his race jurisprudence, despite his protestations of 'impartiality.'"[184]

What most offends Thomas's critics is his argument that the Constitution is color blind, and in an attempt to disparage this argument, they suggest that Thomas has not come to that view impartially but rather based on his own personal experiences. But they get the causation wrong. Thomas argues that the Constitution is color blind not because he felt stigmatized by affirmative action but because the principle of equality in the Declaration of Independence that infuses and underlies the Constitution requires nothing less. What his critics fail to realize is that it represents no departure from impartiality on Thomas's part for him to argue that, in addition to being contrary to the principle of equality, race mixing, affirmative action, and proportional representation based on race are also profoundly damaging to most members of his race.[185] For Thomas, it is the principle of equality that guides his jurisprudence on race, not the harm these policies inflict. In fact, he would oppose these policies as being contrary to constitutional principle even were they shown to be beneficial. As Nicole Stelle Garnett has written: "That Justice Thomas's expressed constitutional commitments are both genuine and self-binding is, in my view, established in the undeniable record of reaching conclusions that run counter to his personal preferences."[186]

The picture that Thomas paints with broad strokes in his opinions on race and equality depicts a people living together under a color-blind constitution where racial categories are irrelevant and individuals, not groups, have rights — where, in the words of John Marshall Harlan in *Plessy*, 'the law regards man as man, and takes no account of his surroundings or of his color when his civil rights as guaranteed by the supreme law of the land are involved."[187] Then and only then does Thomas brush details into the canvas that give vibrancy and poignancy to the picture he has already sketched. These details include his frequent invocation of Frederick Douglass and W. E. B. DuBois; his defense of historically black institutions; his reflections on wearing the badges of inferiority a race-conscious society has imposed on him; and his contempt for those who condescend to argue that all blacks think alike, that blacks can learn only in the presence of whites, and that blacks can succeed only with the assistance of affirmative action.[188] There is obvious passion in these brushstrokes, but they do not define the painting's composition and character. They merely add texture and fill in the empty spaces of the sketch Thomas has already carefully laid out based on the principle of equality in the Declaration of Independence.

Chapter Seven

No Longer Doubting Thomas

On October 1, 2012, Thomas began his twenty-second year of service on the Supreme Court, having at that point written 475 opinions—171 majority opinions, 138 concurrences, and 166 dissents.[1] Over that twenty-one-year period, the Court had decided 1,772 cases, so Thomas's 171 majority opinions represent 10.4 percent of that total, slightly less than his proportionate share of one-ninth, or 11.1 percent. That is not surprising: although he joins in the Court's disposition of nonunanimous cases 70.0 percent of the time, he joins the opinion of the Court disposing of those cases only 60.1 percent of the time. Thomas's 166 dissents (he has averaged 7.9 dissents per term) make him the Court's third most frequent dissenter. During twenty-one years together with Thomas on the Court, Scalia filed 181 dissents (averaging 8.6 per term), and during the nineteen years he served with Thomas before retiring in 2010, Stevens filed 305 dissents (averaging 16.1 per term). No other justice comes close to these numbers.

During his tenure on the Court, Thomas has served with a total of fourteen colleagues. Table 1 shows, for the 1991 through 2011 terms of the Court, the number of years he has served with each of these colleagues and the percentage of cases in which he joined or was joined by each of them in a majority, concurring, or dissenting opinion. Unsurprisingly, Thomas has been aligned with the Court's conservative majority, voting with each member of this contingent at least 70 percent of the time. The justice with whom he is most closely aligned also is no surprise: he has voted with his fellow originalist, Justice Scalia, 84.8 percent of the time. Also worthy of comment is the fact that during Scalia and Thomas's twenty-one years together on the Court, in only 12 cases has one written the majority opinion and the other written a dissent.[2]

Because of how frequently Thomas and Scalia vote together and because of Scalia's reputation as the intellectual anchor of the conservative wing of the Court, Thomas has been maligned and ridiculed by critics as Scalia's "lawn jockey." *Emerge* magazine (owned in part by Time, Inc., and self-servingly described by *Time* magazine in 2000 when *Emerge* ceased publication as "the nation's best black newsmagazine for the past seven years") was especially vituperative. In its November 1996 issue, it depicted Thomas on its cover as a grinning lawn jockey under the headline UNCLE THOMAS: LAWN JOCKEY OF THE FAR RIGHT.

Table 1. Voting Alignments: Thomas and His Colleagues, 1991–2011 Terms of the Court

Justice	Years of Service Together	Percentage Agreement
Rehnquist	14	78.7
White	2	67.8
Blackmun	3	44.4
Stevens	19	54.3
O'Connor	15	70.1
Scalia	21	84.8
Kennedy	21	70.8
Souter	18	53.7
Ginsburg	19	49.2
Breyer	18	49.6
Roberts	7	76.3
Alito	7	73.3
Sotomayor	3	51.2
Kagan	2	56.6

Inside, it included a caricature of Thomas as a shoe-shine boy polishing Scalia's shoes; its editor's note, "We Were Too Kind," included the following statement: "I apologize. Exactly three years ago, shortly after I took over as editor of *Emerge*, we ran a cover illustration of U.S. Supreme Court Justice Clarence Thomas, resplendent with an Aunt Jemima–like handkerchief on his head. In retrospect, we were far too benevolent. Hence, this month's cover with Clarence appropriately attired as a lawn jockey."[3] These outrageous comments have been repeatedly and gleefully quoted in numerous law review articles endorsing this calumny.[4]

Interestingly, the *Washington Post* has reported that the first black justice, Thurgood Marshall, voted with Brennan 94 percent of the time, and yet no one accused Marshall of being Brennan's lawn jockey or shoe-shine boy.[5] More contemporaneously, during their sixteen years together on the Court, Ginsburg voted 84.2 percent of the time with Souter, and during their eighteen years together on the Court, Ginsburg has voted 80.2 percent of the time with Breyer, but likewise, no one has suggested that Ginsburg's votes were not independently cast. When the focus is narrowed to justices voting together in nonunanimous cases, the percentage of cases in which Thomas has voted with Scalia drops 8.9 percent to 75.3 percent, but again and interestingly, the percentage of cases in which Ginsburg voted with Souter drops only 6.2 percent to 78.0 percent. (See Table 2, which shows for the 1997 through 2011 terms of the Court[6] the number

Table 2. Voting Alignments in Nonunanimous Cases: Thomas and
His Colleagues, 1997–2011 Terms of the Court

Justice	Years of Service Together	Percentage Agreement
Rehnquist	8	66.7
Stevens	13	17.0
O'Connor	9	52.7
Scalia	15	75.3
Kennedy	15	55.6
Souter	12	23.4
Ginsburg	15	23.4
Breyer	15	25.1
Roberts	7	66.8
Alito	7	63.8
Sotomayor	3	31.4
Kagan	2	34.7

of years Thomas served with each of his colleagues and the percentage of nonunanimous cases in which Thomas joined or was joined by each of them in a majority, concurring, or dissenting opinion.) And it is worth noting that during their sixteen years together on the Court, in only eight cases did Souter or Ginsburg write a majority opinion from which the other dissented.

There is still another critical matter to consider: has Thomas voted with Scalia or Scalia with Thomas? Put another way, how often has Scalia shined Thomas's shoes?[7] When Blackmun retired from the Supreme Court, he broke a long-standing tradition by releasing all of his Court papers in 2004, just ten years after his retirement and at a point when many of his former colleagues were still active on the High Bench.[8] His files were voluminous and included all the documents from every case he had heard, including the notes that the justices sent to each other as they were deciding these cases. Jan Crawford Greenburg, an ABC News correspondent who covers law and politics, drew heavily from Blackmun's papers when she wrote *Supreme Conflict*. In it, she reports that during the three years Blackmun and Thomas served together—and where Blackmun's paper are revealing on this question—there were numerous instances when Scalia changed his initial vote in critical cases and voted with Thomas after he read draft opinions written by Thomas.[9] In *Hudson v. McMillian*,[10] a case heard during Thomas's second week on the Court, Scalia switched his vote and joined Thomas's dissent; another such case was *Doggett v. United States*.[11] Both of these cases were discussed at length in chapter 5.

Thomas has written 171 majority opinions, but his contributions to the original general meaning of the Constitution have not come from them. His most influential majority opinions addressing constitutional questions are *Kansas v. Hendricks*,[12] *Rubin v. Coors Brewing Company*,[13] and *Alleyne v. United States*.[14] In *Hendricks*, a case of first impression, he held that Kansas did not violate the Constitution's bans on ex post facto lawmaking or double jeopardy when it passed its Sexually Violent Predator Act, which established procedures for the civil commitment of convicted felons who upon their release from prison are likely to engage in "predatory acts of sexual violence." *Rubin* was influential only because Thomas used it to launch a series of opinions protecting commercial speech by holding that a federal law prohibiting beer labels from displaying alcohol content violated the First Amendment. In *Alleyne*, he was finally able to vindicate his view that, because mandatory minimum sentences increase the penalty for a crime, any fact that increases the mandatory minimum is an "element" that must be submitted to the jury and that there is no basis in principle or logic to distinguish facts that raise the mandatory maximum from those that increase the mandatory minimum.

His other major constitutional opinions for the Court merely extended current Court precedents. Examples include *Good News Club v. Milford Central Schools*,[15] where he extended *Lamb's Chapel v. Center Moriches Union Free School District*[16] and *Rosenberger v. Rector and Visitors of the University of Virginia*;[17] *Board of Education of Independent School District No. 92 of Pottawatomie County v. Earls*,[18] where he "appl[ied] the principles articulated"[19] in *Vernonia School District 47J v. Acton*;[20] and *Federal Maritime Commission v. South Carolina State Ports Authority*,[21] where he built on a series of state sovereign immunity cases in order to bar actions against nonconsenting states in federal regulatory agencies.[22]

Thomas's enduring contributions to the Constitution's original general meaning have come from his 138 concurring and 166 dissenting opinions. Concerning federalism, in his concurrences in *United States v. Lopez*[23] and *United States v. Morrison*[24] and his dissent in *Gonzales v. Raich*,[25] he repeatedly rejected those precedents that were responsible for the Court's "rootless and malleable" substantial effects test and that justified Congress's continuing appropriation of the police powers of the states. His reiterated arguments were vindicated when a majority of the justices in *National Federation of Independent Business v. Sebelius* concluded that were they to uphold the Affordable Care Act under Congress's power to regulate commerce, "the idea of limited Government power . . . [would be] at an end."[26] Likewise, in his concurrences in *Pharmaceutical Research and Manufacturers of America v. Walsh*[27] and *Wyeth v. Levine*[28] and his dissents in *Altria Group v. Good*[29] and *Cuomo v. The Clearing House Association*,[30] he led the way in defending not only the statutory text in express preemption cases from the presumption against preemption but also federalism and the power of states to regulate in implied field and obstacle preemption cases.

Concerning freedom of speech and the press, his powerful concurrence in *44 Liquormart v. Rhode Island*,[31] in which he methodically demolished the *Central Hudson* "test," established him as the Court's greatest defender of commercial speech. His dissents in such cases as *Colorado Republican Federal Campaign Committee v. Federal Election Commission*,[32] *Nixon v. Shrink Missouri Government PAC*,[33] and *McConnell v. Federal Election Commission*[34] and his concurrence in *Randall v. Sorrell*[35] led to the vindication of his well-articulated argument in *Citizens United v. FEC*[36] that both campaign contributions and expenditures "involve core First Amendment expression." And his dissent in *Denver AETC v. FCC*[37] and his concurrence in *FCC v. Fox Television*[38] have brought his colleagues to the verge of agreeing that broadcast, cable, and Internet companies should enjoy the same First Amendment protections as the print media.

Concerning other substantive rights, his concurrence in *Printz v. United States*[39] was cited by the Fifth Circuit Court of Appeals in *United States v. Emerson*[40] when it held for the first time that the Second Amendment guarantees an individual right to keep and bear arms for self-defense, and it was decisive in persuading Alan Gura to initiate litigation that culminated in the Supreme Court's decision in *District of Columbia v. Heller*.[41] Thomas's concurrences in *Saenz v. Roe*[42] and especially *McDonald v. Chicago*[43] breathed new life into the largely moribund Privileges or Immunities Clause but in a way that did not allow it to become "yet another convenient tool for inventing new rights, limited solely by the 'predilections of those who happen at the time to be Members of this Court.'"[44] His dissent in *Kelo v. City of New London*[45] contributed to the immediate passage of a resolution in the U.S. House of Representatives denouncing the Court's decision by a vote of 365 to 33 and the passage of legislation restricting takings for the purpose of economic redevelopment in forty-four states.[46] And his graphic depiction of what is involved in a partial-birth abortion in his dissent in *Stenberg v. Carhart*[47] contributed to Congress's passage of the Partial-Birth Abortion Ban Act of 2003 and the Court's affirmation of its constitutionality in *Gonzales v. Carhart*.[48]

Concerning criminal procedural rights, Thomas's concurrences in *United States v. Hubbell*[49] and *White v. Illinois*,[50] his dissent in *Mitchell v. United States*,[51] and his opinion concurring in part and dissenting in part in *Davis v. Washington*[52] reminded his colleagues that the meaning of the word *witness* as found in the Self-Incrimination Clause, the Compulsory Process Clause, and the Confrontation Clause should be consistently interpreted. His concurrences in *Apprendi v. New Jersey*[53] and *Shepard v. United States*[54] and his dissent in *Harris v. United States*[55] helped build on the foundation for Scalia's landmark opinion in *Blakely v. Washington*.[56] His dissent in *Georgia v. McCollum*[57] provided for his colleagues the strongest case against eliminating peremptory challenges for black criminal defendants. And his numerous concurring and dissenting opinions in Eighth Amendment cases provide conclusive evidence that the original general meaning of the Cruel and Unusual Punishments Clause was to place substantive limitations on punishments, not procedural requirements on sentencing.

Finally, concerning questions of race and equal protection, Thomas's concurring opinions in *United States v. Fordice*[58] and *Missouri v. Jenkins*[59] unequivocally rejected the notion of black inferiority. His concurrence in *Parents Involved in Community Schools v. Seattle School District No. 1*[60] and his dissent in *Grutter v. Bollinger*[61] powerfully affirmed that the principles of the Declaration of Independence and of the Equal Protection Clause of the Fourteenth Amendment require nothing less than a color-blind Constitution. And his concurrence in *Holder v. Hall*[62] profoundly challenged the "implicit assumption" of *Thornburg v. Gingles*[63] "that members of racial and ethnic groups must all think alike on important matters of public policy and must have their own 'minority preferred' representatives holding seats in elected bodies if they are to be considered represented at all."[64]

After a long and bruising confirmation battle, Thomas arrived at the Court as damaged goods. And given the liberal predilections of the legal professoriat,[65] law review articles about him during his first decade of service were unrelentingly hostile and derogatory.[66] But during his second decade on the Court and beyond, things changed dramatically; the impact that his concurring and dissenting opinions have had on his colleagues—and the law—became apparent to the legal community, and thoughtful articles taking seriously his opinions and commending his original general meaning jurisprudence are now much more prevalent than those castigating him. They praise him as the "Next 'Great Dissenter,'"[67] as "The Lone Principled Federalist,"[68] and as the emerging "Commercial-Speech Protector."[69] Nat Hentoff—journalist, civil libertarian, and one of the foremost authorities on the First Amendment—has called him the "First Friend" of free speech: "To the incremental surprise and perhaps discomfiture of some of his critics, Justice Clarence Thomas is growing harder to stereotype. He has written as boldly and uncompromisingly in celebration of the First Amendment as did Justices William O. Douglas and William Brennan Jr. in days of yore."[70]

Furthermore, prominent law professors across the ideological spectrum are increasingly acknowledging his intellectual contributions and leadership. Steven G. Calabresi, a conservative professor at Northwestern University School of Law and a cofounder of the Federalist Society, has described Thomas's opinions as "very scholarly, with lots of historical sources," and he views Thomas as "the most principled, even among the conservatives. He has staked out some bold positions, and then the Court has set out and moved in his direction."[71] And prominent liberal law professors agree. Akhil Amar, a liberal professor at Yale Law School, favorably compares Thomas's career with that of Justice Hugo Black: "Both were Southerners who came to the Court young and with very little judicial experience. Early in their careers, they were often in dissent, sometimes by themselves, but they were content to go their own way. But once Earl Warren became Chief Justice the Court started to come to Black. It's the same with Thomas and the Roberts Court. Thomas's views are now being followed by a majority of the Court in case after case."[72] And Sanford Levinson, a left-leaning professor at the University of Texas School of Law, makes the following comparison of Scalia and Thomas: "Scalia is far more influential, because he has spent much of the last two decades campaigning around the nation for his views, but it would not surprise me if future historians find Thomas to be the more intellectually serious of the two."[73]

Not everyone is happy with this outcome, but a growing number of Thomas's critics are honest enough to acknowledge his impact. One example is Tom Goldstein, who is the publisher and cofounder of SCOTUSblog; he teaches Supreme Court litigation at Stanford and Harvard Law Schools, and he has argued twenty-seven cases before the Supreme Court. Goldstein recently wrote: "I disagree profoundly with Justice Thomas's views on many questions, but if you believe that Supreme Court decision-making should be a contest of ideas rather than power, so that the measure of a justice's greatness is his contribution to new and thoughtful perspectives that enlarge the debate, then Justice Thomas is now our greatest justice."[74] Another example is Richard Hasen, a professor at the School of Law at the University of California–Irvine, founding coeditor of *Election Law Journal*, and the principal blogger at Election Law Blog: "[Thomas's] view allows virtually no regulation of campaign advertising, campaign contributions, or expenditures. The Court has been moving his way."[75]

Even Thomas's civil rights opinions are now winning the respect of leftist professors. In an article entitled "Just Another Brother on the SCT? What Justice Thomas Teaches Us about the Influence of Racial Identity," Angela Onwuachi-Willig, a self-described "liberal black womanist," thoughtfully describes Thomas's jurisprudence as "deeply grounded in black conservative thought," and she has argued it is as deserving of respect in the black community as the jurisprudence of Thurgood Marshall. In advancing that argument, she confesses that she has committed "an act that I once thought was impossible: defend Justice Thomas."[76] Mark Tushnet—a socialist professor at Harvard Law School who once argued that Thomas's confirmation was such a mistake that any five-to-four Supreme Court decision in which Thomas was in the majority should be regarded as non-binding[77]—subsequently recanted and has described Thomas as "the most recent representative of a distinguished tradition of black nationalism in its conservative variant."[78] In his book on the Rehnquist Court, he declares that what Thomas "has done on the Court is certainly more interesting and distinctive than what Scalia has done, and, I think, has a greater chance of making an enduring contribution to constitutional law." He concludes his chapter on Thomas by saying that he looks forward to watching "his jurisprudence develop over the next decades," which, he confidently assumes, "is likely to be at least as interesting."[79]

Thomas was a young man when he was appointed to the Court—he was forty-three. He is now well into his second decade of service, and as Tushnet suggests, he intends to serve for decades to come. He has compared himself to a marathon runner who must take the long view and pace himself for the distance. When he interviewed John Eastman for a Supreme Court clerkship, he said: "I'm the marathon runner. You're the sprinter."[80] And Thomas then asked: "Are you ready for the sprint year?" His "sprinter" clerks have helped him lay out a comprehensive original general meaning approach to constitutional interpretation that is having a profound impact on his colleagues and the law professoriat and is guiding in his direction "the tectonic shifts" occurring in the Court's overall jurisprudence.[81]

A condition common to marathon runners is "hitting the wall," manifested by fatigue and a loss of energy. They must break through that wall if they are to reach the finish line. Thomas hit his wall before the race actually began, during his enervating confirmation battle. He arrived at the Court utterly fatigued from the months of personal invective and attacks on his character,[82] but he quickly got his second wind, filing powerful and principled dissents within months of his confirmation. He established his pace early on, and through the years, he has steadily and confidently lengthened his stride.

NOTES

Preface

1. See Ralph A. Rossum, *Antonin Scalia's Jurisprudence: Text and Tradition* (Lawrence: University Press of Kansas, 2006).

2. Clarence Thomas, "Judging," 45 *Kansas Law Review* (November 1996): 7.

Introduction

1. Clarence Thomas, *My Grandfather's Son: A Memoir* (New York: HarperCollins, 2007), 2. Ken Foskett, *Judging Thomas: The Life and Times of Clarence Thomas* (New York: William Morrow, 2004), wonderfully complements Thomas's memoir.

2. Thomas, *My Grandfather's Son*, 4, 6.

3. Ibid., 7–8.

4. Ibid., 28.

5. Ibid., 9–13.

6. Ibid., 25.

7. Ibid., 30–31.

8. Ibid., 37.

9. Ibid., 43–47.

10. Angela Onwuachi-Willig, "Just Another Brother on the SCT? What Clarence Thomas Teaches Us about the Influence of Racial Identity," *Iowa Law Review* 90 (March 2005): 931–1009, 969.

11. Thomas, *My Grandfather's Son*, 51.

12. Onwuachi-Willig, "Just Another Brother?" 968–969.

13. Thomas, *My Grandfather's Son*, 62–63.

14. Ibid., 67–68.

15. Ibid., 78.

16. Onwuachi-Willig, "Just Another Brother?" 968–969.

17. Thomas, *My Grandfather's Son*, 99.

18. Ibid., 113.

19. Ibid., 119, 123.

20. Ibid., 149.

21. Ibid., 191.

22. Nathan W. Dean, "The Primacy of the Individual in the Political Philosophy and Civil Rights Jurisprudence of Justice Clarence Thomas," *George Mason University Civil Rights Law Journal* 14 (Winter 2004): 27–72, 34.

23. Thomas, *My Grandfather's Son*, 193, 197.

24. 347 U.S. 483 (1954).

25. Thomas, *My Grandfather's Son*, 216.

26. *Hearings Before the Committee on the Judiciary, United States Senate, One Hundred Second Congress, First Session, On the Nomination of Clarence Thomas to Be Associate Justice of the Supreme Court of the United States*, Pt. 4, 102nd Cong., at 157–158 (1993).

27. Much ink has been spilled on the topic of Thomas's Senate confirmation as associate justice of the Supreme Court, most of it written by partisans. This topic is ancillary to the focus of this book and has merited but a few paragraphs of discussion. For readers interested in a more detailed and yet balanced account of Thomas's confirmation hearing and Anita Hill's testimony, see Scott Douglas Gerber, *First Principles: The Jurisprudence of Clarence Thomas* (New York: New York University Press, 1999), chap. 1.

28. For an excellent account of Thomas's first year on the Supreme Court, see Jan Crawford Greenburg, *Supreme Conflict: The Inside Story of the Struggle for Control of the*

United States Supreme Court (New York: Penguin, 2007), 109–137.

29. See Mike Sacks, "Clarence's Questions: The Case of the Burning Cross," *Huffington Post*, October 7, 2011, http://www.huffingtonpost.com/2011/10/07/clarence-thomas-questions-cross-burning-case_n_1000569.html.

30. Scott D. Gerber, "Justice for Clarence Thomas: An Intellectual History of Justice Thomas's Twenty Years on the Supreme Court," *University of Detroit Mercy Law Review* 88 (Summer 2011): 667, 675.

31. See interview with Justice Clarence Thomas by Susan Swain, July 29, 2009, C-SPAN, http://supremecourt.c-span.org /Video/JusticeOwnWords/SC_Jus_Thomas .aspx.

32. John Eastman, "Reflections on Justice Thomas's Twenty Years on the Bench," *University of Detroit Mercy Law Review* 88 (Summer 2011): 691–705, 698–699. Eastman adds, "When you do not allow that line of questioning, the oral argument becomes more a game of 'gotcha' and a demonstration that a Justice has read the record, than any attempt to get to the serious crux of the legal issues that are being presented. And if you know Justice Thomas at all, you know that he does not suffer that kind of wasteful effort gladly. So he will sit back peacefully, wishing that the advocates could get more of an argument out than they do, but the notion that his silence is somehow reflective of lack of confidence or of intellect on the bench is just patently absurd." Ibid., 700.

33. Alexander Hamilton, James Madison, and John Jay, *The Federalist*, ed. Jacob E. Cooke (New York: World Publishing, 1961), No. 51, 351. All subsequent citations of *The Federalist* are to this edition.

34. 542 U.S. 507 (2004).

35. 548 U.S. 557 (2006).

36. Clarence Thomas, "The Higher Law Background of the Privileges or Immunities Clause of the Fourteenth Amendment," *Harvard Journal of Law and Public Policy* 12 (Winter 1989): 63, 64.

37. The "tectonic plates" metaphor comes from Eastman, "Reflections," 699.

Chapter 1. Thomas's Original General Meaning Approach to Interpretation

1. Additionally, as Thomas Hobbes reminds us, "precedents prove only what was done, but not what was well done." Hobbes, *A Dialogue between a Philosopher and a Student of the Common Laws of England*, ed. Joseph Cropsey (Chicago: University of Chicago Press, 1971), 129.

2. "Thomas frequently writes concurrences or dissents that stake out legal ground far beyond what any of his colleagues will embrace. Indeed, he is the most willing of all of his colleagues to overrule precedent, what is known in legal jargon as *stare decisis*, or 'let the decision stand,' says Justice Scalia. 'He does not believe in *stare decisis*, period.' Scalia says. 'If a constitutional line of authority is wrong, he would say let's get it right. I wouldn't do that.'" Ken Foskett, *Judging Thomas: The Life and Times of Clarence Thomas* (New York: William Morrow, 2004), 281–282.

3. The term *original general meaning* comes from Gregory E. Maggs's excellent article entitled "Which Original Meaning of the Constitution Matters to Justice Thomas?" *New York University Journal of Law & Liberty* 4 (2009): 494–516, 495. I wish to express my debt of gratitude to Professor Maggs for coining this useful term that so perfectly captures Thomas's originalist approach. I found Maggs's article after I wrote "Thomas's Originalist Understanding of the Interstate, Negative, and Indian Commerce Clauses," *University of Detroit Mercy Law Review* 88 (Summer 2011): 769–826, in which I described Thomas as pursuing an original understanding approach.

4. Lino Graglia, "Interpreting the Constitution: Posner on Bork," *Stanford Law Review* 44 (May 1992): 1019, 1024.

5. Maggs, "Which Original Meaning?" 497.

6. Max Farrand, ed., *The Records of the Federal Convention of 1787*, 4 vols. (New Haven, CT: Yale University Press, 1937), 1:15. (Hereafter cited as Farrand's *Records*.)

7. Maggs, "Which Original Meaning?" 498.

8. 5 *Annals of Congress* 776 (1796).

9. Maggs, "Which Original Meaning?" 498.

10. Ibid., 495.

11. Clarence Thomas, "Judging," *Kansas Law Review* 45 (November 1996): 1, 6.

12. Ibid., 7.

13. 514 U.S. 334, 359 (1995).

14. Maggs, "Which Original Meaning?" 495.

15. I am grateful to Professor Maggs for the examples that follow. Ibid., 499–500.

16. *Federalist* No. 81, 549.

17. Jonathan Elliot, ed., *The Debates in the Several State Conventions on the Adoption of the Federal Constitution as Recommended by the General Convention in Philadelphia in 1787*, 5 vols. (Philadelphia: Lippincott, 1836), 3:555. (Hereafter cited as Elliot's *Debates*.)

18. 2 U.S. 419 (1793).

19. Farrand's *Records*, 2:538.

20. *Federalist* No. 75, 504–505.

21. See Ralph A. Rossum, *Antonin Scalia's Jurisprudence: Text and Tradition* (Lawrence: University Press of Kansas, 2006).

22. Scalia searches out the ordinary meaning of the words used when the provision was adopted, frequently consulting dictionaries of the era. In fact, he consults dictionaries more often than any of his colleagues. See Note, "Looking It Up: Dictionaries and Statutory Interpretation," *Harvard Law Review* 107 (April 1994): 1437, 1439.

23. For Justice Scalia, separation of powers represents such a critical structural principle. See Antonin Scalia, "Originalism: The Lesser Evil," *University of Cincinnati Law Review* 57 (1989): 849, 851.

24. By *the most specific legal tradition*, Scalia means "the most specific level at which a relevant tradition protecting, or denying protection to, the asserted right can be identified." *Michael H. v. Gerald D.*, 491 U.S. 110, 127 n.6 (1989).

25. "What I do when I interpret the American Constitution is, I try to understand what it meant, what was understood by the society to mean when it was adopted. And I don't think it changes since then." "Transcript of Discussion between U.S. Supreme Court Justices Antonin Scalia and Stephen Breyer," American University, Washington College of Law, January 13, 2005, 12.

26. *Callins v. Collins*, 510 U.S. 1141 (1994).

27. See, for example, *Doe v. Chao*, 540 U.S. 614 (2004), where the Court announced that "Souter, J., delivered the opinion of the Court, in which Rehnquist, C. J., and O'Connor, Kennedy, and Thomas, JJ., joined, and in which Scalia, J., joined except as to the penultimate paragraph of Part III and footnote 8." The penultimate paragraph begins: "This inference from the terms of the Commission's mandate is underscored by drafting history showing that Congress cut out the very language in the bill that would have authorized any presumed damages." Ibid., at 622. Footnote 8 contains the sentence: "Congress's use of the entitlement phrase actually contained in the statute, however, is explained by drafting history." Ibid., at 623. Scalia's refusal to join opinions that rely on legislative history is driven by his commitment never to join an opinion in which he does not agree with both the outcome and the reasoning. See Rossum, *Antonin Scalia's Jurisprudence*, 221.

28. *Thompson v. Thompson,* 484 U.S. 174, 191–192 (1988).

29. 530 U.S. 363 (2000).

30. Ibid., at 390–391. Emphasis in the original.

31. Antonin Scalia, *A Matter of Interpretation: Federal Courts and the Law* (Princeton, NJ: Princeton University Press, 1997), 34.

32. See Ralph A. Rossum, "Antonin Scalia and the Rule of Law: The Textualist Foundation of the 'Law of Rules,'" in Anthony A. Peacock, ed., *Freedom and the Rule of Law* (Lanham, MD: Lexington Books, 2010), 115–136.

33. 554 U.S. 570 (2008).

34. Ibid., at 595.

35. Ibid., at 637.

36. Speech in the House of Representatives, August 13, 1789, in *The Annals of Congress,* formally known as *The Debates and Proceedings in the Congress of the United States,* 1:736.

37. Ibid., 734.

38. Respondent's Brief, *District of Columbia v. Heller,* 32.

39. Official Transcript of Oral Argument in ibid., 31–32.

40. See Rossum, *Antonin Scalia's Jurisprudence,* 37–44.

41. Thomas has not used the term *original general meaning;* however, consistent with describing this approach as an incorporation of original intent, original understanding, and original public meaning, he employs all three terms in his opinions and speeches. Thus, he occasionally speaks of *original understanding*—see his opinions in cases such as *United States v. Lopez,* 514 U.S. 549 (1995); *U.S. Term Limits v. Thornton,* 514 U.S. 779 (1995); *Printz v. United States,* 521 U.S. 898 (1997); *Lilly v. Virginia,* 527 U.S. 116 (1999); *United States v. Morrison,* 529 U.S. 598 (2000); *Federal Maritime Commission v. South Carolina,* 535 U.S. 743 (2002); *Utah v. Evans,* 536 U.S. 452 (2002); *Cutter v. Wilkinson,*

544 U.S. 709 (2005); *Gonzales v. Raich,* 545 U.S. 1 (2005); *Morse v. Frederick,* 551 U.S. 393 (2007); *Meadwestvaco v. Illinois Department of Revenue,* 553 U.S. 16 (2008); and *Baze v. Rees,* 553 U.S. 35 (2008). On other occasions, he uses both *original understanding* and *original meaning* interchangeably in the same opinion: see *McIntyre v. Ohio Election Commission,* 514 U.S. 334 (1995); *Rosenberger v. University of Virginia,* 515 U.S. 819 (1995); *Saenz v. Roe,* 526 U.S. 489 (1999); *Apprendi v. New Jersey,* 530 U.S. 466 (2000); and *Harris v. United States,* 536 U.S. 545 (2002). In *Van Orden v. Perry,* 545 U.S. 677 (2005), and *McDonald v. City of Chicago,* 130 S. Ct. 3020 (2010), Thomas uses exclusively the term *original meaning.* When addressing the general public, he has even used the term *original intent;* see his October 16, 2008, Walter B. Wriston Lecture to the Manhattan Institute for Policy Research, "Judging in a Government by Consent," http://www .manhattan-institute.org/video/index .htm?c=10–16–2008%20Wriston%20-%20 Judging%20Government%20Consent.

42. "Assisted by canons and dictionaries, Justice Thomas asks whether the statutory text admits of plain interpretation, and if so, then 'judicial inquiry is complete'; or if there is irreducible ambiguity, and if so looks guardedly beyond. Where he finds that the statute speaks plainly, he takes its expression as conclusive of legislative intent. When he must go beyond, he looks to sources of intent such as clear statement rules and legislative history. He seeks not strict construction but reasonable interpretation. The text is his lodestar." H. Brent McKnight, "The Emerging Contours of Justice Thomas's Textualism," *Regent University Law Review* 12 (1999–2000): 365, 366.

43. Maggs suggests that the "principal theoretical difficulty with Thomas' method is the lack of any apparent or articulated rationale for it." He argues that Thomas has not yet offered a "theory for why

courts should strive to discern and follow an original general meaning." Maggs, "Which Original Meaning?" 514. Scalia's refusal/failure to strengthen his original public meaning interpretation in *District of Columbia v. Heller* by employing the original intent of Madison regarding where he wanted the Second Amendment to be placed in the text of the Constitution (Article I, § 9) offers perhaps the best rationale for why Thomas pursues an original general meaning, whether articulated or not.

44. Philip B. Kurland and Ralph Lerner, *The Founders' Constitution*, 5 vols. (Chicago: University of Chicago Press, 1987).

45. Herbert J. Storing, ed., *The Complete Anti-Federalist*, 7 vols. (Chicago: University of Chicago Press, 1981).

46. John P. Kaminski et al., eds., *The Documentary History of the Ratification of the Constitution*, 26 vols. (Madison: Wisconsin Historical Society Press, 1976–2013).

47. 517 U.S. 843 (1996).

48. Ibid., at 859–860.

49. 544 U.S. 709 (2005).

50. Ibid., at 728. Emphasis in the original.

51. Ibid., at 730.

52. Ibid. See also Thomas's opinion concurring in the judgment in part and dissenting in part in *Davis v. Washington*, 547 U.S. 813, 836 (2006), where, in this Confrontation Clause case, Thomas cited W. Holdsworth's *History of English Law* (1926) and concluded that "many statements that would be inadmissible as a matter of hearsay law bear little resemblance to the . . . evidentiary practices which the Framers proposed the Confrontation Clause to prevent."

53. 544 U.S. at 731. It should be noted here that the opinion in which Thomas employed founding-era materials most extensively and persuasively is his dissent in *U.S. Term Limits, Inc. v. Thornton*, 514 U.S. 779 (1995). See the extensive discussion of this case in chapter 3.

54. "Unlike Justice Scalia, whose jurisprudence exhibits a textualist orientation, Thomas is unapologetic in his defense and exposition of an original understanding of the Constitution, the Declaration of Independence, and the 'higher law' principles that animate those documents. Not since the turn of the century, when members of the Supreme Court frequently appealed to the logic of natural rights and used the Declaration of Independence as a touchstone for interpreting the Constitution, has a single justice played such an integral role in rekindling the seminal debate over the role of natural law and natural rights in constitutional adjudication." Kirk A. Kennedy, "Reaffirming the Natural Law Jurisprudence of Justice Clarence Thomas," *Regent University Law Review* 9 (Fall 1997): 33, 34–35.

55. Scalia, *Matter of Interpretation*, 134. See also *Troxel v. Granville*, 530 U.S. 57, 91 (2000), where Scalia wrote: "In my view, a right of parents to direct the upbringing of their children is among the 'unalienable Rights' with which the Declaration of Independence proclaims 'all Men . . . are endowed by their Creator.' . . . The Declaration of Independence, however, is not a legal prescription conferring powers upon the courts." Scalia occasionally invokes the Declaration, but he does so merely to support a point he is making. See, for example, his dissent in *Neder v. United States*, 527 U.S. 1, 30–31 (1999), in which he argued that a criminal defendant has the right to have the jury determine his guilt of the crime charged and that this includes his commission of every element of the crime charged: "One of the indictments of the Declaration of Independence against King George III was that he had 'subjected us to a Jurisdiction foreign to our Constitution, and unacknowledged by our Laws' in approving legislation 'for depriving us, in many Cases, of the Benefits of Trial by Jury.'"

56. *Hearings Before the Committee on the Judiciary, United States Senate, One Hundred Second Congress, First Session, On the Nomination of Clarence Thomas to Be Associate Justice of the Supreme Court of the United States*, Pt. 1, 102nd Cong., at 114 (1993). (Hereafter cited as *Hearings*.)

57. Clarence Thomas, "The Higher Law Background of the Privileges or Immunities Clause of the Fourteenth Amendment," *Harvard Journal of Law and Public Policy* 12 (Winter 1989): 63, 64.

58. Clarence Thomas, "An Afro-American Perspective: Toward a 'Plain Reading' of the Constitution—The Declaration of Independence in Constitutional Interpretation," *Howard Law Journal* (1987): 691, 693.

59. Ibid., 695.

60. Thomas, "Higher Law Background," 64. See the opening section of chapter 6 for a more extended discussion of Thomas's understanding of the Declaration of Independence.

61. Ibid., 63.

62. Ibid., 6. See Kennedy, "Reaffirming the Natural Law Jurisprudence," 33, 50, and John S. Baker, Jr., "Natural Law and Justice Thomas," *Regent University Law Review* 12 (1999–2000): 471, 500.

63. Thomas, "Higher Law Background," 64.

64. 515 U.S. 200, 240 (1994). See also Scott Douglas Gerber, *First Principles: The Jurisprudence of Clarence Thomas* (New York: New York University Press, 1999), 36–65.

65. 539 U.S. 306 (2003).

66. Ibid., at 378.

67. 163 U.S. 537, 559 (1896). As Thomas stated in "Higher Law Background," 66–67, "Justice Harlan's opinion [in *Plessy*] provides one of our best examples of natural rights or higher law jurisprudence."

68. 130 S. Ct. 3020, 3059–3060 (2010). Emphases added.

69. Thomas, "Judging," 6.

70. Ibid.

71. *Lewis v. Casey*, 518 U.S. 343, 367 (1996).

72. Thomas, "Judging," 7.

73. As Thomas said in an August 10, 1987, speech to the Pacific Research Institute: "One does not strengthen self-government and the Rule of Law by having the non-democratic branch of government make policy. . . . The Court has its dignity, and its power, by virtue of being above and beyond such clamoring." The speech is found in *Hearings*, 166–167.

74. Chief Justice Hughes subsequently qualified these remarks, noting, "The remark has been used, regardless of its context, as if permitting inference that I was picturing constitutional interpretation by the courts as a matter of judicial caprice. This was farthest from my thought. . . . I was speaking of the essential function of the courts under our system of interpreting and applying constitutional safeguards." David J. Danielski and J. S. Tulshin, eds., *The Autobiographical Notes of Charles Evans Hughes* (Cambridge, MA: Harvard University Press, 1973), 143.

75. Thomas, "Judging," 7.

76. Ibid.

77. Ibid.

78. 514 U.S. 334 (1995).

79. Ibid., at 359.

80. Thomas, "Judging," 7.

81. 545 U.S. 1 (2005).

82. 539 U.S. 59 (2003).

83. 550 U.S. 330 (2007).

84. 538 U.S. 644 (2003).

85. 555 U.S. 555 (2009).

86. 556 U.S. 502 (2009).

87. 550 U.S. 124 (2007).

88. 505 U.S. 42 (1992).

89. 514 U.S. 927 (1995).

90. 519 U.S. 433 (1997).

91. 530 U.S. 27 (2000).

92. 530 U.S. 466 (2000).

93. 536 U.S. 545 (2002).

94. 542 U.S. 296 (2004).

95. 543 U.S. 220 (2005).

96. 544 U.S. 13 (2005).

97. In addition to the cases mentioned in the pages that follow, see also *Fogerty v. Fantasy*, 510 U.S. 517, 535–538 (1994); *Farmer v. Brennan*, 511 U.S. 825, 858–862 (1994); *Mitchell v. United States*, 526 U.S. 314, 341–343 (1999); *United States v. Hubbell*, 530 U.S. 27, 49–56 (2000); *Whitman v. American Trucking Association*, 531 U.S. 457, 486–487 (2001); *Cooper Industries v. Leatherman Tool Group*, 532 U.S. 424, 443 (2001); *Sabri v. United States*, 541 U.S. 600, 610–614 (2004); *Grable & Sons Metal Products v. Darue Engineering and Manufacturing*, 545 U.S. 308, 320–322 (2005); *Morse v. Frederick*, 551 U.S. 393, 410–422 (2007); *Federal Communications Commission v. Fox Television Stations*, 556 U.S. 502, 530–535 (2009); and *Carachuri-Rosendo v. Holder*, 130 S. Ct. 2577, 2591 (2010).

98. 502 U.S. 346 (1992).

99. Ibid., at 366.

100. 509 U.S. 25 (1993).

101. 429 U.S. 97 (1976).

102. 509 U.S. at 42. See Thomas's earlier dissent in *Hudson v. McMillian*, 503 U.S. 1, 17–29 (1992). Thomas continues to push for the reconsideration of precedents in criminal procedure. See, for example, his concurrence in *Berghuis v. Smith*, 130 S. Ct. 1382, 1396 (2010): "[The Court's] conclusion . . . seems difficult to square with the Sixth Amendment's text and history. Accordingly, in an appropriate case I would be willing to reconsider our precedents articulating the 'fair cross section' requirement. But neither party asks us to do so here, and the only question before us is whether the state court's disposition was contrary to, or an unreasonable application of, our precedents. I concur in the Court's answer to that question."

103. 545 U.S. 677 (2005).

104. Ibid., at 694.

105. Ibid., at 697.

106. 514 U.S. 334 (1995).

107. Ibid., at 359.

108. Ibid., at 376–377.

109. Ibid., at 370–371.

110. 545 U.S. 469 (2005).

111. Ibid., at 518.

112. Ibid., at 523.

113. 536 U.S. 452 (2002).

114. Ibid., at 489.

115. Ibid., at 490. He insisted that the Court should be guided "by the Census Clause's 'original meaning,' for the Constitution is a written instrument. As such, its meaning does not alter. That which it meant when adopted, it means now." Ibid., at 491.

116. Ibid.

117. Ibid., at 500–501.

118. Ibid., at 493.

119. Ibid., at 503.

120. Ibid., at 506, 510.

121. 514 U.S. 549 (1995).

122. Ibid., at 584.

123. 529 U.S. 598 (2000).

124. Ibid., at 627.

125. 520 U.S. 564 (1997).

126. The negative (or dormant) Commerce Clause is a legal doctrine that holds that the Commerce Clause of Article I, § 8 not only grants power to Congress to regulate commerce among the states but also confers power on the Court to protect the right to engage in interstate trade free from restrictive state regulation.

127. 520 U.S. at 610.

128. 550 U.S. 330 (2007).

129. Ibid., at 349.

130. 541 U.S. 193, 214 (2004).

131. 524 U.S. 498 (1998).

132. 3 U.S. 386 (1798).

133. 524 U.S. at 538–539.

134. See McKnight, "Emerging Contours," 365, 366–384, for a detailed discussion of Thomas's approach to statutory construction. The paragraphs that follow rely heavily on McKnight's insightful analysis.

135. 511 U.S. 350, 356 (1994).

136. See Thomas's statement in *Connecticut National Bank v. Germain*, 503 U.S. 249, 253–254 (1992): "In interpreting a statute a court should always turn first to one, cardinal canon before all others. We have stated time and time again that courts must presume that a legislature says in a statute what it means and means what it says there."

137. Ibid., at 254.

138. 512 U.S. 849, 865 (1994).

139. *Shannon v. United States*, 512 U.S. 573, 582–583 (1994). As Thomas noted, "Courts have no authority to enforce [a] principle gleaned solely from legislative history that has no statutory reference point." Ibid., at 584. See also his dissent in *Small v. United States*, 544 U.S. 385, 406 (2005): "The Court's reliance on the absence of any discussion of foreign convictions in the legislative history is equally unconvincing. Reliance on explicit statements in the history, if they existed, would be problematic enough. Reliance on silence in the history is a new and even more dangerous phenomenon." See also his powerful rejection of the use of legislative history in *Holder v. Hall*, 512 U.S. 874, 727 (1994): "Contrary to the remarkable 'legislative history first' method of statutory construction pursued in *Gingles*, however, I had thought it firmly established that the 'authoritative source' for legislative intent was the text of the statute passed by both Houses of Congress and presented to the President, not a series of partisan statements about purposes and objectives collected by congressional staffers and packaged into a committee report."

140. 503 U.S. 291 (1992).

141. Ibid., at 311.

142. See Thomas's defense of the rule of lenity in his dissenting opinion in *Evans v. United States*, 504 U.S. 255, 289–290 (1992).

143. 503 U.S. at 311–312.

144. In his opinion concurring in part and concurring in the judgment, in which Thomas joined, Scalia observed that "it may well be true that in most cases the proposition that the words of the United States Code or the Statutes at Large give adequate notice to the citizen is something of a fiction, albeit one required in any system of law; but necessary fiction descends to needless farce when the public is charged even with knowledge of Committee Reports." 503 U.S. at 309. Thomas joined Scalia's opinion and agreed with him "that there appears scant justification for extending the 'necessary fiction' that citizens know the law to such extralegal materials." Ibid., at 312.

145. McKnight, "Emerging Contours," 376.

146. In *Koons Buick Pontiac GMC v. Nigh*, 543 U.S. 50, 68 (2004), Thomas suggested that one reason for the Court's inability to adhere to the text was that what Congress had passed was "not a model of the best practices in legislative drafting."

147. 516 U.S. 235 (1996).

148. Ibid., at 254. Emphasis in the original.

149. Ibid., at 262. Emphasis in the original.

150. Ibid., at 263.

151. Ibid., at 256. Emphasis in the original.

152. Ibid., at 256–257.

153. Ibid., at 260.

154. McKnight, "Emerging Contours," 377.

155. 512 U.S. 874 (1994).

156. 478 U.S. 30 (1985).

157. 512 U.S. at 912.

158. Ibid., at 892.

159. Ibid., at 944. See Edith H. Jones, "Justice Thomas and the Voting Rights Act," *Regent University Law Review* 12 (1999–2000): 333.

160. Stephen J. Wermiel, "Clarence Thomas after Ten Years: Some Reflections," *American University Journal of Gender, Social Policy, and the Law* 10 (2002): 315, 321.

161. Ibid. Wermiel also states: "Thomas has outlined an ambitious agenda for himself and the Court. It is a strange trademark for a Justice who consistently tells audiences that an important limitation on the power of the Supreme Court is that it cannot reach out to decide issues not properly presented before the Court." Ibid., 323.

162. 518 U.S. at 367.

163. Thomas, "Judging," 7.

164. "A commitment to bring the Court's jurisprudence into line with the original meaning of the Constitution's text, however, differs from a jurisprudence which either ignores text or gives text a meaning that its words will not bear. The latter implements the will of the judge; the former, the will of the people as embodied in the text of the Constitution, which is the rationale for judicial review as stated in *Marbury*." Baker, "Natural Law and Justice Thomas," 508–509.

Chapter 2. Constitutional Structure and Federalism: The Commerce Clause

1. Clarence Thomas, "Why Federalism Matters," *Drake Law Review* 48 (2000): 231, 234.

2. Interestingly enough, although Thomas has spoken and written extensively on federalism (so much so that this chapter and the next address his understanding of that subject), he has spoken and written very little on separation of powers, the other "double security." In his Opperman Lecture, he spoke briefly of separation of powers, mentioning that "the framers divided the powers of the national government into three branches" in part because "they believed it would create an efficient government." Ibid., 233. He did not elaborate, but he was referencing the fact that the framers knew government would be more efficient if its various functions were performed by separate and distinct bodies. James Wilson, a leading member of the Constitutional Convention, defended the creation of an independent and energetic executive on this exact basis: "In planning, forming, and arranging laws, deliberation is always becoming, and always useful. But in the active scenes of government, there are emergencies, in which the man . . . who deliberates is lost. Secrecy may be equally necessary as dispatch. But can either secrecy or dispatch be expected, when, to every enterprise, mutual communication, mutual consultation, and mutual agreement among men, perhaps of discordant views, of discordant tempers, and discordant interests, are indispensably necessary? How much time will be consumed! and when it is consumed, how little business will be done! . . . If, on the other hand, the executive power of government is placed in the hands of one person, who is to direct all the subordinate officers of that department; is there not reason to expect, in his plans and conduct, promptitude, activity, firmness, consistency, and energy?" Robert Green McCloskey, ed., *The Works of James Wilson* (Cambridge, MA: Belknap Press of Harvard University Press, 1967), 300.

Thomas's only opinions that directly address separation of powers questions are his dissents in two cases dealing with Guantanamo Bay detainees: *Hamdi v. Rumsfeld*, 542 U.S. 507 (2004), and *Hamdan v. Rumsfeld*, 548 U.S. 557 (2006). In both of them, he wrote opinions consistent with his brief discussion in his Opperman Lecture. In *Hamdi*, in which a Court plurality held that the detainee had a right to a hearing allowing him the opportunity to present evidence that he was not an enemy combatant, Thomas insisted that "the Executive Branch, acting pursuant to the powers vested in the President by the Constitution and with explicit congressional approval, has determined that Yaser Hamdi is an enemy combatant and should be detained. This detention falls squarely within the Federal Government's war powers, and we lack the expertise and capacity to second-guess that decision. As such, petitioners' habeas challenge should fail. . . . I do not think that the Federal Government's war powers can be balanced away by this Court. Arguably, Congress could provide for additional procedural protections, but until it does, we have no right to insist upon them." 542 U.S. at 579. And in *Hamdan*, in which a Court plurality held that military commissions set up by the Bush administration to try detainees lacked the power to proceed because their structure and procedures violated both the Uniform Code of Military Justice and the Geneva Conventions, Thomas concluded that its opinion "openly flouts our well-established duty to respect the Executive's judgment in matters of military operations and foreign affairs. The plurality's evident belief that *it* is qualified to pass on the 'military necessity' of the Commander in Chief's decision to employ a particular form of force against our enemies" was simply "antithetical to our constitutional structure." 548 U.S. at 678. Emphasis in the original.

3. Thomas, "Why Federalism Matters," 235.

4. Ibid., 235–236.

5. Ibid., 236–237.

6. Ibid., 237. Emphasis in *The Federalist*.

7. Ibid., 237.

8. Ibid., 237–238.

9. But see *Pierce County v. Guillen*, 537 U.S. 129 (2003), in which Thomas held for a unanimous Court that 1995 amendments to the Intermodal Surface Transportation Efficiency Act of 1991, 105 Stat. 1978, protecting information "compiled or collected" in connection with certain federal highway safety programs from being discovered or admitted in certain federal or state trials, represented a valid exercise of Congress's authority under the Commerce Clause. Both the 1991 act and the 1995 amendment "can be viewed as legislation aimed at improving safety in the channels of commerce and increasing protection for the

instrumentalities of interstate commerce. As such, they fall within Congress' Commerce Clause power." 537 U.S. at 147.

10. 514 U.S. 549 (1995).

11. 18 U.S.C. § 922(q)(1)(A),1988 ed., Supp. V. A *school zone* was defined as "in, or on the grounds of, a public, parochial, or private school" or "within a distance of 1,000 feet from the grounds of a public, parochial or private school." 18 USC § 921(a)(25).

12. 514 U.S. at 551.

13. Ibid., at 559.

14. Ibid., at 567. The act, Rehnquist argued, "has nothing to do with 'commerce' or any sort of economic enterprise, however broadly one might define those terms." It "is not an essential part of a larger regulation of economic activity, in which the regulatory scheme could be undercut unless the intrastate activity were regulated. It cannot, therefore, be sustained under our cases upholding regulations of activities that arise out of or are connected with a commercial transaction, which viewed in the aggregate, substantially affects interstate commerce." Ibid., at 561.

15. Ibid., at 563.

16. Ibid., at 564.

17. Ibid., at 567.

18. Ibid.

19. Ibid., at 600. As Souter said later in his dissent: "It seems fair to ask whether the step taken by the Court today does anything but portend a return to the untenable jurisprudence from which the Court extricated itself almost 60 years ago." Ibid., at 608.

20. Ibid., at 614.

21. Ibid., at 613.

22. Ibid.

23. Ibid., at 616–617. Breyer asserted, albeit without much conviction, that "to hold this statute constitutional is not to 'obliterate' the 'distinction between what is national and what is local'; nor is it to hold that the Commerce Clause permits the Federal Government to 'regulate any

activity that it found was related to the economic productivity of individual citizens,' to regulate 'marriage, divorce, and child custody,' or to regulate any and all aspects of education." Ibid., at 624.

24. Ibid., at 619.
25. See ibid., at 619–625, 631–644.
26. Ibid., at 584.
27. Ibid.
28. Ibid. Emphasis in the original.
29. Ibid., at 584–585.
30. Ibid., at 600. Emphasis in the original.
31. Ibid., at 585.
32. Ibid.
33. Ibid., at 585–586.
34. Ibid., at 586.
35. Ibid., at 586–587.
36. Ibid., at 585.
37. Ibid., at 587–588.
38. Ibid., at 588–589.
39. Ibid., at 589.
40. Ibid. Emphasis in the original.
41. Ibid., at 590. He quoted William Davie, a delegate to the North Carolina Ratifying Convention, who articulated well, at Elliot's *Debates*, vol. 4, p. 20, the close link between agriculture and manufacturing and commerce: "Commerce, sir, is the nurse of [agriculture and manufacturing]. The merchant furnishes the planter with such articles as he cannot manufacture himself, and finds him a market for his produce. Agriculture cannot flourish if commerce languishes; they are mutually dependent on each other."
42. 514 U.S. at 591.
43. Ibid., at 592.
44. Ibid., at 593.
45. 22 U.S. (9 Wheat.) 1 (1824).
46. 514 U.S. at 631.
47. Ibid., at 596.
48. Ibid., at 599.
49. Ibid., at 596.
50. Ibid., at 599. See Thomas's dissent from the Court's denial of a writ of certiorari in *Cargill v. United States*, 516 U.S. 955 (1995). The question in this case was whether the Army Corps of Engineers could, under the Clean Water Act, constitutionally assert jurisdiction over private property based solely on the actual or potential presence of migratory birds that cross state lines. Thomas declared that "in light of *Lopez*, I have serious doubts about the propriety of the Corps' assertion of jurisdiction over petitioner's land in this case." He summarized the corps's claim as follows: "The self propelled flight of birds across state lines creates a sufficient interstate nexus to justify the Corps' assertion of jurisdiction over any standing water that could serve as a habitat for migratory birds. As the Court of Appeals admitted, the Corps' expansive interpretation of its regulatory powers under the Clean Water Act may test the very 'bounds of reason,' and, in my mind, likely stretches Congress' Commerce Clause powers beyond the breaking point." Ibid., at 958. Thomas insisted that he was not challenging "Congress' power to preserve migratory birds and their habitat through legitimate means." But he insisted that did "not give the Corps *carte blanche* authority to regulate every property that migratory birds use or could use as habitat. The point of *Lopez* was to explain that the activity on the land to be regulated must substantially affect interstate commerce before Congress can regulate it pursuant to its Commerce Clause power." He pointed out that "other than the occasional presence of migratory birds," there was "no showing that petitioner's land use would have any effect on interstate commerce, much less a substantial effect. Nor was there any showing that the cumulative effect of land use involving seasonal standing water—water that is wholly isolated from any water used, or usable, in interstate commerce—would have a substantial effect on interstate commerce. This case raises serious and important constitutional questions about the limits of federal land use regulation in the name of the Clean Water Act that provide a

compelling reason to grant certiorari in this case." Ibid., at 959.

51. 514 U.S. at 601.

52. Ibid., n.8.

53. Ibid.

54. Ibid., at 602.

55. Ibid., at 600. See Thomas's spirited defense of the Court's majority opinion in *Lopez* in his dissent (joined by Scalia) to the Supreme Court's denial of certiorari and therefore to its "tacit accept[ance of] the nullification of our recent Commerce Clause jurisprudence," in *Alderman v. United States*, 131 S. Ct. 700 (2010). In this case, the Ninth Circuit ruled that Congress has power under the Commerce Clause to prevent felons from possessing or transporting body armor (in this instance, wearing a bulletproof vest). The Ninth Circuit recognized that *Lopez* had "significantly altered the landscape of congressional power under the Commerce Clause" but held that it was guided "first and foremost" by *Scarborough v. United States*, 431 U.S. 563 (1977)—characterized by Thomas as "a 33-year old statutory interpretation opinion." He found that the Ninth Circuit's "reading of *Scarborough*, by trumping the *Lopez* framework, could very well remove any limit on the commerce power." 131 S. Ct. 702–703. "Fifteen years ago in *Lopez*, we took a significant step toward reaffirming this Court's commitment to proper constitutional limits on Congress' commerce power. If the *Lopez* framework is to have any ongoing vitality, it is up to this Court to prevent it from being undermined by a 1977 precedent that does not squarely address the constitutional issue. Lower courts have recognized this problem and asked us to grant certiorari. I would do so." Ibid., at 703.

56. 521 U.S. 898 (1997).

57. Ibid., at 935.

58. Ibid., at 937. Emphasis in the original.

59. Ibid.

60. Ibid., at 938.

61. 554 U.S. 570 (2008).

62. 521 U.S. at 939. Emphasis in the original.

63. 529 U.S. 598 (2000).

64. Ibid., at 615.

65. Ibid., at 615–616.

66. In his concurrence in *Cutter v. Wilkinson*, though Thomas agreed with his colleagues that the Religious Land Use and Institutionalized Persons Act of 2000 was "entirely consonant with the Establishment Clause," he wondered in a footnote whether Congress had exceeded its authority under the Commerce Clause to pass the law in the first place. He continued, however, to note that the Court had "properly decline[d]" to address this issue since it was "outside the question presented" and was "not addressed by the Court of Appeals." 544 U.S. 709, 727 (2005). Similarly, in his concurrence in *Gonzales v. Carhart*, after questioning whether Congress's Partial-Birth Abortion Ban Act of 2003 constituted "a permissible exercise" of its power under the Commerce Clause, he noted that the question was "not before the Court. The parties did not raise or brief that issue; it is outside the question presented; and the lower courts did not address it." 550 U.S. 124, 169 (2007).

67. 529 U.S. at 627. In *Jones v. United States*, 529 U.S. 848 (2000), Justice Ruth Bader Ginsburg delivered the unanimous opinion of the Court and held that the federal arson statute did not cover the arson of an owner-occupied dwelling that was not used for any commercial purpose. The defendant had tossed a Molotov cocktail through a window into a home owned and occupied by his cousin and was convicted in federal court of arson, in violation of 18 U.S.C.S. § 844(i). On appeal, the defendant argued the statute did not apply to buildings not used for commercial purposes and, relying on *Lopez*, challenged the constitutionality of such an application. The government, however, argued that the residence was "used" in interstate commerce

because it received natural gas and had a mortgage and an insurance policy. The Supreme Court granted certiorari and framed the question as follows: "whether, in light of *United States v. Lopez* (1995), and the interpretive rule that constitutionally doubtful constructions should be avoided, 18 U.S.C. § 844(i) applies to the arson of a private residence; and if so, whether its application to the private residence in the present case is constitutional." 529 U.S. at 852. Ginsburg avoided the constitutional question that would have arisen had the Court read the statute to render the traditionally local criminal conduct a matter for federal enforcement by holding (1) that the provision covered only property currently used in commerce or in an activity affecting commerce, and (2) that an owner-occupied residence not used for any commercial purpose did not qualify. Thomas wrote a concurring opinion, in which Scalia joined, indicating that when an appropriate case arose, he would be open, in light of *Lopez*, to considering the constitutionality of applying the federal arson statute even to certain commercial buildings. "In joining the Court's opinion," he wrote, "I express no view on the question whether the federal arson statute, 18 U.S.C. § 844(i) as there construed, is constitutional in its application to all buildings used for commercial activities." 529 U.S. at 860.

68. 545 U.S. 1 (2005).

69. Ibid., at 22.

70. Ibid., at 33–42.

71. Ibid., at 40.

72. Ibid., at 39–40. See, however, *United States v. Oakland Cannabis Buyers' Cooperative*, 532 U.S. 483 (2001). In this case, the United States obtained an injunction from the U.S. District Court for the Northern District of California prohibiting the cooperative and its director from distributing medical marijuana, authorized under California's Compassionate Use Act of 1996 but in violation of the federal government's Controlled Substances Act. The court subsequently rejected the cooperative's motion to modify the injunction to permit marijuana distributions that purportedly were medically necessary. The U.S. Court of Appeals for the Ninth Circuit reversed the district court's refusal to modify the injunction and remanded the case to the district court, instructing it to consider the criteria for a medical-necessity exception to the CSA's prohibitions. Thomas wrote the majority opinion reversing the Ninth Circuit and holding that, with respect to marijuana, there was no medical-necessity exception, for it was clear from the text of the act that Congress had made a determination that marijuana had no medical benefits worthy of an exception. On first blush, this conclusion would seem contrary to what he would argue in his dissent in *Raich*, but it was not. As Thomas noted near the end of his opinion, the question of the constitutionality of the CSA had not been addressed by the courts below and this case was not the proper vehicle to address that issue. "Finally," he wrote, "the Cooperative contends that . . . the statute exceeds Congress' Commerce Clause powers, violates the substantive due process rights of patients, and offends the fundamental liberties of the people under the Fifth, Ninth, and Tenth Amendments. . . . [We do not] consider the underlying constitutional issues today. Because the Court of Appeals did not address these claims, we decline to do so in the first instance." Ibid., at 494.

73. Ibid., at 59.

74. Ibid., at 61.

75. Ibid., at 63.

76. Ibid., at 64.

77. Ibid.

78. Ibid., at 67.

79. Ibid., at 25.

80. Ibid., at 69.

81. Ibid., at 70.

82. Ibid. Emphasis in the original.

83. Ibid., at 71. In *Gonzales v. Oregon*, 546 U.S. 243 (2006), Justice Anthony Kennedy upheld for a six-member majority a challenge by the state of Oregon to U.S. Attorney General Alberto Gonzales's statutory interpretation of the CSA that would have disrupted physician-assisted suicide under Oregon's Death with Dignity Act (2003). Thomas dissented from this opinion, contrasting the majority opinion in *Oregon* with the majority opinion in *Raich*: "When Angel Raich and Diane Monson challenged the application of the Controlled Substances Act to their purely intrastate possession of marijuana for medical use as authorized under California law, a majority of this Court (a mere seven months ago) determined that the CSA effectively invalidated California's law because 'the CSA is a comprehensive regulatory regime specifically designed to regulate which controlled substances can be utilized for medicinal purposes, *and in what manner.*'" Yet he noted, "Today the majority beats a hasty retreat from these conclusions." Ibid., at 299. Emphasis in the original. He pointed to the "stark contrast" between "*Raich's* broad conclusions about the scope of the CSA as it pertains to the medicinal use of controlled substances" and *Oregon's* conclusion that the CSA was "merely concerned with fighting 'drug abuse' and only insofar as that abuse leads to 'addiction or abnormal effects on the nervous system.'" Ibid., at 300. He found "puzzling" the "majority's newfound understanding of the CSA as a statute of limited reach" because, as he noted, it rested on "constitutional principles that the majority of the Court rejected in *Raich*." The states' "traditional police powers to define the criminal law and to protect the health, safety, and welfare of their citizens" were completely ignored in *Raich*, he noted, but suddenly figured prominently in *Oregon*. Ibid., at 300–301. He concluded: "The Court's reliance upon the constitutional principles that it rejected in *Raich*—albeit

under the guise of statutory interpretation—is perplexing to say the least. Accordingly, I respectfully dissent." Ibid., at 302.

84. 132 S. Ct. 2566 (2012).

85. Ibid., at 2677. Emphasis in the original.

86. Ibid., at 2648.

87. Ibid., at 2655. Emphasis in the original.

88. Recall his comments on judicial review in Thomas, "Why Federalism Matters," 237–238.

89. See Ralph A. Rossum, *Federalism, the Supreme Court, and the Seventeenth Amendment: The Irony of Constitutional Democracy* (Lanham, MD: Lexington Books, 2001).

90. Philip B. Kurland and Ralph Lerner, *The Founders' Constitution*, 5 vols. (Chicago: University of Chicago Press, 1987), 2:232.

91. Farrand's *Records*, 1:52.

92. Ibid., 1:156.

93. Ibid., 1:150.

94. Ibid., 1:155. In Robert Yates's "Notes" for the same day, Dickinson observed that "this mode will more intimately connect the state governments with the national legislature," and Mason was reported as saying: "The second branch of the national legislature should flow from the legislature of each state, to prevent the encroachments on each other, and to harmonize the whole." Ibid., 1:157. Rufus King recorded Mason as follows: "The Danger is that the national, will swallow up the State Legislatures—what will be a reasonable guard agt. this Danger, and operate in favor of the State authorities—The answer seems to me to be this, let the State Legislatures appoint the Senate." Ibid., 1:160.

95. Elliot's *Debates*, 2:306.

96. Ibid., 2:317–318.

97. *Federalist* No. 59, 401.

98. Ibid., No. 37, 234.

99. Farrand's *Records*, 1:53. Emphasis in the original.

100. Ibid.

101. Ibid. Madison appreciated the difficulty of attempting to put into words a precise enumeration. As he argued in *Federalist* No. 37, 236–237, even "when the Almighty himself condescends to address mankind in their own language, his meaning, luminous as it must be, is rendered dim and doubtful, by the cloudy medium through which it is communicated."

102. *Federalist* No. 41, 270. See also Alexander Hamilton's similar statements in *Federalist* No. 31, 194, in which he describes as "maxims in ethics and politics . . . that the means ought to be proportioned to the end; that every power ought to be commensurate with this object, [and] that there ought to be no limitation of a power destined to effect a purpose, which is itself incapable of limitation."

103. *Federalist* No. 48, 333.

104. *Federalist* No. 51, 347–348. The mode of electing the Senate was obviously one such contrivance that the framers employed to keep the general government in its proper place.

105. Farrand's *Records*, 1:54.

106. Ibid., at 2:95.

107. Ibid., at 2:131–132.

108. Ibid., at 2:308.

109. There was no reference in Madison's Notes at that time to the Indian Commerce Clause either because the Virginia Plan that served as the first draft of the Constitution included no language for federal authority over Indian affairs. Madison corrected his oversight on August 18 when he proposed language to grant to the new federal government the power to "regulate affairs with the Indians as well within as without the United States." See ibid., at 2:324.

110. Ibid., at 2:344–345. Though both Edmund Randolph and Elbridge Gerry eventually mentioned the Necessary and Proper Clause among their reasons for refusing to sign the Constitution, they never objected to its wording or sought its elimination when the convention was reviewing the work of the Committee of Detail. See ibid., at 2:563, 632.

111. Several delegates to the convention clearly believed that the Court would have the power of judicial review. Gouverneur Morris, for one, observed that the judiciary should not "be bound to say that a direct violation of the Constitution was law." Ibid., at 2:299. Luther Martin, for another, argued against a proposed council of revision on the grounds that "the constitutionality of laws . . . will come before the judges in their official character. In this character, they have a negative on the laws." Ibid., at 2:76. See also Gerry's comments in ibid., at 2:97. The problem with these statements, however, is that they imply neither a general power to expound the Constitution nor an obligation on the part of the other branches to regard a judicial decision on the constitutionality of their actions as binding. Moreover, statements were also made by other convention delegates unequivocally rejecting judicial review. Thus, for example, John Mercer "disapproved of the doctrine that the judges as expositors of the Constitution should have authority to declare a law void. He thought laws ought to be well and cautiously made, and then to be uncontrollable." Ibid., at 2:298. So, too, did Dickinson, who argued that "as to the power of the Judges to set aside the law, . . . no such power ought to exist." Ibid., at 2:299. See George Anastaplo, *The Constitution of 1787: A Commentary* (Baltimore, MD: Johns Hopkins University Press, 1989), 47–48, who, by proceeding "section by section" through the Constitution, concludes that the Constitution tends toward legislative supremacy and that judicial review is highly suspect; noting the "complete silence in the Constitution about judicial review," he wonders "if it is likely . . . that judicial review was indeed anticipated, when nothing was said about it, considering the care with which [for example] executive review is provided for." See also Ralph A.

Rossum, "The Least Dangerous Branch?" in Peter Augustine Lawler and Robert Martin Schaefer, eds., *The American Experiment: Essays on the Theory and Practice of Liberty* (Lanham, MD: Rowman & Littlefield, 1994), 241–258.

112. *Federalist* No. 78, 524. Emphasis added.

113. See Ralph A. Rossum, "James Wilson and the 'Pyramid of Government': The Federal Republic," *Political Science Reviewer* 6 (1976): 113–142, 133–134.

114. Farrand's *Records*, 2:73. Emphasis added.

115. *Federalist* No. 78, 524. Here is the entire passage: "The complete independence of the courts of justice is peculiarly essential in a limited Constitution. By a limited Constitution, I understand one which contains certain specified exceptions to the legislative authority; such, for instance, as that it shall pass no bills of attainder, no ex-post-facto laws, and the like. Limitations of this kind can be preserved in practice no other way than through the medium of courts of justice, whose duty it must be to declare all acts contrary to the manifest tenor of the Constitution void. Without this, all the reservations of particular rights or privileges would amount to nothing."

116. *Federalist* No. 33, 206. As Hamilton made clear in both *Federalist* No. 59, 401, and during the New York Ratifying Convention (Elliot's *Debates*, 2:306, 317–318), one way the people could "redress the injury" caused by congressional infringement on the "residuary sovereignty" of the states was by electing state legislators who would hold senators responsible for this infringement.

117. See C. H. Hoebeke, *The Road to Mass Democracy: Original Intent and the Seventeenth Amendment* (New Brunswick, NJ: Transaction, 1995).

118. Rossum, *Federalism*, 219–220.

119. In *Camps Newfound/Owatonna v. Town of Harrison*, 520 U.S. 564, 609 (1997),

Thomas indicated why he typically uses the term *negative Commerce Clause*: "Although the terms 'dormant' and 'negative' have often been used interchangeably to describe our jurisprudence in this area, I believe 'negative' is the more appropriate term. See *Oklahoma Tax Commission v. Jefferson Lines, Inc.*, 514 U.S. 175, 200 (1995) (Scalia, J., joined by Thomas, J., concurring in judgment) (The 'negative Commerce Clause' . . . is 'negative' not only because it negates state regulation of commerce, but also because it does *not* appear in the Constitution). There is, quite frankly, nothing 'dormant' about our jurisprudence in this area."

120. Clarence Thomas, "Judging in a Government by Consent," Walter B. Wriston Lecture to the Manhattan Institute for Policy Research, October 16, 2008, http://www.manhattan-institute.org/video/index.htm?c=10–16–2008%20Wriston%20-%20Judging%20Government%20Consent.

121. *Dennis v. Higgins*, 498 U.S. 439, 448 (1991).

122. *Westinghouse Electric Corp. v. Tully*, 466 U.S. 388, 402–403 (1984). Emphasis added.

123. 511 U.S. 93 (1994).

124. 504 U.S. 334 (1992).

125. Ibid., at 95.

126. Ibid., at 99, 100.

127. 511 U.S. 641 (1994).

128. Ibid., at 646.

129. 510 U.S. 355 (1994).

130. Ibid., at 382.

131. 515 U.S. 582 (1995).

132. 516 U.S. 325 (1996).

133. 520 U.S. 564 (1997).

134. Ibid., at 571.

135. Ibid., at 609.

136. Ibid.

137. Ibid., at 611. See Brannon P. Denning, "Justice Thomas, the Import-Export Clause, and *Camps Newfound/Owatonna v. Harrison*," *University of Colorado Law Review* 70 (Winter 1998): 155, 219, who expected that Thomas's "abrupt

volte face would warrant at least a footnote. But in his *Camps Newfound/Owatonna* dissent, Justice Thomas seems either not to recognize the break between his present position and his earlier opinions, or takes care to conceal his shift in position from his audience." Obviously, Thomas did not take sufficient care, as he did not conceal it from Denning!

138. 520 U.S. at 610.

139. 483 U.S. 232, 259–265 (1987). Justice Scalia dissenting.

140. 486 U.S. 888, 895–898 (1988). Justice Scalia concurring in judgment.

141. 520 U.S. at 610. See Michael Greve's criticisms of Thomas's and Scalia's textualist objections to the negative Commerce Clause in *The Upside-Down Constitution* (Cambridge, MA: Harvard University Press, 2012), 358–365.

142. 520 U.S. at 618.

143. Ibid., at 620. He also added that if the Court would abandon the negative Commerce Clause and confine itself to interpreting the Import Export Clause, it would leave to Congress "the policy choices necessary for any further regulation of interstate commerce."

144. 75 U.S. 123 (1869).

145. 520 U.S. at 636.

146. Ibid., at 621. Emphasis in the original. Thomas made his detailed argument from pp. 621–637.

147. Ibid., at 636.

148. Ibid., at 637.

149. Ibid. Emphasis in the original.

150. Ibid., at 640.

151. *American Trucking Association v. Smith*, 496 U.S. 167, 202 (1990).

152. *Camps Newfound/Owatonna v. Town of Harrison*, 520 U.S. at 610.

153. But see Scalia's passing reference at the end of his opinion concurring in part and dissenting in part in *Tyler Pipe v. Washington Department of Revenue*, 483 U.S. 232, 265 (1987), in which he indicated that "rank discrimination against citizens of other

States . . . is regulated not by the Commerce Clause but by the Privileges and Immunities Clause, U.S. Const., Art. IV, § 2, cl. 1 ('The Citizens of each State shall be entitled to all Privileges and Immunities of Citizens in the several States.')." That Clause, however, is limited to "citizens," not "persons," and therefore, would not be available to protect corporations from "rank discrimination."

154. Ibid., at 636.

155. 507 U.S. 60 (1993).

156. Ibid., at 78–79. He has repeated this announcement in *West Lynn Creamery v. Healy*, 512 U.S. 186, 210 (1994); *Barclays Bank v. Franchise Tax Board*, 512 U.S. 298, 332 (1992); and *General Motors Corporation v. Tracy*, 519 U.S. 278, 312 (1997).

157. 507 U.S. at 78–79. See Scalia's concurring or dissenting opinions in which he debated with his colleagues whether a particular state regulation or tax is, in fact, "facially discriminatory" in *American Trucking Association v. Scheiner*, 483 U.S. 266, 305 (1987); *New Energy Company of Indiana v. Limbach*, 486 U.S. 269, 280 (1988); *Amerada Hess v. Division of Taxation, New Jersey Department of the Treasury*, 490 U.S. 66, 80 (1989); *Healy v. Beer Institute*, 491 U.S. 324, 344 (1989); and *Trinova Corporation v. Michigan Department of Treasury*, 498 U.S. 358, 387 (1991).

158. 507 U.S. at 78–79.

159. 539 U.S. 59 (2003).

160. Ibid., at 68. Thomas also quoted the same language from *Camps Newfound* in *Pharmaceutical Research and Manufacturers of America v. Walsh*, 538 U.S. 644, 683 (2003), and *American Trucking Associations, Inc. v. Michigan Public Service Commission*, 545 U.S. 429, 439 (2005).

161. 550 U.S. 330 (2007).

162. Ibid., at 349.

163. Ibid., at 352.

164. Ibid., at 355. Thomas quoted from his opinion in *United Haulers* that the negative Commerce Clause should be "discard[ed]." See also his opinions in

Meadwestvaco Corp. v. Illinois Department of Revenue, 553 U.S. 16, 32 (2008), and *Department of Revenue of Kentucky v. Davis,* 553 U.S. 328, 361 (2008), and *McBurney v. Young,* 133 S. Ct. 1709, 1721 (2013).

165. 544 U.S. 460, 497 (2005).
166. Ibid., at 494.
167. Ibid., at 496.
168. Ibid., at 497.
169. Ibid., at 499.
170. 286 U.S. 131, 139–140 (1932).
171. 544 U.S. at 499.
172. Ibid., at 500.
173. Ibid., at 514.
174. Ibid., at 525.
175. Ibid., at 527.
176. 541 U.S. 193 (2004).
177. Ibid., at 200.
178. Ibid., at 210. *Lara* reached the Supreme Court as a double jeopardy case. Breyer held for the majority that when Congress in 1991 authorized tribes to prosecute nonmember Indians, that was a relaxation of previous restrictions it had placed on the exercise of the tribes' inherent sovereign authority and not a delegation of federal prosecutorial power to them; therefore, a federal prosecution of Billy Jo Lara for assaulting a federal police officer did not violate the Double Jeopardy Clause of the federal constitution's Fifth Amendment, even though he had previously been prosecuted for "violence to a policeman" under the law of an Indian tribe of which he was not a member.
179. "I cannot agree with the Court . . . that the Constitution grants to Congress plenary power to calibrate the 'metes and bounds' of tribal sovereignty. Unlike the Court, I cannot locate such congressional authority in the Treaty Clause, U.S. Const., Art. II, § 2, cl. 2, or the Indian Commerce Clause, Art. I, § 8, cl. 3. Additionally, I would ascribe much more significance to legislation such as the Act of Mar. 3, 1871, that purports to terminate the practice of dealing with Indian tribes by treaty. The making of treaties,

after all, is the one mechanism that the Constitution clearly provides for the Federal Government to interact with sovereigns other than the States." Ibid., at 215.
180. Ibid., at 224. Thomas has held firmly to this belief. See his concurring opinion in *Adoptive Couple v. Baby Girl,* 133 S. Ct. 2552, 2566–2567 (2013): "Although this Court has said that the 'central function of the Indian Commerce Clause is to provide Congress with plenary power to legislate in the field of Indian affairs, neither the text nor the original understanding of the Clause supports Congress' claim to such 'plenary' power."
181. Ibid., at 214–215.
182. Ibid., at 219.
183. Ibid., at 214. He could not understand how the federal government could "regulate the tribes through ordinary domestic legislation and simultaneously maintain that the tribes are sovereigns in any meaningful sense." Ibid., at 225.
184. Ibid., at 226.
185. See Ralph A. Rossum, *The Supreme Court and Tribal Gaming:* California v. Cabazon Band of Mission Indians (Lawrence: University Press of Kansas, 2011), 36–53.
186. *Federalist* No. 42, 284–285.
187. David P. Currie, *The Constitution in Congress: The Federalist Period, 1789–1801* (Chicago: University of Chicago Press, 1997), 3.
188. *McCulloch v. Maryland,* 17 U.S. 316, 407 (1819).
189. Currie, *Constitution in Congress,* 4.
190. Ibid., 5.
191. W. B. Allen, ed., *Works of Fisher Ames,* 2 vols. (Indianapolis, IN: Liberty Fund, 1983), 2:877.
192. 1 Stat. 49 (1789).
193. 1 Stat. 50 (1789).
194. 1 Stat. 54 (1789).
195. 1 Stat. 67 (1789).
196. 1 Stat. 137 (1790).
197. 1 Stat. 332 (1793).

198. 1 Stat. 469 (1796).

199. 1 Stat. 743 (1799).

200. 2 Stat. 139 (1802).

201. 30 U.S. 1 (1831).

202. Ibid., at 30.

203. Ibid., at 16.

204. Ibid.

205. Ibid., at 17.

206. Ibid.

207. Ibid., at 18.

208. 470 U.S. 226 (1985).

209. Ibid., at 247.

210. See Bryan H. Wildenthal, "Federal Labor Law, Indian Sovereignty, and the Canons of Construction," *Oregon Law Review* 86 (2007): 413–531.

211. *Cohen's Handbook of Federal Indian Law* (Newark, NJ: LexisNexis, 2005), 119–122.

212. 198 U.S. 371 (1905).

213. Ibid., at 380.

214. 207 U.S. 564 (2008). "By a rule of interpretation of agreements and treaties with the Indians, ambiguities occurring will be resolved from the standpoint of the Indians. And the rule should certainly be applied to determine between two inferences, one of which would support the purpose of the agreement and the other impair or defeat it." Ibid., at 576–577.

215. 426 U.S. 373 (1976). "Finally, in construing this 'admittedly ambiguous' statute, we must be guided by that 'eminently sound and vital canon' that 'statutes passed for the benefit of dependent Indian tribes . . . are to be liberally construed, doubtful expressions being resolved in favor of the Indians.'" Ibid., at 392.

216. 373 U.S. 546 (1963). "The Court in *Winters* concluded that the Government, when it created [by executive order] that Indian Reservation, intended to deal fairly with the Indians by reserving for them the waters without which their lands would have been useless. *Winters* has been followed by this Court as recently as 1939 in *United States v. Powers*, 305 U.S. 527.

We follow it now and agree that the United States did reserve the water rights for the Indians effective as of the time the Indian Reservations were created." Ibid., at 600.

217. Although the Supreme Court will typically employ these canons of construction, several qualifications need to be noted. To begin with, as the Court made clear in *Northern Cheyenne Tribe v. Hollowbreast*, 425 U.S. 649 (1976), it will not apply these canons if the contesting parties are an Indian tribe and a class of individuals consisting primarily of tribal members. Additionally, the Court has announced in a series of opinions that there are three categories of federal law where the canons do not presumptively apply; these encompass unexpressed exceptions from federal taxation, *Chickasaw Nation v. United States*, 534 U.S. 84 (2001); most federal criminal laws, *United States v. Dion*, 476 U.S. 734 (1986); and the reach of the Federal Power Act, *Federal Power Commission v. Tuscarora Indian Nation*, 362 U.S. 99 (1960).

218. Philip P. Frickey, "Marshalling Past and Present: Colonialism, Constitutionalism, and Interpretation in Federal Indian Law," *Harvard Law Review* 107 (December 1993): 381–439, 424.

219. *Cohen's Handbook*, 121.

220. 526 U.S. 172 (1999).

221. Ibid., at 195.

222. Ibid., at 196.

223. Ibid., at 200.

224. Ibid., at 221.

225. Ibid., at 223. Emphasis in the original. "The 1837 Treaty at issue here did not reserve 'the right of taking fish at all usual and accustomed places, in common with citizens of the Territory' like those involved in *Tulee* and *Puyallup Tribe*. Rather, it provided that: 'The *privilege* of hunting, fishing, and gathering the wild rice, upon the lands, the rivers and the lakes included in the territory ceded, is guaranteed to the Indians, during the pleasure of the President of the United States.'" Ibid., at 226.

226. Ibid. Emphasis in the original. See also his refusal to apply the canons in his dissent in *United States v. White Mountain Apache Tribe*, 537 U.S. 465, 481–86 (2003).

227. 508 U.S. 679 (1993). See also his unanimous decisions for the Court in *Alaska v. Native Village of Venetie Tribal Government*, 522 U.S. 520 (1998), and *Cass County v. Leech Lake Band of Chippewa Indians*, 524 U.S. 103 (1998).

228. Ibid., at 687.

229. Ibid., at 690.

230. Ibid., at 693. Thomas was not at all persuaded by Justice Harry Blackmun's argument in dissent: "The majority supposes that the Tribe's right to regulate non-Indian hunting and fishing is incidental to and dependent on its treaty right to exclusive use of the area and that the Tribe's right to regulate was therefore lost when its right to exclusive use was abrogated. This reasoning fails on two counts. First, treaties 'must . . . be construed, not according to the technical meaning of [their] words to learned lawyers, but in the sense in which they would naturally be understood by the Indians.' I find it implausible that the Tribe here would have thought every right subsumed in the Fort Laramie Treaty's sweeping language to be defeated the moment they lost the right to exclusive use of their land. Second, the majority's myopic focus on the Treaty ignores the fact that this Treaty merely confirmed the Tribe's pre-existing sovereignty over the reservation land. Even on the assumption that the Tribe's treaty-based right to regulate hunting and fishing by non-Indians was lost with the Tribe's power to exclude non-Indians, its *inherent* authority to regulate such hunting and fishing continued." Ibid., at 700–701. Emphasis in the original.

231. 555 U.S. 379 (2009).

232. Ibid., at 389. Emphasis in the original.

233. Ibid., at 390. Emphasis in the original. Interestingly, Scalia did not disassociate himself from this use of legislative history.

234. Ibid., at 413–414.

Chapter 3. Constitutional Structure and Federalism: Other Federalism Questions

1. Catherine M. Sharkey, "Against Freewheeling, Extratextual Obstacle Preemption: Is Clarence Thomas the Lone Principled Federalist?" *New York University Journal of Law & Liberty* 5 (2010): 63, 67–68. I wish to express my gratitude to Professor Sharkey for her very instructive and thoughtful article, on which I heavily rely in my discussion of federal preemption.

2. Ibid., 68. See Michael Greve's criticisms of Thomas's preemption jurisprudence in *The Upside-Down Constitution* (Cambridge, MA: Harvard University Press, 2012), 368–372.

3. Sharkey, "Against Freewheeling," 74. Sharkey notes, "It is true that the net effect of express preemption will likely be no role (or no significant role) for states in regulatory enforcement or as providers of compensation for injuries. This might strike at the heart of a true federalist, but, for Thomas, fidelity to text trumps, at least where Congress has enacted legislation in accordance with constitutional principles." Ibid., 78.

4. Ibid., 74.

5. 532 U.S. 141 (2001). See also his opinion for the Court in *District of Columbia v. Greater Washington Board of Trade*, 506 U.S. 125 (1992), and his unanimous opinion for the Court in *Aetna Health, Inc. v. Davila*, 542 U.S. 200 (2004).

6. 532 U.S. at 146.

7. 463 U.S. 85, 97 (1983).

8. 532 U.S. at 147–148.

9. Ibid., at 148.

10. Ibid., at 148–149. See also Thomas's dissent for a four-member minority in *Rush Prudential v. Moran*, 536 U.S. 355, 400 (2002), also dealing with the preemptive

effect of ERISA: "Allowing disparate state laws that provide inconsistent external review requirements to govern a participant's or beneficiary's claim to benefits under an employee benefit plan is wholly destructive of Congress's expressly stated goal of uniformity in this area."

11. 532 U.S. at 150. See also *Lorillard Tobacco Co. v. Reilly*, 533 U.S. 525, 572–590 (2001), in which Thomas in a concurrence agreed that the Federal Cigarette Labeling and Advertising Act preempted Massachusetts's regulations governing cigarette advertising. See as well *Pliva v. Mensing*, 131 S. Ct. 2567 (2011), in which Thomas held, for a five-member majority, that federal drug regulations applicable to generic drug manufacturers directly conflicted with and thus preempted various state claims.

12. 555 U.S. 70, 91–112 (2008). See also *Bates v. Dow Agrosciences*, 544 U.S. 431, 455–459 (2005), where Thomas's argument was fully developed.

13. The state of Maine argued that the Altria Group acted fraudulently because research showed that smokers of "light" cigarettes unconsciously engage in compensatory behaviors that negate the effect of the tar- and nicotine-reducing features of these cigarettes. As Justice Stevens explained for the Court majority, "By covering filter ventilation holes with their lips or fingers, taking larger or more frequent puffs, and holding the smoke in their lungs for a longer period of time, smokers of 'light' cigarettes unknowingly inhale as much tar and nicotine as do smokers of regular cigarettes. 'Light' cigarettes are in fact more harmful because the increased ventilation that results from their unique design features produces smoke that is more mutagenic per milligram of tar than the smoke of regular cigarettes." 555 U.S. at 72.

14. 15 U.S.C. § 1333.

15. 15 U.S.C. § 1331.

16. 15 U.S.C. § 1334(b) and 1334(c).

17. 555 U.S. at 77.

18. Ibid., at 79.

19. 505 U.S. 504 (1992).

20. 555 U.S. at 84.

21. Ibid., at 91.

22. Ibid., at 91–92. Thomas denied that the *Cipollone* plurality opinion was a "binding precedent," but he said that even if it were, "the Court 'should not hesitate to allow our precedent to yield to the true meaning of an Act of Congress.'" Ibid., at 108.

23. Ibid., at 92.

24. 544 U.S. 431, 457 (2005).

25. 555 U.S. at 99.

26. Ibid., at 107.

27. Ibid., at 108–109.

28. Ibid., at 111–112.

29. *Bates v. Dow Agrosciences*, 544 U.S. at 457.

30. However, there are also occasions when Thomas understands Congress to have spoken clearly and determined not to preempt state law. See Thomas's majority opinions in two ERISA cases—*Lockheed Corp. v. Spink*, 517 U.S. 882 (1996), and *California Division of Labor Standards Enforcement v. Dillingham Construction*, 519 U.S. 316 (1997)—as well as his opinions in two National Traffic and Motor Vehicle Safety Act cases—*Freightliner Corp. v. Mynick*, 514 U.S. 280 (1995), for which Thomas wrote the majority opinion, and *Williamson v. Mazda Motor of America*, 131 S. Ct. 1131 (2011), for which he wrote an opinion concurring in the judgment.

31. But consider his unanimous opinion for the Court in *Entergy Louisiana v. Louisiana Public Services Commission*, 539 U.S. 39 (2003), where Thomas found the state to be preempted from enforcing its regulatory regime based on precedent.

32. 513 U.S. 265, 292 (1995). See also his dissent in *Doctor's Associates, Inc. v. Casarotto*, 517 U.S. 681, 689 (1996).

33. See, for example, *English v. General Electric Co.*, 496 U.S. 72, 79 (1990), and

Rice v. Santa Fe Elevator Corp., 331 U.S. 218, 230 (1947).

34. See, for example, *Rice v. Santa Fe Elevator Corp.*, 331 U.S. at 230.

35. 520 U.S. at 617. But see his unanimous opinion for the Court in *Kurns v. Railroad Friction Products Corp.*, 132 S. Ct. 1261 (2012), in which he held that the petitioners' state-law claims alleging defective design and failure to warn about the presence of asbestos fell within the field of locomotive equipment regulation preempted by the federal Locomotive Inspection Act. "Congress may, of course, expressly pre-empt state law, but 'even without an express provision for preemption, we have found that state law must yield to a congressional Act' when 'the scope of a [federal] statute indicates that Congress intended federal law to occupy a field exclusively.' We deal here only with the latter, so-called field pre-emption." Ibid., at 1265–1266.

36. See *English v. General Electric Co.*, 496 U.S. at 79.

37. Caleb Nelson, "Preemption," *Virginia Law Review* 86 (March 2000): 225, 228.

38. Ibid., 228–229.

39. He joined Souter's dissent in *Gade v. National Solid Wastes Management Association*, 505 U.S. 88, 114–122 (1992), rejecting the Court plurality's use of obstacle preemption to conclude that an Illinois licensing act related to hazardous waste conflicted with the federal Occupational Safety and Health Act (OSHA) of 1970.

40. 555 U.S. 555, 582–604 (2009).

41. Ibid., at 594, 604, 583.

42. "The text of the statutory provisions and the accompanying regulatory scheme governing the FDA drug approval process, therefore, establish that the FDA's initial approval of a drug is not a guarantee that the drug's label will never need to be changed. And nothing in the text of the statutory or regulatory scheme necessarily insulates Wyeth from liability state law simply because

the FDA has approved a particular label. In sum, the relevant federal law did not give Wyeth a right that the state-law judgment took away, and it was possible for Wyeth to comply with both federal law and the Vermont-law judgment at issue here. The federal statute and regulations neither prohibited the stronger warning label required by the state judgment, nor insulated Wyeth from the risk of state-law liability. With no 'direct conflict' between the federal and state law, then, the state-law judgment is not pre-empted." Ibid., at 593–594.

43. Ibid., at 590. He was relying on Nelson, "Preemption," 228n15. Nelson served as a law clerk to Justice Thomas during the 1994–1995 term of the Court.

44. Alito wrote: "This case illustrates that tragic facts make bad law. The Court holds that a state tort jury, rather than the Food and Drug Administration, is ultimately responsible for regulating warning labels for prescription drugs. That result cannot be reconciled with . . . general principles of conflict pre-emption. I respectfully dissent." 555 U.S. at 604.

45. Ibid., at 584.

46. Ibid., at 586.

47. Ibid., at 587–588. "Preemption must turn on whether state law conflicts with the text of the relevant federal statute or with the federal regulations authorized by that text." Ibid., at 588. See the discussion that follows on "*Chevron* deference."

48. Ibid., at 602.

49. Ibid., at 604.

50. 132 S. Ct. 2492 (2012).

51. Ibid., at 2422.

52. Ibid., at 2524.

53. Ibid., at 2525. See also his concurrence in the judgment in *Hillman v. Maretta*, 133 S. Ct. 1943, 1955 (2013); his concurring opinion in *American Trucking Association v. Los Angeles*, 133 S. Ct. 2096, 2106 (2013); and his dissenting opinion in *Arizona v. Inter-Tribal Council*, 133 S. Ct. 2247, 2261–2270 (2013).

54. Sharkey, "Against Freewheeling," 68.

55. A classic example of Thomas's willingness to engage in *Chevron* deference is *National Cable & Telecommunications Association v. Brand X Internet Services*, 545 U.S. 967 (2005).

56. 467 U.S. 837 (1984).

57. Where there is no ambiguity in a federal statute, Thomas flatly rejects agency interpretations regarding preemption: See his opinions in *Bates v. Dow Agrosciences*, 544 U.S. at 455–459, and *CSX Transportation, Inc. v. Easterwood*, 507 U.S. 658, 676 (1993).

58. 538 U.S. 644, 681 (2003).

59. 557 U.S. 519 (2009).

60. Ibid., at 529.

61. Ibid., at 537.

62. Ibid., at 555.

63. Ibid. "A federal agency's construction of an ambiguous statutory term may clarify the preemptive scope of enacted federal law, but that fact alone does not mean that it is the agency, rather than Congress, that has effected the pre-emption." Ibid., at 555–556.

64. Ibid., at 556.

65. 130 S. Ct. 1949 (2010).

66. 18 U.S.C. § 4248.

67. 521 U.S. 346 (1997). Thomas explained why: "Kansas argues that the Act's definition of 'mental abnormality' satisfies 'substantive' due process requirements. We agree. Although freedom from physical restraint 'has always been at the core of the liberty protected by the Due Process Clause from arbitrary governmental action,' that liberty interest is not absolute. The Court has recognized that an individual's constitutionally protected interest in avoiding physical restraint may be overridden even in the civil context. . . . Accordingly, States have in certain narrow circumstances provided for the forcible civil detainment of people who are unable to control their behavior and who thereby pose a danger to the public health and safety. We have consistently upheld such involuntary commitment statutes provided the confinement takes place pursuant to proper procedures and evidentiary standards. It thus cannot be said that the involuntary civil confinement of a limited subclass of dangerous persons is contrary to our understanding of ordered liberty." Ibid., at 356–357.

68. 130 S. Ct. at 1954.

69. Ibid., at 1963.

70. Ibid., at 1964.

71. Ibid., at 1965.

72. Ibid., at 1970.

73. 17 U.S. 316 (1819).

74. 130 S. Ct. at 1971.

75. Ibid., at 1972. Thomas was quoting Justice Tom C. Clark's majority opinion in *Kinsella v. United States ex rel. Singleton*, 361 U.S. 234, 247 (1960).

76. 130 S. Ct. at 1974.

77. Ibid. Emphasis in the original. Thomas wrote, "The Court observes that Congress has the undisputed authority to 'criminalize conduct' that interferes with enumerated powers; to 'imprison individuals who engage in that conduct'; to 'enact laws governing [those] prisons'; and to serve as a 'custodian of its prisoners.'" From this, the Court assumed that the civil-commitment statute must also be a valid exercise of congressional power because it is "'reasonably adapted' to *those* exercises of Congress' incidental—and thus unenumerated—authorities." But, he continued, "that is not the question. The Necessary and Proper Clause does not provide Congress with authority to enact any law simply because it furthers *other laws* Congress has enacted in the exercise of its incidental authority; the Clause plainly requires a showing that every federal statute 'carr[ies] into Execution' one or more of the Federal Government's *enumerated* powers." Ibid., at 1976. Emphases in the original.

78. Ibid., at 1981.

79. Ibid., at 1982.

80. Ibid., at 1983.

81. 514 U.S. 779 (1995).

82. See Richard Albert's very insightful treatment of *Thornton* in "The Next Constitutional Revolution," *University of Detroit Mercy Law Review* 88 (Summer 2012): 707, 720–723.

83. 395 U.S. 486 (1969).

84. 514 U.S. at 782.

85. Ibid., at 831.

86. In his opinion, Thomas addressed at length dozens of objections to the argument made by Stevens in his majority opinion. What follows is his principal argument concerning the Tenth Amendment and the meaning of the Qualifications Clauses; it leaves many intriguing details unaddressed. Readers interested in his opinions should read it in its entirety.

87. 514 U.S. at 845.

88. Ibid., at 846.

89. Ibid., at 850.

90. Ibid., at 847.

91. Ibid., at 848.

92. Ibid., at 850. See David N. Mayer, "Justice Clarence Thomas and the Supreme Court's Rediscovery of the Tenth Amendment," *Capital University Law Review* 25 (1996): 339–423.

93. 514 U.S. at 802.

94. Ibid., at 851. Emphasis in the original.

95. Ibid., at 852.

96. Ibid., at 861–862. See also Thomas's use of the Tenth Amendment in his opinion concurring in the judgment in part and dissenting in part in *Northwest Austin Municipal Utility District Number One v. Holder*, 557 U.S. 193 (2009).

97. 514 U.S. at 865.

98. Ibid., at 806.

99. Thomas readily acknowledged that the Qualifications Clauses "prevent the individual States from abolishing all eligibility requirements for Congress. This restriction on state power reflects the fact that when the people of one State send immature, disloyal, or unknowledgeable representatives to Congress, they jeopardize not only their own interests but also the interests of the people of other States. Because Congress wields power over all the States, the people of each State need some guarantee that the legislators elected by the people of other States will meet minimum standards of competence." Relying on statements made in the Federal Convention by George Mason and Alexander Hamilton and by James Madison in *The Federalist*, he argued that "the Qualifications Clauses provide that guarantee: They list the requirements that the Framers considered essential to protect the competence of the National Legislature." Ibid., at 869.

100. Ibid., at 867–868.

101. Ibid., at 888.

102. Ibid., at 867.

103. Ibid., at 870.

104. Ibid., at 877.

105. Ibid., at 879.

106. Ibid., at 903–904.

107. Ibid., at 904.

108. Ibid., at 905–913.

109. Ibid., at 914.

110. Ibid., at 918.

111. Ibid.

112. Ibid., at 925–926.

113. Ibid., at 926. See also Thomas's concurrence in the judgment in *Cook v. Gralike*, 531 U.S. 510, 530 (2001).

114. 369 U.S. 186 (1962).

115. Ibid., at 217.

116. 517 U.S. 44 (1996).

117. Ibid., at 69–70.

118. Ibid., at 54.

119. Ibid., at 68. *Chisholm v. Georgia*, 2 U.S. 419 (1793).

120. 514 U.S. at 69–70.

121. Ibid., at 108.

122. Ibid., at 111.

123. 517 U.S. at 111.

124. 521 U.S. 261 (1997).

125. 527 U.S. 627 (1999).

126. 527 U.S. 666 (1999).

127. For my criticisms of Scalia's state sovereign immunity jurisprudence, see Ralph A. Rossum, *Antonin Scalia's Jurisprudence: Text and Tradition* (Lawrence: University Press of Kansas, 2006), 106–114.

128. 527 U.S. 706 (1999).

129. 528 U.S. 62 (2000).

130. In truth, Thomas concurred in part and dissented in part. He concurred in part because he agreed that Congress lacked the power to abrogate state sovereign immunity for suits charging states with discrimination based on an individual's age, but he dissented in part because he did not think that Congress had made its intention to abrogate "unmistakably clear" in the text of the ADEA. 528 U.S. at 99.

131. 531 U.S. 356 (2001).

132. 535 U.S. 743, 753 (2002).

133. But see Thomas's unanimous opinion for the Court in *Northern Insurance Company of New York v. Chatham County, Georgia*, 547 U.S. 189 (2006), in which he held that an entity that does not qualify as an "arm of the State" for Eleventh Amendment purposes cannot assert sovereign immunity as a defense to an admiralty suit.

134. Chief Justice Rehnquist and Justices O'Connor, Scalia, Kennedy, and Thomas made up this majority.

135. 535 U.S. at 753.

136. Ibid., at 760.

137. Ibid., at 751.

138. Ibid., at 760.

139. Ibid., at 777. Emphasis in the original.

140. Clarence Thomas, "Judging," *Kansas Law Review* 45 (November 1996): 1, 6.

141. 514 U.S. at 926.

142. 538 U.S. 721 (2003).

143. 541 U.S. 509 (2004).

144. 546 U.S. 356 (2006). See also *Sossamon v. Texas*, 131 S. Ct. 1651 (2011), in which a Texas prison inmate sued the state of Texas seeking injunctive and monetary relief under the Religious Land Use and Institutionalized Persons Act of 2000. The act allowed injured parties to seek "appropriate relief." Justice Thomas wrote, for a six-member majority (Sonia Sotomayor dissented and was joined by Stephen Breyer; Elena Kagan did not participate), holding that the phrase *appropriate relief* was not so free from ambiguity that the Court could conclude that the states, by receiving federal funds, had unequivocally expressed intent to waive their sovereign immunity to suits for damages. Strictly construing that phrase in favor of the sovereign, he concluded that it did not include suits for damages against a state. The issue here, of course, is different from the other cases that have been discussed. It raises the question of whether states have consented to waive their immunity in return for federal funds, not whether Congress can abrogate their immunity without their consent.

145. But see *Coleman v. Court of Appeals of Maryland*, 132 S. Ct. 1327 (2012), in which the Court held that Congress lacked the power under § 5 of the Fourteenth Amendment to abrogate state sovereign immunity in order to allow state employees to sue under the self-care provision of the Family and Medical Leave Act. Thomas joined the judgment of the Court and wrote a concurring opinion.

146. *Cotton Petroleum Corp. v. New Mexico*, 460 U.S. 136, 192 (1989).

147. Ibid. See also Chief Justice Rehnquist's words in this opinion for the Court in *Seminole Tribe of Florida v. Florida*, 517 U.S. 44, 62 (1996), which Thomas joined: "If anything, the Indian Commerce Clause accomplishes a greater transfer of power from the States to the Federal Government than does the Interstate Commerce Clause. This is clear enough from the fact that the States still exercise some authority over interstate trade but have been divested of virtually all authority over Indian commerce and Indian tribes."

Thomas's willingness to sign on to that sentence may be explained by the fact that *Seminole Tribe* invalidated Congress's power under the Indian Commerce Clause to abrogate state sovereign immunity in the Indian Gaming Regulatory Act.

148. Sharkey, "Against Freewheeling," 68.

149. 130 S. Ct. at 1974.

150. 514 U.S. at 851. Emphasis in the original.

151. Clarence Thomas, "Why Federalism Matters," *Drake Law Review* 48 (2000): 231, 235. See also Mayer, "Justice Clarence Thomas," 410: "Justice Thomas showed his appreciation of the fundamental fact that the Tenth Amendment was not about 'states' rights.' Rather, it was designed to protect not only the powers of state governments but also the powers of the people themselves."

Chapter 4. Thomas's Original General Meaning Approach to Substantive Rights

1. 540 U.S. 712 (2004).

2. Ibid., at 734–735.

3. Ibid., at 726–734.

4. 132 S. Ct. 694, 710–711 (2012).

5. *Utah Highway Patrol Association v. American Atheists, Inc.*, 132 S. Ct. 12, 13, 22. Thomas dissenting from the denial of certiorari.

6. Ibid., at 14.

7. Ibid., at 21–22.

8. Ibid., at 17–19.

9. 515 U.S. 819 (1995).

10. See Thomas's similar argument regarding viewpoint discrimination in violation of freedom of speech in *Good News Club v. Milford Central Schools*, 533 U.S. 98 (2001).

11. 515 U.S. at 852–853.

12. Ibid., at 855–856.

13. Ibid., at 858.

14. Ibid., at 859–860.

15. 530 U.S. 793 (2000).

16. Ibid., at 827.

17. Ibid., at 829.

18. 536 U.S. 639 (2002).

19. 542 U.S. 1 (2004).

20. 545 U.S. 677 (2005).

21. 536 U.S. at 676.

22. Ibid., at 684.

23. Ibid., at 677.

24. 330 U.S. 1 (1947).

25. 163 U.S. 537, 555 (1896).

26. 536 U.S. at 678.

27. Ibid. Thomas cited two justices in support of his argument: Justice Robert Jackson in *Beauharnais v. Illinois*, 343 U.S. 250, 294 (1952), and the second Justice John Marshall Harlan in *Roth v. United States*, 354 U.S. 476, 503–504.

28. 536 U.S. at 679.

29. Ibid., at 679–680. "Converting the Fourteenth Amendment from a guarantee of opportunity to an obstacle against educational reform distorts our constitutional values and disserves those in the greatest need." Ibid., at 684.

30. 542 U.S. at 45.

31. Ibid., at 45–46. See Richard F. Duncan, "Justice Thomas and Partial Incorporation of the Establishment Clause: Herein of Structural Limitations, Liberty Interests, and Taking Incorporation Seriously," *Regent University Law Review* 20 (2007): 37–56.

32. 505 U.S. 577 (1992).

33. 542 U.S. at 46.

34. Ibid., at 45, 46, 49.

35. Ibid., at 49–51.

36. Ibid., at 52. As he would say the next year in his concurrence in *Cutter v. Wilkinson*, 544 U.S. 709, 729: "To proscribe Congress from making laws 'respecting an establishment of religion' was to forbid legislation respecting coercive state establishments."

37. Leonard Levy, *The Establishment Clause* (New York: Macmillan, 1986), 4.

38. 542 U.S. at 54. See James A. Campbell, "Newdow Calls for a New Day in

Establishment Clause Jurisprudence: Justice Thomas's 'Actual Legal Coercion Standard' Provides the Necessary Renovation," *Akron Law Review* 39 (2006): 541–592.

39. 545 U.S. at 649.

40. Ibid., at 697–698. As he said in his dissent from the denial of certiorari in *Utah Highway Patrol Association v. American Atheists, Inc.*, 132 S. Ct. at 21, "Even if the Court does not share my view that the Establishment Clause restrains only the Federal Government, and that, even if incorporated, the Clause only prohibits 'actual legal coercion,' the Court should be deeply troubled by what its Establishment Clause jurisprudence has wrought."

41. 514 U.S. 334 (1995).

42. Ibid., at 359.

43. By so doing, Thomas has won the praise of Nat Hentoff, civil libertarian and free speech activist, who has stated: "[Thomas] has written as boldly and uncompromisingly in celebration of the First Amendment as did Justices William O. Douglas and William Brennan, Jr., in days of yore." Quoted in Steven B. Lichtman, "Black Like Me: The Free Speech Jurisprudence of Clarence Thomas," *Penn State Law Review* 114 (Fall 2009): 415, 461.

44. David L. Hudson, Jr., "Justice Clarence Thomas: The Emergence of a Commercial-Speech Protector," *Creighton Law Review* 35 (April 2002): 485, 501.

45. 507 U.S. 410, 438–439 (1993).

46. 514 U.S. 476 (1995).

47. Ibid., at 482.

48. 316 U.S. 52 (1942).

49. 425 U.S. 748 (1976).

50. 447 U.S. 557, 566 (1980).

51. 514 U.S. at 480.

52. 533 U.S. 525, 590 (2001).

53. Ibid., at 590.

54. 517 U.S. 484 (1996).

55. Lichtman, "Black Like Me," 427.

56. 517 U.S. at 528.

57. Clarence Thomas, "Judging," *Kansas Law Review* 45 (November 1996): 1, 7.

58. 517 U.S. at 527.

59. Ibid., at 528. Emphasis in the original.

60. Ibid., at 522. Thomas pointed to "some historical materials" to support his contention. To begin with, he referenced Stevens's principal opinion: "Indeed, commercial messages played such a central role in public life prior to the founding that Benjamin Franklin authored his early defense of a free press in support of his decision to print, of all things, an advertisement for voyages to Barbados. Franklin, An Apology for Printers, June 10, 1731, reprinted in 2 *Writings of Benjamin Franklin* 172 (1907)." Ibid., at 495–496. And he gave considerable attention to the Brief for American Advertising Federation et al. as *Amici Curiae* 12–24, which "cited authorities for propositions that commercial activity and advertising were integral to life in colonial America and that Framers' political philosophy equated liberty and property and did not distinguish between commercial and noncommercial messages." Ibid., at 522.

61. 517 U.S. at 518. "I would adhere to the doctrine . . . that all attempts to dissuade legal choices by citizens by keeping them ignorant are impermissible." Ibid., at 526.

62. Ibid., at 520.

63. 521 U.S. 457, 505 (1997).

64. 527 U.S. 173, 197 (1999).

65. 535 U.S. 357, 377 (2002).

66. 521 U.S. at 477.

67. See Jennifer R. Franklin, "Peaches, Speech, and Clarence Thomas: Yes, California, There Is a Justice Who Understands the Ramifications of Controlling Commercial Speech," *Regent University Law Review* 12 (1999–2000): 627–647.

68. 521 U.S. at 504.

69. Ibid., at 505. Emphasis in the original.

70. Ibid., at 506. See also Thomas's brief concurring opinion in *United States v. United Foods*, 533 U.S. 405, 418–419 (2001), in which he reaffirmed his *Glickman*

dissent. See also his concurring opinion in *Johanns v. Livestock Marketing Association,* 544 U.S. 550, 567 (2005), in which he cited his concurrence in *United Foods* and "continue[d] to believe that 'any regulation that compels the funding of advertising must be subjected to the most stringent First Amendment scrutiny,'" but since in this case "the regulation compels the funding of speech that is the government's own," he, "like the Court," could "see no analytical distinction between 'pure government speech funded from general tax revenues' and speech funded from targeted exactions" from U.S. beef producers.

71. 424 U.S. 1 (1976).

72. *Nixon v. Shrink Missouri Government PAC,* 528 U.S. 377, 410 (2000). Justice Thomas dissenting.

73. *Colorado Republican Federal Campaign Committee v. Federal Election Commission,* 518 U.S. 604, 636 (1996). Justice Thomas concurring in the judgment and dissenting in part.

74. Ibid., at 641. Steven B. Lichtman has written: "It is not an understatement to suggest that Thomas [has] played a pivotal and even dominant role in the escalation of conflict on the Court over the rules for—and constitutional status of—political money." Lichtman, "Black Like Me," 431.

75. 528 U.S. at 410.

76. Ibid., at 411. He then quoted James Madison: "'The value and efficacy of [the right to elect the members of government] depends on the knowledge of the comparative merits and demerits of the candidates for public trust, and on the equal freedom, consequently, of examining and discussing these merits and demerits of the candidates respectively.' Madison, Report on the Resolutions (1799), in 6 *Writings of James Madison* 397 (G. Hunt ed. 1906)."

77. 528 U.S. at 412. Emphasis in the original.

78. 518 U.S. at 635–636.

79. Ibid., at 636.

80. 528 U.S. at 416.

81. 518 U.S. at 636.

82. 470 U.S.480 (1985).

83. 518 U.S. at 637.

84. Ibid., at 639–640.

85. Ibid., at 641. See also his opinion concurring in the judgment in *Buckley v. American Constitutional Law Foundation,* 525 U.S. 182, 206–215 (1999), a case dealing with state election law and therefore closely related to campaign finance regulation. In it, he subjected Colorado's statutory provisions governing the ballot-initiative process to strict scrutiny and on that basis found unconstitutional—because not narrowly tailored—the state's requirements that circulators of initiative petitions be registered voters and wear identification badges indicating their names and whether they were paid or unpaid as well as its requirement that the proponents of initiatives report the names and addresses of all paid circulators and the amount they were paid.

86. 518 U.S. at 641.

87. Ibid., at 643.

88. 533 U.S. 431, 465 (2001): "As an initial matter, I continue to believe that *Buckley v. Valeo* should be overruled."

89. 539 U.S. 146, 164 (2003): "I continue to believe that campaign finance laws are subject to strict scrutiny."

90. 548 U.S. 230, 266 (2006): "The illegitimacy of *Buckley* is further underscored by the continuing inability of the Court to apply *Buckley* in a coherent and principled fashion. As a result, *stare decisis* should pose no bar to overruling *Buckley* and replacing it with a standard faithful to the First Amendment."

91. 540 U.S. 93 (2003).

92. 494 U.S. 652, 659–660 (1990).

93. 540 U.S. at 274.

94. Ibid., at 264.

95. Ibid., at 283.

96. Ibid., at 283–284.

97. Ibid., at 286.

98. 558 U.S. 310 (2010).

99. Transcript of Oral Argument, *Citizens United v. Federal Election Commission*, No. 08-205, March 24, 2009, 27.

100. 558 U.S. at 913.

101. 514 U.S. at 359.

102. Ibid.

103. Ibid., at 360.

104. Ibid., at 361.

105. Ibid., at 361–370.

106. Ibid., at 361.

107. 540 U.S. at 275–276.

108. Ibid., at 276–277.

109. 130 S. Ct. at 914.

110. Ibid., at 980–981.

111. Ibid., at 981–982. Emphasis in the original.

112. Ibid., at 982.

113. 518 U.S. 727 (1996).

114. Ibid., at 812.

115. 395 U.S. 367 (1969).

116. Ibid., at 389.

117. 518 U.S. at 813–814.

118. 512 U.S. 622 (1994).

119. 395 U.S. at 390.

120. 518 U.S. at 816.

121. Ibid., at 824. Thomas faulted the act's leased and public access requirements for being "a type of forced speech," but since the constitutionality of these requirements was not before the Court, he simply stated that "the position adopted by the Court in *Turner* ineluctably leads to the conclusion" that the federal access requirements burden the free speech rights of the cable operators and must be subjected to strict scrutiny. Ibid., at 820–821. And he parried the argument that Kennedy made in his concurrence that the act's requirements for public access channels were permissible as these channels were public forums. He pointed out that cable systems "are not public property," that "government control over private property cannot justify designation of that property as a public forum," that "we have expressly stated that neither governmental ownership nor government control will guarantee public access to property," and

that "petitioners' attempt to redistribute cable speech rights in their favor must fail." Ibid., at 827, 829, 831.

122. Ibid., at 832.

123. 535 U.S. 564, 566–585 (2002).

124. 413 U.S. 15 (1973). Based on *Miller,* Congress in COPA defined "material that is harmful to minors" as "any communication, picture, image, graphic image file, article, recording, writing, or other matter of any kind that is obscene or that—(A) the average person, applying contemporary community standards, would find, taking the material as a whole and with respect to minors, is designed to appeal to, or is designed to pander to, the prurient interest; (B) depicts, describes, or represents, in a manner patently offensive with respect to minors, an actual or simulated sexual act or sexual contact, an actual or simulated normal or perverted sexual act, or a lewd exhibition of the genitals or post-pubescent female breast; and (C) taken as a whole, lacks serious literary, artistic, political, or scientific value for minors." 47 U.S.C. § 231(e)(6).

125. Lichtman, "Black Like Me," 442.

126. 556 U.S. 502 (2009).

127. Ibid., at 530.

128. 438 U.S. 726 (1978).

129. 556 U.S. at 530.

130. Ibid., at 531–532.

131. Ibid., at 533.

132. Ibid., at 534.

133. 132 S. Ct. 2307, 2321 (2012).

134. Ibid., at 2321.

135. 505 U.S. 377 (1992).

136. Ibid., at 383, 386.

137. 515 U.S. 753 (1995).

138. Ibid., at 770.

139. Ibid., at 771–772.

140. 538 U.S. 343 (2003).

141. Ibid., at 354.

142. Ibid., at 388.

143. Ibid., at 389.

144. Clarence Thomas, *My Grandfather's Son* (New York: HarperCollins, 2007), 21–22. See also p. 257: "As a child in the Deep

South, I'd grown up fearing the lynch mobs of the Ku Klux Klan."

145. 538 U.S. 391. Thomas is famous for going years at a time between asking a question during oral argument. But in this case, he interrupted Deputy Solicitor General Michael Dreeben's argument in favor of the law's constitutionality by asking: "Mr. Dreeben, aren't you understating the . . . the effects of . . . of the burning cross? . . . I indicated, I think, in the Ohio case [*Pinette*] that the cross was not a religious symbol and that it . . . was intended to have a virulent effect. And I think that what you're attempting to do is to fit this into our jurisprudence rather than stating more clearly what the cross was intended to accomplish and, indeed, that it is unlike any symbol in our society." Dreeben replied: "Well, I don't mean to understate it, and I entirely agree with Your Honor's description of how the cross has been used as an instrument of intimidation against minorities in this country." Thomas then broke in again and declared (leaving little doubt about how he would vote in this case): "There was no other purpose to the cross. There was no communication of a particular message. It was intended to cause fear . . . and to terrorize a population." Transcript of Oral Argument in *Virginia v. Black*, No. 01-1107, December 11, 2002, 22–24.

146. 538 U.S. at 394 n.2.

147. Ibid., at 394–395. As in *Virginia v. Black*, so, too, in *Dawson v. Delaware*, 503 U.S. 159 (1992), Thomas was the lone dissenter. In *Dawson*, the Court overturned the death sentence given to a member of the Aryan Brotherhood prison gang; it concluded that the introduction of his membership in the gang at the sentencing stage of his trial proved nothing more than his and the gang's abstract beliefs, not that he or the gang had committed or endorsed any unlawful or violent acts, and therefore violated his freedom of association under the First Amendment. Just as in *Virginia v. Black*,

Thomas denied that there was any First Amendment issue present; what mattered for him was Dawson's conduct, not his beliefs. Thomas pointed out that in an effort to prove his good character, Dawson had introduced his membership in Alcoholics Anonymous (AA). Joining AA involved conduct on Dawson's part, as did his joining the Aryan Brotherhood. "Membership in AA might suggest a good character, but membership in the Aryan Brotherhood just as surely suggests a bad one. The jury could not have assessed Dawson's overall character without both." Ibid., at 175. See Stephen F. Smith, "Clarence X? The Black Nationalist behind Justice Thomas's Constitutionalism," *New York University Journal of Law & Liberty* 4 (2009): 583, 592.

148. 538 U.S. at 398–399.

149. 530 U.S. 703 (2000).

150. 538 U.S. at 399–400.

151. 551 U.S. 393 (2007).

152. 393 U.S. 503 (1969).

153. Ibid., at 506.

154. Ibid., at 513.

155. 478 U.S. 675 (1986).

156. Ibid., at 682.

157. 484 U.S. 260 (1988).

158. Ibid., at 273.

159. 551 U.S. at 408–409.

160. Ibid., at 410–411.

161. Ibid., at 411.

162. Ibid., at 412.

163. Ibid., at 417.

164. Ibid., at 418–419.

165. Ibid., at 419–420.

166. Ibid., at 420–421.

167. Ibid., at 422. In Matthew D. Bunker and Clay Calvert, "Contrasting Concurrences of Clarence Thomas: Deploying Originalism and Paternalism in Commercial and Student Speech Cases," *Georgia State University Law Review* 26 (Winter 2010): 321, 323–324, the authors criticize Thomas for expanding protection for commercial speech and "elevat[ing] advertisers up from the ranks of second-

class First Amendment citizens" but, in
"jarring contrast," "simultaneously yearning
to obliterate constitutional protection for
the speech of public school students and
relegate them to a constitutional status below
that of federal prisoners." Although they
even include *originalism* in the title, they
show little appreciation for what it means
in Thomas's jurisprudence. Compare their
comments with Richard W. Garnett, "Can
There Really Be 'Free Speech' in Public
Schools?" *Lewis & Clark Law Review* 12
(Spring 2008): 45, 47: "Thomas filed, to the
horror of some and the fascination of others,
another 'yes, I really mean it about this
originalism business!' concurrence."

168. 131 S. Ct. 2729 (2011).
169. Ibid., at 2751.
170. Ibid., at 2751–2759.
171. Ibid., at 2759–2760.
172. 554 U.S. 570 (2008).
173. See Ralph A. Rossum, "Antonin
Scalia and the Rule of Law: The Textualist
Foundation of the 'Law of Rules,'" in
Anthony A. Peacock, ed., *Freedom and the
Rule of Law* (Lanham, MD: Lexington
Books, 2010), 115–136, for a lengthy
treatment of Scalia's majority opinion.
174. 130 S. Ct. 3020 (2010).
175. Ibid., at 3050
176. Ibid., at 3059–3060.
177. See Michael P. Zuckert,
"Congressional Power under the Fourteenth
Amendment—The Original Understanding
of Section Five," *Constitutional Commentary*
3 (1986): 123–147.
178. 526 U.S. 489 (1999).
179. 83 U.S. 36 (1873).
180. 526 U.S. at 527. In *McDonald*,
Thomas spoke of the Court's "marginalization
of the Clause." 130 S. Ct. 3061.
181. 83 U.S. at 78.
182. Ibid., at 79.
183. Ibid., at 80.
184. Ibid., at 101.
185. Michael Kent Curtis, "Resurrecting
the Privileges and Immunities Clause and

Revising the *Slaughter-House Cases* without
Exhuming *Lochner*: Individual Rights and
the Fourteenth Amendment," *Boston College
Law Review* 38 (December 1966): 105.
186. 296 U.S. 404 (1935).
187. 309 U.S. 83 (1040).
188. 321 U.S. 1 (1944).
189. 526 U.S. at 521.
190. Ibid., at 528. Thomas anticipated
his *Saenz* dissent in his article entitled "The
Higher Law Background of the Privileges
and Immunities Clause of the Fourteenth
Amendment," *Harvard Journal of Law and
Public Policy* 12 (Winter 1989): 63–70.
191. See Brannon P. Denning and Glenn
H. Reynolds, "Five Takes on *McDonald v.
Chicago*," *Journal of Law and Politics* 26
(Winter 2011): 273–303.
192. Transcript of Oral Argument,
McDonald v. Chicago, No. 08-1521, 4.
193. Ibid., at 6–7. Unsurprisingly, given
his exchange with Gura, Scalia declined
to join Thomas's originalist argument
concerning privileges and immunities.
194. 92 U.S. 542 (1876).
195. 130 S. Ct. at 3060.
196. In his concurring opinion, Scalia
wrote: "I join the Court's opinion. Despite
my misgivings about Substantive Due Process
as an original matter, I have acquiesced in the
Court's incorporation of certain guarantees
in the Bill of Rights 'because it is both long
established and narrowly limited.' *Albright v.
Oliver*, 510 U.S. 266, 275 (1994) (Scalia, J.,
concurring). This case does not require me
to reconsider that view, since straightforward
application of settled doctrine suffices to
decide it." 130 S. Ct. at 3050.
197. Ibid., at 3062.
198. Ibid., at 3063.
199. 5 U.S. 137 (1803).
200. 130 S. Ct. at 3063.
201. Ibid., at 3063–3065.
202. Ibid., at 3066.
203. Ibid., at 3068–3071. See David
C. Durst, "Justice Clarence Thomas's
Interpretation of the Privileges and

Immunities Clause: *McDonald v. City of Chicago* and the Future of the Fourteenth Amendment," *University of Toledo Law Review* 42 (Summer 2011): 933, 936, who doubts that Thomas sufficiently clarified "how the Court should address the question of constitutionally unenumerated rights."

204. 130 S. Ct. at 3072.

205. Ibid., at 3072, 3074. Thomas declared that there was "much else" in the legislative record to which he could turn. "Many statements by Members of Congress corroborate the view that the Privileges and Immunities Clause enforced constitutionally enumerated rights against the States. I am not aware of any statement that directly refutes that proposition." Ibid., at 3075.

206. Ibid., at 3076.

207. Despite Thomas's detailed historical account, not everyone has been persuaded. See Lawrence Rosenthal and Joyce Lee Malcolm, "*McDonald v. Chicago*: Which Standard of Scrutiny Should Apply to Gun-Control Law?" *Northwestern University Law Review Colloquy* 105 (November 2010): 85–113. In this debate between these two scholars, Rosenthal accuses Thomas of engaging in "law office history" (ibid., at 111) and wonders why, if "the public understood that the Fourteenth Amendment made all constitutionally enumerated rights binding on the states," there was no "effort in the ratifying states to make their own laws consistent with these enumerated rights." He gives a specific example: the ratification of the Fourteenth Amendment "did nothing to halt a trend in the states toward prosecution by information, despite its inconsistency with the Fifth Amendment's Grand Jury Clause. This is not what one would expect had there been a general understanding that the Fourteenth Amendment had rendered all enumerated constitutional rights applicable to the states. About this historical evidence, Justice Thomas offers no comment." Ibid., at 108–109. It is worth noting, however, that Rosenthal chooses as his sole example the

one criminal procedural right that the Court has not incorporated to apply to the states, even under substantive due process.

208. 130 S. Ct. at 3076.

209. Ibid., at 3085.

210. Ibid., at 3086.

211. Ibid., at 3087.

212. Ibid., at 3088.

213. Ibid.

214. 505 U.S. 1003 (1992).

215. 512 U.S. 374 (1994).

216. 515 U.S. 1116 (1995).

217. Ibid., at 1118.

218. Nancie G. Marzulla, "Clarence Thomas and the Fifth Amendment: His Philosophy and Adherence to Protecting Property Rights," *Regent University Law Review* 12 (2000): 549, 567. See also Marzulla, "The Textualism of Clarence Thomas: Anchoring the Supreme Court's Property Rights Jurisprudence in the Constitution," *American University Journal of Gender, Social Policy & the Law* 10 (2002): 351, 373–375.

219. 524 U.S. 498 (1998).

220. 3 U.S. 386 (1798).

221. 524 U.S. at 538.

222. As Thomas said in his concurring opinion in *United States v. Playboy Entertainment Group*, 529 U.S. 803, 830 (2000), "The 'starch' in our constitutional standards cannot be sacrificed."

223. 524 U.S. 539.

224. 535 U.S. 302 (2002).

225. Ibid., at 355–356. Emphasis in the original.

226. 545 U.S. 469 (2005).

227. Ibid., at 479–480.

228. Ibid., at 506.

229. Ibid., at 509.

230. Ibid., at 510–511.

231. Ibid., at 513. For a critique of Thomas's review of this history, see David L. Breau, "Justice Thomas' *Kelo* Dissent, or 'History as a Grab Bag of Principles,'" *McGeorge Law Review* 38 (2007): 373–404.

232. 198 U.S. 45 (1905).

233. See, for example, Thomas's disparaging comments about *Lochner* in *United States v. Lopez*, 514 U.S. 549, 601 (1995); *United Haulers Association v. Oneida-Herkimer Solid Waste Management Authority*, 550 U.S. 330, 355 (2007); *Morse v. Frederick*, 551 U.S. at 421; *MeadWestvaco Corp. v. Illinois Department of Revenue*, 553 U.S. 16, 34 (2008); and *McDonald v. Chicago*, 130 S. Ct. at 3062.

234. 164 U.S. 112, 161–162 (1896).

235. 545 U.S. at 515–516.

236. 160 U.S. 668, 680 (1896).

237. 545 U.S. at 517.

238. Ibid., at 521.

239. Ibid., at 522.

240. Ibid., at 523.

241. 505 U.S. 833 (1992).

242. 410 U.S. 113 (1973).

243. *Gonzales v. Carhart*, 550 U.S. 124, 169 (2007).

244. 530 U.S. 914 (2000).

245. Ibid., at 1020.

246. Ibid., at 980. Emphasis in the original.

247. Ibid., at 982.

248. Ibid., at 984–985.

249. Ibid., at 987. Thomas noted partial-birth abortion gained prominence when Dr. Martin Haskell presented a paper entitled "Dilation and Extraction for Late Second Trimester Abortion" at the National Abortion Federation's September 1992 Risk Management Seminar. In that paper, Haskell described his version of the procedure in detail, which Thomas quoted at length. Among other things, Haskell provided instruction on how the fetus's head could be held in the vagina so that a live birth could be prevented and the abortion performed. Ibid., at 987–999. He also quoted the testimony of a nurse who had observed a partial-birth abortion procedure: "The baby's little fingers were clasping and unclasping, and his little feet were kicking. Then the doctor stuck the scissors in the back of his head, and the baby's arms jerked out, like

a startle reaction, like a flinch, like a baby does when he thinks he is going to fall. The doctor opened up the scissors, stuck a high-powered suction tube into the opening, and sucked the baby's brains out. Now the baby went completely limp." Ibid., at 1007.

250. Ibid., at 1007–1008.

251. 550 U.S. 124, 169 (2007).

252. See Mary Kate Kearney, "Justice Thomas in *Grutter v. Bollinger*: Can Passion Play a Role in a Jurist's Reasoning?" *St. John's Law Review* 78 (Winter 2004): 1535, who defends Thomas's passion. And see also Ronald Turner, "On *Parents Involved* and the Problematic Praise of Justice Clarence Thomas," *Hastings Constitutional Law Quarterly* 37 (Winter 2010): 225–242, who is harshly critical of his passion.

Chapter 5. Thomas's Original General Meaning Approach to Criminal Procedural Rights

1. 503 U.S. 1 (1992).

2. "The Youngest, Cruelest Justice," *New York Times*, February 27, 1992, A 24.

3. 503 U.S. at 8–9.

4. Ibid., at 18.

5. 429 U.S. 97 (1976).

6. 217 U.S. 349 (1910).

7. 503 U.S. at 18–19.

8. Ibid., at 28.

9. 509 U.S. 25 (1993).

10. Ibid., at 37.

11. Ibid., at 38.

12. To repeat, Thomas understands that the Due Process Clause of the Fifth and Fourteenth Amendments would provide redress of these injuries.

13. 509 U.S. at 38. Emphasis in the original.

14. Ibid., at 38–39.

15. Ibid., at 39. Emphasis in the original.

16. Ibid.

17. Ibid.

18. 429 U.S. at 104.

19. 509 U.S. at 42.

20. Ibid.

21. Ibid. Emphasis in the original. In *Farmer v. Brennan*, 511 U.S. 825, 861–862 (1994), Thomas declared that given "[my] serious doubts concerning the correctness of *Estelle* . . . to cover challenges to conditions of confinement, I believe the scope of the *Estelle* 'right' should be confined as narrowly as possible"; rather than dissenting, however, he concurred in the judgment because the Court had taken "a step in the right direction by adopting a restrictive definition of deliberate indifference." Because the respondents did not ask the Court to revisit *Estelle*, because no one had briefed or argued the question, and because "*stare decisis* counsels hesitation in overruling dubious precedents," Thomas concurred in the Court's judgment. "In doing so, however, I remain hopeful that in a proper case the Court will reconsider *Estelle* in light of the constitutional text and history." In *Overton v. Bazzetta*, 539 U.S. 126, 145 (2003), Thomas concurred in the judgment of the Court that prisoners do not have a right to noncontact prison visitation but for a different reason: "In my view, for the reasons given in *Hudson*, regulations pertaining to visitations are not punishments within the meaning of the Eighth Amendment." In *Erickson v. Pardus*, 551 U.S. 89, 95 (2007), Thomas dissented from a per curiam opinion that relied on *Estelle*, citing his dissents in *Hudson* and *Helling*. In *Wilkins v. Gaddy*, 130 S. Ct. 1175, 1180–1181 (2010), Thomas again mentioned his dissents in *Hudson* and *Helling*: "I continue to believe that *Hudson* was wrongly decided. . . . [However,] no party to this case asks us to overrule *Hudson*. Accordingly, I concur in the Court's judgment."

22. 3 U.S. 386 (1798).

23. 524 U.S. 498 (1998).

24. Ibid., at 538–539.

25. 514 U.S. 499 (1995).

26. See also *Kansas v. Hendricks*, 521 U.S. 346 (1997), in which Thomas denied that Kansas had violated the Constitution's ban on ex post facto lawmaking when it passed its Sexually Violent Predator Act, which established procedures for the civil commitment of persons who, due to a "mental abnormality" or a "personality disorder," are likely to engage in "predatory acts of sexual violence." In his majority opinion in this five-to-four case, he concluded that "where the State has 'disavowed any punitive intent'; limited confinement to a small segment of particularly dangerous individuals; provided strict procedural safeguards; directed that confined persons be segregated from the general prison population and afforded the same status as others who have been civilly committed; recommended treatment if such is possible; and permitted immediate release upon a showing that the individual is no longer dangerous or mentally impaired, we cannot say that it acted with punitive intent. We therefore hold that the Act does not establish criminal proceedings and that involuntary confinement pursuant to the Act is not punitive. Our conclusion that the Act is nonpunitive thus removes an essential prerequisite for Hendricks' . . . *ex post facto* claim." Ibid., at 368–369. See also ibid., at 370–371.

27. Ibid., at 504. He cited Justice Samuel Chase's opinion in *Calder v. Bull*, 3 U.S. at 391–392.

28. 514 U.S. at 505.

29. Ibid., at 507.

30. Ibid., at 511.

31. Ibid., at 513.

32. Ibid., at 514. In *Stogner v. California*, 539 U.S. 607 (2003), Thomas joined Justice Kennedy's dissent that found no ex post facto violation had occurred when California enacted a 1993 statute extending the limitations period for crimes of sex-related child abuse and authorizing prosecution for criminal acts allegedly committed many years before—even if the original limitations period had expired—as long as the prosecution began within one year of

an alleged victim's first complaint to the police. As Kennedy declared: "California has enacted a retroactive extension of statutes of limitations for serious sexual offenses committed against minors. The new period includes cases where the limitations period has expired before the effective date of the legislation. To invalidate the statute in the latter circumstance, the Court tries to force it into the second category of [Justice Chase's opinion in *Calder v. Bull*] http://www
.lexisnexis.com.ezproxy.libraries
.claremont.edu/lnacui2api/mungo/lexseestat
.do?bct=A&risb=21_T13964031512&
homeCsi=6443&A=0.14332570998046135
&urlEnc=ISO-8859-1&&citeString=3%20
Dall.%20386&countryCode=USA, which prohibits a retroactive law 'that aggravates a crime, or makes it greater than it was, when committed.' These words, in my view, do not permit the Court's holding, but indeed foreclose it. A law which does not alter the definition of the crime but only revives prosecution does not make the crime 'greater than it was, when committed.' Until today, a plea in bar has not been thought to form any part of the definition of the offense." Ibid., at 633.

33. 519 U.S. 433 (1997).

34. Ibid., at 450. Thomas's exasperation with the Court's emerging ex post facto jurisprudence and its requirement that it ascertain whether changes in sentencing practices carry with them risks of increasing the measure of punishment that are more than merely speculative was clear in his dissent in *Peugh v. United States*, 133 S. Ct. 2072, 2093 (2013): "Today's opinion also demonstrates the unworkability of our ex post facto jurisprudence. Under our current precedent, whenever a change in the law creates a 'risk' of an increased sentence, we must determine whether the risk is 'sufficient' see Morales, 514 or sufficiently 'significant' to violate the Ex Post Facto Clause. Our analysis under that test has devolved into little more than an exercise in judicial intuition. I would return to the original meaning of the Clause as stated in Justice Chase's classic *Calder* formulation, under which laws of this sort are ex post facto only when they retroactively increase the punishment 'annexed to the crime.'"

35. 519 U.S. at 451. Emphasis in the original.

36. Ibid., at 449. On similar grounds, Thomas joined Justice Stevens's majority opinion in *Carmell v. Texas*, 529 U.S. 513 (2002). A Texas statute that went into effect after Scott Carmell committed sexual offenses against his stepdaughter authorized conviction for these offenses on the victim's testimony alone — contrary to the previous statute that required the victim's testimony plus other corroborating evidence to convict. Carmell was convicted on his stepdaughter's testimony alone on certain charges and appealed his conviction under the new statute, arguing that it was an unconstitutional ex post facto law. In a five-to-four decision, the Supreme Court agreed, on the grounds that the new statute altered the legal rules of evidence and required less or different testimony than the law required at the time the offense was committed.

37. 521 U.S. 346 (1996).

38. Ibid., at 361. Emphasis in the original.

39. Ibid., at 362.

40. Ibid., at 363. Emphasis in the original.

41. Ibid., at 364.

42. Ibid., at 368–369, 371.

43. 531 U.S. 250 (2001).

44. Ibid., at 270. Emphasis in the original.

45. Ibid., at 270–271.

46. Ibid., at 273.

47. 538 U.S. 84 (2003).

48. Ibid., at 106.

49. Ibid., at 107.

50. 526 U.S. 559 (1999).

51. Ibid., at 563.

52. 267 U.S. 132 (1925).

53. 526 U.S. at 564.

54. Ibid., at 564–565. Emphasis in the original.

55. 540 U.S. 551 (2004).
56. Ibid., at 571.
57. Ibid., at 572.
58. Ibid., at 573.
59. 514 U.S. 927 (1995).
60. Ibid., at 930.
61. Ibid., at 934.
62. 531 U.S. 32 (2000).
63. 428 U.S. 543 (1976).
64. 496 U.S. 444 (1990).
65. 531 U.S. at 56.
66. 536 U.S. 822 (2002).
67. Ibid., at 838.
68. 547 U.S. 103 (2006).
69. Ibid., at 145.
70. 547 U.S. 843 (2006).
71. Ibid., at 846.
72. 534 U.S. 112 (2001).
73. 547 U.S. at 830.
74. 133 S. Ct. 1552 (2013).
75. Ibid., at 1574.
76. 232 U.S. 383 (1914).
77. 367 U.S. 643 (1961).
78. See Thomas's majority opinion in *United States v. Mezzanatto*, 513 U.S. 196 (1995).
79. 524 U.S. 357 (1998).
80. Ibid., at 364.
81. Ibid., at 364–365.
82. Ibid., at 365.
83. Ibid., at 369. Thomas never conceded that the search in question was unconstitutional: "We express no opinion regarding the constitutionality of the search." Ibid., at 362. One of the conditions of Scott's parole was that he would refrain from "owning or possessing any firearms or other weapons," and he signed a parole agreement that further provided: "I expressly consent to the search of my person, property and residence, without a warrant by agents of the Pennsylvania Board of Probation and Parole. Any items, the possession of which constitutes a violation of parole/reparole shall be subject to seizure, and may be used as evidence in the parole revocation process." Ibid., at 360. Because Thomas held that the

exclusionary rule would not be applied in this case, the question of whether the search was, in fact, unconstitutional was irrelevant. Of course, had the Court found the search to be constitutional, Thomas could not have found that the exclusionary rule did not apply to parole revocation hearings.

84. 380 U.S. 609 (1965).
85. 526 U.S. 314 (1999).
86. Ibid., at 331.
87. Ibid., at 336.
88. Ibid., at 341.
89. Ibid., at 343.
90. Ibid. See also Thomas's concurrence in the judgment in *Salinas v. Texas*, 133 S. Ct. 2174, 2184 (2013): "We granted certiorari to decide whether the Fifth Amendment privilege against compulsory self-incrimination prohibits a prosecutor from using a defendant's pre-custodial silence as evidence of his guilt. The plurality avoids reaching that question and instead concludes that Salinas' Fifth Amendment claim fails because he did not expressly invoke the privilege. I think there is a simpler way to resolve this case. In my view, Salinas' claim would fail even if he had invoked the privilege because the prosecutor's comments regarding his pre-custodial silence did not compel him to give self-incriminating testimony."
91. 530 U.S. 27 (2000).
92. Ibid., at 49.
93. Ibid., at 49–50.
94. Ibid., at 50.
95. Ibid., at 51.
96. Ibid., at 52.
97. Ibid., at 53.
98. Ibid., at 54–55. Thomas noted that Marshall's argument was accepted by the Court in the executive privilege case of *United States v. Nixon*, 418 U.S. 683 (1974).
99. 25 F. Cas. 30 (CC Va. 1807).
100. 530 U.S. at 55.
101. 425 U.S. 391 (1976).
102. 530 U.S. at 56.

103. 502 U.S. 346 (1992).

104. Ibid., at 359.

105. Ibid., at 365.

106. Ibid., at 365–366.

107. 547 U.S. at 840. He acknowledged that once the police officer arrived at her home, he asked the wife about her husband's past abusive conduct, but he contended that "the primary purpose of his inquiry was to assess whether [the husband] constituted a continuing danger to his wife, requiring further police presence or action." Ibid., at 841.

108. 554 U.S. 353 (2008).

109. Ibid., at 378.

110. 557 U.S. 305 (2009).

111. Ibid., at 330.

112. 131 S. Ct. 1143 (2011).

113. Ibid., at 1167. See Thomas's concurrence in the judgment in *Williams v. Illinois*, 132 S. Ct. 2221 (2012), where he relied on his opinion in *Bryant* and advocated the adoption of "a reading of the Confrontation Clause that respects its historically limited application to a narrow class of statements bearing indicia of solemnity." He rejected the attempt of the plurality opinion, written by Justice Alito, to distinguish between those who testify to make "inherently inculpatory" statements and those who testify to make other statements that are merely "helpful to the prosecution" (rejecting the former but accepting the latter) as having "no foundation in the text of the Amendment" and as diminishing "the Confrontation Clause's protection in cases where experts convey the contents of solemn, formalized statements to explain the bases for their opinions. These are the very cases in which the accused *should* 'enjoy the right . . . to be confronted with the witnesses against him.'" Ibid., at 2264. Emphasis in the original.

114. 530 U.S. 466 (2000).

115. Ibid., at 499.

116. Ibid., at 501.

117. Ibid., at 521.

118. Ibid., at 522. See his more recent argument to the same effect in *United States v. O'Brien*, 130 S. Ct. 2169, 2184 (2010). Thomas concurred in the judgment of the Court that the fact that a firearm was a machine gun was an element to be proved to the jury beyond a reasonable doubt, not a sentencing factor to be proved to the judge at sentencing. "In my view, it makes no difference whether the sentencing fact 'vaults a defendant's mandatory minimum sentence' by many years or only 'incremental[ly] changes' it by a few. Nor does it make a difference whether the sentencing fact 'involve[s] characteristics of the offender' or 'characteristics of the offense,' or which direction the other factors in the Court's five-factor test may tilt. One question decides the matter: If a sentencing fact either 'raises the floor or raises the ceiling' of the range of punishments to which a defendant is exposed, it is, 'by definition [an] elemen[t].'"

119. 477 U.S. 79 (1986).

120. 530 U.S. at 500.

121. Ibid., at 518.

122. 536 U.S. 545 (2002).

123. Ibid., at 573.

124. Ibid., at 579.

125. 133 S. Ct. 2151 (2013).

126. Ibid., at 2163.

127. 544 U.S. 13, 26–28 (2005).

128. 523 U.S. 224 (1998). In *Apprendi*, Thomas confessed that it had been an "error" on his part when he "succumbed" to join the majority opinion in *Almendarez-Torres*. 530 U.S. at 521.

129. 544 U.S. at 27.

130. Ibid., at 27–28. See Thomas's concurrence in the judgment in *Descamps v. United States*, 133 S. Ct. 2276, 2295 (2013): "The only reason Descamps' ACCA enhancement is before us is 'because this Court has not yet reconsidered *Almendarez-Torres v. United States*, which draws an exception to the *Apprendi* line of cases for judicial factfinding that concerns a

defendant's prior convictions.' Regardless of the framework adopted, judicial factfinding increases the statutory maximum in violation of the Sixth Amendment. However, because today's opinion at least limits the situations in which courts make factual determinations about prior convictions, I concur in the judgment."

131. 542 U.S. 296 (2004).

132. Ibid., at 303–304. Emphasis in the original.

133. See, for example, O'Connor's comments at ibid., 323–324: "The consequences of today's decision will be as far reaching as they are disturbing. Washington's sentencing system is by no means unique. Numerous other States have enacted guidelines systems, as has the Federal Government. Today's decision casts constitutional doubt over them all and, in so doing, threatens an untold number of criminal judgments. Every sentence imposed under such guidelines in cases currently pending on direct appeal is in jeopardy. And . . . all criminal sentences imposed under the federal and state guidelines since *Apprendi* was decided in 2000 arguably remain open to collateral attack."

134. 543 U.S. 220 (2005).

135. Ibid., at 245–268.

136. Ibid., at 284–285.

137. Ibid., at 314.

138. Ibid., at 315.

139. Ibid., at 316–317.

140. Ibid., at 317.

141. Ibid., at 317–318. See Thomas's elaborations of his dissent in *Booker* in his dissenting opinion in *Kimbrough v. United States*, 552 U.S. 85, 114–116 (2007), and his dissenting opinion in *Pepper v. United States*, 131 S. Ct. 1229, 1257–1258 (2011): "I would apply the Guidelines as written in this case because doing so would not violate the Sixth Amendment. The constitutional problem arises only when a judge makes 'a finding that raises the sentence beyond the sentence that could have lawfully been imposed

by reference to facts found by the jury or admitted by the defendant.'"

142. 419 U.S. 522 (1975).

143. Ibid., at 530.

144. 130 S. Ct. 1382 (2010).

145. Ibid., at 1396.

146. See, for example, *Irvin v. Dowd*, 366 U.S. 717 (1961).

147. 504 U.S. 127 (1992).

148. Ibid., at 148. Thomas also dissented from O'Connor's opinion on two other matters. First, he rejected her conclusion that Riggins did not have a full and fair trial because Mellaril had side effects that interfered with his ability to participate in his defense; he argued that "Riggins has failed to allege specific facts to support his claim that he could not participate effectively in his defense. He has not stated how he would have directed his counsel to examine or cross-examine witnesses differently. He has not identified any testimony or instructions that he did not understand." Ibid., at 149–150. Second, he also rejected her conclusion that Nevada violated Riggins's substantive liberty interest in avoiding unwanted medication under the Fourteenth Amendment's Due Process Clause by contending that Riggins failed to "argue below for reversal on his conviction" on that ground. Ibid., at 152.

149. 549 U.S. 70 (2006).

150. 425 U.S. 501 (1976).

151. 475 U.S. 560 (1986).

152. 549 U.S. at 75–76.

153. Ibid., at 77.

154. Ibid., at 81. Although he wrote a unanimous opinion in *Musladin* in 2006, in *Deck v. Missouri*, 544 U.S. 622 (2005), Thomas, joined by Scalia, dissented from Breyer's majority opinion holding that *Holbrook v. Flynn* prohibited the use of visible shackles during a capital trial's guilt phase unless doing so is justified by an essential state interest, such as courtroom security specific to the defendant on trial. He rejected the precedents Breyer cited,

claiming that even though they represented recent practice, they did not determine whether the Fourteenth Amendment, "as properly and traditionally interpreted, i.e., as a statement of law, not policy preferences," embodied a right to be free from visible physical restraints at trial. Ibid., at 650. He also argued that "wholly apart from the propriety of shackling a defendant at trial, due process does not require that a defendant remain free from visible restraints at the penalty phase of a capital trial. Such a requirement has no basis in tradition or even modern state practice. Treating shackling at sentencing as inherently prejudicial ignores the common-sense distinction between a defendant who stands accused and a defendant who stands convicted." Ibid., at 651. Building on that point, he stated that "capital sentencing jurors know that the defendant has been convicted of a dangerous crime. It strains credulity to think that they are surprised at the sight of restraints. Here, the jury had already concluded that there was a need to separate Deck from the community at large by convicting him of double murder and robbery. Deck's jury was surely aware that he was jailed; jurors know that convicted capital murderers are not left to roam the streets. It blinks reality to think that seeing a convicted capital murderer in shackles in the courtroom could import any prejudice beyond that inevitable knowledge." Ibid., at 652–653.

155. 100 U.S. 303 (1880).
156. Ibid., at 309.
157. 380 U.S. 202 (1965).
158. 476 U.S. 79 (1986).
159. Ibid., at 87.
160. 499 U.S. 400 (1991).
161. 500 U.S. 614 (1991).
162. 505 U.S. 42 (1992).
163. Ibid., at 57.
164. Ibid., at 59.
165. Ibid., at 70.
166. Ibid., at 59–60.
167. Ibid., at 60.

168. Ibid., at 61.
169. Ibid., at 61–62. The answer to peremptories on the basis of sex came soon enough. In *J. E. B. v. Alabama ex rel. T. B.*, 511 U.S. 127 (1994), a six-member majority held that making peremptory challenges based solely on a prospective juror's sex is unconstitutional. Thomas joined Scalia's dissent, as did Chief Justice Rehnquist.
170. 505 U.S. at 62. See Thomas's dissent in *Synder v. Louisana*, 552 U.S. 472, 487 (2008), in which the Court held, by a seven-to-two majority, that the prosecutor's proffered reasons for striking two black prospective jurors were mere pretexts for racial discrimination in violation of *Batson*. He charged the Court "with only paying lip-service to the pivotal role of the trial court. The Court second-guesses the trial court's determinations in this case merely because the judge did not clarify which of the prosecutor's neutral bases for striking Mr. Brooks was dispositive. . . . When the grounds for a trial court's decision are ambiguous, an appellate court should not presume that the lower court based its decision on an improper ground, particularly when applying a deferential standard of review."
171. 523 U.S. 392 (1998).
172. Ibid., at 404.
173. Ibid., at 403.
174. Ibid., at 406.
175. Ibid., at 404.
176. Ibid., at 407. See Calvin J. TerBeek, "Write Separately: Justice Clarence Thomas's 'Race Opinions' on the Supreme Court," *Texas Journal of Civil Liberties and Civil Rights* 11 (Spring 2006): 185, 198–199.
177. 505 U.S. 647 (1992).
178. 407 U.S. 514 (1972). The four criteria were whether delay before trial was uncommonly long; whether the government or the criminal defendant was more to blame for that delay; whether, in due course, the defendant asserted his right to a speedy trial; and whether he suffered prejudice as a result of the delay.

179. 505 U.S. at 657.

180. Ibid., at 659.

181. Ibid., at 650–660.

182. Ibid., at 668–669.

183. Ibid., at 669. Emphasis in the original.

184. Ibid., at 670–671.

185. Ibid., at 671. Emphasis in the original.

186. 464 U.S. 501 (1984).

187. 130 U.S. 721 (2010).

188. Ibid., at 726.

189. Ibid., at 727.

190. 553 U.S. 35 (2008). In this case, it was the judgment of Chief Justice Roberts and six of his colleagues that Kentucky's use of a three-drug lethal injection method of capital punishment was not cruel and unusual punishment.

191. Ibid., at 94.

192. Ibid., at 95–96.

193. Ibid., at 97.

194. Ibid., at 98.

195. Ibid., at 99.

196. Ibid., at 101.

197. 506 U.S. 461, 490 (1993).

198. *Shafer v. South Carolina*, 532 U.S. 36, 58 (2001). See also *Kelly v. South Carolina*, 534 U.S. 246, 265 (2002): "Today's decision allows the Court to meddle further in a State's sentencing proceedings under the guise that the Constitution requires us to do so. I continue to believe, without qualification, that 'it is not this Court's role to micromanage state sentencing proceedings.'"

199. 548 U.S. 163 (2006).

200. Ibid., at 174.

201. 408 U.S. 238 (1972).

202. 506 U.S. at 487. It should be noted that Thomas never addresses the fact that a mandatory death penalty scheme does not eliminate explicit discretion but merely transfers it to the prosecutor, who may be no less prejudiced than the jury.

203. 492 U.S. 302 (1989).

204. 489 U.S. 288 (1989).

205. 506 U.S. at 479.

206. Ibid., at 493–494.

207. Ibid., at 495. See also Thomas's rejection of *Penry* in *Tennard v. Dretke*, 542 U.S. 274, 294–295 (2004).

208. 130 S. Ct. 2011 (2010).

209. Ibid., at 2043.

210. But see *United States v. Bajakajian*, 524 U.S. 321 (1998), in which Thomas held for a five-member majority (the other justices being Stevens, Souter, Ginsburg, and Breyer) that the forfeiture of the entire $357,144 that Bajakajian was carrying when he failed to report to customs officials that he was transporting abroad more than $10,000 in currency violated the Eighth Amendment's Excessive Fines Clause because such a forfeiture was grossly disproportionate to the gravity of his offense. But, of course, focusing on proportionality was appropriate in this case; the Excessive Fines Clause, by definition, requires the employment of the proportionality principle.

211. 130 S. Ct. at 2044. See Thomas's brief opinion in *Ewing v. California*, 542 U.S. 11, 32 (2003), in which he concurred in the Court's judgment that California's three-strikes law did not violate the Eighth Amendment; though the plurality found that Ewing's sentence of twenty-five years to life for committing a third felony (the theft of three golf clubs) was not "grossly disproportionate" to his crime, Thomas simply noted that the Cruel and Unusual Punishments Clause "contains no proportionality principle."

212. 130 S. Ct. at 2045–2046.

213. Ibid., at 2046. Emphasis in the original.

214. Ibid., at 2047. Emphasis in the original.

215. Ibid., at 2028.

216. Ibid., at 2048.

217. Ibid., at 2058.

218. 132 S. Ct. 2455 (2012).

219. 501 U.S. 957 (1991).

220. 132 S. Ct. 2486.

Chapter 6. Thomas's Original General Meaning Approach to Questions of Race and Equality

1. 347 U.S. 483, 494 (1954).

2. See Marshall's lengthy dissent in *Milliken v. Bradley*, 418 U.S. 717, 781–814 (1974).

3. See Marshall's opinion concurring in part and dissenting in part in *Regents of the University of California v. Bakke*, 438 U.S. 265, 387–402 (1978); his concurrence in the judgment in *Fullilove v. Klutznik*, 448 U.S. 448, 517–522; and his dissent in *City of Richmond v. Croson*, 488 U.S. 469, 528–561 (1989). Marshall joined Justice Brennan's majority opinion in *Metro Broadcasting v. Federal Communications Commission*, 497 U.S. 547 (1990), expressly overturned five years later in *Adarand Constructors v. Pena*, 515 U.S. 200 (1995), in an opinion in which Thomas joined.

4. See Chief Justice Warren's opinion in *Allen v. State Board of Elections*, 393 U.S. 544 (1969), which Marshall joined; Marshall's lengthy dissent in *Mobile v. Bolden*, 446 U.S. 55, 103–140 (1980); and Justice Brennan's opinion for the Court in *Thornburg v. Gingles*, 478 U.S. 30 (1986), which Marshall joined.

5. Clarence Thomas, "Affirmative Action Goals and Timetables: Too Tough? Not Tough Enough?" *Yale Law and Policy Review* 5 (Spring-Summer 1987): 402–411.

6. Clarence Thomas, "An Afro-American Perspective: Toward a 'Plain Reading' of the Constitution—The Declaration of Independence in Constitutional Interpretation," 1987 *Howard Law Review* (1987): 691, 700: "Brennan [in his opinion in *Bakke*] insists that Justice Harlan's phrase [that the "Constitution is color-blind"] 'has never been adopted by this Court as the proper meaning of the Equal Protection Clause. Indeed, we have expressly rejected this proposition on a number of occasions.' Justice Brennan at least frankly

acknowledged the opposition of the racial preference policies to color-blind principles, even going so far as to cite with approval the ethnic Japanese exclusion cases."

7. 347 U.S. at 494 n.11. As Thomas pointed out, Clark's studies "could just as easily have been used *in support* of segregation, as against it." Thomas, "Afro-American Perspective," 698. Emphasis in the original.

8. 163 U.S. 537, 553 (1896). See Thomas, "Afro-American Perspective," 699–700: "*Brown* was a missed opportunity, as all its progeny, whether they involve busing, affirmative action, or redistricting. The task of those involved in securing the freedom of all Americans is to turn policy toward reason rather than sentiment, toward justice rather than sensitivity, toward freedom rather than dependence—in other words, toward the spirit of the Founding. These steps would validate the *Brown* decision, by replacing the Warren opinion with one resting on reason and moral and political principles, as established in the Constitution and the Declaration of Independence, rather than on feelings. Justice Harlan's *Plessy* opinion is a good example of thinking in the spirit of the Founding. His arguments can be fully appreciated only in light of the Founders' intentions."

9. See Clarence Thomas, *My Grandfather's Son: A Memoir* (New York: HarperCollins, 2007), 227.

10. Ibid., 271.

11. A. Leon Higginbotham, Jr., "An Open Letter to Justice Clarence Thomas from a Federal Judicial Colleague," *University of Pennsylvania Law Review* 140 (January 1992): 1005–1028.

12. Ibid., 1007.

13. Ibid., 1011, 1014.

14. Ibid., 1015.

15. Ibid., 1018–1019.

16. Ibid., 1020–1021.

17. Ibid., 1025.

18. Ibid., 1027.

19. Scott Douglas Gerber, *First Principles: The Jurisprudence of Clarence Thomas* (New York: New York University Press, 1999), 14–15.

20. Mark V. Tushnet, "Clarence Thomas: The Constitutional Problems," *George Washington University Law Review* 63 (March 1995): 466–478. A decade later, Tushnet would recant; see his "Clarence Thomas's Black Nationalism," *Howard Law Review* 47 (Winter 2004): 323–339.

21. Note, "Lasting Stigma: Affirmative Action and Clarence Thomas's Prisoners' Rights Jurisprudence," *Harvard Law Review* 112 (April 1999): 1331, 1333. As Gerber points out, there have also been "at least fifteen books" published on the subject of Thomas's confirmation. Gerber, *First Principles*, 15.

22. Angela Onwuachi-Willig, "Just Another Brother on the Supreme Court? What Justice Clarence Thomas Teaches Us about the Influence of Racial Identity," *Iowa Law Review* 90 (March 2005): 931, 977 n.218. Four years earlier, Higginbotham had delivered the Matthew O. Tobriner Memorial Lecture at Hastings College of Law, entitled "Justice Clarence Thomas in Retrospect," *Hastings Constitutional Law Quarterly* 45 (August 1994): 1405–1433, 1428. Among his other calumnies, Higginbotham suggested that Thomas's votes and judicial opinions revealed "many aspects of racial self-hatred that sometimes trigger the perverse conclusions he reaches."

23. Onwuachi-Willig, "Just Another Brother," 977.

24. Clarence Thomas, "The Higher Law Background of the Privileges or Immunities Clause of the Fourteenth Amendment," *Harvard Journal of Law and Public Policy* 12 (Winter 1989): 63, 64. See his Address on the Occasion of the Dedication of the Donald P. Kennedy Hall at Chapman University School of Law, *Chapman Law Review* 3 (Spring 2000): 3–5. See also Thomas, "Civility," *South Texas Law Review* 39 (June

1998): 655–661. Finally, see Andrew Peyton Thomas, *Clarence Thomas: A Biography* (San Francisco: Encounter Books, 2002), 308, where the author describes the Declaration as Thomas's "lodestar for interpreting the Constitution on matters of race."

25. Thomas, "Higher Law Background," 64. Thomas explained what consent means: "In the American regime, this means by majority rule, *but not just by any majority rule* . . . Thomas Jefferson, in his first presidential inaugural address, observed: 'All, too, will bear in mind this sacred principle that, though the will of the majority is in all cases to prevail, that will, to be rightful, must be reasonable. Let the minority possess their equal rights which equal law must protect . . . and to violate would be oppression.'" Emphasis in the original.

26. Thomas, "Afro-American Perspective," 700. See also Thomas, "Higher Law Background," 63–64, where he references the "higher law political philosophy of the Founding Fathers" and makes clear he means "the fundamental principle that all men are created equal."

27. Thomas, "Afro-American Perspective," 693. "If the Constitution is not a logical extension of the principles of the Declaration of Independence, important parts of the Constitution are inexplicable. One should never lose sight of the fact that the last words of the original Constitution as written refer to the Declaration of Independence, written just eleven years earlier." Thomas, "Higher Law Background," 65. Some may wonder how, if Thomas believes that all men are created equal and the Constitution is the fulfillment of the principles of the Declaration of Independence, the Constitution in Article I, § 2 could declare that for purposes of representation, slaves counted as "three-fifths" of a person. He might offer several replies. The delegates from the slave states were those who sought to have their slaves counted as full persons because it would have enhanced their states'

power in the new national government. The delegates from the North did not want them to be represented at all because they would not be given the franchise. A compromise was reached by the delegates, employing a precedent agreed to under the Articles of Confederation for apportioning requisitions on the states, based on their ability to contribute. The compromise was not based on an agreement that blacks were inferior; rather, it was based on the recognition that black slave labor was less productive (they deemed it to be only three-fifths as productive) as free white labor because a free man will work for himself much harder than a slave will work for his master. Frederick Douglass, so often quoted by Thomas and referenced in the passage to which this note is attached, dismissed this provision and the original Constitution's two other accommodations of slavery (Article I, § 9's twenty-year ban on importing slaves and Article IV, § 2's Fugitive Slave Clause) by noting that the word *slave* never appeared in any of their provisions and by insisting that "the Federal Government was never, in its essence, anything but an anti-slavery government. It was purposely so framed as to give no claim, no sanction to the claim, of property in man. If in its origin slavery had a relation to the government, it was only as the scaffolding to the magnificent structure, to be removed as soon as the building was completed." Frederick Douglass, "Address for the Promotion of Colored Enlistments," July 6, 1863, in *The Life and Writings of Frederick Douglass*, ed. Philip S. Foner (New York: International Publishers, 1950), 3:365.

28. Thomas, "Afro-American Perspective," 692. Judge Higginbotham claimed to have read all of Thomas's articles and speeches. Yet he could not fathom why Thomas called himself a conservative. See Higginbotham, "Open Letter," 1018–1019. He must have missed Thomas's "Higher Law Background," 69–70: "And what can be more conservative than the revolutionary principle that

America was founded on—that all men are created equal? . . . Just before he died in 1826, [Thomas Jefferson] wrote: 'All eyes are opened or opening to the rights of man. The general spread of the light of science has already laid open to every view the palpable truth . . . that the mass of Mankind has not been born, with saddles on their backs, nor a favored few booted and spurred, ready to ride them legitimately by the grace of God.'"

29. Clarence Thomas, "Why Federalism Matters," Dwight D. Opperman Lecture, *Drake Law Review* 48 (2000): 231, 232.

30. Roy P. Basler, ed., *Collected Works of Abraham Lincoln*, 8 vols. (New Brunswick, NJ: Rutgers University Press, 1953), 4:168–169. Emphasis in the original. See Douglas W. Kmiec's introduction of Justice Thomas at "The Justices Speak: Reflection—The Second Annual William French Smith Memorial Lecture: A Conversation with Justice Clarence Thomas," *Pepperdine Law Review* 37 (December 2009): 7, 8. Thomas "has been the only member of the Court to take seriously the insight of Abraham Lincoln that recalls the old spiritual proverb that 'a word fitly spoken is like an apple of gold in a frame of silver.'"

31. Thomas, "Afro-American Perspective," 703.

32. Thomas, "Why Federalism Matters," 232.

33. Basler, *Collected Works*, 2:398–410.

34. Thomas, "Higher Law Background," 65–66.

35. Thomas, "Afro-American Perspective," 692.

36. Ibid., 702: "The proper way to interpret the Civil War Amendments is as extensions of the promise of the original Constitution which in turn was intended to fulfill the promise of the Declaration."

37. Basler, *Collected Works*, 2:493.

38. Frederick Douglass, "Fourth of July Oration," in Herbert J. Storing, ed., *What Country Have I?* (New York: St. Martin's Press, 1970), 38. Douglass concluded his

oration as follows: "Allow me to say, in conclusion, notwithstanding the dark picture I have this day presented of the state of the nation, I do not despair of this country. There are forces in operation, which must inevitably work the downfall of slavery. 'The arm of the Lord is not shortened,' and the doom of slavery is certain. I, therefore, leave off where I began, with hope. While drawing encouragement from the Declaration of Independence, the great principles it contains, and the genius of American Institutions, my spirit is also cheered by the obvious tendencies of the age."

39. Thomas, "Afro-American Perspective," 703.

40. Thomas distinguished the term *color-blind society* from *color-blind Constitution*: "Clearly the two do not mean the same thing. The former, much broader in scope, is certainly beyond the power of legislation alone to bring about. The latter, however, is very much a political matter, and a necessary condition for a color-blind society." Ibid., 700 n.37.

41. Ibid., 703. Harlan referred to the Declaration of Independence as "our political Bible." See Linda Przybyszewski, *The Republic According to John Marshall Harlan* (Chapel Hill: University of North Carolina Press, 1999), 64, who writes that, for Harlan, the post–Civil War Amendments "constitutionalized the universal equality that the founders promised in the Declaration of Independence." Ibid., 49.

Thomas acknowledges that Justice Harlan's assertions were "marred by a reference to the dominant white race and an opprobrious reference to Chinese immigrants," and after discussing them at some length, he concludes that "whatever Harlan's personal beliefs, the strength of those universal principles of equality and liberty provides the means for resolving contradictions between principle and practice." Thomas, "Afro-American Perspective," 701–702. See Christopher E.

Smith, "Clarence Thomas: A Distinctive Justice," *Seton Hall Law Review* 28 (1997): 1, 10–12, who argues that "Thomas's confident posture belies evident 'blind spots' in his understanding of constitutional history and original intent"; he also faults Thomas for not confronting "the manifestly un-color blind polices of racial segregation perpetuated by the Framers of the Fourteenth Amendment." Smith questions how Thomas can rely on the Declaration for support of a color-blind constitution when Thomas Jefferson owned slaves, did not contribute to the drafting of the Constitution, and wrote the Declaration close to a hundred years prior to the drafting of the Fourteenth Amendment. "Thomas does not appear inclined to express misgivings or self-doubt, especially about originalism, and thus he positions himself to collide with the many documented impediments that make it difficult, if not impossible, to adhere actually and consistently to an originalist approach to constitutional interpretation." See also Samuel Marcosson, "Colorizing the Constitution of Originalism: Clarence Thomas at the Rubicon," *Law and Equality* 16 (Summer 1998): 429, who wonders whether Thomas, had he been on the Court when it decided *Loving v. Virginia*, 388 U.S. 1 (1967), would have joined the Court in striking down Virginia's miscegenation law "on the basis of color-blindness" or dissented "as an originalist." Ibid., 430. Smith and Marcosson show themselves to be ignorant of Lincoln's recognition that, given human nature, the principles of the Declaration, even "though never perfectly attained," as a "standard maxim" would "be constantly approximated, and thereby constantly spreading and deepening its influence, and augmenting the happiness and value of life to all people of all colors everywhere." Basler, *Collected Works*, 2:398–410. Smith and Marcosson also show that they did not read, or read carefully, Thomas's reflections in "Afro-American Perspective."

42. Thomas, "Afro-American Perspective," 701. See also Thomas's dissent in *Grutter v. Bollinger*, 539 U.S. 306, 378 (2003).

43. See Hanna L. Weiner, "The Next 'Great Dissenter'? How Clarence Thomas Is Using the Words and Principles of John Marshall Harlan to Craft a New Era of Civil Rights," *Duke Law Journal* 58 (October 2008): 139–176, and Nathan W. Dean, "The Primacy of the Individual in the Political Philosophy and Civil Rights Jurisprudence of Justice Clarence Thomas," *George Mason University Civil Rights Law Review* 14 (Winter 2004): 27–72. See also Gerber, *First Principles*, 50: "What motivates [Thomas's] approach to civil rights and the post–Civil War Amendments is his conception of civil rights as an *individual* rather than a group concern." Emphasis in the original. See Thomas's chapter, "Civil Rights as a Principle versus Civil Rights as an Interest," in David Boaz, ed., *Assessing the Reagan Years* (Washington, DC: Cato Institute, 1988), 391–402.

44. Thomas, "Affirmative Action Goals and Timetables," 402. "I consider goals and timetables to be at best a relatively weak and limited weapon against existing forms of discrimination." Ibid., 403.

45. Ibid., 406.

46. Ibid., 406–407. "Any preferences given should be directly related to the obstacles that have been unfairly placed in those individuals' paths, rather than on the basis of race or gender, or on other characteristics that are often poor proxies for true disadvantage." Ibid., 410.

47. Ibid., 411.

48. "Rather than offer the individuals pity or handouts, we should provide them with the tools that may allow them to help themselves." Ibid., 410.

49. Clarence Thomas, "Victims and Heroes in the 'Benevolent State,'" *Harvard Law and Public Policy Review* 19 (Spring 1996): 671. Thomas delivered the same set of remarks in the James McClure Memorial Lecture in Law, delivered at the University of Mississippi Law School. See Thomas, "James McClure Memorial Lecture," *Mississippi Law Review* 65 (Spring 1996): 463–475.

50. Thomas, "Victims and Heroes," 672.

51. Ibid., 679.

52. Ibid., 683.

53. Clarence Thomas, "Comments of Justice Clarence Thomas," *Thurgood Marshall Law Review* 23 (Fall 1997): 5, 6.

54. Ibid., 7.

55. As Thomas said in *Adarand Constructors v. Pena*, racial paternalism "is at war with the principle of inherent equality that underlies and infuses our Constitution." 515 U.S. at 240.

56. 515 U.S. 70, 114 (1995).

57. Jeffrey Rosen, "Moving On," *New Yorker*, April 29, 1996, 66–73, 66.

58. *Parents Involved in Community Schools v. Seattle School District No. 1*, 551 U.S. 701, 749 (2007): "Racial imbalance is not segregation, and the mere incantation of terms like resegregation and remediation cannot make up the difference."

59. Speaking from firsthand experience, Thomas writes in his memoir about his efforts to land a job upon graduating from Yale Law School: "I set my sights on Atlanta, but I also interviewed with firms in New York, Washington, and Los Angeles that were recommended by my classmates, who assured me that I'd have no difficulty finding a job. They were wrong. One high-priced lawyer after another treated me dismissively, making it clear that they had no interest in me despite my Ivy League pedigree. Many asked pointed questions unsubtly suggesting that they doubted I was as smart as my grades indicated. . . . By late December I had yet to receive a single job offer. Now I knew what a law degree from Yale was worth when it bore the taint of racial preference." Thomas, *My Grandfather's Son*, 86–87.

60. 512 U.S. 874, 906–907 (1994).

61. 505 U.S. 717 (1992).

62. Ibid., at 745.

63. These were the words from Justice White's majority opinion. Ibid., at 729.

64. Ibid., at 745.

65. Ibid., at 746–747. Emphasis in the original.

66. Ibid., at 747–748. Emphasis in the original.

67. Ibid., at 748–749.

68. Ibid., at 749. Emphasis in the original. See also Thomas, *My Grandfather's Son*, 141–142.

69. 515 U.S. 70 (1995).

70. *Missouri v. Jenkins*, 495 U.S. 33 (1990).

71. Ibid., at 77.

72. Kennedy wrote an opinion concurring in part and concurring in the judgment, joined by Chief Justice Rehnquist and Justices O'Connor and Scalia.

73. 515 U.S. at 89.

74. Ibid., at 138, 114.

75. Ibid., at 114, 135.

76. Ibid., at 115–116.

77. Ibid., at 116.

78. Ibid., at 119.

79. Ibid., at 120–121.

80. Ibid., at 121.

81. Ibid., at 122–123.

82. Ibid., at 123.

83. Ibid., at 124–131, 127.

84. Ibid., at 131.

85. Ibid., at 132–133.

86. Ibid., at 137.

87. Ibid., at 136–137. Emphasis in the original. A representative law review article commenting on Thomas's concurrence in *Jenkins* is Jared A. Levy, "Blinking at Reality: The Implications of Justice Clarence Thomas's Influential Approach to Race and Education," *Boston University Law Review* 78 (April 1998): 575–618, 578: "If other political, legal, and economic leaders follow Thomas's lead, the purposes behind the Fourteenth Amendment will be subverted, and black schoolchildren will be left to attend deteriorating and unequal schools for at least another generation." But of course, four years later in *Zelman v. Simmons-Harris*, 536 U.S. 639 (2002), Thomas voted to uphold a non-raced-based way to ensure that black schoolchildren will not attend "deteriorating and unequal schools" — vouchers. See Tomiko Brown-Nagin, "The Transformative Racial Policies of Justice Thomas? The *Grutter v. Bollinger* Opinion," *University of Pennsylvania Journal of Constitutional Law* 7 (February 2005): 787–807, 791–792. "As his decisions in *Zelman* and *Jenkins* demonstrate, Justice Thomas's objections to the agenda favored by liberal civil rights groups seem to turn on remedial considerations rather than on indifference to bias. He categorically rejects race-conscious remedies. Thus, Justice Thomas's support for the Cleveland voucher program that primarily benefited poor, minority children turned, in part, on the fact that the program was not explicitly race conscious. But, he has questioned explicitly race-conscious remedies in school desegregation and affirmative action cases because, as he sees it, they are premised on an assumption of black deficiency, and therefore perpetuate the very stigma they were designed to remediate. Justice Thomas's opinions about how best to remedy racial inequality in education certainly are subject to debate. But his disagreement with conventional, liberal perspectives on the best remedies for racial discrimination does not mean that he is unconcerned about the welfare of African Americans."

88. 551 U.S. 701 (2007).

89. 539 U.S. 306 (2003).

90. 551 U.S. at 725.

91. Ibid., at 724–725.

92. Ibid., at 787.

93. Ibid., at 867.

94. Ibid., at 748. See J. Harvie Wilkinson III, "The Seattle and Louisville School Cases: There Is No Other Way," *Harvard Law Review* 121 (November 2007): 158–185.

95. 551 U.S. at 759.

96. Ibid., at 839.

97. Ibid., at 765–766.

98. Ibid., at 772. Thomas then turned to the remarks of Judge Constance Baker Motley, a close associate of Thurgood Marshall at the NAACP and the first black woman to be appointed a federal district court judge: "Marshall had a 'Bible' to which he turned during his most depressed moments. The 'Bible' would be known in the legal community as the first Mr. Justice Harlan's dissent in *Plessy*. I do not know of any opinion which buoyed Marshall more in his pre-*Brown* days." Ibid., at 773.

99. Ibid., at 774–776.

100. Ibid., at 777–778.

101. Ibid., at 778–779.

102. Ibid., at 780–782.

103. Ibid., at 782 n.30.

104. 515 U.S. 200 (1995).

105. Ibid., at 240.

106. Ibid., at 210–211. See Thomas's earlier majority opinion in *Northeastern Florida Chapter of the Associated Contractors of America v. City of Jacksonville*, 508 U.S. 656, 666 (1993), in which he held that a party challenging a racial set-aside program has standing to sue upon a demonstration that it "is able and ready to bid on contracts and that a discriminatory policy prevents it from doing so on an equal basis."

107. 539 U.S. 306 (2003).

108. Ibid., at 322.

109. Ibid., at 328.

110. Ibid., at 329.

111. Ibid., at 334.

112. Ibid., at 337. A companion case to *Grutter* was *Gratz v. Bollinger*, 539 U.S. 244 (2003), which addressed the constitutionality of a far less subtle racial preference program of the University of Michigan's undergraduate College of Literature, Science, and the Arts. Unlike the Law School's use of race, which O'Connor held was narrowly tailored because the race of applicants was not the defining feature of their applications, the undergraduate college's policy challenged in *Gratz*

automatically awarded every applicant from an underrepresented racial or ethnic minority group twenty points of the one hundred points needed to guarantee admission. In *Gratz*, the Court struck down the state's mechanistic approach for achieving a diverse student body at the undergraduate level. In his majority opinion, Chief Justice Rehnquist was forced to accept the principle announced in *Grutter* that diversity constituted a compelling state interest for employing racial preferences, but he was able to declare for a six-member majority (the four dissenters in *Grutter*—Rehnquist, Scalia, Kennedy, and Thomas—plus O'Connor and Breyer) that "the University's policy, which automatically distributes . . . one-fifth of the points needed to guarantee admission, to every single 'underrepresented minority' applicant solely because of race, is not narrowly tailored to achieve the interest in educational diversity that respondents claim justifies their program." Ibid., at 270. Thomas joined Rehnquist's opinion and wrote a brief concurring opinion to reiterate that "a State's use of racial discrimination in higher education admissions is categorically prohibited by the Equal Protection Clause." Ibid., at 281.

113. 539 U.S. at 330.

114. Ibid., at 331.

115. Ibid., at 332.

116. Ibid., at 343.

117. 536 U.S. 639 (2002).

118. Ibid., at 349–350. Emphasis in the original.

119. Ibid., at 350. There is one area where Thomas is willing to defer to state officials concerning issues of racial classifications: prison administration. In *Johnson v. California*, 543 U.S. 499 (2005), in a five-to-three opinion, O'Connor held that California's unwritten policy of placing new or transferred inmates with cellmates of the same race during initial evaluation had to be reviewed under strict scrutiny, not under the standard of *Turner v. Safley*,

482 U.S. 78 (1987), requiring only that the policy be "reasonably related" to a legitimate penological interest. Thomas disagreed: "The Constitution has always demanded less within the prison walls. Time and again, even when faced with constitutional rights no less 'fundamental' than the right to be free from state-sponsored racial discrimination, we have deferred to the reasonable judgments of officials experienced in running this Nation's prisons. There is good reason for such deference in this case. California oversees roughly 160,000 inmates in prisons that have been a breeding ground for some of the most violent prison gangs in America—all of them organized along racial lines. In that atmosphere, California racially segregates a portion of its inmates, in a part of its prisons, for brief periods of up to 60 days, until the State can arrange permanent housing. The majority is concerned with sparing inmates the indignity and stigma of racial discrimination. California is concerned with their safety and saving their lives. I respectfully dissent." 543 U.S. at 524. He was convinced that California's policy would be upheld under strict scrutiny on remand but saw no need to second-guess the policy in the first place. He called to mind O'Connor's opinion in *Grutter:* "Two Terms ago, in upholding the University of Michigan Law School's affirmative-action program, this Court deferred to the judgment by the law school's faculty and administrators on their need for diversity in the student body. Deference would seem all the more warranted in the prison context, for whatever the Court knows of administering educational institutions, it knows much less about administering penal ones. The potential consequences of second-guessing the judgments of prison administrators are also much more severe." Ibid., at 543.

120. 539 U.S. at 350–351.
121. Ibid., at 354.
122. Ibid., at 355 n.3.

123. Ibid., at 355.
124. Ibid., at 356.
125. Ibid., at 357–358.
126. Ibid., at 361.
127. Ibid., at 362. The Court over time had built up a First Amendment argument that an aspect of free speech is "academic freedom" and that "academic freedom includes the right of an institution of higher education not only to teach what it wants but also to whom it wants." See Justice Felix Frankfurter's opinion concurring in the judgment in *Sweezy v. New Hampshire,* 354 U.S. 234, 263 (1957): "It is the business of a university to provide that atmosphere which is most conducive to speculation, experiment and creation. It is an atmosphere in which there prevail 'the four essential freedoms' of a university—to determine for itself on academic grounds who may teach, what may be taught, how it shall be taught, and who may be admitted to study." As he was establishing for the first time in a Supreme Court opinion a justification to discriminate on the basis of race to advance the interest of "diversity," Justice Powell quoted approvingly Frankfurter's language in his solo opinion in *Regents of the University of California v. Bakke,* 438 U.S. 265, 312 (1978).
128. 518 U.S. 515 (1996). Thomas recused himself in this case because his son, Jamal, was a student at the Citadel, which, like the Virginia Military Institute, was a publicly supported university with an exclusively male admission policy at that time.
129. 539 U.S. at 366.
130. Ibid., at 366–367. Thomas also referenced the "facially-neutral 'percent plans'" used in Texas and Florida. Ibid., at 369.
131. Ibid., at 370–371.
132. Ibid., at 371.
133. Ibid., at 372.
134. Ibid., at 373. See Mary Kate Kearney, "Justice Thomas in *Grutter v. Bollinger:* Can Passion Play a Role in a Jurist's Reasoning?" *St. John's Law Review* 78 (Winter 2004):

15, 26–27: "Justice Thomas's dissent has received widespread attention and criticism. Commentators have questioned his opposition to affirmative action on different grounds. Many of those critics assume that he has been the beneficiary of affirmative action policies, and they are offended that he is opposing those very policies that they believe have led him to his current position on the Supreme Court. In their estimation, Justice Thomas does not have the moral authority to make the case against affirmative action because he 'is himself one of the most notorious affirmative action hires in history.' The problems with these criticisms are twofold. First, they assume without proof that Justice Thomas's achievements are related to the color of his skin and not to his abilities. Second, they validate one of the concerns that he expressed in his opinion: that affirmative action policies lead people to believe that minorities who reach high levels cannot possibly be there on the basis of merit."

135. 539 U.S. at 378.

136. 133 S. Ct. 2411 (2013).

137. Ibid., at 2415.

138. Ibid., at 2422.

139. Ibid., at 2424–2425.

140. Ibid., at 2426–2427.

141. Ibid., at 2428.

142. Ibid., at 2430.

143. Ibid., at 2431.

144. See *Holder v. Hall*, 512 U.S. 874, 893 (1994).

145. See *Hunt v. Cromartie*, 526 U.S. 541, 546 (1999).

146. See *Northwest Austin Municipal Utility District Number One* [NAMUDNO] *v. Holder*, 557 U.S. 193 (2009).

147. See the comments of Edith H. Jones, chief judge of the US Court of Appeals for the Fifth Circuit, in "Justice Thomas and the Voting Rights Act," *Regent University Law Review* 12 (1999–2000): 333. "Justice Thomas's arguments are strong; only a few critics have dared tackle them on the merits."

148. 512 U.S. at 891.

149. Ibid., at 892–893. Thomas made a similar argument in his dissenting opinion in *Morse v. Republican Party of Virginia*, 517 U.S. 186, 277 (1996). He rejected the plurality's contention that a party's imposition of a registration fee to attend its state convention at which candidates for statewide office are nominated was a procedure "with respect to voting." "Based on the statutory definition of 'voting,' I conclude that the registration fee is not the type of election-related change with which the Act concerns itself."

150. 512 U.S. at 892.

151. Ibid., at 895. See Thomas's description of these tests and devices in his dissenting opinion in *Lopez v. Monterey County*, 525 U.S. 266, 297 (1999).

152. 393 U.S. 544 (1969).

153. 512 U.S. at 895–896.

154. Ibid., at 897.

155. Ibid., at 899. Emphasis in the original.

156. Ibid., at 901.

157. 520 U.S. 471 (1997).

158. Ibid., at 491–492. Emphases in the original.

159. 478 U.S. 30 (1986).

160. 512 U.S. at 902–903, 935. "The last clause in the subsection [of § 2 of the Voting Rights Act] states in unmistakable terms that 'nothing in this section establishes a right to have members of a protected class elected in numbers equal to their proportion in the population.'" Ibid., at 927.

161. Ibid., at 903.

162. Ibid., at 905–906.

163. Ibid., at 913–914.

164. Ibid., at 944–945. See Daniel M. O'Keefe, "Stare Decisis: What Should the Supreme Court Do When Old Laws Are Not Necessarily Good Laws? A Comment on Justice Thomas' Call for Reassessment in the Supreme Court's Voting Rights Jurisprudence," *St. Louis University Law Journal* 40 (Winter 1996): 261–302.

165. 517 U.S. 952 (1996).

166. Ibid., at 999.

167. Ibid., at 1000.

168. Ibid., at 1002–1003.

169. 526 U.S. at 543–544.

170. 478 U.S. 109 (1986).

171. 526 U.S. at 551. Emphasis in the original.

172. Ibid., at 553–554.

173. 557 U.S. 193, 216 (2009).

174. 383 U.S. 301, 358 (1966).

175. 557 U.S. at 213.

176. Ibid., at 216.

177. Ibid., at 216–217.

178. Ibid., at 224–225.

179. Ibid., at 225–226. In the 2013 case of *Shelby County v. Holder*, 133 S. Ct. 2612 (2013), Chief Justice Roberts held for a five-member majority that Congress acted unconstitutionally when it reauthorized in 2006 § 4 of the Voting Rights Act, containing the formula for determining which states and jurisdictions are covered by § 5's preclearance requirements. It found that although the coverage formula was logical in both theory and practice when Congress established it in 1965, it no longer had a logical relation to the present day. Thomas joined that majority but wrote a concurring opinion to explain that, as in *NAMUDNO*, he would have found § 5 of the Voting Rights Act unconstitutional as well: "While the Court claims to 'issue no holding on § 5 itself,' its own opinion compellingly demonstrates that Congress has failed to justify 'current burdens' with a record demonstrating 'current needs.' By leaving the inevitable conclusion unstated, the Court needlessly prolongs the demise of that provision. For the reasons stated in the Court's opinion, I would find § 5 unconstitutional." Ibid., at 2632.

180. See andre douglas pond cummings, "*Grutter v. Bollinger*, Clarence Thomas, Affirmative Action, and the Treachery of Originalism: 'The Sun Don't Shine Here in This Part of Town,'" *Harvard Blackletter Law*

Journal 21 (Spring 2005): 1–73, 58. See also John O. Calmore, "Airing Dirty Laundry: Disputes among Privileged Blacks—From Clarence Thomas to 'The Law School Five,'" *Howard Law Journal* 46 (Winter 2003): 175–227, 192. Thomas's jurisprudence "is deeply personal and his black identity and biography stand closely behind his Supreme Court votes and opinions."

181. Calvin J. TerBeek, "Writing Separately: Justice Clarence Thomas's 'Race Opinions' on the Supreme Court," *Texas Journal on Civil Liberties and Civil Rights* 11 (Spring 2006): 185–209, 208.

182. Kendall Thomas, "Reading Clarence Thomas," *National Black Law Journal* 18 (2004): 224, 236–338.

183. The quotation is from Clarence Thomas, "Judging," *Kansas Law Review* 45 (November 1996): 1, 4. Critics who cite this passage include cummings, "*Grutter v. Bollinger*," 59, and Ronald Turner, "On *Parents Involved* and the Problematic Praise of Justice Clarence Thomas," *Hastings Constitutional Law Quarterly* 37 (Winter 2010): 225–242, 227.

184. See cummings, "*Grutter v. Bollinger*," 60.

185. Stephen F. Smith, "Clarence X? The Black Nationalism behind Justice Thomas's Constitutionalism," *New York University Journal of Law & Liberty* 4 (2009): 583–625, 585.

186. Nicole Stelle Garnett, "'But for the Grace of God There Go I'": Justice Thomas and the Little Guy," *New York University Journal of Law & Liberty* 4 (2009): 626–647, 629. Garnett mentions three cases. In his dissent in *Lawrence v. Texas*, 539 U.S. 558, 605–606 (2003), in which the Court struck down Texas's antisodomy statute, Thomas explained, "I write separately to note that the law before the Court today 'is uncommonly silly.' If I were a member of the Texas Legislature, I would vote to repeal it. Punishing someone for expressing his sexual preference through noncommercial

consensual conduct with another adult does not appear to be a worthy way to expend valuable law enforcement resources. Notwithstanding this, I recognize that as a member of this Court I am not empowered to help petitioners and others similarly situated. My duty, rather, is to 'decide cases agreeably to the Constitution and laws of the United States.' And, I 'can find [neither in the Bill of Rights nor in any other part of the Constitution] a general right of privacy,' or as the Court terms it today, the 'liberty of the person both in its spatial and more transcendent dimensions.'" In his concurrence in *Bennis v. Michigan*, 516 U.S. 442, 454 (1996), in which the Court held that an innocent-owner defense is not mandated by the Due Process Clause in cases of civil forfeiture, he declared, "This case is ultimately a reminder that the Federal Constitution does not prohibit everything that is intensely undesirable." "Improperly used, forfeiture could become more like a roulette wheel employed to raise revenue from innocent but hapless owners whose property is unforeseeably misused . . . than a component of a system of justice." However, he continued, when the property sought to be forfeited (Mrs. Bennis's automobile) "has been entrusted by its owner to one who uses it for crime" (her husband, who had an assignation with a prostitute in it), the Constitution "assigns to the States and to the political branches of the Federal Government the primary responsibility for avoiding that result." Ibid., at 457. And in *Hudson v. McMillian*, 503 U.S. 1, 28 (1992), already discussed in chapter 5, he stated, "Abusive behavior by prison guards is deplorable conduct that properly evokes outrage and contempt. But that does not mean that it is invariably unconstitutional." Garnett could have added a good number of other examples, as discussed in chapter 1.

187. 163 U.S. 537, 559 (1896).

188. Wilkinson, "Seattle and Louisville School Cases," 165.

Chapter 7. No Longer Doubting Thomas

1. The statistical information presented in this chapter in both the text and the tables has been compiled from the *Harvard Law Review*'s annual review and statistical analysis of the work of the Supreme Court in its November issues. See *Harvard Law Review* 106 (November 1992): 376; 107 (November 1993): 372; 108 (November 1994): 372; 109 (November 1995): 340; 110 (November 1996): 367; 111 (November 1997): 431; 112 (November 1998): 355; 113 (November 1999): 400; 114 (November 2000): 390; 115 (November 2001): 539; 116 (November 2002): 453; 117 (November 2003): 480; 118 (November 2004): 497; 119 (November 2005): 415; 120 (November 2006): 372; 121 (November 2007): 436; 122 (November 2008): 516; 123 (November 2009): 382; 124 (November 2010): 411; 125 (November 2011): 362; and 126 (November 2012): 388.

2. In the following five cases, Thomas wrote the majority opinion to which Scalia dissented: *United States v. Rodriquez-Moreno*, 526 U.S. 275 (1999); *Olympic Airways v. Husain*, 540 U.S. 644 (2004); *National Cable & Telecommunications Association v. Brand X Internet Services*, 545 U.S. 967 (2005); *Washington State Grange v. Washington State Republican Party*, 552 U.S. 442 (2008); and *Montana v. Wyoming*, 131 S. Ct. 1765 (2011). And in the following seven cases, Scalia wrote the majority opinion to which Thomas dissented: *United States by & ex rel. IRS v. McDermott*, 507 U.S. 447 (1993); *Clark v. Suarez Martinez*, 543 U.S. 371 (2005); *Buckeye Check Cashing, Inc. v. Cardegna*, 546 U.S. 440 (2006); *MedImmune Inc. v. Genentech, Inc.*, 549 U.S. 118 (2007); *Cuomo v. The Clearing House Association*, 557 U.S. 519 (2009); *Brown v. Entertainment Merchants Association*, 131 S. Ct. 2729 (2011); and *Arizona v. Inter-Tribal Council*, 133 S. Ct. 2247 (2013). Except for *Brown*, a First Amendment case, they all involve questions

of statutory construction, not constitutional interpretation.

3. George E. Curry and Trevor W. Coleman, "Editor's Note: We Were Too Kind," *Emerge*, November 1996, 38.

4. See, in particular, John O. Calmore, "Airing Dirty Laundry: Disputes among Privileged Blacks—From Clarence Thomas to 'The Law School Five,'" *Howard Law Journal* 46 (Winter 2003): 175, 180, and andre douglas pond cummings, "*Grutter v. Bollinger*, Clarence Thomas, Affirmative Action and the Treachery of Originalism: 'The Sun Don't Shine Here in This Part of Town,'" *Harvard Blackletter Journal* 21 (Spring 2005): 1. See also Vincent T. Bugliosi, "None Dare Call It Treason," *Nation*, February 5, 2001, 11, who called Justice Scalia "the Court's right-wing ideologue" and described Justice Thomas as "his Pavlovian puppet . . . who doesn't even try to create the impression that he's thinking." These calumnies have so pervaded popular culture that Jon Stewart, in *America (The Book): A Citizen's Guide to Democracy Inaction* (New York: Grand Central Publishing, 2004), 101, referred to Thomas as Scalia's "sock puppet."

5. Michael A. Fletcher and Kevin Merida, "Jurist Embraces Image as a Hard-Line Holdout," *Washington Post*, October 11, 2004, A1. See also Calvin J. TerBeek, "Write Separately: Justice Clarence Thomas's 'Race Opinions' on the Supreme Court," *Texas Journal of Civil Liberties & Civil Rights* 11 (Spring 2006): 185, 202.

6. The *Harvard Law Review* began reporting on nonunanimous cases for the first time in its statistical analysis of the 1997 term of the Court. See *Harvard Law Review* 112 (November 1998): 355.

7. "Thomas is different. There was no close competition for the seat he got, but the others who were considered . . . were more or less standard Federalist Society conservatives. *They* might have been Scalia's clones. Not Thomas." Mark V. Tushnet, *A*

Court Divided: The Rehnquist Court and the Future of Constitutional Law (New York: W. W. Norton, 2005), 72. Emphasis in the original.

8. In 1997, Justice Blackmun gave his personal papers to the United States for inclusion in the collections of the Library of Congress. At the time of his gift, he stipulated that they should not be opened to the general public until five years after his death; he died in Arlington, Virginia, on March 4, 1999, and his papers were opened on that date in 2004.

9. Jan Crawford Greenburg, *Supreme Conflict: The Inside Story of the Struggle for Control of the United States Supreme Court* (New York: Penguin Books, 2007), 109–137.

10. 503 U.S. 1 (1992).

11. 505 U.S. 647 (1992).

12. 521 U.S. 346 (1996).

13. 514 U.S. 476 (1995).

14. 133 S. Ct. 2151 (2013).

15. 533 U.S. 98 (2001).

16. 508 U.S. 384 (1993).

17. 515 U.S. 819 (1995).

18. 536 U.S. 822 (2002).

19. Ibid., at 827.

20. 515 U.S. 646 (1995).

21. 535 U.S. 743 (2002).

22. Mark V. Tushnet offers an explanation for why Thomas has written no major constitutional opinions for the Court: "His willingness to handle complex cases involving statutory interpretation and economic regulation limited what he had to say about major constitutional questions in the Rehnquist years." Tushnet, *Court Divided*, 103.

23. 514 U.S. 549 (1995).

24. 529 U.S. 598 (2000).

25. 545 U.S. 1 (2005).

26. 132 S. Ct. 2566, 2648 (2012).

27. 538 U.S. 644 (2003).

28. 555 U.S. 555 (2009).

29. 555 U.S. 70, 91–112 (2008).

30. 557 U.S. 519 (2009).

31. 517 U.S. 484 (1996).

32. 518 U.S. 604 (1996).

33. 528 U.S. 377 (2000).

34. 540 U.S. 93 (2003).

35. 548 U.S. 230 (2006).

36. 558 U.S. 310 (2010).

37. 518 U.S. 727 (1996).

38. 556 U.S. 502 (2009).

39. 521 U.S. 898 (1997).

40. 270 F.3d 203 (5th Cir. 2001).

41. 554 U.S. 570 (2008). See Jeffrey Toobin, "Annals of Law: Partners—Will Clarence and Virginia Thomas Succeed in Killing Obama's Health-Care Plan?" *New Yorker*, August 29, 2011, http://www.newyorker.com/reporting/2011/08/29/110829fa_fact_toobin?currentPage=all. In his interview with Gura, Toobin, author of *The Nine: Inside the Secret World of the Supreme Court* (New York: Anchor Books, 2008), reports that Gura told him: "When a Supreme Court Justice indicates interest in a dormant constitutional question, people take note, especially if it's a question that's otherwise generating a lot of controversy. It was highly influential."

42. 526 U.S. 489 (1999).

43. 130 S. Ct. 3020 (2010).

44. 526 U.S. at 528.

45. 545 U.S. 469 (2005).

46. Ilya Somin, "The Limits of Backlash: Assessing the Political Response to *Kelo*," *Minnesota Law Review* 93 (June 2009): 2100, 2109–2111.

47. 530 U.S. 914 (2000).

48. 550 U.S. 124 (2007).

49. 530 U.S. 27 (2000).

50. 502 U.S. 346 (1992).

51. 526 U.S. 314 (1999).

52. 547 U.S. 813 (2006).

53. 530 U.S. (2000).

54. 544 U.S. 13, 26–28 (2005).

55. 536 U.S. 545 (2002).

56. 542 U.S. 296 (2004).

57. 505 U.S. 42 (1992).

58. 505 U.S. 717 (1992).

59. 515 U.S. 70 (1995).

60. 551 U.S. 701 (2007).

61. 539 U.S. 306 (2003).

62. 512 U.S. 874 (1994).

63. 478 U.S. 30 (1986).

64. 512 U.S. at 903.

65. See Scott D. Gerber, "Justice for Clarence Thomas: An Intellectual History of Justice Thomas's Twenty Years on the Supreme Court," *University of Detroit Mercy Law Review* 88 (Summer 2011): 667, 676–683.

66. "Probably because of the legacy of Justice Thomas's bitter confirmation process, it is quite hard to locate serious academic commentary on Justice Thomas's Supreme Court opinions that is even passingly dispassionate or written by someone without an obvious ax to grind." Mark V. Tushnet, "Clarence Thomas's Black Nationalism," *Howard Law Journal* 47 (Winter 2004): 323, 339.

67. Hannah L. Weiner, "The Next 'Great Dissenter'? How Clarence Thomas Is Using the Words and Principles of John Marshall Harlan to Craft a New Era of Civil Rights," *Duke Law Journal* 58 (October 2008): 139.

68. Catherine M. Sharkey, "Against Freewheeling, Extratextual Obstacle Preemption: Is Justice Clarence Thomas the Lone Principled Federalist?" *New York University Journal of Law & Liberty* 5 (2010): 63.

69. David L. Hudson, Jr., "Justice Clarence Thomas: The Emergence of a Commercial-Speech Protector," *Creighton Law Review* 35 (April 2002): 485.

70. Nat Hentoff, "First Friend: Justice Clarence Thomas Has Written as Ardently in Defense of Free Speech as Liberal Icon William Brennan Jr. Ever Did," *Legal Times*, July 3, 2000, 62.

71. Toobin, "Annals of Law."

72. Ibid.

73. Ibid.

74. Tom Goldstein, "The John Roberts Method," *New Republic*, June 30, 2009,

http://www.tnr.com/articles/politics/the-john
-roberts-method.

75. Toobin, "Annals of Law."

76. Angela Onwuachi-Willig, "Just
Another Brother on the SCT? What Justice
Thomas Teaches Us about the Influence of
Racial Identity," *Iowa Law Review* 90 (2005):
931, 934. See Onwuachi-Willig, "Using the
Master's 'Tool' to Dismantle His House: Why
Justice Clarence Thomas Makes the Case for
Affirmative Action," *Arizona Law Review* 47
(2005): 113. In her *Iowa Law Review* article,
she is at pains to point out that her use of
the word *tool* was not meant as a criticism
of Thomas.

77. Mark V. Tushnet, "Clarence Thomas:
The Constitutional Problems," *George*
Washington University Law Review 63
(March 1995): 466–478.

78. Tushnet, "Clarence Thomas's Black
Nationalism," 339.

79. Tushnet, *Court Divided*, 72, 103.

80. John Eastman, "Reflections on Justice
Thomas's Twenty Years on the Bench,"
University of Detroit Mercy Law Review 88
(Summer 2011): 691, 692.

81. The "tectonic plates" metaphor comes
from Eastman, ibid., 699.

82. As he said in his memoir, "What
I needed was a vacation, not another
marathon." Clarence Thomas, *My
Grandfather's Son* (New York: HarperCollins,
2007), 285.

INDEX